"Stringing Proverbs Together"

The Proverbial Language

in

Miguel de Cervantes's *Don Quixote*

Wolfgang Mieder

"Proverbium"
in cooperation with the
Department of German and Russian

The University of Vermont
Burlington, Vermont
2016

Supplement Series

of

Proverbiam
Yearbook of International Proverb Scholarship

Edited by Wolfgang Mieder

Volume 38

The cover illustration (1687) is the frontispiece
of John Phillips's (1631-1706) translation
*The History of the Most Renowned Don Quixote of Mancha,
and His Trusty Squire Sancho Panza.*
London: Thomas Hodgkin, 1687.

ISBN 978-0-9846456-3-3

Manufactured in the United States of America
by Queen City Printers Inc.
Burlington, Vermont

Contents

Preface v

1. Identification of the Proverbial Materials
   (Paremiography) 1

2. Interpretation of the Proverbial Texts
   (Paremiology) 9

3. The Proverbial *Don Quixote* as Translated
   World Literature 17

4. Cervantes as Paremiographical Paremiologist 29

5. Proverbs by the Narrator and Minor
   Characters 39

6. Proverbial Wisdom Employed by Teresa Panza 55

7. Don Quixote's Unexpected Proverb Repertoire 65

8. Sancho Panza's Messages as the Proverbial
   Wise Fool 81

9. Sancho Panza's Bottomless Sack of Proverbs 101

10. Ten Translations of the String of Proverbs in
    Chapter 43 129

    Index of Proverbs and Proverbial Expressions 157

    Bibliography 299

Preface

About ten years ago my colleague and friend Prof. Juan Maura of the Department of Romance Languages and Linguistics at the University of Vermont asked me to participate in the annual Hispanic Forum on our campus. Not being a Hispanist and having only an extremely limited knowledge of the Spanish language, I nevertheless accepted this honor and prepared a lecture on the proverbial expression "to tilt at windmills" which is an allusion to Don Quixote's infamous fight against windmills that he imagines to be giants. The phrase has gained international dissemination even though it does not appear in Miguel de Cervantes Saavedra's novel *Don Quixote* (also spelled *Don Quijote*) as such. As I prepared for my lecture, the research expanded to such a degree that I published my findings a year later as a book entitled *"Tilting at Windmills". History and Meaning of a Proverbial Allusion to Cervantes' "Don Quixote"* (Burlington, Vermont: The University of Vermont, 2006).

With this effort I thought I had satisfied my Spanish friend Juan, who together with his dear wife Tania has been a treasured colleague and special friend for close to three decades. But now, with the four hundredth anniversary of Cervantes's death at hand, Juan Maura is organizing yet another Hispanic Forum. As he was looking for possible speakers, it seemed quite natural for him during one of his frequent visits to my office in the Department of German and Russian one floor below his in the Waterman Building to ask me once again to participate. While I was touched by his request, my first inclination was to decline his invitation. I did not think that I was really qualified to speak a second time on Cervantes. I got away with it once without making a fool out of myself, but now I was afraid to be forced into the role of the fool Sancho Panza. But Juan Maura has the fighting spirit of a Spanish matador, and before I knew it, he had twisted both of my arms and I agreed to give the matter serious thought.

I had read the entire *Don Quixote* for my study on tilting at windmills, and as it is my custom with everything I read, I had diligently marked the numerous proverbs and proverbial expressions that appear in this long novel. I pulled the book from my bookshelves and leafed through it, feeling ever more like Sancho Panza, foolish enough to have made a pact with Juan Maura and now, small as Sancho but not as rotund, wondering what I could possibly pontificate about. To be honest, an idea actually came to me in a relatively short time. After all, the novel is a treasure trove of proverbs, and it happens to be the case that I know a few things about proverbial folk wisdom. So, happily encouraged, I informed my Don Quixote called Juan Maura that I would prepare a lecture about the use, function, and meaning of proverbs in Cervantes's *magnum opus*.

Relieved that Juan and I had teamed up for another scholarly adventure, I set out to fight the scholarly windmills of the vast scholarship on the *Don Quixote*. One book and article after the other found their way into my offices at the university and at home. As I tackled many publications in Spanish, I felt that as long as they dealt with proverbial matters, I could actually make some sense of them. Of course, there was no way that I could possibly conquer the challenge of reading the novel in Spanish. This fact gave me nightmares, but then I realized that masterworks of world literature are read, appreciated, and studied by thousands of people worldwide in excellent translations. Even if some of us are bi- or trilingual, perhaps having adequate reading knowledge of two or three additional foreign languages, there would still be hundreds of literary works that would be accessible only in the form of translations. So I made my peace with this matter and stuck to Edith Grossman's relatively new and acclaimed translation *Don Quixote* (New York: Harper Collins, 2003) that served me well in my previous study. It reached somewhat of a best-seller status upon its publication and therefore enjoyed a wide distribution in the English-speaking world. There would have been a good dozen other English translations to choose from, but having done some comparative analysis of how the various translators dealt with the vexing problem of translating the proverbial language, I felt very comfortable with Grossman's handling of these proverbial matters.

As always happens, once I got started this research project grew beyond any proportion that I had imagined. After all, I at first wanted to prepare but a lecture to be a good sport to my Spanish colleagues. Well, to make a long story short, I started sometime in January and matters expanded week after week. The number of secondary sources on this novel belonging to the one hundred most valued works of world literature is utterly amazing. And it was rewarding to find much of it in the Bailey/Howe Library here at the University of Vermont. It was with particular pleasure that I made use of the three books on Cervantes by John Weiger who was the Dean of the College of Arts and Sciences when I arrived at the University of Vermont in 1971. I shall forever be thankful that he hired me at that time. Other sources were obtainable by way of our superb interlibrary loan office. As with all of my projects, I am deeply thankful to my colleagues and friends who once again have supplied me with English, French, German, Russian, and Spanish materials for this study. With their help and the support of various colleagues and friends, I am putting the finishing touches on this project on Bastille Day in the middle of July. It was not my intention to make a book out of this, but that is what has happened after several months of intensive but enjoyable work. Of course, now I have the challenge of reducing the book to a lecture of reasonable length for the Hispanic Forum that will take place in mid-October 2016. I won't be able to string too many proverbs together at that time, but I am sure that my new-found friend Sancho Panza will understand.

As can be seen from the table of contents, I have divided my study into ten chapters. The first two chapters survey the various attempts at identification of the proverbs and proverbial expressions contained in the novel as well as the interpretation of the role they play in this literary work. Together they amount to a detailed research report concerning the paremiographical and paremiological scholarship during the past two centuries. The third chapter discusses the problems that translators of *Don Quixote* have faced. The novel has been translated into at least fifty languages with twenty of them having appeared in English between 1612 and 2009. The next chapter looks at Cervantes as a proverb collector of sorts as well as his more theoretical deliberations on proverbs as such, arguing that he was somewhat of a paremiographical paremiologist. Chapters 5-8 deal with the use and function of proverbs by the narrator and minor characters, the proverbial wisdom employed by Teresa Panza, Don Quixote's unexpected proverb repertoire, and Sancho Panza's messages as the proverbial wise fool. The climax of these deliberations based on numerous contextualized references and comments from scholarly studies is the discussion of Sancho Panza's bottomless sack of proverbs in the ninth chapter. The last chapter offers ten translations for the sake of viii

comparison of the string of proverbs by Sancho from chapter 43. This is followed by a comprehensive "Index of Proverbs and Proverbial Expressions" that lists all 714 proverbial texts (386 proverbs, 327 proverbial expressions, and 1 wellerism) in their literary contexts, of which quite a few are discussed in the various chapters. Finally, there is an extensive bibliography of the ten translations and the many references cited from international Cervantes and proverb scholarship.

As I worked on this book, there were two Spanish colleagues and friends who were steadily on my mind. The one is Professor Juan Maura, for whom I have the highest respect and admiration as a teacher and scholar and who has taught me so much about his native Spain and to whom I now owe two books on Cervantes. The other is Professor Julia Sevilla Muñoz from the Universidad Complutense at Madrid, distinguished paremiologist and founding editor of the exquisite yearbook *Paremia*, and herself an expert on the proverbs in the *Don Quixote*. As paremiologists we not only form a mutual admiration club but also join forces in serving the international community of proverb scholars and students. It is then with deep appreciation and great admiration that I dedicate this book to my special friends Juan Maura and Julia Sevilla Muñoz.

Wolfgang Mieder   Summer 2016

1. Identification of the Proverbial Materials (Paremiography)

While the amassment of proverbs and proverbial expressions in Miguel de Cervantes Saavedra's *Don Quixote* (1605/1615) amounts to an impressive collection of proverbial lore current in Spain at his time, it must be remembered that this fascination and preoccupation with folk wisdom was evident throughout Europe. Erasmus of Rotterdam's *Adagia* (1500ff.) encouraged other humanists to publish proverb collections in Latin, but there was an equal interest to compiling proverb dictionaries in various vernacular languages as well, with Martin Luther even putting together his own collection in 1530 that served him well to render the Bible into German (Mieder 2011). But there were also iconographical illustrations of proverbs in the form of woodcuts, carvings, and illustrated broadsheets, with Pieter Bruegel's celebrated oil painting "The Netherlandish Proverbs" (1559) representing the quintessential artistic accomplishment (Mieder 2004b). There can be no doubt that the sixteenth and the first half of the seventeenth centuries were the golden age for the proverb in Europe both in its oral and written form. François Rabelais in France, Hans Sachs in Germany, and William Shakespeare in England, to name but three major authors, are known for their proverbial prowess (Mieder and Bryan 1996), and the literature of the Spanish "siglo de oro" did not lack behind, as can be seen from the rich proverbial language in the works of Lope Félix de Vega Carpio, Tirso de Molina, and Pedro Calderón de la Barca (Hayes 1936, González Martín 1997). There also appeared major Spanish proverb collections, among them Pedro Vallés, *Libro de refranes* (1549), Hernán Nuñez, *Refranes o proverbios en romance* (1555), Juan de Mal Lara, *La philosophía vulgar* (1568), and Gonzalo de Correas, *Vocabulario de refranes* (1627). In fact, even though Cervantes employed proverbs from oral tradition, it has now been established that he most likely also had access to the collection by Vallés, since 174 out of his 241 proverbs correspond directly to those of the collection (see the comparative list in Cull 2014: 150-160). Regarding the origin and distribution of some of these proverbs employed by Cervantes that go back to classical Greek and Latin, the Bible, and medieval Latin, see Joseph Haller's voluminous bilingual (Spanish and German) collection *Altspanische Sprichwörter und sprich-wörtliche Redensarten* (1883) that contains detailed comparative treatises for 555 proverbs and proverbial expressions current in Spain before and around the time of Cervantes.

Due to several understandable reasons scholars differ considerably regarding the actual number of proverbs in *Don Quixote*. Some of them only count those texts that are cited by Cervantes as complete proverbs and leaving out mere allusions or intentional modifications. Others also include proverbial expressions and proverbial comparisons, resulting in much higher numbers. Their representation in lists also differ greatly, ranging from mere enumerations without indication of where in the first or second part of the novel and in what individual chapters the texts appear to scholarly compilations with detailed annotations including references to proverb collections. One of the earliest lists is included at the end of the fourth volume of M. de Aulnayes French translation *L'Ingénieux Chevalier Don Quixote de la Manche* (1832). It contains about 271 texts in Spanish with French translations arranged alphabetically by the French keywords. Neither the two parts nor the chapters of the novel are mentioned, and there are also no annotations in this unscholarly compilation (Aulnaye 1821: IV, 401-440). Even less valuable is Emma Thompson's *Wit and Wisdom of Don Quixote* (1867) which on 161 pages retells major portions of the novel by interspersing the prose with proverbs translated into English, once again without any references to where they appear in the novel.

Things are much improved in Ulick Ralph Burke's collection of *Sancho Panza's Proverbs, and Others Which Occur in "Don Quixote"* (1872) that lists 286 numbered proverbs on 44 pages in Spanish and literal English translations together with references to the parts and chapters of the novel. The texts are arranged alphabetically by Spanish keywords, making it a bit difficult for no-speakers of Spanish to locate the proverbs. Two years later José Coll y Vehí published his invaluable compilation *Los refranes del Quijote* (1874) that contains 263 numbered entries, each with about one page of commentary including contextualized passages and scholarly references. The compiler also includes a scholarly introduction to Spanish proverbs (v-xxv), a list of the chapters with their proverbs (218-226), a list of the proverbs in other works by Cervantes (227-228), an alphabetical list of all proverbs in *Don Quixote* (229-232), and a similar list for proverbs in Cervantes's other works (233-238). It is a shame that the lists about the additional works do not include any page numbers, but Terrence L. Hansen's article "Folk Narrative Motifs, Beliefs, and Proverbs in Cervantes' *Exemplary Novels*" (1959) helps to rectify this shortcoming of an otherwise major scholarly resource. And interestingly, John Ormsby included a useful list of 252 proverbs and proverbial expressions in Spanish with English translations in the fourth volume of his still valuable *Don Quixote* translation (1885: IV, 367-252). In his very recent translation of the novel James H. Montgomery has also provided a list of "Selected Proverbs, Maxims, and Passages from the *Don Quixote*" in English only (2009: 835-844).

Twenty years later A. López del Arco published his *Refranes de Sancho Panza. Aventuras y desventuras, malicias y agudezas del escudero de don Quijote* (1905) with only the first few pages (7-20) presenting a disappointing helter-skelter list of Spanish proverbs from the novel. Of delightful general value is, however, Elías Olmos Canalda's bibliophile compilation *Los refranes del "Quijote"* (1940) with its justified republication in 1998. It lists 283 proverbs with short explanations and references to parts and chapters of the novel. Together with its handsome illustrations it is a florilegium of folk wisdom to be enjoyed by general readers and enthusiasts of *Don Quixote*. J. Leyva's much newer collection *Refranes, dichos y sentencias de "Quijote"* (2004) is quite similar. It lists 290 texts in the context of the novel. Each entry takes up one page with some notes at the bottom with the index (pp. 301-319) presenting an alphabetically arranged list that includes phraseologisms that appear in the main entries. In the same year, Miguel Requena provided a mere alphabetical list of "Los refranes del *Quijote*" (2004) with part and chapter numbers that really offers no additional information.

On a much more scholarly level, Enrique de Cárcer y de Sobíes published his massive (666 large pages printed in two columns) polyglot lexicon *Las frases del "Quijote". Su exposición, ordenación y comentarios, y su versión á las lenguas francesa, portugesa, italiana, catalana, inglesa y alemana*

(1916). He arranged his rich materials consecutively, presenting the proverbs and other phraseologisms for each chapter as a unit. Each entry begins with the proverbial text with explanatory comments, the contextualized reference from *Don Quixote*, additional references from other works, appearances in proverb collections, and finally a list of French, Portuguese, Italian, Catalan, English, and German equivalents or translations. A large alphabetically arranged index (581-659) of all registered proverbs, proverbial expressions, and other phraseologisms and their variants is included. This oversize volume is of highest paremiographical value and should be part of any further study on the phraseologisms contained in this acclaimed novel. It goes far beyond proverbial matters in the narrow sense of addressing primarily proverbs and proverbial expressions. Unfortunately this pioneering work appears to have disappeared from the scholarly radar screen since it does not appear in the bibliographies of Jesús Cantera Ortiz de Urbina, Julia Sevilla Muñoz, and Manuel Sevilla Múnoz's *Refranes, otras paremias y fraseologismos en "Don Quijote de la Mancha"* (2005) and Hugo O. Bizzarri's *Diccionario de paremias cervantinas* (2015) that could well have benefited from the about 1350 (my count) detailed monographs (ranging from a solid paragraph to three pages in length) that include many variants in addition to the primary proverbial texts from the novel.

Even after this early *magnum opus,* scholars continued their paremiographical work, with Juan Suñé Bengaes's *Fraseología de Cervantes* (1929) considerable collection of proverbs, proverbial expressions, and other phraseologisms being somewhat informative but fading in comparison to Cárcer y de Sobiés's scholarly treatise. Katharine B. Woodward's master's thesis *Proverbs in "Don Quixote"* (1930) is of even less value in that it merely lists 227 proverbs and proverbial expressions on forty-four double-spaced pages with English equivalents or translations and the location of the texts in the novel. Next the well-known Spanish folklorist Antonio Castillo de Lucas listed and commented on 57 (42 from *Don Quixote*) medically related proverbs in "Refranes de aplicación médica en *El Quijote*" (1943), and some forty years later Ceslso Bañeza Román assembled an annotated list of 49 Biblical proverbs from *Don Quixote* in his "Refranes de origen bíblico en Cervantes" (1989, see also

Hatzfeld 1949: 196-204). In between Gloria Diaz Isaacs published "Los Refranes del *Quijote*" (1974) that contains an alphabetically arranged list of 209 proverbs with very short explanatory comments for readers in Panama. It is, after all, of much interest to see what proverbs of the *Don Quixote* survive in the Spanish language in Central and South America. Thus the Columbian proverb scholar Jaime Sierra García included 171 alphabetically listed proverbs in his book chapter on "El refrán antioqueño en la obra de Cervantes" (1994: 328-351; see also Sierra García 1997), and there is also Róbinson Ayala Mejíra's exquisite Salvadorian study *Ecos de "Don Quijote" en el habla moderna de El Salvador: Los refranes españoles y su transmisión oral* (2007) that provides two lists of 318 proverbs out of *Don Quixote*, the one in chronological order as to their appearance in the two parts and chapters of the novel (140-154), the other in straight alphabetical order (155-169). Based on a survey with 255 participants the author was able to show that modern Salvadorians continue to use many of the proverbs from *Don Quixote* in their oral communication today.

Various lists of the proverbs contained in *Don Quixote* continue to be assembled that vary in the number of texts and the mode of presentation. With all of this attention, it is amazing that they don't necessarily build on each other and that there appears to be no standardized compilation. In any case, somewhat unexpectedly perhaps, R.M. Flores lists 139 numbered and chronologically arranged "Sayings and Proverbs" with reference to parts and chapters of the novel in the enlightening book *Sancho Panza Through Three Hundred Seventy-Five Years of Continuations, Imitations, and Criticism, 1605-1980* (1982b: 215-222). The author includes sayings (proverbial expressions), but it is not clear how the relatively small number of texts was reached. María Cecilia Colombi in her valuable study *Los refranes en el "Quijote": texto y contexto* (1989b) arrives at a useful list of 171 alphabetically arranged proverbs (111-136) with information of the parts, chapters, and page numbers where they appear in the novel. She also refers to their appearance in Gonzalo Correas's major proverb collection *Vocabulario de refranes y frases proverbiales* (1627). Of course, this list is only the paremiographical prerequisite to her literary and folkloric interpretation of the proverbs in their narrative context. Building on these and earlier findings, Jesús Cantera Ortiz de Urbina, Julia Sevilla Muñoz, and Manuel Sevilla Muñoz published their excellent scholarly book *Refranes, otras paremias y fraseologismos en "Don Quijote de la Mancha"* (2005) in celebration of the four hundredth anniversary of the appearance of the first part of the novel in 1605. It was my great honor to serve as its editor and to publish it as volume 17 of the Supplement Series of *Proverbium: Yearbook of International Proverb* Scholarship here at the University of Vermont in Burlington, Vermont (USA).They too look at the function of the proverbs in their literary context and present a richly annotated alphabetically arranged list of 388 proverbs and proverbial expressions (49-116; texts plus parts and chapters of the novel, references from major Spanish proverb collections, and variants). There are also alphabetically arranged lists of numerous "Máximas y sentencias" (117-131), "Frases hechas, expresiones, locuciones, modismos, idiotismos" (133-172), "Saludos, exclamaciones, juramentos" (173-178), and "Latinismos" (179-189). For the Latin texts the authors provide explanatory comments, but for all the rest only the parts and chapters of appearance are listed. And, of course, some of these maxims, sententious remarks, etc. might well be considered to be "classical" proverbs or proverbial expressions (see p. 16 and 49: "paremias clásicas") that would/could drive the number of 388 texts up somewhat. But to be sure, both this study and that by María Colombi are major modern accomplishments in the paremiographical investigation of Cervantes's *Don Quixote*.

True to the folkloric prevalence of the number three, there is yet one additional absolutely unique scholarly *summum bonum* to register. Hugo O. Bizzarri drew attention to what magisterial study he was working on with untiring diligence in his article "Apuntes para la realización de un 'diccionario de refranes, frases proverbiales y sentencias cervantinas'" (2011). Four years later, in September of 2015 and in time for the four hundredth anniversary of the publication of the second part of *Don Quixote*, I received an autographed copy of Hugo O. Bizzarri's *Diccionario de paremias cervantinas* (2015), a voluminous and all-inclusive study of 621 pages printed in two dense columns that will never be surpassed! It is a lexicon *par excellence* in which the entire proverbial materials found in the works of Cervantes are registered according to their alphabetically arranged keywords. The texts are listed in their literary contexts and this is followed by variants and references from other literary works as well as proverb collections. Bizzarri also includes explanatory commentaries, and as one would expect, each "monograph" ends with a special bibliography. Some of the approximately 1365 (my count) entries might only comprise half a column, while others reach four densely printed columns. In the world's annals of paremiography, Hugo Bizzarri's *Diccionario de paremias cervantinas* deserves to be listed among the very best. It is the final chapter in the long paremiographical journey towards the complete identification and explanation of the many proverbial treasures contained in the fabulous works of Cervantes. Many scholars have contributed to this scholarly effort, but Hugo Bizzarri has far surpassed any previous efforts. His dictionary became a "classic" the minute it appeared in print, and it will inform all future work on the proverbial prowess of Miguel de Cervantes Saavedra.

2. Interpretation of the Proverbial Texts (Paremiology)

The identification of the rich proverbial materials in Cervantes's *Don Quixote* is but one side of the coin with paremiologists having also looked at linguistic, stylistic and functional aspects of the proverbs and proverbial expressions in this novel. Identification (paremiography) is after all only the first step in literary proverb investigations with the interpretation (paremiology) being the necessary second task to discover how, why, when, and by whom the proverbial language is instantiated by Cervantes in his prose (Taylor 1948: 221, Dundes 1965: 136-137, Mieder 1974: 889). Ferdinand Denis hinted at this in his early "Essai sur la philosophie de Sancho" (1834) that does, however, only touch tangentially on the novel in its general survey of folk wisdom as such with "Sancho" standing in for the common voice of the people. Much later Américo Castro included a chapter on the "Refranes" in his insightful book *El pensamiento de Cervantes* (1925: 190-195) in which he relates Cervantes's fascination with proverbs to Erasmus of Rotterdam's preoccupation with them and shows, not surprisingly so, that many of the proverbs employed by Cervantes can also be found in Juan de Mal Lara's early proverb collection *La philosophía vulgar* (1568). About ten years later the great Cervantes scholar Francisco Rodríguez Marín made the important point in his short essay "Las frases del *Quijote*" (1916) that Cervantes did not just include actual proverbs but also plenty of proverbial expressions and other phraseologisms in his most important literary work. A similar point was then made by Amado Alonso in his article "Las prevaricaciones idiomáticas de Sancho" (1948) that illustrates by way of some contextualized references how proverbial language is manipulated especially by Sancho in order to achieve a comical effect.

But the more detailed analysis of the use and function of proverbs has its serious beginning with Eleanor O'Kane's study on "The Proverb: Rabelais and Cervantes" (1950). She is well aware of the fact that the time of these two authors was the golden age of proverbs with scholars like Erasmus of Rotterdam and other humanists publishing major proverb collections all over Europe, with well-known literary authors integrating them into their works, with reformers using them in their religious treatises and sermons, with artists depicting proverbs in woodcuts, in books and on broadsheets, and with Pieter Bruegel the Elder illustrating them in his famous oil painting "The Netherlandish Proverbs" (1559). Proverbs and proverbial expressions were clearly in the air, on the paper, and on the canvas, with Cervantes being a major player in this predominance of proverbs and proverbial expressions in all modes of communication ranging from the didactic and straightforward use of them to their manipulative corruptions for the sake of satire, irony, and humor (Mieder 2009). What would William Shakespeare's plays be without their proverbial dialogues that often involve wordplay, where would Martin Luther's linguistic prowess be without his effective use of proverbial folk speech, and what would François Rabelais's novels be without their colorful amassments of proverbial lore? But the mere accumulation of proverbs is one thing and their meaningful integration or truncated allusion to them is quite another. As O'Kane points out, considerable skill is necessary for "the *crossing* of two or more proverbs and the *twisting* of one part of a single proverb, generally by substituting one word for another" (1950: 366). She feels that it is the "dexterity of handling proverbs" and especially in using proverbs as a "psychological resource" (O'Kane 1950: 366, 368) in the dialogues especially between Don Quixote and Sancho Panza that sets Cervantes apart from mere *tours de force* compilations. Little wonder that Francisco Lacosta entitled his similar essay as "El infinito mundo de los proverbios: *Don Quijote*" (1965), showing by way of many examples how rich the proverbial language was during the Spanish *siglo de oro* with Cervantes being a major player (see Chevalier 1993: 253-259, Avalle-Arce 1984: 134). That this is particularly true for the proverbial language of the wise fool Sancho is amply exemplified by numerous textual references in Ángel Rosenblat's chapter on "El refranero y el habla de Sancho" (1971b). There is no doubt that Cervantes has captured the popular folk speech in his novel that basically includes all linguistic registers from the profane to the sublime (Rosenblat 1971a). And, of course, it is not only the proverbial language but also the many other types of phraseologisms that add to the often humorous tone of the novel's prose and dialogues (Zucker 1973).

The 1970s brought four significant articles by the French paremiologist Monique Joly from the Université de Caen in Normandy, where I was a student in the summer semesters of 1965 and 1966. She republished them in her book *Études sur "Don Quichotte"* (1996: 205-297). This section of her studies begins with the article "Le discours métaparémique dans *Don Quichotte* (1984) that investigates the occurrences and the users of proverbial language in the many discourses of the novel. This is followed by the relatively short Spanish article "De paremiología cervantina: una reconsideración del problema" (1991) that looked in particular at Sancho Panza's ambiguous use of proverbs. The third article is actually Joly's earliest contribution to the paremiological aspects of the novel, and as its title "Aspectos del refrán en Mateo Alemán y Cervantes" (1971) implies, it is a comparative analysis of which half is dedicated to Cervantes's contemporary writer Mareo Alemán (1547-1614). By numerous contextualized examples Joly shows that while Cervantes employs folk speech in his own unique way, he is certainly not alone in his fascination with proverbial matters. The fourth and final article with the telling title "Ainsi parlait Sancho Pança" (1975) looks at Sancho's incredible repertoire of proverbs and proverbial expressions that has made him into a paremiological legend.

The next high point in the paremiological scholarship on *Don Quixote* was reached with María Cecilia Colombi's American dissertation *Los refranes en "Don Quijote"* (1988) that was published in a revised form one year later as *Los refranes en el "Quijote": texto y contexto* (1989b). This book begins with a detailed survey of Spanish proverb scholarship and also looks at the structure and semantics of Spanish proverbs. This is followed by a linguistic and stylistic analysis of how Cervantes integrated proverbs into his narrative and the various dialogues. The point is made that certain introductory formulas direct the reader's attention to the ensuing proverb, a clear indication of the importance that he saw in integrating such a plethora of folk proverbs. The study concludes with a chapter on proverbs as direct or indirect speech acts. Of course there is also the annotated list of the 171 proverbs that form the basis of Colombi's insightful discussion of these texts in their literary context. I still remember my excitement when María Colombi, who was teaching at the University of Massachusetts at Amherst not too far from Vermont, submitted her article "Los refranes en el *Quijote*: Discurso autoritario y des-autor-itario [*sic*]" (1990) to me for publication in *Proverbium: Yearbook of International Proverb Scholarship*. By way of a number of contextualized examples she shows how proverbs exhibit a certain traditional authority that can, however, also be questioned in certain situations. Cervantes was clearly aware of the fact that proverbs are not universal truths and that they can be criticized or ridiculed.

Pilar María Vega Rodríguez followed in the footsteps of María Colombi's analysis with her general "Consideraciones paremiológicas cervantinas" (1990). She deals with the basic definition issues of proverbs, proverbial expressions, and sententious remarks while also stressing the fact that such formulaic language often exists in variants. This is followed by a discussion of various functions that proverbs perform in *Don Quixote*, stressing that Cervantes is keen to go beyond the more traditional didactic purpose of proverbs by employing them in innovative fashion to add creative expressiveness to the various speakers within the novel. Part of this is, of course, Cervantes's inclination towards wordplays and puns, as Rodríguez's later article "De nuevo sobre *El Quijote*: novela de burlas" (1999) shows.

As is to be expected, the last twenty years have seen a continuation of the interest in what role the proverbial predominance in *Don Quixote* has played in keeping this old novel on the list of the one hundred best literary works in the world. The fact that the distinguished paremiologist Julia Sevilla Muñoz from the Universidad Complutense de Madrid began publishing her superb yearbook *Paremia* in 1993 has been at least in part instrumental in maintaining this scholarly activity. It began with Louis Combet's short article about "La fonction occulte des proverbes dans le *Don Quichotte*" (1997) in which he discusses the religious, moral, and social function of a number of proverbs. He followed this up a year later with a more important contribution on "Les refranes dans le *Quichotte* d'Avellaneda" (1998, see also Álvarez Curiel 1999)). This is the only study that has investigated the use of proverbs in Alonso Fernández de Avellaneda's novel *Don Quijote de la Mancha* (1614) that continues and imitates the first part of Cervantes's *Don Quixote* and that appeared to Cervantes's displeasure prior to his own second part in 1615. The imitator incorporated merely 66 proverbs (including 6 duplicates) and thus cannot possibly hold the candle to Cervantes's ingenious and massive proverbial style. Almost exactly a hundred years later the French author Robert Challe (1659-1720) published yet another *Continuation de l'hstoire de l'admirable Don Quichotte de la Manche* (1713), and it is good to have Laurent Versini's informative article "Les proverbes de Sancho: De Cervantès à Challe" (2003) on this matter. Challe does not seem to have been influenced by Cervantes's proverbs in particular. He has only 12 proverbs out of his total of 145 in common with the original *Don Quixote*.

The other *Paremia* articles include first of all Ángel Estévez Molinero's discussion of "Paremias de Sancho, parénesis de Don Quijote y algunos entretenidos razonamientos" (1999), elaborating on a few proverbial dialogues how Sancho and Don Quixote communicate with each other. This is followed by Nieves Rodríguez Valle's study of "Paremias en *El Quijote* de 1605 como estrategias literarias" (2005) that explains how Cervantes used proverbs as a literary strategy to show that there is not just one truth but that much in life is relative, including the truth value of proverbs. Three years later he published his paper "La 'creación' de refranes en el *Quijote*" (2008) in which he discusses a number of proverb-like texts in *Don Quixote* that have not been found in proverb collections of literary works before him. However, it is argued that they have become proverbial later because of the incredible influence that the *Don Quixote* has had on the Spanish language and culture during the past four hundred years (see also Rodríguez Valle 2010). The traditional proverbs and Cervantes's own creations from his novel continue to have considerable influence today when efforts are on foot to use them in the instruction of the Spanish language to foreign speakers. Julia Sevilla Muñoz refers to the instructional use of "Cervantes's" proverbs in her report on "Presupuestos paremiológicos de una propuesta metodológica para la enseñanza de los refranes a través de *El Quijote*" (2005) which María Teresa Barbadillo de la Fuente followed up a year later with her similar report "Presupuestos didácticos para la enseñanza de los refranes a través de *El Quijote*" (2006).

Moving on from the research contained in the Spanish *Paremia* yearbook, it is of value to mention Alberto Zuluaga's German contribution "Verwendungsverfahren und Funktionen phraseologischer Äußerungen in *El Quijote*" (1997) that he presented somewhat similarly in Galician a few years later as "Interpretación textolingüística de fraseoloxismos quixotescos" (2005) in the seventh volume of the valuable *Cadernos de fraseoloxía galega*. He looks at the various types of phraseologisms employed by Cervantes from a linguistic point of view, stressing semantic-stylistic aspects and once again pointing out that at least for proverbs as such Cervantes often cites introductory formulas to draw special attention to this folk wisdom no matter for what purpose it is being used by the speakers. He also discusses modifications and mere allusions to such elements of folk speech by citing a number of contextualized examples.

Of course, as has been mentioned previously, the important relatively recent book *Refranes, otras paremias y fraseologismos en "Don Quijote de la Mancha"* (2005) by Jesús Cantera Ortiz de Urbina, Julia Sevilla Muñoz, and Manuel Sevilla Muñoz has, in addition to its scholarly collection of the proverbs, proverbial expressions, and other types of phraseologisms from *Don Quixote*, an important first chapter (pp. 11-47) that analyzes the distribution of these proverbial materials throughout the two parts and their chapters of the novel, provides a short discussion of Cervantes's view of folk speech, and looks at various functions and modifications of proverbs in particular. In comparison, Hugo O. Bizzarri's voluminous *Diccionario de paremias cervantinas* (2015) has only a very short and disappointing four-page introduction. It would have been a good idea for him to reprint his informative article "Los refranes en Cervantes" (2003) that he had published twelve years earlier. In it he discusses the paremiological tradition of which Cervantes was a major part, he looks at the early proverb collections of that time by Hernán Nuñez (1555), Juan de Mal Lara (1568), and Gonzalo de Correas (1627) as well as Erasmus of Rotterdam (1500ff.). While Cervantes most likely was aware of the latter's *Adagia*, he might even have known his influential *The Praise of* Folly (1509), with "the Erasmian notion of the 'wise fool' percolating into *Don Quixote*, though more on association with Sancho than with his master" (Riley 1986a: 53, see also González Echevarría 2001:

273, Martín 2002: 164)). He also explains Cervantes's inclination towards folk language and his awareness of the use and abuse of proverbs in actual discourse. Just as in actual speech acts of that time and still today, proverbs function as authoritative and ethical bits of wisdom, but they are by no means sacrosanct and can also be manipulated to express humor or ill will. This valid discussion has more recently been continued by Sonia Fournet-Perot in her excellent article on "Les proverbes dans *'El ingenioso hidalgo' don Quijote de la Mancha*: des stéréotypes linguistiques et culturels révélateurs de la complexité du message cervantin" (2009). While stressing the humor and irony that are brought about by the stringing together of proverbs *ad nauseam*, they are by no means simplistic elements of folk speech. Metaphorical proverbs clearly play an important stylistic and semantic role in this masterful novel, and yes, they are part and parcel of the complexity of Miguel de Saaveera Cervantes's message of his timeless novel *El ingenioso hidalgo Don Quijote de la Mancha*.

3. The Proverbial *Don Quixote* as Translated World Literature

It is doubtful that Cervantes wrote his unequivocally Spanish novel with the idea in mind that it would be translated into at least fifty languages. But with the first part of his novel having already appeared in English translation by Thomas Shelton in 1612, he might well have thought of the possibility of at least some translations when he has Don Quixote early in the second part of the novel from 1615 make the observation that "One of the things that must give the greatest contentment to a virtuous and eminent man is to see, while he is still alive, his good name printed and published in the languages of different peoples" (475; all English texts and their page numbers are from Edith Grossman's 2003 translation). He certainly was very cognizant of the art of translation necessary to make the classics of Greek and Roman antiquity available to Spanish readers. And he was, of course, also aware of the linguistic prowess of Erasmus of Rotterdam and other humanists of his time, with the same being true for the skillful translators of the Bible into the vernacular languages of Europe. All of this clearly occupied his literary mind, in fact so much so that he included a treatise of sorts in his *Don Quixote* that is a treasure trove for an unlimited number of subject matters. And typically for Cervantes, he has Don Quixote create a perfect metaphor for it all:

> "It seems to me that translating from one language to another, unless it is from Greek and Latin, the queens of all languages, is like looking at Flemish tapestries from the wrong side, for although the figures are visible, they are covered by threads that obscure them, and cannot be seen with the smoothness and color of the right side; translating easy languages does not argue for either talent or eloquence, just as transcribing or copying from one paper to another does not argue for those qualities. And I do not wish to infer from this that the practice of translating is not deserving of praise, be-

cause a man might engage in worse things that bring him even less benefit." (873-874)

The German novelist Thomas Mann, who describes in his account "Voyage with *Don Quixote*" (1934) how he read Cervantes's novel on the ship that carried him into exile from Nazi-Germany to the United States, stated that this is an "admirable critique of the nature of translation" and that "the metaphor [of the Flemish tapestries] is striking" (Mann 1934: 29). Little wonder that Ilan Stavans entitled his survey of various English translations of the novel "Flemish Tapestries" (2015: 172-204), thereby signaling that none of them are so perfect that they equal the art of the original. In general, translators have the choice of puritanically sticking to the text or in a more liberal way trying to "capture the spirit, style, and tone of the original work but not intending to replicate that work precisely in a different language" (Parr and Vollendorf 2015c: 18-19). In the case of the *Don Quixote*, it has been observed that "the Spaniards are correct when they claim that *Don Quixote*, like much verbal humor, is to some extent untranslatable. Some levels of style and some chivalric archaisms and proverbs can be reproduced in English, but the vivid dialogue [...] can only be explained, never translated" (Eisenberg 1984: 66). And yet, translators around the world have valiantly attempted to render the novel into various target languages with numerous translation attempts existing for some of the major world languages (Cobelo 2009).

It is true that some proverbs, proverbial expressions, and other phraseologisms can be translated without any particular problem. Regarding proverbs as such, this is true for older texts that can be traced back to Greek and Roman antiquity that were spread via the Latin *lingua franca* and humanists like Erasmus of Rotterdam throughout Europe. Such classical proverbs as "Big fish eat little fish", "One swallow does not make a summer", "One hand washes the other", and "Love is blind" were loan translated and exist in equal wording as common European proverbs. The same is true for such Bible proverbs as "He who digs a pit for others, falls in himself" (Prophets 26:27), "There is nothing new under the sun" (Ecclesiastes 1:9), "A prophet is not without honor save in his own country" (Matthew 13:57), and the golden rule "Do unto others as you would have them do unto you" (Matthew 12:7). Yet another group of common European proverbs are those that were coined during the Middle Ages in Latin and then subsequently translated into the vernacular language, including such well-known proverbs as "New brooms sweep clean", "Strike while the iron is hot", "The pitcher goes so long to the well until at last it breaks", and "All that glitters is not gold" (Paczolay 1997, Mieder 2014: 60-63). But every language has large numbers of proverbs that are indigenous to that culture (Krauss 1946 and 1959), and it is with these unique texts that translators have great problems. They can translate them literally, they can try to find equivalent proverbs in the target language, they can paraphrase them, or they can simply ignore them. Translators might well employ all four possibilities in dealing with this vexing problem, depending also on whether they are attuned to proverbial language and its cultural background at all. Not only need proverbs to be identified as "culturally marked models", they also require interpretation by the translator in order to find an appropriate wording in the other language (Zurdo Ruiz-Ayúcar 2014: 35).

It is a fascinating undertaking to take a look at how various translators have rendered the proverbial language of *Don Quixote* into their respective languages. Maryse Privat has compared the rendition of a total of 34 proverbs in three French translations in her articles "Traduction et proverbes dans le *Don Quijote*" (1997) and "Quelques proverbes du *Don Quijote* vus dans trois traductions françaises" (1999), and Galit Hasan-Rokem has analyzed how four Hebrew translators have dealt with three proverbs in her theoretical and interpretive paper on "Literary Forms and Orality: Proverbs in the Hebrew Translations of *Don Quijote*" (2007). More comprehensive work, but dealing with only one translation, has been done by María Jesús Barsanti Vigo in her valuable study *Estudio paremiológico contrastivo de la traducción de "El Quijote" de Ludwig Tieck* (2003) on how the German Romantic author Ludwig Tieck dealt with the proverbial language in his *Don Quixote* (1799-1800) translation. By way of a linguistic and functional analysis she shows that this first German translation coped quite successfully with this paremiological complexity (see also Barsanti Vigo 2006 and 2010). As one would expect there have been other German translations of the *Don Quixote*, and Ernest W.B. Hess-Lüttich includes a small section in his general article on "Sprichwörter und Redensarten als Übersetzungsproblem" (1983) where he contrasts the translation of two Spanish proverbial expressions in five German translations. One year later , Margaret Axnick, upon my suggestion, completed her M.A. thesis *Probleme der deutschen Sprichwortübersetzungen aus Miguel de Cervantes' "Don Quijote" – eine vergleichende sprachliche und literarische Studie* (1984) in which she compared the translation attempts of five German translators for 139 proverbs. This detailed study clearly shows how the translators during a time span of over one hundred years have dealt quite differently with the proverbial originals. There are a few cases where all translators agree, as for example the German rendering of "Una golondrina sola no hace verano" as "Eine Schwalbe macht noch keinen Sommer" (One swallow doesn't make a summer). This is hardly a surprise, since this proverb belongs, as stated before, to the common European stock of proverbs. But in most cases only two and sometimes three translations are in agreement, and for a few proverbs not one of the five translators offered a German proverb equivalent.

Regrettably there are no such studies for the numerous extant English and American English translations! It would be a great undertaking for a research team to compile a comparative list of all the proverb translation attempts during the past 400 years by the following twenty translators together with an analysis to see what translation might receive the crown for its proverbiality (Stavans 2015: 177):

1612 Thomas Shelton (2nd part 1620)	1888 Henry Edward Watts
1687 John Phillips	1910 Robinson Smith
1700 Peter Anthony Motteux	1949 Samuel Putnam
1700 John Stevens	1950 John Michael Cohen
1742 Charles Jarvis	1954 Walter Starkie
1755 Tobias Smollett	1995 Burton Raffel
1769 George Kelley	2000 John Rutherford
1864 T.T. Shore	2003 Edith Grossman
1881 Alexander J. Duffield	2005 Tom Lathrop
1885 John Ormsby (revised by Joseph R. Jones and Kenneth Douglas in 1981)	2009 James H. Montgomery

It is, of course, not necessarily a good sign to learn that Joseph R. Jones and Kenneth Douglas, having American college students in mind, revised John Ormsby's translation from 1885 in their Norton Critical Edition of 1981 by "occasionally sacrificing rare and obsolete words or proverbs in favor of contemporary equivalents, thereby circumventing the need for esoteric notes and allowing a more immediate comprehension of the text" (Bjornson 1984b: 10). It can also hardly be taken as a compliment when J.M. Cohen's 1950 translation is characterized as "a straightforward modernizing version, [being] over-inclined to take the easy way out when faced with the difficulties Cervantes's ways of using language present" (Russell 1985: 110). In any case, Ilan Stavans, who reports that he read *all* of the translations, reports that in doing so, "one witnesses the changes of the English language through time, from its Elizabethan variety in the early seventeenth century to the one used today, four hundred years later. The linguistic transformation becomes obvious against this historical procession: spelling and conjugations have changed; verb choices are different; and while articles and pronouns appear to be the most stable, they too have undergone a change in function" (Stavans 2015: 178). Surely, this evolution of the English language will also come to the fore if the proverbial language of all these translations were to be compared.

Michael J. McGrath has provided an impressive introductory article for such an undertaking with his survey "Tilting at Windmills: *Don Quijote* in English" (2006). He begins with an obvious fact that is true for other literary masterpieces of the world as well: "Unfortunately, there are many readers who are unable to read the novel in its original language, and those who depend upon an English translation may read a version that is linguistically and culturally quite different from the original" (McGrath 2006: 7). He then provides informed comments on eight modern and easily accessible translations by Samuel Putnam (1949), John Michael Cohen (1950), Walter Starkie (1964), Joseph R. Jones and Kenneth Douglas (1981), Burton Raffel (1995), John Rutherford (2000), Edith Grossman (2003), and Tom Lathrop (2007). While his interest is not especially in how the translators handled the proverbial language, there a few isolated comments that relate to this topic. For example, there is the comment that "while Cohen translates the majority of Sancho's

sayings with his own words, he inserts occasionally English sayings that resemble closely the original" (12), and he also men-
tions that "Jones deals with proverbs in two ways. If the meaning
of the proverb is obvious, he substitutes it with a rhyming translation that sounds like a proverb. In addition, Jones replaces
proverbs that are difficult to understand with other well-known
proverbs" (13). Had he referred to the other translations, he
would doubtlessly have made similar statements since the perfect
reproduction of the proverbial origin is a definite impossibility.
And he also quite correctly points out that "while accuracy is a
necessary component of a successful translation, the translator
should not sacrifice a translation that makes sense in favor of one
that is accurate but difficult to understand" (22). By chance he
cites as one of his examples a Spanish proverbial expression with
its various translation attempts:

> Another passage that requires translators to choose between
> literal accuracy and making sense is the following statement
> by Sancho Panza, who comments on the presence of the in-
> terpolated novel "El curioso impertinente" in Cide Hamete
> Benengeli's adventures of Don Quijote and Sancho, from
> Part II, Chapter 3: "Yo apostaré que ha mezclado el hi de
> perro berzas con capachaos". Sancho, of course, compares
> the presence of the interpolated novel within the larger novel
> to mixing cabbage (*berzas*) with baskets (*capachos*). Not all
> of the translators, however, chose a translation that makes
> sense in lieu of the one that is accurate. As a result, the read-
> er must make sense of the translation. For example, Put-
> nam's and Jones/Douglas's translations of mixing "cabbages
> with baskets" is literal and requires the reader to ponder its
> significance. Although not as literal, Starkie's translation "a
> pretty kettle of fish of everything" is equally ambiguous. The
> other translations, while less accurate, make more sense:
> Cohen, "a fine mix-up of everything"; Raffel, "all sorts of
> silly stuff"; Rutherford, "right old hotch-potch"; Grossman,
> "apples and oranges", and Lathrop, "mixed everything up".
> (McGrath 2006: 22-23)

These translation problems are clearly not restricted to proverbial
matters alone, for what are translators to do with the archaic
style, ironic twists, wordplays, puns, and intended nonsensical

statements in the novel? Much of this is part of the humorous tone that is also present in some of the proverbial utterances. McGrath offers an interesting example in this regard for the problematic translation of the originally Italian proverbial expression "Cercar Maria per Ravenna" that appears in the *Don Quixote* with a slight modification of the female name to Marica. The origin and meaning of "To look for Maria in Ravenna" goes back to a folk narrative and has three basic meanings: (1) to look uselessly for something that is right in front of someone, (2) to look for things where they are not to be found, and (3) to look for something for one's own harm and shame (see Mulinacci 1990). Things are even more complicated since the same sentence includes the second proverbial expression "To look for a student in Salamanca" with a similar meaning. Here then are McGrath's revealing observations on various translation attempts that reflect the almost insurmountable challenges of rendering but this one onomastic sentence into meaningful English:

> The translators cannot agree on how best to translate Cervantes' humor in the following line from Part II, Chapter 10: "Y más, que así será buscar a Dulcinea por el Toboso como a Marica por Rávena, o al bachiller en Salamanca". Of course, Cervantes compares locating Dulcinea, whom neither Don Quijote nor Sancho have ever seen, to finding a needle in a haystack. Unless the reader knew that *Marica* is the diminutive of *María* and that Ravenna is a city in northern Italy, the first allusion could not be appreciated. For this reason, either an accurate translation that does not sacrifice the meaning of the phrase or a footnote is needed. Unfortunately, not all the translators recognized the potential problems associated with a faulty translation of "Marica por Rávena":

> Putnam: Marica in Rávena
> Cohen: little Maria in Ravenna
> Starkie: needle in a haystack
> Jones/D.: María in Ravenna
> Raffel: one Marica out of all the Marcias in Ravenna
> Rutherford: a girl called Maria in Madrid
> Grossman: María in Ravenna
> Lathrop: Marica in Ravenna

Putnam, Cohen, Jones/Douglas, and Grossman rely on the reader's knowledge to understand their translations. Starkie, Raffel, and Rutherford provide more explanatory translations; Starkie's, however, ignores completely the cultural content of Cervantes' allusion. While Lathrop's translation is similar to Putnam's, Lathrop provides for the reader a lengthy footnote that explains the meaning of "Marica in Ravenna":

Ravenna is that city in northern Italy, near the Adriatic Sea, south of Venice and east of Bologna. *Marica* is an affectionate diminutive for *María*. But wouldn't it be easy to find lots of Maricas in Ravenna?

With respect to the comparison of finding "Dulcinea por el Toboso" to locating "al bachiller en Salamanca," there exist subtle misinterpretations. According to the *Diccionario de autoridades*, *bachiller* is "El primer grado que se da en las Universidades a los que han oído y estudiado alguna facultad: como Artes, Teología, Leyes, Cánones, Medicina, después de haber cursado en ellas el tiempo derterminado para recibirle." An accurate translation, therefore, is one that reflects the idea of a college graduate or at least a student. An endnote accompanies Putnam's translation, "bachelor in Salamanca": "Salamanca was full of bachelors of arts". Cohen, Jones/Douglas, Grossman, and Lathrop translate *bachiller* as "bachelor." Without an explanatory footnote, the comparison becomes finding Dulcinea in Toboso with locating a bachelor, or an unmarried man, in Salamanca. This meaning, however, clearly was not Cervantes' intention. The other translations are more accurate:

Starkie: scholar in Salamanca
Raffel: college graduate in Salamanca
Rutherford: student in Salamanca (McGrath 2006: 32-33)

Clearly McGrath has provided a telling explanation of the difficulties that might arise from the translation of just one sentence of *Don Quixote*, but it might have been helpful to state that Cervantes is in fact coupling two proverbial expressions in this case with the same meaning, the one having originated in Italy and the other in Spain (see Bizzarri 2015: 496-497). In any case, he finishes his long article with the following insightful observation: "Translators of *Don Quixote* aspire to an impossible goal: a perfect rendering of one of the most complex and ingenious novels ever written. In order to do so, however, a translation of the novel must make sense, both linguistically and culturally, to the reader. For this reason, a reader must consider, when selecting a translation, the year in which the translation first appeared and the translator's country of origin" (37). In the case of translating proverbial language, it must be acknowledged that there are, for example, differences that do at times appear in the phraseologisms of British and American English.

The opinions of what modern American English translations (Putnam 1949, Joseph/Douglas 1981, Raffel 1995, Grossman 2003, Lathrop 2007, Montgomery 2009) might be "the best" differ widely. McGarth gives the nod to Jones/Douglas and Lathrop (38), while Daniel Eisenberg in his "The Text of *Don Quixote* as Seen by Its Modern English Translators" (2006) appears to skirt the issue by stating that "there is no one translation that will serve every purpose" (120, see also Thacker 2015: 41-44). I must, however, admit that he is quite critical of Edith Grossman's translation (see p. 108) that had been recommended to me by my Spanish colleagues in our Department of Romance Languages when I, relatively late in my life, decided to read *Don Quixote* in 2005 as I began the work on my book *"Tilting at Windmills". History and Meaning of a Proverbial Allusion to Cervantes' "Don Quixote"* (2006a-b). Grossman's translation had received glowing reviews in the media, with Tom Lathrop beginning his substantial scholarly review "Edith Grossman's Translation of *Don* Quixote" (2006) with the following laudatory paragraph:

> The spectacular success of Edith Grossman's translation is the best thing that has ever happened to Cervantes in this country. It was published on October 21, 2003, and two months later, on Christmas Eve, 2003, it rose to be the ninth-best-selling book at Amazon.com.
>
> What this means is that thousands, or even hundreds of thousands of people, have experienced reading this book in recent months, a great boon to *cervantistas'* (or at least *my*) desire to see a *Quijote* on everyone's bookshelf. Our collective hats should collectively be tipped in the direction of

New York's Upper West Side to congratulate Edith Grossman on her achievement.

> This is a trade book [HarperCollins] destined for the
> general reader, and in this role Grossman's text is ideal –
> you read it, you get the story, you get lots of footnotes – in
> an altogether readable format. (Lathrop 2006: 237)

This is quite some praise by Tom Lathrop who, at the time of
writing this review, was himself busy finishing his very own
translation as *Don Quixote. Fourth-Centenary Translation.* Illustrated by Jack Davis (Newark, Delaware: European Masterpieces, 2007). Of course, what follows are almost twenty pages of
very detailed and critical corrections or amendments to Grossman's translation, among them also the following two paragraphs relating to proverbial texts:

> Finding the right word in a second language for plays on
> words in the original language can be sticky. [...] Proverbs
> [and proverbial expressions] are another problem, and the
> translation handles some of them very well by giving appro-
> priate English equivalents. Sancho says: "the proverb fits:
> bird of a feather flock together" (610 [also on p. 515]) for the
> Spanish "dime con quien andas; decirte he quién eres." After
> Maese Predo's ape escapes, he says: "It would be like pull-
> ing teeth to get him back" (653 [should be p. 633]). This is a
> good English equivalent for the Spanish, which says: "me
> han de sudar los dientes." In a scene where Sancho apologiz-
> es to don Quijote, he says: "If I talk too much, it comes more
> from weakness than from malice, and to err is human, to for-
> give divine" (646). A fine equivalent for "quien yerra y se
> enmienda, a Dios se encomienda."
>
> On the other hand, the translation sometimes misses the
> boat, such as when Ginés de Pasamonte says that demanding
> that the galley slaves go to El Toboso is "like asking pears
> from an elm tree" (172) with similar variants [i.e., to ask the
> elm tree for pears] of the same expression on pp. 726 [should
> be p. 716] and 799. Wouldn't "trying to get blood from a
> turnip" be the best equivalent? Similarly, when don Quijote
> speaks of Durandarte, he says that he was "of pure flesh and
> pure bone" (606) – wouldn't "pure flesh and blood" be bet-
> ter? And as for "Zamora was not won in an hour" (922),

wouldn't "Rome was not built in a day" be more logical?
(Lathrop 2006: 239-240)

Just to take issue with this last example, I would argue that Edith
Grossman actually made the right decision by her literal translation of the Spanish "Zamora" proverb referring to the famous
battle at that location in in July 901. There appears to be no reason to replace this culturally specific equivalent with the common European proverbs "Rome was not built in a day" since the
context makes it clear to an English reader what the Spanish
proverb means (see Bizzarri 2015: 615-616, Paczolay 1997: 449-
451). In any case, Tom Lathrop concludes his review by stating
that "I have a warning to make: serious students of literature in
translation should consider looking elsewhere for more faithful
translations, such as Starkie and the discontinued and lamented
Ormsby-Douglas-Jones version [and since 2007 his own translation with notes]. There are just too many things that just are not
right, or are confusing, in this translation" (240). This is a somewhat harsh judgment and certainly contradicts the positive eval-
uation by the well-known literary scholar Harold Bloom who
wrote an introduction to the Grossman translation (xxi-xxxv). As
a novice to Cervantes's *Don Quixote*, I must admit that I thor-
oughly enjoyed reading this translation that as a best-seller conquered its market. Since it obviously is the most widely distributed and available modern translation of *Don Quixote*, I feel justified to base my proverbial study on Edith Grossman's valiant
attempt to make the novel accessible in a readable translation.
For better or worse, I shall take her translations of proverbs, proverbial expressions, and other phraseologisms at face value
without an analysis in each case of how successful the English
renditions are to be judged. As I said before, a comparative analysis of the proverbial material in the twenty English translations
must wait for a future effort by a research team. Of importance
for my study is that Edith Grossman has succeeded in maintaining the rich proverbial language especially in the dialogues between Don Quixote and Sancho Panza, thereby assuring that this
particular trademark of the novel is not lost. This certainly contradicts Vladmir Nabokov's too negative judgment of *Don Quixote* translations: "Proverbs: Sancho, of the second part especially, is a bursting bag of old saws and sayings. To the readers of
translations this Breughelian [*sic*] side of the book is as dead as

cold mutton" (1951-1952: 29). The 714 proverbial texts (386 proverbs, 327 proverbial expressions and comparisons, and 1 wellerism; these numbers include duplicates) that I have identified and presented in the "Index of Proverbs and Proverbial Expressions" are ample proof that Edith Grossman has succeeded splendidly in keeping the rich proverbial language of the novel alive in her celebrated translation.

4. Cervantes as Paremiographical Paremiologist

There can be no doubt that Cervantes was very much aware of the great interest in collecting proverbs during his age that had begun with scholars like Erasmus of Rotterdam, other humanists, protestant reformers, and others interested in assembling the proverbs of the various developing languages in Europe. One can surely imagine that he too enjoyed the rich proverbial tradition of Spain that he could see presented in such collections as Pedro Vallés's *Libro de refranes* (1549) and Juan de Mal Lara's *La philosophía vulgar* (1568), with Sancho Panza being a folksy and ridiculed mirror of this obsession with proverbs (Neumeister 1994: 206-207). At the same time, however, he might well have realized that such compilations are in fact filled with contradictory pieces of folk wisdom. Proverbs are not universal truths but rather limited generalizations that are valid only in certain situations. Such proverb pairs as "Nothing ventured, nothing gained" and "Look before you leap" or "Absence makes the heart grow fonder" and "Out of sight, out of mind" make clear that proverbs are not a logical philosophical system, but each proverb in itself can be employed effectively as a communicative strategy in a context where its underlying insight is appropriate (Mieder 2004a: 133-134). This basic fact must have had its special appeal to Cervantes that lead him to include numerous dialogues in his novel that enumerate proverbs as being valid or invalid. That he did in fact "theorize" about this traditional wisdom can be seen from a number of pertinent passages that draw special attention to the nature and use of proverbs.

Again and again Cervantes draws attention to the fact that a particular proverb happens to be the perfect fit in the context at hand, as for example:

> "And by any chance do the enchanted sleep, Señor?" asked Sancho.
>
> "No, certainly not," responded Don Quixote. "At least, in the three days I have been with them not one of them closed an eye, and neither did I."
>
> "Here," said Sancho, "the proverb fits: birds of a feather flock together; your grace flocks with enchanted people who

fast and stay awake, so it's no surprise you don't sleep while you're with them." (610)

On another occasion, when Sancho bombards Don Quixote with several proverbs from his never-ending repertoire, the latter has to agree that they are perfectly appropriate under the situation at hand (Hart 2002: 47):

> "I'll go and come back very quickly," said Sancho, "and swell that heart of yours, which can't be any bigger now than a hazelnut, and remember what they say: a good heart beats bad luck, and where there is no bacon, there are no stakes [Sancho misquotes the proverb; actually: "To think there's bacon when there's not even a hook to hang it on"], and they also say that a hare leaps out when you least expect it [that is, Life is full of surprises.]. I'm saying this because if we didn't find my lady's palaces or castles last night, now that it's day I think I'll find them when I least expect to, and once I've found them, just leave everything to me."
> "Well, Sancho," said Don Quixote, "you certainly bring in proverbs that suit our affairs perfectly, and I hope God gives me as much good fortune in my desires." (514)

By twice employing the introductory formula "they [people] say", Sancho shrewdly adds some traditional authority to his arguments that help to convince his master while uplifting his spirits.

Another interesting case in point is when Don Quixote in one of his depressed moods wants to let himself die of hunger by refusing to eat. Here Sancho tries to convince him otherwise by way of explaining to him that he should rather believe in the proverb "Let Marta die but keep her belly full" that argues for a continuation of life:

> "That means," said Sancho, not stopping his rapid chewing, "that your grace doesn't agree with the proverb that says, 'Let Marta die but keep her belly full.' I, at least, don't plan to kill myself; instead, I plan to do what the shoemaker does when he pulls on the leather with his teeth and stretches it until it reaches as far as he wants: I'll stretch my life by eating until it reaches the end that heaven has arranged for it; you should know, Señor, that there's no greater madness than wanting to despair, the way your grace does; believe me, after you eat

something, you should sleep a little on the green featherbed of this grass, and you'll see that when you wake up you'll feel much relieved." (843)

And "Don Quixote complied, thinking that Sancho's words were those of a philosopher, not a fool" (843). As Sancho grows in stature towards the end of the novel, Don Quixote has to realize that at times it is he who acts like a fool, with the irony being that one of those proverbs for which he so often ridiculed his squire actually saves his life.

With all his criticism of Sancho's constant use of proverbs, Don Quixote, and Cervantes himself as well, is perfectly aware of their value. Already in the first part of the novel, where Sancho has not really vexed him with his proverbial cannonades as yet, he employs a proverb to add credence to his statement:

> "'Tis a common proverb, O beauteous lady, that diligence is the mother of good fortune, and in many grave and serious matters experience hath shown that solicitude canst bring a doubtful matter to a successful conclusion, but nowhere is this truth clearer than in questions of war, in which celerity and speed canst disrupt the enemy's plans and achieve victory ere the adversary prepareth his defenses." (399)

That the common proverb is true is certainly implied here, but this truth value of proverbs is taken to an extreme by the father of a captive. He actually employs two proverbs, namely "The Church, the sea, or the royal house" (see Quint 2003: 287-288) and "Better the king's crumbs than the noble lord's favors", a clear indication that not only Sancho amasses proverbs:

> "What I [the father of a captive] have decided is to divide my fortune into four parts: three I will give to you [his three sons], each one receiving exactly the same share, and the fourth I will retain to keep me for the time it pleases heaven to grant me life. But after each of you has his share of the estate, I would like you to follow the path I indicate. There is a proverb in our Spain, one that I think is very true, as they all are, for they are brief maxims taken from long, judicious experience; the one I have in mind says: 'The Church, the sea, or the royal house'; in other words, whoever wishes to be successful and wealthy should enter the Church, or go to sea as a mer-

chant, or enter the service of kings in their courts, for, as they say: 'Better the king's crumbs than the noble lord's favors.' I say this because I would like, and it is my desire, that one of you should pursue letters, another commerce, and the third should serve the king in war, for it is very difficult to enter his service at court, and although war does not provide many riches, it tends to bring great merit and fame." (335)

That proverbs cannot possibly be true at all times and situations, is wonderfully explained by Sancho, and indirectly by Cervantes as well, in this insightful comment by Sancho, who proves himself to be much wiser than Don Quixote makes people think:

"I know more proverbs than a book, and so many of them come into my mouth at one time when I talk that they fight with one another to get out, but my tongue tosses out the first ones it finds, even if they're not to the point. But I'll be careful from now on to say the ones that suit the gravity of my position, because in a well-stocked house, supper is soon cooked; and if you cut the cards, you don't deal; and the man who sounds the alarm is safe; and for giving and keeping, you need some sense." (733-734)

So Sancho's incredible proverb repertoire is like one of those printed proverb collections, and when he wants to draw on one, competing proverbs want to come to the fore, some as true in a particular case, others as being not at all to the point. As Don Quixote says: "Look, Sancho, I am not saying that an appropriate proverb is wrong, but loading and stringing together proverbs any which way makes your conversation lifeless and lowborn" (734). Cervantes shows his awareness here that proverb instantiation is no easy matter as anybody knows who has learned proverbs by way of foreign language study. To choose the fitting proverb from a memorized list is no easy matter.

But how about the following all-inclusive statement by Don Quixote quite early in the novel (see Nuessel 1999: 259-260)? Does he not actually like proverbs here by telling Sancho that they are all true? Too bad that Sancho does not recall this high praise for proverbs by his master when in the second part of the novel he ridicules his squire for them:

"It seems to me, Sancho, that there is no proverb that is not true, because all of them are judgments based on experience, the mother of all knowledge, in particular the one that says: 'One door closes and another opens.' I say this because if last night fortune closed the door on what we were seeking, deceiving us with fulling hammers, now she opens wide another that will lead to a better and truer adventure; if I do not succeed in going through this door, the fault will be mine, and I shall not be able to blame my ignorance of fulling hammers or the dark of the night." (153)

Here Don Quixote elaborates on the truth of the proverb "One door closes and another opens". At the end of the novel, he once again emphasizes the truth of a proverb, this time even by referring to it as one that Sancho – by now recognized as being quite wise – likes to cite:

"I have never heard you speak, Sancho," said Don Quixote, "as elegantly as now, which leads me to recognize the truth of the proverb that you like to quote: 'It is not where you were born but who your friends are now that counts.'"

"Ah, confound it, Señor!" replied Sancho. "Now I'm not the one stringing proverbs together; they also drop two by two from your grace's mouth better than they do from mine, but between my proverbs and yours there must be this difference: your grace's come at the right time, while mine are out of place, but in fact they're all proverbs." (904)

Sancho, the ever humble servant, tells his master that whether he likes it or not, he has used proverbs from time to time. Sure, Don Quixote does employ his proverbs in a more sensical fashion, but Sancho is far too subservient here at the close of their joint adventures. He too has moments where his nonsensical amassment of proverbs turns to sensible talk that actually educates Don Quixote. How better to phrase all of this than to say categorically "in fact they're all proverbs!"

There is another metaparemiological dialogue between Sancho and Don Quixote where Cervantes shows himself as a theoretician with deep insights into proverbial folk wisdom (Hasan-Rokem 2007: 195). In utter frustration because of the repeatedly received reprimands due to his natural inclination towards proverbs, Sancho defends his wisdom that fits, proverbially speaking,

"like pears in a wicker basket" and then capitulates in the face of
so much authoritative opposition by citing the proverb "Al buen
callar llamen Sancho" (Golden silence is what they call Sancho;
or, The one who knows how to be silent is called Sancho) that
carries his very own name. First Sancho cites numerous proverbs
that explain how he will act as the future governor of an *ínsula*,
and then follows the extraordinary exchange between the two
central figures:

> "I know how to sign my name very well," responded San-
> cho, "because when I was steward of a brotherhood in my
> village, I learned to make some letters like the marks on
> bundles, and they told me that they said my name; better yet,
> I'll pretend that my right hand has been hurt, and I'll have
> somebody else sign for me; there's a remedy for everything
> except death, and since I'll be in charge of everything, I can
> do whatever I want; then, too, when your father's the magis-
> trate... [you're safe when you go to trial]. And being a gov-
> ernor, which is more than being a magistrate, just let them
> come and they'll see what happens! No, let them make fun
> of me and speak ill of me: they'll come for wool and go
> home shorn; and when God loves you, your house knows it;
> and the rich man's folly passes for good judgment in the
> world; and since that's what I'll be, being a governor and a
> very generous one, which is what I plan to be, nobody will
> notice any faults in me. No, just be like honey and the flies
> will go after you; you're only worth as much as you have,
> my grandmother used to say; and you won't get revenge on a
> well-established man."
>
> "O, may you be accursed, Sancho!" said Don Quixote at
> this point. "May sixty thousand devils take you and your
> proverbs! For the past hour you have been stringing them to-
> gether and with each one giving me a cruel taste of torment.
> I assure you that one day these proverbs will lead you to the
> gallows; because of them your vassals will take the gover-
> norship away from you, or rise up against you. Tell me,
> where do you find them, you ignorant man, and how do you
> apply them, you fool, when to say only one that is really ap-
> plicable, I have to perspire and labor like a ditchdigger?"
>
> "By God, my lord and master," replied Sancho, "your
> grace complains about very small things. Why the devil does

it trouble you when I make use of my fortune, when I have no other, and no other wealth except proverbs and more proverbs? And right now four have come to mind that are a perfect fit, like pears in a wicker basket, but I won't say them, because golden silence is what they call Sancho."

"That Sancho is not you," said Don Quixote, "because not only are you not golden silence, you are foolish speech and stubborn persistence, but even so I should like to know which four proverbs came to mind just now that were so to the point, because I have been searching my mind, and I have a good one, and I cannot think of a single proverb."

"Which ones could be better," said Sancho, "than 'Never put your thumbs between two wisdom teeth' and 'There's no answer to get out of my house and what do you want with my wife' and 'Whether the pitcher hits the stone or the stone hits the pitcher, it's bad luck for the pitcher'? They're all just fine. Because nobody should take on his governor or the person in authority because he'll come out of it hurt, like the man who puts his finger between two wisdom teeth, and if they're not wisdom teeth but just plain molars, it doesn't matter; and there's no reply to what the governor says, like the 'Leave my house and what do you want with my wife.' As for the stone and the pitcher, even a blind man can see that. So whoever sees the mote in somebody else's eye has to see the beam in his own, so that nobody can say about him: 'The dead woman was frightened by the one with her throat cut.' And your grace knows very well that the fool knows more in his own house than the wise man does in somebody else's."

"That is not so, Sancho," responded Don Quixote, "for the fool knows nothing whether in his own house or in another's, because on a foundation of foolishness no reasonable building can be erected. Enough of this now, Sancho, for if you govern badly, the fault will be yours and mine the shame; but it consoles me that I did what I had to do and advised you with all the truth and wisdom of which I am capable: now I am relieved of my obligation and my promise. May God guide you, Sancho, and govern you in your governorship, and free me of the misgivings I still have that you will turn the entire ínsula upside down, something I could

avoid by revealing to the duke who you are, and telling him
that this plump little body of yours is nothing but a sack
filled with proverbs and guile." (735-736)

Much has been made of the "Sancho" proverb (for other proverbs with this name see Jehenson and Dunn 2006: 137) that was
current in a number of variants before Cervantes employed it in
his *Don Quixote* as a rather ironic self-characterization of his
squire (Morel-Fatio 1882, Colombi 1989a, Sevilla Muñoz 1993:
359-361). It has been suggested that it is this very proverb in the
sense of "Silence is golden" that might have lead Cervantes to
call the infamous squire Sancho Panza, with his last name referring to his small but rotund stature (Hasan-Rokem 2007: 189-
190, Bizzarri 2015: 534-535). The paremiological insight of this
discourse is, of course, that proverbs are not universally applicable, because this specific Sancho Panza is way too talkative especially in his proverb bombardments.

And yet, Don Quixote also talks in proverbs even though he
employs them with much less frequency and a much more limited repertoire. By typical self-praise, he claims that he, in apparent contradistinction to Sancho's expertise, uses proverbs only
appropriately and then defines them one more time:

> "Look, Sancho," responded Don Quixote, "I say proverbs
> when they are appropriate, and when I say them they fit like
> the rings on your fingers, but you drag them in by the hair,
> and pull them along, and do not guide them, and if I remem-
> ber correctly, I have already told you that proverbs are brief
> maxims derived from the experience and speculation of wise
> men in the past, and if the proverb is not to the point, it is not
> a maxim, it is nonsense." (902)

The proverbial expression "to fit like a ring on one's finger" is
an absolutely appropriate metaphor to express the correct instantiation of a proverb that in its brevity must be to the point. And
yes, proverbs are based on observed experience and wise insights. But Don Quixote is wrong in his assumption that the simple folk might not have the wisdom to create and use proverbs
correctly. Lord John Russell's proverb definition "A proverb is
the wit of one, and the wisdom of many" (1823) that has long
become proverbial in its own right (Mieder 2004a: 9) implies
that anybody can formulate a sentence that might become pro-

verbial by being accepted and repeated over time. Even Sancho Panza might succeed at this, and even though he at times goes overboard with his strings of proverbs that only occasionally make no sense in the underlying context, this nonsense can quickly be turned around into sense when he does employ them with traditional authority as experienced folk wisdom.

Cervantes, as collector and interpreter of proverbs, definitely had a keen interest in and knowledge of the complexity of these traditional bits of wisdom. Just as "in structure and style, as on the level of meanings, nothing in *Don Quixote* is simple" (Gerhard 1982: 26), so it is with the proverbs that are part of Cervantes's "age of hybridity" and the "cultural polyphony [that] resonates throughout Cervantes's novel" (Jehenson and Dunn 2006: 128 and 129). As the novel confronts the reader with a "barrage of adventures, encounters, speeches, and general display of humanity" (Durán and Rogg 2006: 106), the ever-present stories and proverbs "jostle each other for expression" (Riley 1962: 125). The simple fact that proverbs can contradict each other and that as metaphors they can be quite ambiguous served Cervantes well in his desire to write a new type of novel that is based on a multitude of antitheses (Hatzfeld 1947: 95, Durán 1974: 126, Dunn 1984: 83), and such "conceptual polarities [as] madness-sanity, illusion-reality, appearances-truth, fiction-fact, art-life, poetry-history, romance-novel, idealism-realism, theory-practice, mind-matter, spirit-flesh" (Riley 1986a: 133). Things are simply not obvious or clear in this novel of duality, ambiguity, and uncertainty (Cassou 1947: 12, Serrano-Plaja 1970: 16, Gerhard 1982: 28, Russell 1985: 107-109) that in its multivalency contains wisdom (Bloom 1994: 160) that at least in part is evident in the proverbial dialogues of Don Quixote and Sancho Panza. In those cases where these two discuss the actual nature of proverbs, Cervantes as a "wisdom writer" (Bloom 1994: 145) steps forth as a *bona fide* paremiographical paremiologist as Benjamin Franklin and Ralph Waldo Emerson in due course will as multi-talented writers with their keen interest in proverbs (Mieder 1993: 98-134, and 2014: 261-283). They all enjoyed to descant upon the multifaceted and fascinating world of proverbs.

5. Proverbs by the Narrator and Minor Characters

Even though scholars have for the most part restricted their comments primarily to the use of proverbs in the dialogues between Sancho Panza and Don Quixote, they actually appear throughout the novel albeit with much higher frequency in the second part. Seemingly Cervantes had become convinced that he had touched a nerve with Sancho's limited proverbial speech in the first part and consequently made it the signature for his wise fool as he continued the account of his adventures as Don Quixote's squire. While the proverbial dialogues between his two major male characters are definite highpoints of his novel, he also has minor figures rely on proverbs just like other writers of the *siglo de oro* did with much gusto (Riley 1986a: 126-127, Versini 2003: 30, Jehenson and Dunn 2006: 138, Ayala Mejíra 2007: 82-84). Being a man of his time, Cervantes does by no means restrict his use of proverbs to the direct discourse of his numerous characters that appear in part in "the narration of tales simply interpolated holus-bolus in the middle of the main plot" (Russell 1985: 48), but also employs them quite naturally as the narrator of the fascinating adventures of his knight errant Don Quixote and his squire Sancho Panza. In fact, as all of the proverbs within the massive novel "in which hundreds of characters, situations, vistas, themes, plots and subplots are merged" (Spitzer 1948: 197, see also El Saffar 1975: 15, Vrtunski 1985, Riley 1986b: 63) are surveyed, their omnipresence becomes to a certain degree a red thread of wisdom that ties this "barrage of adventures, encounters, speeches, and general display of humanity" (Durán and Rogg 2006: 106) together. This complex novel that has been compared to "windmills of the mind" (Armas 2015: 112) in reference to the famous adventure of the windmills of the eighth chapter (58-65) is then, at least in small part, also a compendium of "an enormous diversity of speechtypes" that as "speech-acts" become social codes of the "voices" of Cervantes's time (Cascardi 2002a: 62, Rivers 1984: 115). The renowned Hispanist Leo Spitzer has analyzed this incredible variety of language with its satirical or humorous puns and wordplays in his seminal essay on "Linguistic Perspectivism in the *Don Quixote*" (1948, see Corley 1917, Gorfkle 1993: 102-103). Including his own voice as the narrator, "Cervantes blends [linguistic] registers, dialects, idiolects, archaic speech and epic speech, gravity, levity, puns, jokes, proverbs, and comical prevarications, in a *tour de force* of linguistic acrobatics" (Martín 2002: 172). Speaking of the narrator, Cervantes begins his novel with a telling "Prologue" to the "Idle Reader" whose second sentence includes the proverb "Like begets like" as an apology for the possible artistic shortcomings of his literary creation:

> Without my swearing to it, you can believe that I would like this book, the child of my understanding, to be the most beautiful, the most brilliant, and the most discreet, that anyone could imagine. But I have not been able to contravene the natural order; in it, like begets like. And so what could my barren and poorly cultivated wits beget but a history of a child who is dry, withered, capricious, and filled with inconstant thoughts never imagined by anyone else? (3)

The proverb appears to underscore the author's claim that his novel might just be no good, but this statement is, of course, a tongue-in-cheek understatement and a clear indication of the ironic intent of the proverbial message in this context. Not many lines later, still in the same paragraph, Cervantes continues in this vein, telling his prospective readers to be as critical of his account as they wish:

> I do not wish to go along with the common custom and implore you, almost with tears in my eyes, as others do, dearest reader, to forgive or ignore the faults you may find in this my child, for you are neither kin nor his friend, and you have a soul in your body and a will as free as anyone's, and you are in your own house, where you are lord, as the sovereign is master of his revenues, and you know the old saying: under the cover of my cloak I can kill the king. Which exempts and excuses you from all respect and obligation, and you can say anything you desire about this history without fear that you will be reviled for the bad things or rewarded for the good that you might say about it. (3-4)

Having brought his proverbial disclaimer to a conclusion, Cervantes zeroes in on Don Quixote who has decided to be a knight errant ready for adventures that will entail the search for a beautiful lady. Adapting the proverb "A man without a woman is like a tree without leaves" to his newly found chivalrous identity, he is ready to go:

> Having cleaned his armor and made a full helmet out of a simple headpiece, and having given a name to his horse and decided on one for himself, he realized that the only thing left for him to do was to find a lady to love; for the knight without a lady-love was a tree without leaves or fruit, a body without a soul. (23)

Here it is the narrator who informs the reader of this truth, but later in the novel it becomes clear that this is a stated leitmotif for Don Quixote's struggles:

> "I [Don Quixote] have said it many times before, and now I say it again: the knight errant without a lady is like a tree without leaves, a building without a foundation, a shadow without a body to cast it." (671)

Cervantes clearly also likes the proverb "The devil never sleeps" and employs it three times in order to introduce or comment on fateful events befalling his hero:

> As luck and the devil, who is not always sleeping, would have it, grazing in that valley was a herd of Galician ponies tended by some drovers from Yanguas, whose custom it is to take a siesta with their animals in grassy, well-watered places and sites, and the spot where Don Quixote happened to find himself. (103)

> At that very moment the devil, who never sleeps, willed the arrival at the inn of the barber from whom Don Quixote had taken the helmet of Mambrino, and Sancho Panza the donkey's gear that he had exchanged for his own. (389)

> And so, disconsolate and hoarse, they returned to their village and told their friends, neighbors, and acquaintances what had happened to them in their search for the donkey, each exaggerating the other's talent for braying, all of which was learned and circulated in nearby towns. And the devil, who never sleeps, and loves to sow and plant quarrels and discord wherever he goes, spreading mischief on the wind and creating disputes out of nothing, ordered and arranged matters so

that people from other towns, when they saw someone from our village, would bray. (622-623)

There is no particular deep meaning to this proverb, and this is more or less also the case with the proverb "The cat chased the rat, the rat chased the rope, the rope chased the stick" that is cited as a humorous introduction to the struggle that breaks out in an inn that Don Quixote imagines to be a castle (Gerhard 1982: 91-92):

> And, as the old saying goes, the cat chased the rat, the rat chased the rope, the rope chased the stick: the muledriver hit Sancho, Sancho hit the girl, the girl hit Sancho, the innkeeper hit the girl, and all of them acted so fast and furiously that they did not let up for an instant; then, the best part was that the innkeeper's lamp went out, and since they were in darkness, everyone hit everyone with so little mercy that wherever their hands landed they left nothing whole and sound. (115)

Cervantes's narrative employment of proverbs is not always that straight-forward. At times he relinquishes their formulaic structure for the sake of the flow of his prose. In those instances, the proverbs lose their sapiential message, as in this case of the altered proverb "Hunger is the best sauce:

> After riding a short while between two hills, they found themselves in a broad, secluded valley, where they dismounted, and Sancho lightened the donkey's load, and they stretched out on the green grass, and with hunger as their sauce, they had breakfast, lunch, dinner, and supper all at once, satisfying their stomachs. (140)

In the "Prologue" to the second part, Cervantes makes use of the proverb "It is better for a soldier to be dead in combat than safe in flight" in order to refer indirectly to his own fate at the battle of Lepanto, where he was wounded:

> If my wounds do not shine in the eyes of those who see them, they are, at least, esteemed by those who know where they were acquired; it seems better for a soldier to be dead in combat than safe in flight, and I believe this so firmly that even if I could achieve the impossible now, I would rather have taken part in that prodigious battle than to be free of wounds and not to have been there. (454)

He continues in this apologetic way by applying the two proverbs "A poor man may have honor, but not a villain" and "Need may cloud nobility, but not hide it completely" to himself and his literary work that hopefully will be valued:

> A poor man may have honor, but not a villain; need may cloud nobility, but not hide it completely; if virtue sheds her light, even along the crags and cracks of poverty, it will be esteemed by high, noble spirits, and so be favored. (458)

And then he concludes his second prologue with a paragraph that includes the proverbial expression "To be cut from the same cloth" and the proverb "Abundance of things makes people esteem them less", thereby stating that the second part of his *Don Quixote* will follow closely the first and thus face the danger of being considered too repetitive and thus little appreciated. After all, as a second proverb in this final paragraph states, only "Scarcity of things lends a certain value":

> I do not wish to say more to you except to tell you to consider that this second part of *Don Quixote,* which I offer to you now, is cut by the same artisan and from the same cloth as the first, and in it I give you a somewhat expanded Don Quixote who is, at the end, dead and buried, so that no one will dare tell more tales about him, for the ones told in the past are enough, and it is also enough that an honorable man has recounted his clever follies and does not want to take them up again; for abundance, even of things that are good, makes people esteem them less, and scarcity, even of bad things, lends a certain value. (458)

The other authorial intrusions are not that subjective but rather mere narrative observations stating that the proverbs cited are general truths applicable to the situation at hand. Clearly "Time is swift" (Time flies) and "When in Rome, do as the Romans do" are classical proverbs that have been loan translated throughout Europe:

> But since time is swift and there is no obstacle that can stop it, the hours raced by and morning soon arrived. Seeing which Don Quixote left the soft featherbed, and, by no means slothful, dressed in his chamois outfit and put on the traveling boots in order to hide the misfortune of his stocking. (753)

All at the same time, they [pilgrims] raised their arms and the wineskins into the air, their mouths pressed against the mouths of the wineskins and their eyes fixed on heaven, as if they were taking aim; they stayed this way for a long time, emptying the innermost contents of the skins into their stomachs, and moving their heads from one side to the other, signs that attested to the pleasure they were receiving.

Sancho watched everything, and not one thing caused him sorrow; rather, in order to comply with a proverb that he knew very well – "When in Rome, do as the Romans do" – he asked Ricote for his wineskin and took aim along with the rest and with no less pleasure than they enjoyed. (812)

The second example is interesting from a stylistic point of view, since the narrator is quoting the proverb for Sancho, who most likely would have had it in his repertoire. Regarding the unforgettable squire, Cervantes makes the following proverbial remark that speaks of his colorful rhetoric: "Sancho made so many comical remarks that all the servants in the house, and everyone else who heard him, hung on his every word" (864). That is doubtfully true and also especially in regard to his proverbial language that is so very prevalent in the second part of the *Don Quixote*.

While proverbs are not plentiful in the narrative prose, they certainly appear throughout the novel in the dialogues of most characters and not only in those of the three major players Don Quixote and Sancho and Teresa Panza (Jehenson and Dunn 2006: 140). Speaking of Sancho, here is a perfectly fitting proverb by a duchess to describe him:

"That our good Sancho is comical is something I esteem greatly, because it is a sign of his cleverness; for wit and humor, Señor Don Quixote, as your grace well knows, do not reside in slow minds, and since our good Sancho is comical and witty, from this moment on I declare him a clever man." (656)

Later she says with much irony "Everything said here by our good Sancho [...] are Catonian sentences. [...] Well, well, to say it in his fashion, under a poor cloak you can find good drinker" (682). In other words, Sancho is slowly but surely proving himself to be wiser than originally thought. While he might not cite proverbs from Cato used in medieval Latin schools, he is, of course, only too aware of his at times somewhat coarse folk proverbs. This is wonderfully obvious in an exchange between the duke and Sancho. Following the duke's proverbial lead "There's many a slip between the cup and the lip", Sancho retorts with a string of three proverbs:

> "That may be so," replied Sancho, "but if you pay your debts, you don't worry about guaranties, and it's better to have God's help than to get up early, and your belly leads your feet, not the other way around; I mean, if God helps me, and I do what 1 ought to with good intentions, I'll be sure to govern in grand style. Just put a finger in my mouth and see if I bite or not!" (686)

Of course, Don Quixote immediately ridicules Sancho's proverbial rhetoric:

> "God and all his saints curse you, wretched Sancho," said Don Quixote, "as I have said so often, will the day ever come when I see you speak an ordinary coherent sentence without any proverbs? Señores, your highnesses should leave this fool alone, for he will grind your souls not between two but two thousand proverbs brought in as opportunely and appropriately as the health God gives him, or me if I wanted to listen to them." (686)

But the duchess, and good for her, defends Sancho's overuse of proverbs, by stating how much she enjoys listening to them. Her comment foreshadows exactly what readers of the *Don Quixote* have in fact enjoyed for four hundred years:

> "Sancho Panza's proverbs," said the duchess, "although more numerous than those of the Greek Commander, because of their brevity are no less estimable. As far as I am concerned, they give me more pleasure than others that may be more fitting and more opportune." (686-687)

The reference to the "Greek Commander" is actually to Hernán Nuñez, who compiled his famous proverb collection *Refranes o proverbios* in 1555, and which might well have been one of the collections that Cervantes used as a source for his many proverbs.

While this is plain folk speech, there is in contrast the educated Sansón Carrasco, who shows his erudition by integrating Latin proverbs and proverbial expressions (see Percas de Ponseti 1988:

6) in addition to Spanish proverbs during a comical discussion with Don Quixote and Sancho Panza about the value of the book that had been published about them (part 2, chapter 3). There has been some criticism about the publication, but proverbially speaking, "'There is no book so bad,' said the bachelor, 'that it does not have something good in it'" (479). And to defend authors from too much criticism, he quotes the famous classical phrase "From time to time even Homer nods" from Horace's *Ars poetica*:

> "All this is true, Señor Don Quixote," said Carrasco, "but I should like those censurers to be more merciful and less severe and not pay so much attention to the motes in the bright sun of the work they criticize, for if *aliquando bonus dormitat Homerus,* they should consider how often he was awake to give a brilliant light to his work with the least amount of shadow possible; and it well may be that what seem defects to them are birthmarks that often increase the beauty of the face where they appear; and so I say that whoever prints a book exposes himself to great danger, since it is utterly impossible to write in a way that will satisfy and please everyone who reads it." (479)

And Carrasco has one more Latin proverb in store, and with its wisdom that "The number of fools is infinite" Cervantes succeeds in adding plenty of irony to his statement:

> "The one that tells about me," said Don Quixote, "must have pleased very few."
>   "Just the opposite is true [said Carrasco]; since *stultorum infinitus est numerus,* an infinite number of people have enjoyed the history, though some have found fault and failure in the author's memory, because he forgets to tell who the thief was who stole Sancho's donkey." (479-480)

Isn't Carrasco actually saying here that the people who have read the first part of the *Don Quixote* novel must be fools?

    It should also be noted that Sancho is not the only character who amasses proverbs, although he is doubtlessly the master of stringing proverbs together. Here is a paragraph that has Doña Rodríguez cite the proverbial expression "to not come up to (touch) the sole of someone's shoe" as well as the two proverbs "All that is not gold that glitters" and "Walls have ears":

"Your grace [Don Quixote] should keep in mind that my daughter is an orphan, and well-bred, and young, and possessed of all those gifts that I have mentioned to you, for by God and my conscience, of all the maidens that my mistress has, there is none that can even touch the sole of her shoe, and the one they call Altisidora, the one they consider the most elegant and spirited, can't come within two leagues of my daughter. Because I want your grace to know, Señor, that all that glitters is not gold; this little Altisidora has more vanity than beauty, and more spirit than modesty, and besides, she's not very healthy: she has breath so foul that you can't bear to be near her even for a moment. And then, my lady the duchess ... But I'd better be quiet, because they say that the walls have ears." (771)

Close to Sancho's proverb strings is also a dialogue in the interspersed account of "The Man Who Was Recklessly Curious" (first part, chapter 34). It is a splendid scene between Camila and her maid Leonala that develops into a duel of the four proverbs "By giving quickly, one gives twice", "What costs less is valued less", "Love sometimes flies and sometimes walks", and "Good lovers need to have the four Ss":

It happened once, when Camilla found herself alone with her maid, she said:

"I am mortified, my dear Leonela, to see how lightly I valued myself, for I did not even oblige Lotario to pay with time for the complete possession of my desire; I gave it to him so quickly, I fear he will judge only my haste or indiscretion, not taking into account that he urged me so strongly I could no longer resist him."

"Do not be concerned, Señora," responded Leonela. "Giving quickly is of little significance, and no reason to lessen esteem, if, in fact, what one gives is good and in itself worthy of esteem. They even say that by giving quickly, one gives twice" [see Erler 1986].

"They also say," said Camila, "that what costs less is valued less."

"The argument doesn't apply to you," responded Leonela, "because love, I've heard it said, sometimes flies and sometimes walks; it runs with one, and goes slowly with another; it cools some and burns others; some it wounds, and others it kills; it begins the rush of its desires at one point, and at the same point it ends and concludes them; in the morning it lays siege to a fortress, and by nightfall it has broken through, because there is no power that can resist it. [...] Besides, Señora Camila, [said Leonela], you would not have given yourself or surrendered so quickly if you had not first seen in Lotario's eyes, words, sighs, promises, and gifts all his soul, or not seen in it and its virtues how worthy Lotario was of being loved. If this is true, do not allow those qualms and second thoughts to assault your imagination, but be assured that Lotario esteems you as you esteem him, and live contented and satisfied that although you were caught in the snare of love, it is he who tightens it around you with his admiration and esteem. He not only has the four Ss that people say good lovers need to have, but a whole alphabet as well. (293-294)

The last proverb stating that "Good lovers need to have the four Ss" implies the four Spanish words *sabio* ("wise"), *solo* ("alone"), *solicito* ("solicitous"), and *secreto* ("secretive"), indicating that Loratio possesses these attributes and many more. It is also noteworthy that the proverb "By giving quickly, one gives twice" goes back to the classical Latin "Bis dat qui cito dat" that is found once again in most European languages (Erler 1986).

In the adventure with the Knight of the Wood and his Squire of the Wood, Don Quixote and Sancho encounter a pair that appears to be a mirror image of both of them. In fact, the two squires have a lot to speak about their masters and their expectations. The personalized citation of the Biblical proverb "In the sweat of thy face (brow) shalt thou eat bread" (Genesis 3:19) seems to be a fitting description of their fate:

The Squire of the Wood said to Sancho: "We have a difficult life, Señor, those of us who are squires to knights errant: the truth is we eat our bread by the sweat of our brows, which is one of God's curses on our first parents."

"You could also say," added Sancho, "that we eat it in the icy cold of our bodies, because who suffers more heat and cold than we wretched squires of knight errantry? If we ate, it would be easier because sorrows fade with a little bread, but

sometimes we can go a day or two with nothing for our breakfast but the wind that blows." (533)

They even admit to each other that their masters are crazy, with
the Squire of the Wood taking the proverbial lead here. In one
long sentence he strings the proverbs "Greed tears the sack" and
"Other people's troubles kill the donkey" as well as the proverbial
expression "to hit someone right in the face" together:

> "I [Sancho] want to see them [his wife and children] again so
> much that I pray God to deliver me [...] from this dangerous
> squirely work that I've fallen into for a second time, tempted
> and lured by a purse with a hundred *ducados* [...]; and the
> devil places before my eyes, here, there, not here but over
> there, a sack filled with *doblones*, and at every step I take I
> seem to touch it with my hand, and put my arms around it, and
> take it to my house, and hold mortgages, and collect rents, and
> live like a prince, and when I'm thinking about that, all the tri-
> als I suffer with the simpleton of a master seem easy to bear,
> even though I know he's more of a madman than a knight."
>
> "That," responded the Squire of the Wood, "is why they
> say that it's greed that tears the sack, and if we're going to talk
> about madmen, there's nobody in the world crazier than my
> master, because he's one of those who say: 'Other people's
> troubles kill the donkey,' and to help another knight find the
> wits he's lost, he pretends to be crazy and goes around looking
> for something that I think will hit him right in the face when
> he finds it." (535)

This is followed by a short exchange without proverbial language:

> "Is he in love, by any chance?"
> "Yes," said the Squire of the Wood, "with a certain Casil-
> dea of Vandalia, the crudest lady in the world, and the hardest
> to stomach, but indigestibility isn't her greatest fault; her other
> deceits are growling in his belly, and they'll make themselves
> heard before too many hours have gone by." (535)

But now it is Sancho's turn to show his proverbial prowess by
linking the proverbs "There's no road so smooth that it doesn't
have a stumbling block", "They cook beans everywhere", "Craziness has more companions than wisdom", and "Misery loves
company" together that befit their situation:

"There's no road so smooth," replied Sancho, "that it doesn't have some obstacle or stumbling block; they cook beans everywhere, but in my house they do it by the potful; craziness must have more companions and friends than wisdom. But if what they say is true, that misery loves company, then I can find comfort with your grace, because you serve a master who's as great a fool as mine." (535-536)

But when the Squire of the Wood refers to his master as a "scoundrel", Sancho defends Don Quixote as an honorable man who is "as innocent as a baby" as the proverbial comparison has it:

"A fool, but brave," responded the Squire of the Wood, "and more of a scoundrel than foolish or brave."
"Not mine," responded Sancho. "I mean, there's nothing of the scoundrel in him; mine's as innocent as a baby; he doesn't know how to harm anybody, he can only do good to everybody, and there's no malice in him: a child could convince him it's night in the middle of the day, and because he's simple I love him with all my heart and couldn't leave him no matter how many crazy things he does." (536)

And yet, the Squire has the last word in this interchange, returning with his quite appropriate observation that "If the blind leads the blind, they will both fall into the ditch" (Matthew 15:14) to yet another Biblical proverb with considerable authority:

"Even so, Señor," said the Squire of the Wood, "if the blind man leads the blind man, they're both in danger of falling into the ditch. Brother, we'd better leave soon and go back where we came from; people who look for adventures don't always find good ones." (536)

Thus ends a telling proverbial dialogue between the two squires who, although of limited means and no formal education, have plenty of common sense and certainly plenty of wisdom. When one considers the apparent delight that Cervantes takes in such proverb strings, it is surprising that he did not incorporate two or three more between the two street-smart squires.

There is one more minor character who is quite skillful in using proverbial language. In fact, Cervantes introduces the 62. chapter about Don Antonio Moreno with the proverb "Jests that cause pain are no jests":

Don Antonio Moreno was the name of Don Quixote's host, a wealthy and discerning gentleman, very fond of seemly and benign amusements, who, finding Don Quixote in his house, sought ways to make his madness public without harming him; for jests that cause pain are not jests, and entertainments are not worthwhile if they injure another. (864)

In order to have some fun with him and to show Don Quixote's craziness, Don Antonio and his friends attach a sign to Don Quixote's back that reads in large letters *"This is Don Quixote of La Mancha"* (867). As Don Quixote rides through the streets on a mule, people call out his name so that Don Quixote gets the impression that he is indeed well-known as a knight errant. Of course, Don Antonio plays along with this impression, using the proverbs "Fire cannot be hidden" and "Virtue will be recognized" to underscore the deserved fame of Don Quixote:

He [Don Quixote] said: "Great is the prerogative contained within knight errantry, rendering the man who professes it well-known and famous everywhere on earth, for your grace will observe, Señor Don Antonio, that even the boys in this city, who have never seen me before, know who I am."

"That is so, Señor Don Quixote," responded Don Antonio, "for just as fire cannot be hidden and enclosed, virtue cannot fail to be recognized, and that which is achieved through the profession of arms exceeds and outshines all others." (867)

When an unnamed Castilian steps forth and threatens to destroy the charade by calling Don Quixote a madman who should return home "'and stop this nonsense that is rotting your brain and ruining your mind'" (867), Don Antonio saves the situation by upholding Don Quixote's conviction that he is indeed a virtuous knight errant with the proverb "Virtue must be honored":

"Brother [a Castilian]," said Don Antonio, "go on your way, and don't give advice to people who don't ask for it. Señor Don Quixote of La Mancha is a very prudent man, and we who accompany him are not dolts; virtue must be honored wherever it is found; go now, and bad luck to you, and stop minding other people's business." (867)

Thus, even though all of this was a prank at Don Quixote's expense, Don Antonio and his friends in the long-run play along with him and let him remain in his fantasy world.

There are several other minor characters who employ a proverb, but they are of no particular consequence for the novel and can be taken as an indicator of Cervantes being in tune with people's use of proverbs in their everyday conversations. Here is a small contextualized list of various speakers and their proverbs. Since some of them are mere allusions, I state the speakers and the standard proverbs first before citing the proverbial texts in their contexts:

Anselmo: Fire shows the worth of gold.
"The desire that plagues me [Anselmo] is my wondering if Camila, my wife, is as good and perfect as I think she is, and I cannot learn the truth except by testing her so that the rest reveals the worth of her virtue, as fire shows the worth of gold." (275)

Barber: Time will tell.
The barber recounted: "'You, cured?' said the madman. 'Well, well, time will tell; go with God, but I vow by Jupiter, whose majesty I represent on earth, that on account of the sin that Sevilla commits today by taking you out of this madhouse and calling you sane, I must inflict on her a punishment so severe that its memory will endure for all eternity, amen.'" (464)

Butler: The devil hides behind the cross.
"It also seems to me," said the butler, "that your grace [Sancho] shouldn't eat anything that is on this table because it was prepared by nuns, and as the saying goes, behind the cross lurks the devil." (761)

Commissary: Don't go around looking for a three-legged cat.
The commissary responded: "He [Don Quixote] wants us to let the king's prisoners go, as if we had the authority to free them or he had the authority to order us to do so! Your grace, Señor, be on your way, and straighten that basin you're wearing on your head, and don't go around looking for a three-legged cat [i.e., Don't go looking for trouble]." (170)

Don Lorenzo: Every rule has its exception.
"This humility does not seem a bad thing to me," responded Don Quixote, "because there is no poet who is not arrogant and does not think himself the greatest poet in the world."
"Every rule has its exception," responded Don Lorenzo, "and there must be some who are great and do not think so." (569)

Goatherd: No lock protects a maiden better than her own virtue.
The goatherd said: "Her father [a farmer] watched over her [his daughter], and she watched over herself, for there are no locks or bars or bolts that protect a maiden better than her own modesty and virtue." (434)

Knight of the Mirrors: One egg resembles another.
"To that we respond," said the Knight of the Mirrors, "that you resemble the knight I vanquished as much as one egg resembles another; but since you say that enchanters pursue him, I do not dare to state whether you are the aforementioned or not." (544)

Niece: To look (come) for wool and come back shorn.
"Who can doubt it?" said the niece. "But, Señor Uncle [Don Quixote], who has involved your grace in those disputes? Wouldn't it be better to stay peacefully in your house and not wander around the world searching for bread made from something better than wheat, never to think that many people go looking for wool and come back shorn?" (55)

Page: Truth will rise above a lie. Oil rises above water.
"No matter who doubts it," responded the page, "the truth is what I have said, and truth will always rise above a lie, as oil rises above water." (789)

Priest: What is lost today is won tomorrow.
"Be still, my friend," said the priest, "for it is God's will that fortune changes, and that what is lost today is won tomorrow; your grace should tend to your health now, for it seems to me your grace must be fatigued, if not badly wounded." (53)

Prisoner: Where there's life there's hope.

"The case was proved, nobody showed me favor, I [a prisoner] had no money, I almost had my gullet in a noose, they sentenced me to six years in the galleys, and I agreed: it's a punishment for my crime; I'm young; just let me stay alive, because where there's life there's hope." (167)

As can be seen from these examples, the proverbs are simply used as generalizations or explanations without playing any particular role in the message of the novel. There is, however, one more exchange between a galley slave and Don Quixote that deserves to be cited:

"What?" Don Quixote repeated, "Men also go to the galleys for being musicians and singers?" "Yes, Señor," responded the galley slave, "because there's nothing worse than singing when you're in difficulty." "But I have heard it said," said Don Quixote, "that troubles take wing for the man who can sing." "Here just the opposite is true," said the galley slave. "Warble once, and you weep the rest of your days." (165)

This is only a very short verbal exchange, but it shows that Cervantes is very much aware of the contradictory nature of proverbs (Mieder 2004: 134). Much has been made of the polarization, dualism, and paradox that are inherent to this novel (Williamson 1984: 157), and the contrast of the proverb pair "Troubles take wing for the man who can sing" and "Warble once, and you weep the rest of your days" is certainly part of this antithetical aspect.

6. Proverbial Wisdom Employed by Teresa Panza

Nobody can possibly match Sancho Panza's proverbial prowess, but there can be no doubt that his down-to-earth peasant wife Teresa Panza does have an impressive proverb repertoire that would be more evident if she were playing a larger role in the novel. The fifth chapter of the second part contains a particularly rich proverbial dialogue between Teresa and Sancho with the latter telling his wife with great excitement that he will leave again with Don Quixote and that their lives will drastically change for the better once he receives the governorship of an *ínsula* in due course. It is here where two people from the lower strata of society talk in proverbs to underscore their respective arguments with the authority of tradition. It begins with Teresa stressing that her husband has so changed that she does not even understand his peasant speech any longer to which Sancho responds with the proverb that "God understands all things":

> "Look, Sancho," replied Teresa, "ever since you became a knight errant's servant your talk is so roundabout nobody can understand you."
>
> "It's enough if God understands me, my wife," responded Sancho, "for He understands all things, and say no more about it for now." (486)

But the discussion does not stop there, even though Sancho says proverbially that he will fall down dead if he were not to receive his governorship. To this Teresa retorts with the proverb "Let the chicken live even if she has the pip," where the chicken metaphor has to be understood as somewhat of a demasculinization of Sancho. As she tries to convince her husband to be happy with his lot be it ever so poor, she adds the proverb "The best sauce in the world is hunger" to conclude her argument for the *status quo*:

> "I'll tell you, Teresa," responded Sancho, "that if I didn't expect to be the governor of an ínsula before too much more time goes by, I'd fall down dead right here."
>
> "Not that, my husband," said Teresa, "let the chicken live even if she has the pip; may you live, and let the devil

take all the governorships there are in the world; you came out of your mother's womb without a governorship, and you've lived until now without a governorship, and when it pleases God you'll go, or they'll carry you, to the grave without a governorship. Many people in the world live without a governorship, and that doesn't make them give up or not be counted among the living. The best sauce in the world is hunger, and since poor people have plenty of that, they always eat with great pleasure." (486)

The argument could have stopped there, but then the good woman reminds her husband of their children Sanchico and Mari Sancha, using the proverb "A daughter is better off badly married than happily kept" to remind him that the daughter is looking for a husband:

> "But look, Sancho: if you happen to find yourself a governor somewhere, don't forget about me and your children. Remember that Sanchico is already fifteen, and he ought to go to school if his uncle the abbot is going to bring him into the Church. And don't forget that our daughter, Mari Sancha, won't die if we marry her; she keeps dropping hints that she wants a husband as much as you want to be a governor, and when all is said and done, a daughter's better off badly married than happily kept."
>
> "By my faith, Teresa," responded Sancho, "if God lets me have any kind of governorship, I'll marry Mari Sancha so high up that nobody will be able to reach her unless they call her Señora." (486-487)

Of course, good old Sancho immediately returns to the fantasy of being a rich governor who will be able to plan the fanciest wedding for her to a nobleman. Teresa will have nothing of it, arguing that they should be content with their life as it is. In order to convince Sancho of this view, she cites a proverb and a proverbial expression, giving him some of his own folk medicine as it were:

> "Be content with your station," responded Teresa, "and don't try to go to a higher one; remember the proverb that says: 'Take your neighbor's son, wipe his nose, and bring him into your house.' Sure, it would be very nice to marry our María

to some wretch of a count or gentleman who might take a notion to insult her and call her lowborn, the daughter of peasants and spinners! Not in my lifetime, my husband! I didn't bring up my daughter for that! You bring the money, Sancho, and leave her marrying to me." (487)

But Sancho will not let go of his *idée fixe* and, tit for tat, continues the argument with two proverbs and proverbial phrase. By using the introductory formula "the old folk say" with the proverbs "If you don't know how to enjoy good luck when it comes, you shouldn't complain if it passes you by" and "If luck comes knocking, don't shut the door in its face" he adds considerable traditional authority to his statement. The proverbial metaphor of the "favorable wind" that should be followed strengthens his argument even more:

> "Come here, you imbecile, you troublemaker," replied Sancho. "Why do you [Teresa] want to stop me now, and for no good reason, from marrying my daughter to somebody who'll give me grandchildren they'll call *Lord* and *Lady*? Look, Teresa: I've always heard the old folks say that if you don't know how to enjoy good luck when it comes, you shouldn't complain if it passes you by. It wouldn't be a good idea, now that it's come knocking, to shut the door in its face; we should let the favorable wind that's blowing carry us along." (487)

And yet, Teresa is by no means an imbecile, and she argues against a high society marriage of their daughter by three times stating that the proverbial "to put on airs" is not for her. In her excitement, she misquotes the proverb "Where kings go laws follow" as "Where laws go kings follow" and then concludes her tirade with the anti-feministic proverb "La mujer honrada, la pierna quebrada, y en casa" (To keep a woman honorable break her leg and keep her in the house; see Bizzarri 2015: 375-376). Of course, in this particular case Teresa interprets the proverb to mean that María is better off staying at home than moving away from her social environment. She does not mean to insult her daughter with it, a fine example of the polysemanticity of proverbs. Besides, she also adds the somewhat less drastic proverb "For a chaste girl, work is her fiesta" to it all:

"Do you hear what you're saying, husband?" responded Teresa. "Well, even so, I'm afraid that if my daughter becomes a countess it will be her ruin. You'll do whatever you want, whether you make her a duchess or a princess, but I can tell you it won't be with my agreement or consent. Sancho, I've always been in favor of equality, and I can't stand to see somebody putting on airs for no reason. They baptized me Teresa, a plain and simple name without any additions or decorations or trimmings of *Dons* or *Doñas;* my father's name was Cascajo, and because I'm your wife, they call me Teresa Panza, though they really ought to call me Teresa Cascajo. But where laws go kings follow, and I'm satisfied with this name without anybody adding on a *Doña* that weighs so much I can't carry it, and I don't want to give people who see me walking around dressed in a countish or governorish way a chance to say: 'Look at the airs that sow is putting on! Yesterday she was busy pulling on a tuft of flax for spinning, and she went to Mass and covered her head with her skirts instead of a mantilla, and today she has a hoopskirt and brooches and airs, as if we didn't know who she was.' If God preserves my seven senses, or five, or however many I have, I don't intend to let anybody see me in a spot like that. You, my husband, go and be a governor or an insular and put on all the airs you like; I swear on my mother's life that my daughter and I won't set foot out of our village: to keep her chaste, break her leg and keep her in the house; for a chaste girl, work is her fiesta. You go with your Don Quixote and have your adventures, and leave us with our misfortunes, for God will set them right if we're good; I certainly don't know who gave him [Don Quixote] a *Don,* because his parents and grandparents never had one." (488)

In the context of Teresa's and Sancho's argument, the questionable proverb clearly "functions dialogically as a defense of Teresa, her family and also a proverbial collective authority" (Ciallella 2007: 27, see also Ciallella 2003: 278). It should, however, be noted here that Sancho uses the proverb later when he is governor of his *ínsula* in its chauvinistic sense. In fact, he adds two other antifeministic proverbs to it, making it a triadic proverbial attack on women:

"Nothing's been lost," responded Sancho. "Let's go, and we'll leave your graces [a young maiden and her brother] at your father's house; maybe he hasn't missed you. And from now on don't be so childish, or so eager to see the world; an honorable maiden and a broken leg stay in the house; and a woman and a hen are soon lost when they wander; and a woman who wants to see also wants to be seen. That's all I'll say." (781)

Perhaps readers of the seventeenth century saw some humor in this string of proverbs, but to modern students of the novel Sancho does not gain positive points with these stereotypical invectives that unfortunately are current in all cultures (Schipper 2003). But on the other hand, when Sancho uses the proverb on a third occasion as a mere allusion and the change of "woman" to "governor", there is a certain sense of irony or humor at play.

"No," responded Sancho, "a good governor and a broken leg stay at home. How nice if weary merchants came to see him and he was in the woods enjoying himself! What a misfortune for the governorship!" (686)

All of this is a sign of Cervantes's mastery of the adaptability of proverbs to ever new situations where one and the same proverb can take on different functions and meanings. In paremiological terms, this very phenomenon of proverbs has been referred to as polysituativity, polyfunctionality, and polysemanticity (Krikmann 1974: 15-50, Mieder 2004a: 9 and 132).

But to return to the scene between Teresa and Sancho, he is by no means letting the argument go, and like the pot calling the kettle black, even reproaches his wife of her use of proverbs:

"Now I'll say," replied Sancho, "that you must have an evil spirit in that body of yours. God save you, woman, what a lot of things you've strung together willy-nilly! What do Cascajo, brooches, proverbs, and putting on airs have to do with what I'm saying? Come here, you simple, ignorant woman, and I can call you that because you don't understand my words and try to run away from good luck. If I had said that my daughter ought to throw herself off a tower or go roaming around the way the Infanta Doña Urraca wanted to [allusion to the ballad of Doña Urraca's desire to go wandering],

you'd be right not to go along with me; but if in two shakes
and in the wink of an eye I dress her in a *Doña* and put a *my
lady* on her back for you, and take her out of the dirt and put
her under a canopy and up on a pedestal in a drawing room
with more velvet cushions than Moors in the line of the Almohadas of Morocco, why won't you consent and want what
I want?" (488-489)

This question gives Teresa one final opportunity to employ a
proverb in this duel that she cannot win:

> "Do you know why, Sancho?" responded Teresa. "Because
> of the proverb that says: 'Whoever tries to conceal you, re-
> veals you!' Nobody does more than glance at the poor, but
> they look closely at the rich; if a rich man was once poor,
> that's where the whispers and rumors begin, and the wicked
> murmurs of gossips who crowd the streets like swarms of
> bees." (489)

Sancho remains resolved, with Teresa with tears stating in des-
peration "'I don't understand you, my husband'" (490). Indeed,
"Teresa's proverbial speech [can be seen] as part of an egalitari-
an discourse of domesticity that she shares with Sancho"
(Ciallella 2007: 25), but there is no feminist emancipation here
in the early seventeenth century.

But Teresa changes her tune in the splendidly humorous 50.
Chapter of the second part, where a page brings a letter to her
and their daughter Sanchica announcing that Sancho has in fact
been named the governor of an *ínsula*. The reactions are euphor-
ic, with the gullible Teresa stating "By my faith, we're not poor
relations anymore! We have a nice little governorship! And if the
proudest of the gentlewomen tries to snub me, I'll know how to
put her in her place!" (786). And then this, with the page, a priest
and a bachelor bearing witness:

> "O daughter [Sanchica], you certainly are right!" responded
> Teresa. "And all of this good fortune, and some even greater
> than this, my good Sancho predicted for me, and you'll see,
> daughter, how he doesn't stop until he makes me a countess;
> it's all a matter of starting to be lucky; and I've heard your
> good father say very often – and he loves proverbs as much
> as he loves you – that when they give you the calf, run over

with the rope; when they give you a governorship, take it; when they give you a countship, hold on to it tight, and when they call you over with a nice present, pack it away. Or else just sleep and don't answer when fortune and good luck come knocking at your door!"

"And what difference does it make to me," added Sanchica, "if they say when they see me so proud and haughty: 'The dog in linen breeches ... and all the rest?"

Hearing this, the priest said:

"I can't help thinking that everyone in the Panza family was born with a sack of proverbs inside; I've never seen one of them who isn't always scattering proverbs around in every conversation they have."

"That's true," said the page, "for Señor Governor Sancho says them all the time, and even though many are not to the point, they still give pleasure, and my lady the duchess and my lord the duke praise them a good deal." (788-789)

Teresa bears witness to the fact that Sancho is particularly invested in proverbs, and then she quotes one of his favorite proverbs "When they give you the calf, run over with the rope" that she applies in a series of more specific variations to the new role as a fine lady to herself. And the daughter in anticipation of her new haughty social position chimes in as a budding proverbialist by saying that it will not make a difference if people were to comment that "'The dog in linen breeches' ... and all the rest". The complete proverb states "The dog in linen breeches says how crude, how crude" that is aimed at the poor who for whatever reason prosper and then belittle their old friends. Little wonder that the astonished priest speaks of "the Panza family [being] born with a sack of proverbs inside" that they "always scatter around in every conversation". The page seconds this claim by pointing to Señor Governor Sancho citing them also "all the time" even though they might not be appropriate. There is no doubt that this scene is part of "the broadly comic strain of mockery, laughter, and slapstick that has its roots in popular tradition" (Martín 2002: 168).

There is one more verbal exchange in this special chapter worth mentioning. Even though Cervantes does not employ the proverb "Like mother, like daughter", Sanchica is equally enthralled about being uplifted by her father's new position as the

62   *Proverbial Wisdom Employed by Teresa Panza*

governor of an *ínsula*, and she is ready to join her father by following the page:

"I should be the one to go," said Sanchica. "Señor, your
grace [the page] can let me ride on the horse's hindquarters,
because I'd be very happy to see my father."

"The daughters of governors should not travel the roads
unescorted but should be accompanied by coaches and litters
and a large number of servants."

"By God," responded Sanch[ic]a, "I can ride a donkey as
well as a coach. You must think I'm very hard to please!"

"Be quiet, girl," said Teresa. "You don't know what
you're saying, and this gentleman is right; time changes the
rhyme: when it's Sancho, it's Sancha, and when it's governor, it's Señora, and I don't know if I'm saying something or
not." (789-790)

Attitudes certainly change quickly or "Time changes the rhyme",
a proverb that Sancho employs in one of his proverb strings later
in the novel as well (821).

Teresa does not only speak proverbs, she also includes them
in two letters which come as somewhat of a surprise realizing
that her husband Sancho can neither read nor write. One would
have thought that she is illiterate as well. But in any case, in her
letter to the duchess she alludes to the proverb "When you have a
good day, put it in the house," which is somewhat equivalent to
"Make hay while the sun shines". As the following reference
shows, Teresa certainly has bought into the deceptive claim that
Sancho has become a governor on his *ínsula*:

*Señora of my soul, I've decided, with your grace's permis-
sion, to put this good day in my house by going to court and
leaning back in a carriage and making their eyes pop, for
there are thousands who are already envious of me; and so I
beg Your Excellency to tell my husband to send me some
money, and to make it enough, because at court expenses are
high: bread sells for a real, and a pound of meat costs thirty
maravedís, which is a judgment [a sin, crime], and if he
doesn't want me to go, he should let me know soon, because
my feet are itching to get started.* (801-802)

In the second letter t her husband Sancho she continues along this line by telling him she was almost totally overcome with happiness because of his governorship. The proverb "Sudden joy can kill just like great sorrow" is certainly a fitting folk expression for her state of being:

> *I received your letter, Sancho of my soul, and I can tell you and swear to you as a Catholic Christian that I practically went crazy with happiness. Just think, my husband: when I heard that you were a governor, I thought I'd fall down dead from sheer joy, because you know, people say that sudden joy can kill just like great sorrow.* (802)

But there is a second proverb in this letter that is the perfect fit for her set of mind. She wants to join Sancho to see what their life will be like in his new exquisite surroundings. After all, her mother already had taught her the proverb "You have to live a lot to see a lot":

> *And you know, dear husband, my mother used to say you had to live a lot to see a lot: I say this because l plan to see more if I live more, because I don't plan to stop until I see you as a landlord or a tax collector, for these are trades, after all, in which you always have and handle money, though the devil carries off anyone who misuses them.* (802-803)

As can be seen, Teresa Panza relies on folk proverbs to back up her feelings and thoughts, citing them as summaries of commonly observed experiences and thereby sanctioning her own behavior. From a paremiological point of view, it is a shame that Teresa Panza does not occupy more space in the novel. Her proverbial rhetoric would certainly have been a welcome addition to that of her husband Sancho Panza.

7. Don Quixote's Unexpected Proverb Repertoire

Judging by scholars who have commented on the use and function of proverbs in Cervantes's *Don Quixote*, the conclusion would have to be reached that, except in some of the rich proverb dialogues between the knight errant and his squire, Don Quixote is not prone to employ such folk wisdom in his rhetoric that reflects an educated man. In other words, Teresa and Sancho Panza fit the stereotypical view that people of little education and of the lower social strata are naturally inclined towards citing formulaic proverbs instead of expressing themselves in more intellectual sentences of their own. It is, of course true, that Don Quixote does enjoy philosophical deliberations in which he integrates literary quotations and classical Latin adages, but he is by no means free from relying on traditional proverbs when they suit him for whatever purpose he might have in mind (Burke 1872: v-vi). A case in point is a letter of advice that Don Quixote writes to Sancho regarding the latter's role as the governor of his *ínsula*. While it is somewhat ironic that he is addressing Sancho, who is more or less illiterate, by mail at all, he means well and gives him the proverbial advice that he should "Choose the middle between two extremes":

> *Be a father to virtues and a stepfather to vices. Do not always be severe, or always mild, but choose the middle way between those two extremes; this is the object of wisdom. Visit the prisons, the slaughterhouses, and the market squares, for the presence of the governor in these places is of great importance: it consoles the prisoners, who can hope for a quick release; it frightens the butchers, who then make their weights honest; it terrifies the marketwomen, and for the same reason.*
> (794)

There is no comprehension problem in this down-to-earth statement. But what is poor Sancho to make of the last paragraph of this letter that is rather nebulous to start with and that includes a classical quotation turned proverb in Latin? As Leonardo Tarán has shown in his enlightening study "'Amicus Plato sed magis amica veritas': From Plato and Aristotle to Cervantes" (1984), the proverb "Be a friend to Plato, but a better friend to the truth" originated in ancient Greece and was translated into Latin that helped spread it throughout Europe. However, it was also loan translated into Arabic, and Arabic authors helped to distribute it in Spain. As is so often the case with classical proverb lore, the proverb also appears in Erasmus of Rotterdam's *Adagia* (1500ff.) and it should be no surprise that Cervantes gained knowledge of it. But how about good old Sancho? How is he to understand the Latin proverb? Not to worry, Cervantes or Don Quixote thought of everything. As the reader learns, Sancho might have learned Latin since becoming governor:

> *A matter has been presented to me that I believe will discredit me with the duke and duchess, but although it concerns me a great deal, at the same time it does not concern me at all, for, in the end, I must comply with my profession rather than with their desires; as the saying goes: Amicus Plato, sed magis amica veritas. I say this to you in Latin because I assume you must have learned it after you became a governor. (794-795)*

Nevertheless, early readers must have seen considerable humor in all of this, while modern educated readers, for whom the old *lingua franca* of Latin is quite remote, find themselves looking for a footnote to decipher the meaning of the proverb. It is fair then to argue that the apparent epistolary humor is most likely lost today.

What these two proverbs show is the basic complexity of Don Quixote, who "is a bit cracked but not in the least stupid" (Mann 1934: 27) and who, "as a righter of wrongs, makes eminent sense" (Hutman 1984: 123). In fact, "he is not completely and irreparably mad" and "occasionally becomes a teacher" (Durán 1974: 105). He is indeed a most ambiguous character, who has plenty of "lucid intervals during which he behaves, and, particularly, speaks with apparent prudence and good sense" (Russell 1985: 74, see also Durán 1974: 95). This comes definitely through in his usually didactic use of proverbs that shows him in the role of a teacher, something that has unfortunately been overlooked in the many interpretations of the novel. There can be no doubt that Cervantes has very consciously placed proverbs in the mouth of his major character in order to make statements that make plenty of sense and mirror general rules of social behavior. One thing is for certain, Don Quixote does not make light of folk wisdom but employs proverbs for the most part as truths without ridiculing them.

He might question the wisdom of some of them, especially when Sancho amasses them into seemingly contradictory statements, but in general he recognizes their value as valid verbal signs of human behavior. Interestingly, John Weiger begins his chapter on "Names and Deeds" in his significant study *In the Margins of Cervantes* (1988) with the epigraph "Cada uno es hijo de sus obras", calling it an "apparent commonplace" (1988: 165) without stating explicitly that it is in fact the well-known Spanish proverb "Each man is the child of his deeds". It happens to be Don Quixote's very first proverb that is uttered long before the proverbialist Sancho Panza strikes the reader with his proverbial treasures (Casalduero 1947: 88). After having protected a boy from being mistreated by someone whom he thinks to be a knight, this short but significant exchange takes place:

> The boy said: "This master of mine is no knight and he's never received any order of chivalry; he's Juan Haldudo the rich man, and he lives in Quintanar."
> "That is of no importance," replied Don Quixote. "For there can be knights among Haldudos, especially since each man is the child of his deeds." (37)

In many ways this proverb is a fitting characterization of the trials and tribulations that Don Quixote will endure, always in the strong conviction, as he states later in the novel, that "it is fitting to put into practice my profession [as a knight errant]: to right wrongs and come to the aid and assistance of the wretched" (163).

The second proverb cited by Don Quixote, "Una golondrina sola no hace verano" (One solitary swallow does not a summer make), has an ancient Greek beginning and is known throughout Europe (Paczolay 1997: 49-53). Don Quixote employs it in one of his early discussions about the fact that "there cannot be a knight errant without a lady, because it is as fitting and natural for them to be in love as for the sky to have stars" (90). When an unnamed traveler contradicts him in this conviction by citing an example of a knight who did not undertake adventures for love, Don Quixote brushes this singular fact aside by appropriately applying said proverb:

"Even so," said the traveler, "it seems to me that if I remember correctly, I have read that Don Galaor, brother of the valorous Amadís of Gaul, never had a specific lady to whom he could commend himself, and despite this he was not held in any less esteem, and was a very valiant and famous knight." To which Don Quixote responded: "Señor, one swallow does not a summer make. Furthermore, I happen to know that this knight was secretly very much in love, even though his courting all the lovely ladies he found attractive was a natural inclination that he could not resist. However, it is clearly demonstrated that there was one lady whom he had made mistress of his will, and to her he commended himself very frequently and very secretly, because he prided himself on being a secretive knight." (90)

Don Quixote might well have stopped with the proverb since it served his argument perfectly by insisting that this knight without love is the exception to the rule. Instead he tells a white lie about the knight actually having had a love relationship. Apparently he sensed the need to validate his claim that every knight errant has to have a lady love. In any case, in one of the rare comments about Don Quixote's use of proverbs, Howard Mancing argues that "Don Quixote, trapped, reacts in a manner that anticipates the classic Sancho Panza, by citing a proverb – and then by contradicting himself with an outright lie" (1982a: 12).

This scene is by no means the norm for Don Quixote who employs most of his proverbs in a cautionary, didactic, or moralistic fashion. Here, for example, is a double-barreled proverbial shot of this type for his squire Sancho:

"Even though, I want you to know, brother Sancho," replied Don Quixote, "that there is no memory that time does not erase, no pain not ended by death." (107)

Poor Sancho can't escape the sermonic application of proverbs by his master, who uses them more than he will later admit. And he is clearly aware that he is citing folk wisdom by drawing attention to it with introductory formulas like "as it is said", "what they say", "those who say", and "the adage that says". He does not refer directly to proverbs in these isolated instances, leaving this term to be used when provoked into discussions by Sancho's frequent use of them. Instead, he prefers at least in this one case the term "adage" which represents a more sophisticated designation used by such humanists as Erasmus of Rotterdam:

Self-praise is self-debasement.
"Believe me, beauteous lady, thou canst call thyself fortunate of having welcomed into this thy castle my person, which I [Don Quixote] do not praise because, as it is said, self-praise is self-debasement, but my squire wilt tell thee who I am. I say only that I shall keep eternally written in my memory the service that thou hast rendered me, so that I may thank thee for it as long as I shall live." (111)

A new sin demands a new penance.
"As you value your life, Sancho, do not speak of this [Sancho's earlier comment about Dulcinea] again," said Don Quixote, "for it brings me grief; I forgave you then, and you know what they say: a new sin demands a new penance." (257)

One should build a silver bridge for the enemy who flees.
Don Quixote, stumbling here and falling there, began to run as fast as he could after the herd of bulls, shouting:
"Stop, wait, you villainous rabble! A single knight awaits you, one who does not concur or agree with those who say that one should build a silver bridge for the enemy who flees!"
But not even this could stop the speeding runners, and they paid no more attention to his threats than to the clouds of yesteryear. (841)

Hell is filled with the ungrateful.
Don Quixote said: "Although some say pride is the greatest sin men commit, I say it is ingratitude, for I am guided by the adage that says hell is filled with the ungrateful. This sin is one I have attempted to flee, as much as it was possible for me to do so, since I first reached the age of reason; if I cannot repay the good deeds done for me with other deeds, in their place I put the desire I have to perform them, and if that is not enough, I proclaim those good deeds far and wide, because the person who tells about and proclaims the good deeds that have been performed on his behalf would also recompense them with other deeds if he could, because most of the time those who receive are subordinate to those who give." (839)

Of special interest in this regard is the following statement to Sancho that includes the introductory formula "as the saying goes" and then, to the dismay of the uneducated squire, cites the mere first half of the Latin proverb "Quando caput dolet caetera membra dolent":

> "That was right and proper," responded Sancho, "because, according to your grace, misfortunes afflict knights errant more than their squires."
>
> "You are wrong, Sancho," said Don Quixote. "As the saying goes, *Quando caput dolet—*"
>
> "I don't understand any language but my own," responded Sancho.
>
> "I mean," said Don Quixote, "that when the head aches, all the other members ache, too; since I am your lord and master, I am your head, and you my part, for you are my servant; for this reason, the evil that touches or may touch me will cause you pain, and yours will do the same to me."
>
> "That's how it should be," said Sancho. (470)

Don Quixote should have known better than to bring a partial Latin proverb into play, with Sancho's response that he only understands his own language of Spanish being able to stand generally for the frequent miscommunications between them. It is also of interest to note that Don Quixote actually contradicts the proverb as he translates and explains it for Sancho. According to the proverb, Sancho should feel the pain of his master and not Don Quixote that of his squire. And yet, Don Quixote adds that "yours [the aches of his squire] will do the same". The quick-witted Sancho catches exactly what his master has just said and agrees wholeheartedly with "That's the way it should be". There is much irony if not humor in this, and a sign that Sancho even with such succinct comebacks "frequently holds the floor conversationally" (Russell 1985: 66). But a scene like this would hardly justify considering "*Don Quixote* as a funny [or even hilarious] book" (Eisenberg 1984: 62 and 64). There is something deeper in this short exchange approximately in the middle of the novel. Don Quixote might not yet be aware of the fact that he and Sancho are growing ever closer together as partners in friendship as they continue with their adventures. P.E. Russell's observation "that behind the fun of his story [Cervantes] presented situations and issues for which

laughter was not the only possible response" (1985: 83) is definitely applicable here. Sancho's implication that what is true for
his master also holds for him as his servant begins to show that
"Don Quixote and Sancho Panza are [at the end] not opposites;
more than that, they adopt each other's traits in the course of their
association. [This] can be seen as a dialectical process. [...] By the
end [...] Sancho has been largely 'quixotized', while Quixote has
been sufficiently 'sanchified' to be ready to abandon the dream by
which he had come to live" (Watt 1996: 212). There certainly is
much wisdom in this observation by a priest around the beginning
of the second part of the novel" "May God help them, and let us
be on the alert: we'll see where all the foolishness in this knight
and squire will lead, because it seems to me as if both were made
from the same mold, and that the madness of the master, without
the simplicity of the servant, would not be worth anything" (470,
Johnson 1983: 142, Watt 1996: 214). This rather odd couple –
somewhat reminiscent of such modern "clones" like Charles
Dickens's Mr. Pickwick and Sam Weller in his novel *The Pickwick Papers* (1836, see Gale 1973, Flores 1982a: 59-68), Arthur
Conan Doyle's Sherlock Holmes and Dr. Watson, Dean Martin
and Jerry Lewis, Jack Klugman and Tony Randall, and others
(Stavans 2015: 28) – "might be seen as one head with two faces,
or as the complementing halves of a single soul (Stavans 2015:
26). In a way, "Sancho the wise fool, his master the sane madman" (Parr and Vollendorf 2015b: 10) are strange soul mates tied
together by their basic humanity despite of their different educational and social backgrounds (González Echevarría 2005b: 8).

But to return to the proverbial muttons, Don Quixote does use
proverbs and phrases that refer to classical themes that would not
be cited by Sancho with his more earthy phraseology, to wit his
master's use of the proverbial expressions "before one can say
credo", "to be (get) between Scylla and Charybdis" and "to be a
Gordian knot":

"Did I not tell you so?" said Don Quixote. "Wait, Sancho.
And I shall do them [crazy things] before you can say Credo."
(204)

"They [students] stumble and fall, pick themselves up and fall
again, until they reach the academic title they desire; once this
is acquired and they have passed through these shoals, these

Scyllas and Charybdises, as if carried on the wings of good fortune, we have seen many who command and govern the world from a chair, their hunger turned into a full belly, their cold into comfort, their nakedness into finery, and their straw mat into linen and damask sheets, the just reward for their virtue. But their hardships, measured against and compared to those of a soldier and warrior, fall far behind." (330)

"The companionship of one's own wife is not merchandise that, once purchased, can be returned, or exchanged, or altered; it is an irrevocable circumstance that lasts as long as one lives: it is a rope that, if put around one's neck, turns into the Gordian knot, and if the scythe of Death does not cut it, there is no way to untie it." (578)

"If Alexander the Great cut the Gordian knot, saying: 'It does not matter if it is cut or untied,' and that did not keep him from being the universal lord of all Asia, then in the disenchantment of Dulcinea it might not matter if I whip Sancho against his will, for if the condition of this remedy is that Sancho receive some three thousand lashes, what difference does it make to me if he administers them himself or if another does, since the essence of the matter is that he receive them regardless of where they come from." (850)

It is not Don Quixote's habit to repeat proverbial language as in the case with the "Gordian knot" phrase. But he does so one more time with the proverb "Time reveals all things", which will, of course, eventually also be the case for both Don Quixote and Sancho Panza as they "live through a process beginning with pride and presumption and a consequent unawareness of their limitations, moving toward self-discovery through suffering, and culminating in confession and repentance" (Allen 1979: 34):

"I prefer to remain silent, because I do not wish anyone to say that I am lying, but Time, which reveals all things, will disclose the truth to us when we least expect it." (323-324)

"Events will tell the truth of things, Sancho," responded Don Quixote, "for time, which reveals all things, brings everything into the light of day even if it is hidden in the bowels of the earth." (627-628)

Over time both characters gain "self-knowledge [that] is a prerequisite for the self-mastery that constitutes Don Quixote's victory in the end" (Allen 1979: 22) and that leads Sancho back to his normal station in life with his family. Howard Mancing has spoken of "this evolutionary process [towards] self-knowledge" (1982b:215) of both Don Quixote and Sancho, with Harold Bloom echoing this by speaking of the "knight and squire alike having to sustain a new consciousness" (1994: 159) and L.A. Murillo designating the novel a "story of a self-transformation" (1990: 5). John Weiger, in his insightful book *The Individuated Self. Cervantes and the Emergence of the Individual* (1979) speaks of this as "the process of *becoming* an individual" (1979: 3) in the sense of gaining an identity. To be sure, the proverb "Time reveals all things" serves as a telling metaphor for this development of both Don Quixote and Sancho Panza.

There is then at the end of the novel a certain human equality between Don Quixote and Sancho Panza, "a bond between the two, who beneath the surface enjoy the intimacy of equality" (Bloom 1994: 149). While the knight errant could not yet have known the life-oriented proverb "All men are created equal" from the American *Declaration of Independence* (Mieder 2015), he cites the proverb "All are equal in the grave" to explain to Sancho that at least death will equalize matters:

> "Well, the same thing happens in the drama and business of this world, where some play emperors, others pontiffs, in short, all the figures that can be presented in a play, but at the end, which is when life is over, death removes all the clothing that differentiated them, and all are equal in the grave."
>
> "That's a fine comparison," said Sancho, "though not so new that I haven't heard it many times before, like the one about chess: as long as the game lasts, each piece has its particular rank and position, but when the game's over they're mixed and jumbled and thrown together in a bag, just the way life is tossed into the grave."
>
> "Every day, Sancho," said Don Quixote, "you are becoming less simple and more intelligent." (527)

This definitely brings to mind William Shakespeare's quotation from his play *As You Like It* (1599) turned proverb: "All the world's a stage" (II,7). Perhaps Cervantes did know the comedy from his compatriot who died almost at the same day as Cervantes in 1616.

As this reference shows, Don Quixote does acknowledge that Sancho as his companion is gaining in knowledge. And so he enjoys lecturing Sancho by way of proverbial wisdom, perhaps thinking justifiably that his simple squire will best understand his didactic messages in this language. The following examples show this straight-forward educational approach:

> A mouth without molars is like a mill without a millstone.
> "I should rather have lost an arm, as long as it was not the one that wields my sword. For I must tell you, Sancho, that a mouth without molars is like a mill without a millstone, and dentation is to be valued much more than diamonds." (133)

> No leaf quivers on a tree unless God wills it.
> "Trust in God, Sancho," said Don Quixote, "that everything will turn out well and perhaps even better than you expect; not a leaf quivers on a tree unless God wills it." (477)

> All times are not the same.
> "What you say is correct, Sancho," said Don Quixote, "but you must realize that not all times are the same, nor do they always follow the same course, and what common people generally call omens, which are not founded on any natural cause, the wise man must consider and judge to be happy events." (835)

> The anger of lovers often ends in curses.
> "Altisidora, it seems, loved me dearly; she gave me the three nightcaps, which you [Sancho] know about, she wept at my departure, she cursed me, she reviled me, she complained, despite all modesty, publicly; all of these were signs that she adored me, for the anger of lovers often ends in curses." (898-899)

> Love shows no restraint.
> "You should know, Sancho," said Don Quixote, "that love shows no restraint, and does not keep within the bounds of reason as it proceeds, and has the same character as death: it attacks the noble palaces of kings as well as the poor huts of shepherds, and when it takes full possession of a heart, the first thing it does is to take away fear and shame." (836)

Actually, Don Quixote does not only know from own experience that love has no constraint, he also has no control over plugging in proverbs in order to explain matters. Early in the novel, when Sancho has barely uttered a single proverb (he starts on p. 106), Don Quixote is quick in stringing the three proverbs "God provides all things", "The sun shines on the good and the evil", and "Rain falls alike on the just and unjust" together, albeit without identifying them as such:

> "But be that as it may, mount your donkey, my good Sancho, and follow me, for God, who provides all things, will not fail us, especially since we are so much in His service, when He does not fail the gnats in the air, or the grubs in the earth, or the tadpoles in the water. He is so merciful that He makes His sun to shine on the good and the evil and His rain to fall on the just and the unjust." (132)

Much later, close to the end, Don Quixote first cites the Spanish equivalent "Zamora was not won in an hour" of the classical proverb "Rome was not built in a day" that naturally also exists in Spanish (Paczolay 1997: 449-451) and then adds the folk proverb "The donkey will endure the load, but not an extra load" to it as part of his argument that enough is simply enough (Johnson 1983: 189):

> "On your life, friend [Sancho], let the matter stop here, for this remedy seems very harsh to me, and it would be a good idea to take more time: Zamora was not won in an hour. You have given yourself more than a thousand lashes, if I have counted correctly: that is enough for now, for the donkey, speaking coarsely, will endure the load, but not an extra load." (922)

Such unprovoked reliance on proverbs is also evident when Don Quixote wants to enlighten others besides Sancho. This fact has surely been overlooked by scholars commenting on the proverbs in the novel. Here are a couple of references in point:

Comparisons are odious.
"'Stop right there, Señor Don Montesinos,' I [Don Quixote] said then. 'Your grace should recount this history in the proper manner, for you know that all comparisons are odious, and there is no reason to compare anyone to anyone else. The peerless Dulcinea of Toboso is who she is, and Señora Be-

lerma is who she is, and who she was, and no more should be
said about it.'

To which he responded [with the proverbial expression
"to bite one's tongue"]:

'Señor Don Quixote, may your grace forgive me, for I
confess that I erred and misspoke when I said that Señora
Dulcinea would barely be the equal of Señora Belerma, for it
was enough for me to have realized, by means of I am not certain what conjectures, that your grace is her knight, and I
would rather bite my tongue than compare her to anything but
heaven itself.'" (609)

The beginning of health lies in knowing the disease.
"Señor Roque, the beginning of health lies in knowing the
disease, and in the patient's willingness to take the medicines
the doctor prescribes; your grace is ill, you know your ailment, and heaven, or I should say God, who is our physician,
will treat you with the medicines that will cure you, and which
tend to cure gradually, not suddenly and miraculously." (858)

There are also occasions where Don Quixote merely alludes or
truncates well-known proverbs, where "the crucial recognizable
phrase [i.e., part] serves to call forth the entire proverb". This
"minimal recognizable unit or the *kernel* of the proverb" (Norrick
1985: 45, Mieder 2004: 7) permits native speakers to recognize
the traditional text, but matters are naturally more difficult if one
deals with a foreign language. This can well be seen from these
two examples:

Love is blind.
"If all people who love each other were to marry," said Don
Quixote, "it would deprive parents of the right and privilege to
marry their children to the person and at the time they ought to
marry; if daughters were entitled to choose their own husbands, one would choose her father's servant, and another a
man she saw walking on the street, who seemed to her proud
and gallant, although he might be a debauchee and a braggart;
for love and affection easily blind the eyes of the understanding, which are so necessary for choosing one's estate, and the
estate of matrimony is at particular risk of error, and great
caution is required, and the particular favor of heaven, in order
to choose correctly." (578)

There is no honey without gall.

"Now, when I intended to place you [Sancho] in a position where, despite your wife, you would be called Señor, now you take your leave? Now you go, when I had the firm and binding intention of making you lord of the best ínsula in the world? In short, as you have said on other occasions, there is no honey ... [Nothing is perfect]. You are a jackass, and must be a jackass, and will end your days as a jackass, for in my opinion, your life will run its course before you accept and realize that you are an animal." (646)

Things are a bit more complex with this third reference. The underlying proverb is "It doesn't matter if the pitcher hits the stone or the stone hits the pitcher: it will be bad for the pitcher":

"Therefore, from this day forward, we must treat each other with more respect and refrain from mockery, because no matter why I lose my temper with you [Sancho], it will be bad for the pitcher. The rewards and benefits that I have promised you will come in time, and if they do not, your wages, at least, will not be lost, as I have already told you." (151-152)

Who is to understand this in an English translation since this proverb does not exist in that language? It was thus absolutely essential that Edith Grossman in her literal translation of part of the Spanish proverb provides an explanatory footnote. Add to this that this proverb actually summarizes the entire mutual relationship between Don Quixote and Sancho Panza on their numerous adventures, it is of utmost importance to understand its fundamental message.

That these characters do at times agree with each other proverbially, can be seen from their use of the proverb "It is better to lose with too many cards than too few" even though their occurrence in the novel are separated by almost 150 pages. Sancho as the more skillful proverbialist adds the proverb "A word to the wise is sufficient" to his statement:

[Don Quixote said:] "It is better to lose with too many cards than too few, because 'This knight is reckless and daring' sounds better to the ear of those who hear it than 'This knight is timid and cowardly.'" (566-567)

"I [Sancho] involved myself, and I can involve myself as a squire who had learned the terms of courtesy in the school of your grace, the most courteous and polite knight in all courtliness; in these things, as I have heard your grace say, you can lose as much for a card too many as for a card too few, and a word to the wise is sufficient." (704)

With the understandable scholarly emphasis on the inescapable proverb duels between Don Quixote and Sancho Panza with their strings of proverbs, it has been overlooked that the two of them also communicate in a calmer fashion with each other where each cites but one proverb or proverbial expression to make a point or add some metaphorical expressiveness to a discussion. In this first discourse it is Sancho who employs the proverbial expression "to have on the tip of one's tongue" with Don Quixote volunteering the proverb "No speech is pleasing if it is long":

Sancho said to his master: "Señor, does your grace wish to give me leave to talk a little? After you gave me that harsh order of silence, more than a few things have been spoiling in my stomach, and one that I have now on the tip of my tongue I wouldn't want to go to waste." "Say it," Don Quixote said, "and be brief, for no speech is pleasing if it is long." (157)

On another occasion it is the knight errant who initiates the proverb "There is a remedy for everything except death" to put forth an optimistic view of the future, with his squire being a bit more realistic in citing the cautionary proverb "There's many a slip between the cup and the lip":

"There is a remedy for everything except death," responded Don Quixote, "for if we have a ship along the coast, we can embark on that even if the whole world attempts to prevent it."
      "Your grace paints a very nice picture and makes it seem very easy," said Sancho, "but there's many a slip 'tween cup and lip, and I'll depend on the renegade, who looks to me like an honest and good-hearted man." (884)

Just a few pages later towards the end of the long novel, there is yet another unique proverb exchange between the two heroes based on the two "fortune" proverbs "Fortune is fickle" and "Each man is the architect of his own fortune".

> "Señor, it is as fitting for valiant hearts to endure misfortune as it is for them to rejoice in prosperity; and I [Sancho] judge this on the basis of my own experience, for if I was happy when I was governor, now that I'm a squire on foot, I'm not sad, because I've heard that the woman they call Fortune is drunken, and fickle, and most of all blind, so she doesn't see what she's doing and doesn't know who[m] she's throwing down or raising up."
>
> "You sound very philosophical, Sancho," responded Don Quixote, "and you speak very wisely; I do not know who taught that to you. What I can say is that there is no fortune in the world, and the things that happen in it, whether good or bad, do not happen by chance but by the particular providence of heaven, which is why people say that each man is the architect of his own fortune." (893)

There is no nonsensical slapstick humor here at the end but rather a philosophical discussion of what life is all about, and even if Myriam Jehenson and Peter Dunn refer to the second proverb in their revealing article "Discursive Hybridity: Don Quixote's and Sancho Panza's Utopias" (2006: 134), they fail to recognize the double proverb entendre of this dialogue.

And finally, who would have thought it, Don Quixote has the last proverbial word about two pages before the very end of this long novel. Here he is, not the fictitious Don Quixote of La Mancha any longer but the all too real Alonso Quixano who close to death has recovered his reason. He knows that he will not try to go on any more adventures in search of his imagined love Dulcinea as an honorable knight errant on his horse Rocinante and with his squire Sancho on his donkey. To proclaim the end, he cites the proverb "There are no birds today in yesterday's nests" that has become proverbial in the English language by way of the Thomas Shelton translation of *Don Quixote* in 1620 (Wilson 1970: 60-61, Mieder et al. 1992: 52):

> "Señores," said Don Quixote, "let us go slowly, for there are no birds today in yesterday's nests. I was mad, and now I am sane; I was Don Quixote of La Mancha, and now I am, as I have said, Alonso Quixano the Good. May my repentance and sincerity return me to the esteem your graces once had for me." (937)

Thus, not only does Don Quixote rely on folk wisdom to express his return to sanity, he also lives on by the truth of this proverb in the hearts and minds of readers who have enjoyed and will continue to be enlightened by this extraordinary opus of world literature.

8. Sancho Panza's Messages as the Proverbial Wise Fool

Much has been said and written about the fascinating character of Sancho Panza, but Don Quixote, who in the novel knows his squire best, has perfectly well described this unforgettable figure:

"Sancho Panza is one of the most amusing squires who ever served a knight errant; at times his simpleness is so clever that deciding if he is simple or clever is a cause of no small pleasure; his slyness condemns him for a rogue, and his thoughtlessness confirms him as a simpleton; he doubts everything, and he believes everything; when I think that he is about to plunge headlong into foolishness, be comes out with perceptions that raise him to the skies. In short, I would not trade him for any other squire." (674)

Earlier in the novel, Don Quixote says to Sancho "'Devil take you for a peasant! What intelligent things you say sometime! One would think you had studied!'" (263). Sancho responds honestly "'By my faith, I don't know how to read'" (263). And there is a similar dialogue later on between the knight errant and his squire:

"Every day, Sancho," said Don Quixote, "you are becoming less simple and more intelligent."

"Yes, some of your grace's intelligence has to stick to me," responded Sancho, "for lands that are barren and dry on their own can produce good fruits if you spread manure on them and till them; I mean to say that your grace's conversation has been the manure that has fallen on the barren soil of my dry wits; the time that I have served you and talked to you has been the tilling; and so I hope to produce fruits that are a blessing and do not go to seed or stray from the paths of good cultivation that your grace has made in my parched understanding." (527-528)

What a wonderful earthy metaphor by the peasant Sancho that has plenty of scatological humor in it by indirectly comparing Don Quixote's words to "manure". But the knight errant has a sense of humor, as the narrator relates in a most telling paragraph that relates to Sancho's vast proverb knowledge:

Don Quixote laughed at Sancho's pretentious words but thought that what he said about the change in him was true, because from time to time he spoke in a manner that amazed Don Quixote, although almost always, when Sancho wanted to speak in an erudite and courtly way, his words would plummet from the peaks of his simplicity into the depths of his ignorance; the area in which he displayed the most elegance and the best memory was in his use of proverbs, regardless of whether or not they had anything to do with the subject, as has been seen and noted in the course of this history. (528)

It would have been a good idea for the narrator to mention in this statement of the twelfth chapter of the second part that this observation would not really hold true for the first part that had appeared in print ten years earlier. The at least at times unwarranted stringing together of proverbs is much more prevalent in the sequel. What is true, however, for the entire novel is that when Sancho uses proverbs one or at most two at a time they make perfect sense in their contexts as expressions of commonsensical folk wisdom (Hernandez 1984: 219, Landa 2013: xviii-xix). His personality is based on "that sound empirical common sense, that spontaneous wisdom which goes by the name of mother-wit" (Madariaga 1934: 130). His character clearly stands out because of "his astuteness, his ability to turn situations to his material advantage, his self-confidence, his inconsequential loquacity, his refusal to be intimidated by superior social rank, and his habit of turning to wisdom of poplar proverbs to comment on situations" (Russell 1985: 79). Leaving aside his infamous "strings of proverbs" for now that at times appear somewhat arbitrary or illogical for humorous affect, it can rightfully be claimed that there is plenty of sensical "candor and ingenuousness encapsulated in his proverbs" (Finello 1994: 86). As the following examples will reveal, the individually cited "proverbs are utilized in a functional [and sensical] way" (Casalduero 1947: 88), and this "oral, traditional culture [of proverbs] is close to common sense and worthy of respect" (Durán and Rogg 2006: 102).

P.E. Russell has observed correctly that "Cervantes, finding Sancho growing in potential and importance to the story as it proceeds, improvises new traits for him. The constant use of popular proverbs, which we now think as a special feature of Sancho's speech, is not in fact introduced until chapter 19 [I would say with chapter 15]" (1985: 44). After Don Quixote started the reliance on proverbs with "Each man is the child of his deed" (37) and "One swallow does not a summer make" (90) in chapters four and thirteen respectively, Sancho finally enters the proverbial field in the fifteenth chapter with not one but two proverbs coupled together, indicating right at the beginning that he will play the dominant role in the application of them. And let it be said here and now that that the wisdom of "It takes a long time to know a person" and "Nothing in life is certain" does not only make good sense in this context but that the proverbs actually fit the entire developmental narrative towards individuation:

> "Your grace, see if you can stand up, and we'll help Rocinante, though he doesn't deserve it, because he's the main reason for this beating. I [Sancho] never would have believed it of Rocinante; I always thought he was a person as chaste and peaceable as I am. Well, like they say, you need a long time to know a person, and nothing in this life is certain." (105-106)

And as Don Quixote does on various occasions, Sancho also employs introductory formulas as "like they say" to draw attention to the fact that he is citing insights sanctioned by generations of common folk. He does the same for proverbial expressions that do not express wisdom but that are standard expressions said ("as they say) by people. In the following short statement he ties the three proverbial phrases "not to know one's right foot from the left", "to go from pillar to post", and "to go from bad to worse" together:

> "And what's clear to me [Sancho] in all this is that in the long run, these adventures we're looking for will bring us so many misadventures that we won't know our right foot from our left. And the better and smarter thing, to the best of my poor understanding, would be for us to go back home now it's harvesttime, and tend to our own affairs, and stop going from pillar to post and from bad to worse, as they say." (125)

Sancho has a preference for the "as they say" formula, as can be seen from the references that contain the proverbial expression "to kick at thorns" and the three proverbs "Let the dead go to the grave and the living to the loaf of bread", "When they give you a heifer (calf), don't forget the rope", and "When good comes along, lock it in your house":

> Sancho Panza said: "Oh, Señor, heaven, moved by my tears and prayers, has willed Rocinante not to move, and if you persist, and spur and urge him on, that will anger Fortune, and it will be, as they say, like kicking at thorns." (144)

> "Señor, your grace has come to the end of this dangerous adventure more safely than all the others I have seen […]. The donkey is carrying what it should, the mountains are nearby, hunger is pressing, and there's nothing else to do but withdraw as fast as we can and, as they say, let the dead go to the grave and the living to the loaf of bread." (140)

> "Sancho I was born, and Sancho I plan to die; but even so, if heaven should be so kind as to offer me, without too much trouble or risk, an ínsula or something else like that, I'm not such a fool that I'd turn it down, because, as they say: 'When they give you a heifer, don't forget to bring a rope,' and 'When good comes along, lock it in your house.'" (483-484)

The third example is of interest since Sancho quite naturally adds a second proverb to his metaphorical animal proverb that carries the same meaning by emphasizing that one must be prepared to take advantage of a good situation (Mancing 1982b: 175). Much later in the novel, Sancho returns to the animal proverb, but this time he breaks its traditional structure by personalizing it as a self-characterization:

> Sancho responded: "I'm more clean than gluttonous, and my master, Don Quixote, here before you [Don Antonio], knows very well that we both can go a week on a handful of acorns or nuts. It's true that if somebody happens to give me a calf, I come running with the rope; I mean, I eat what I'm given, and take advantage of the opportunities I find, and anybody who says I'm dirty and stuff myself when I eat doesn't know what he's talking about, and I'd say it another way if I didn't see so many honorable beards at this table." (865)

The proverb might not even be recognized in this case since it has lost its traditional wording and structure. But Sancho knows very well why in this next reference he draws special attention to the proverb "The one who hurts you, is the one who loves you" with the introductory formula "I've heard people say". After all, he wants to be rewarded for his trials and tribulations that he is enduring on account of his knight errant, and the proverb adds plenty of authority to his argument:

> "At least," responded Sancho, "your grace knew how to place the lance, aiming for my head and hitting me on the back, thanks be to God and the care I took to move to the side. Well, well, it all comes out in the end, for I've heard people say: 'The one who hurts you is the one who loves you,' and I've also heard that great gentlemen, after speaking harshly to a servant, give him breeches, though I don't know what they give after beating him with a lance, unless knights errant give ínsulas after a beating, or kingdoms on dry land." (151)

On another occasion Sancho doesn't just call on people in general but rather on "wise men" to add credence to his argument:

> "Your grace [Don Quixote] is right," responded Sancho, "because according to wise men, you shouldn't blame the packsaddle for the donkey's mistake, and since your grace is to blame for what happened, you should punish yourself and not turn your anger against your battered and bloody arms, or the gentle Rocinante, or my tender feet by wanting them to walk more than is fair." (894)

Next he calls on the "truth" claim of the proverbs "A bird in hand is worth two in the bush" and "A man must be a man, and a woman a woman" to underscore his explanation or argument:

> Sancho said to his master: "Señor, what a fool I would've been if I'd chosen the spoils of the first adventure your grace completed as my reward instead of your three mares' foals! It's true, it's true: a bird in hand is worth two in the bush." (526-527)

> "If I tried to work out exactly how much my salary would be, it was to please my wife; when she puts her hand to convincing you of something, no mallet can press down the hoops of a barrel the way she can press you to do what she wants, but the truth is, a man must be a man, and a woman a woman, and since I'm a man everywhere, which I cannot deny, I also want

> to be a man in my own house, no matter who's inside; and so, there's nothing more to do except for your grace to prepare your will and its codicil so it can't be resoaked [*sic*], and for us to be on our way soon." (501)

This "man – woman" proverb is not necessarily meant in a chauvinistic fashion, since Sancho uses it primarily to assert himself while acknowledging in addition that his wife is a strong woman.

As one would expect, there are occasions when Sancho introduces a piece of folk wisdom by calling it by its proper "proverb" name. This is the case in his humorous explanation of marriage partners:

> "Try telling that to my wife!" said Sancho Panza, who so far had been listening in silence. "The only thing she wants is for everybody to marry their equal, following the proverb that says 'Like goes to like.' What I'd like is for this good Basilio, and I'm growing very fond of him, to marry Señora Quiteria; people who keep people who love each other from marrying should rest in peace, world without end, and I was going to say the opposite." (578)

There is also the following interchange between Don Quixote and his squire, where Sancho refers specifically to the fact that he is citing the proverb "For giving and keeping, you need some brains" to put an end to his master's benevolent imagination by way of a proverbial reality check:

> The man uncovered it [a wooden image carved in relief], and it seemed to be St. Martin astride a horse as he divided his cape with the poor man; and as soon as he saw it, Don Quixote said:
>
> "This knight was another Christian seeker of adventures, and I believe he was more generous than brave, as you can see, Sancho, for he is dividing his cape with the poor man and giving him half, and no doubt it must have been winter then; otherwise, he was so charitable he would have given him the entire cape."
>
> "That couldn't have been the reason," said Sancho, "but he must have been paying attention to the proverb that says: 'For giving and keeping you need some brains.'" (833)

Especially telling is finally also Sancho's employment of the proverb "Do what your master tells you and sit with him at the table" that he designates as his proverbial *modus operandi* in his role as the subservient squire of his knight errant:

> "Well, if that's true," responded Sancho, "and your grace at every step insists on finding nonsensical things, or whatever you call them, there's nothing I can do but obey, and bow my head, and follow the proverb that says, 'Do what your master tells you and sit with him at the table.'" (648)

While there might be some irony here, it is certainly not a humorous summary of Sancho's position. But the proverbially astute Sancho knows quite well that a proverb could be found to contradict what he has just claimed. In the following example he first quotes the proverb "It's good to live a long time, because then you see a lot" and then counters it with "If you have a long life, you go through a lot of bad times":

> "I'm saying, Señora [a duchess]," he [Sancho] responded, "that in the courts of other princes I've heard that when the tables are cleared they pour water over your hands, but not lather on your bread; and that's why it's good to live a long time, because then you see a lot; though they also say that if you have a long life, you go through a lot of bad times, though going through one of these washings is more pleasure than trouble." (670)

It is important to point out here that when Sancho strings proverbs together, they usually support each other by expressing the same idea in more or less the same way by using different metaphors. The following, by Sancho's standards, short accumulations of four and then three proverbs make this quite clear:

> "Nothing but one insult after another, though she [Dulcinea] must know the proverb that says that a jackass loaded down with gold climbs the mountain fast, and gifts can break boulders, and God helps those who help themselves, and a bird in hand is worth two in the bush." (694)

> "Señor," responded Sancho, "withdrawing is not running away, and waiting is not sensible when danger outweighs hope, and wise men know to save something for tomorrow

and not risk everything in a single day. And you should know that even though I'm rough and lowborn, I still know something about what people call proper behavior." (174)

Not surprisingly the strengthening of an explanatory statement by way of two proverbs is more common with the similar pieces of folk wisdom implying the correctness of what is being argued:

> If you pay your debts, you don't worry about guaranties.
> In a prosperous house supper is soon on the stove.
> "That is true," responded Sancho, "but if you pay your debts, you don't worry about guaranties, and in a prosperous house supper's soon on the stove; I mean that nobody has to tell me things or give me any advice: I'm prepared for anything, and I know something about everything." (654)

> Every sheep with its mate.
> Let no man stretch his leg farther than the length of the sheet.
> Sancho said: "I'll go back to walking on my feet on level ground, and if they're not adorned with cutout shoes of Cordoban leather, they won't lack for sandals made of hemp. Every sheep with its mate, and let no man stretch his leg farther than the length of the sheet, and now let me pass, it's getting late." (808-809).

> There are always **wins** and losses.
> To think there's bacon when there's not even a hook to hang it on.
> Sancho said: "Señor, your grace should lift up your head and be glad, if you [Don Quixote] can, and give thanks to heaven that even though you were toppled to the ground, you didn't break any ribs; and since you know there are always wins and losses, and you may have the hook but not the bacon, forget about the doctor because you don't need him to be cured of what's ailing you, and let's go back home and stop going around looking for adventures in places and countries we don't know." (889)

The "hook – bacon" proverb is repeated towards the very end of the novel, but here is one of those very rare occasions where the proverb is inappropriate since Sancho intends to say that despite his impoverished appearance he has brought money home to his family:

"Husband, why are you traveling like this, on foot and foot-sore and, it seems to me, looking more like a misgoverned fool than like a governor?"

"Be quiet, Teresa," responded Sancho, "because often you can have hooks and no bacon; let's go home, and there you will hear wonderful things. I have money, which is what matters, that I earned by my own labor, and with no harm to anybody."

"Bring the money, my good husband," said Teresa, "no matter if you earned it here or there; no matter how you did it, you won't have thought up new ways of earning it." (931)

This being Sancho's last utterance of a proverb, it seems strange and somewhat inexplicable that he would come up with this mis-application (see translator's note on p. 931), unless he is equating "hooks" with money and "not having bacon" with having no valuable clothing in some bizarre fashion. It is doubtful that he is playing with words here or that he wants to be funny.

It should also be noticed that Sancho is merely alluding to the proverb which makes matters even more complex. He usually quotes proverbs *verbatim*, but here are two references where he pulls the proverbs "The proof of the pudding is in the eating" and "Trout are not caught with a bare line" only partially out of his stuffed bag of proverbs:

"As for the giant's head, or, I should say, the slashed wine-skins, and the blood being red wine, by God I'm not mistaken, because the wounded wineskins are there, at the head of your grace's bed, and the red wine has formed a lake in the room; if you don't believe me, the proof is in the pudding [variant of the longer proverb "The proof of the pudding is in the eating"], I mean, you'll have your proof when his grace the inn-keeper asks you to pay damages for everything." (325)

"It comes to a total of eight hundred twenty-five *reales*. I'll take that out of your grace's [Don Quixote's] money, and I'll walk into my house a rich and happy man, though badly whipped; because trout aren't caught ... , and that's all I'll say." (920)

Clearly Sancho and also Cervantes could count on their contemporaries to know such standard proverbs, but what has gotten into the so-called simpleton Sancho quite early in the novel when he quotes Cato's "Evil to him who seeks evil":

> "Your grace should pay careful attention, because here I [Sancho] go. 'Once upon a time, and may good come to all and evil to him who seeks it ...' And, Señor, your grace should notice that the beginnings the ancients gave to their tales didn't come out of nowhere; this was a maxim of the Roman Cato Nonsensor, and it says: 'Evil to him who seeks it,' which fits here like the ring on your finger and means that your grace should stay put and not go looking for evil anywhere, and we should take another route, nobody's forcing us to continue on this one with so many frightening things to scare us." (144-145)

Modern readers will appreciate Edith Grossman's footnote in this case: "Sancho is alluding to Cato the Censor, or *Cato Censorio*, who was popularly considered to be a source of proverbs and sayings; in the process, he mispronounces his title, calling him *zonzorino*, which suggests 'simpleminded'" (145). There might be some intellectual humor here for the educated readers of Cervantes's time, but that is somehow lost today. It has repeatedly been observed that over the stretch of this voluminous novel Don Quixote and Sancho grow closer to each other in language and behavior, i.e., there is a certain sanchification of Don Quixote and a quixotification of Sancho (Romero Flores 1951: 186-227, Nabokov 1951-1952: 22, Watt 1996: 213, González- Echevarría 2001: 272), with Roger Abrahams and Barbara Babcock in their seminal article on "The Literary Use of Proverbs" (1977) making this salient point: "Cervantes uses proverbs as a means of dramatizing the changing relationship between Quixote and Sancho Panza. Sancho's adoption of the Quixotic frame of reference is marked by his interlarding common sayings with quotations from Don's books of chivalry. As Sancho increasingly assumes his master's high style of communication, Quixote indulges himself in a series of proverbs. Thus, their 'quotative' behaviors become a significant expression of their inversion of roles" (1977:425-426). All of this is indeed so over the course of the novel, but it seems a bit premature for Sancho to have gained knowledge about Cato this early. Of course, by labelling Cato as a simpleton, Sancho shows at this point that he is still far from proper comprehension and internalization of the scholarly knowledge he is picking up from his master.

In any case, he shows his wits well by properly employing the non-metaphorical classical proverb "Evil to him who seeks it" in his argument to stop Don Quixote of going after further adventures as knight errant to right the wrong and evil in the world. In fact he is so convinced of his correct and appropriate use of the proverb that he adds the proverbial expression "to fit like a ring on one's finger" to stress the perfect match of the proverb for the situation at hand. Such folk metaphors add considerably to Sancho's characterization as plain speaker, something that was set up by Cervantes in the prologue to his novel: "There is no reason for you to go begging for maxims from philosophers, counsel from Holy Scripture, fictions from poets, orations from rhetoricians, or miracles from saints; instead you should strive, in plain speech, with words that are straightforward, honest, and well-placed, to make your sentences and phrases sonorous and entertaining, and have them portray, as much as you can and as far as is possible, your intention, making your ideas clear without complicating and obscuring them" (8). Folksy proverbial expressions used to add colloquial and colorful language in the dialogues of the narrative are an integral part of Cervantes's entertaining style. There is no didactic or philosophical intent here, but simply expressive folk speech that brings authentic life to the prose. The following examples stand for numerous others that are listed in their narrative contexts in the "Index of Proverbs and Proverbial Expressions":

> To not come up to (touch) the sole of someone's shoe.
> "I have seen some governors," said Sancho, "who, in my opinion, don't come up to the sole of my shoe, and even so they're called lordship and are served their food on silver." (477)

> To try to shoe someone.
> "No doubt about it, the good man must think we're asleep here; well, just let him try to shoe us, and he'll know if we're lame or not. What I can say is that if my master would take my advice, we'd already be out in those fields righting wrongs and undoing injustices, which is the habit and custom of good knights errant." (482)

> To ask the elm tree for pears.
> "Id' like to see him [a horse]," responded Sancho, "but thinking that I'll climb up on him, either in the saddle or on his

hindquarters, is asking the elm tree for pears. I can barely stay on my donkey, and that's on a packsaddle softer than silk, and now they want me to sit on the hindquarters made of wood, without even a pillow or cushion!" (716)

There is also an occasion where Sancho first uses the proverbial expression "to grease someone's palm" and then follows that up with the proverb "If the abbot sings he eats his supper" to explain his self-serving intentions even further:

> "Well, I swear that if they bring me another patient [like Altisidora], before I cure anybody they'll have to grease my palm, because if the abbot sings he eats his supper, and I don't want to believe that heaven gave me this virtue to use for others at no charge." (919)

Most of the time Sancho brings a proverb into play in order to provide an explanation to strengthen an argument. The proverbs add considerable authority to these statements while also enhancing his deliberations through their metaphorical language. Thus, when Sancho tries to talk Don Quixote out of yet another dangerous adventure, he relies on the cautionary proverb "Whoever goes looking for danger perishes" to get his point across:

> "Señor, I don't know why your grace wants to embark on this fearful adventure; it's night, nobody can see us here, we can turn around and get away from the danger, even if we don't drink anything for three days, and since there's nobody here to see us, there's nobody to call us cowards; besides, I've heard the sermons of our village priest, and your grace knows him very well, and he says that whoever goes looking for danger perishes; so it isn't a good idea to tempt God by undertaking something so terrible that you can't get out of it except through some miracle." (142-143)

Commenting on this statement, Howard Mancing observes that Sancho "appeals to recognized authority – in this case the local priest – citing the truism, both popular and Christian, that 'quien busca el peligro perece en él' ('he who seeks danger perishes in it'), and the logical corollary that 'no es bien tentar a Dios' ('it is not right to tempt God'), and offering the opinion that God, who intervened to spare Don Quijote in earlier adventures, might exhaust his patience" (1982b: 75).

This kind of serious discussion can be contrasted with situations where Sancho has a bit of fun with a metaphorical proverb. This is the case when he takes the animal proverb "A hare leaps up when you least expect it" to get out of the pickle that there might just be a lady as beautiful as Dulcinea of Toboso:

> "It can't be denied but must be affirmed that my lady Dulcinea of Toboso is very beautiful, but the hare leaps up when you least expect it; I've heard that this thing they call nature is like a potter who makes clay bowls, and if he makes a beautiful bowl, he can also make two, or three, or a hundred: I say this because, by my faith, my lady the duchess is as good-looking as my mistress the lady Dulcinea of Toboso." (656)

It can't be denied that the image of beauties being compared to rabbits does have a comical effect, and modern readers might just additionally be reminded of the *Playboy* bunnies as well.

Here then are but a few additional examples that are part of Sancho's rhetoric based on such traditional folk speech patterns, with the proverb "Never mention (talk of) a rope in the house of a man who has been hanged" having gained currency in English by way of Shelton's *Don Quixote* translation (Wilson 1970: 684):

> Greed makes the sack burst.
> I left my home and my children and my wife to serve your grace, thinking I would be better off, not worse; but just as greed makes the sack burst, it has torn my hopes apart when they were brightest for getting that wretched, ill-starred ínsula your grace has promised me so often. (143)

> Fear has many eyes.
> "That's true," said Sancho, but fear has many eyes and can see things under the ground, let alone high in the sky; even so, it stands to reason that it won't be long until daylight." (143)

> The devil never sleeps.
> "I didn't know her [Torralba]," responded Sancho. "But the man who told me this story said it was true and correct that I certainly could, when I told it to somebody else, affirm and swear that I had seen it all. And so, as the days came and went, the devil who never sleeps and is always stirring up trouble, turned the love that the goatherd had for the shepherdess into hate and ill will." (145)

Never mention (talk of) a rope in the house of a man who has been hanged.

"I say that your grace is correct in everything," responded Sancho, "and that I am an ass. But I don't know why my mouth says ass, when you shouldn't mention the rope in the hanged man's house." (201)

A bird in the hand is better than a vulture in the air.

"Take my advice, and forgive me, and get married right away in the first town where there's a priest, or else here's our own licentiate, and he'll do a wonderful job. Remember that I'm old enough to give advice, and the advice I'm giving you [Don Quixote] now is exactly right, and a bird in the hand is better than a vulture in the air." (262)

Let sleeping dogs lie.

"I have never seen a squire," replied the Knight of the Wood, "who would dare speak when his master was speaking: at least, there stands mine, as big as his father, and no one can prove he has even moved his lips while I am speaking."

"Well, by my faith," said Sancho, "I have spoken, and can speak, in front of any ... enough said, we'll let sleeping dogs lie." (532)

A good name is worth more than great wealth.

"So nobody should blame me, and since I have a good reputation, and I've heard my master say that a good name's worth more than great wealth, just let them pass this governorship on to me and they'll see marvels, because whoever's been a good squire will be a good governor." (682)

Where there is music, there can be nothing bad (no harm).

Then something else was heard, not a noise, but the sound made by soft and harmonious music, which made Sancho very happy, and which he took as a good omen; and so, he said to the duchess, from whose side he had moved not one iota:

"Señora, where there is music, there can be nothing bad." (689-690)

A full belly gives courage.

"I don't deny it," responded Sancho, "and for now give me a piece of bread and about four pounds of grapes, because they really can't be poisoned, and I can't get by without eating, and if we have to be ready for those battles that are threatening us, we'll need to be well-fed, because a full belly gives you courage and not the other way around." (761)

If you give the cat what you were going to give the mouse, your troubles will be over.
The duke said to Tosilos: "Is it true, O knight, that you declare yourself defeated, and that pressed by your timorous conscience, you wish to marry this maiden?"
"Yes, Señor," responded Tosilos.
"He's doing the right thing," said Sancho Panza, "because if you give the cat what you were going to give the mouse, your troubles will be over." (826)

This last example is especially telling in regard to Sancho's frequent use of animal proverbs as expressions of human behavior that is reminiscent of the close relationship between fables and proverbs (Carnes 1988). But speaking of animals brings to mind this touching scene between Sancho and his beloved donkey:

The gray [the donkey] was lying on his back, and Sancho Panza moved him around until he had him on his feet, though he could barely stand; he took a piece of bread out of the saddlebags, which had experienced the same unfortunate fall, and gave it to his donkey, who thought it did not taste bad, and Sancho said to him, as if he could understand:
"Griefs are better with bread." (818)

In light of Sancho's rotund small body and his constant craving for food, this scene in all of its heartfelt compassion has a bit of humor in it for the reader.
Naturally, Sancho as the man of the house also has plenty of advice to his wife Teresa, as the appearance of the two proverbs "Nothing costs less or is cheaper than good manners" and "The man who sounds the alarm is safe" in a letter to her show:

My lady the duchess kisses your hands a thousand times; send her back two thousand, because there's nothing that costs less or is cheaper, as my master says, than good manners. (699)

The man who sounds the alarm is safe, and it'll all come out in the wash of the governorship; what does make me very sad is that they've told me that if I try to take something away

*from it, I'll go hungry afterwards, and if that's true it won't be
very cheap for me, though the maimed and wounded already
have their soft job in the alms they beg; so one way or another, you'll be rich and have good luck.* (699)

Altogether their relationship does not appear to be especially romantic. At least applying the proverb "Honey is not for the donkey's mouth" to Teresa and telling her proverbially "to sew up her
mouth" do not show great love but rather who rules the roost in
the Panza home:

> "I'll show them to you at home," said Panza, "and for now be
> happy, because if it's God's will that we go out again in
> search of adventures, in no time you'll see me made a count,
> or the governor of an ínsula, and not any of the ones around
> here, but the best that can be found."
>
> "May it please God, my husband, because we surely need
> it. But tell me, what's all this about ínsulas? I don't under-
> stand."
>
> "Honey's not for the donkey's mouth," responded San-
> cho. "In time you will, dear wife, and even be amazed to hear
> yourself called ladyship by all your vassals."
>
> "What are you saying, Sancho, about ladyships, ínsulas,
> and vassals?" responded Juana Panza, which was the name of
> Sancho's wife; they were not kin, but in La Mancha wives
> usually take their husbands' family name.
>
> "Don't be in such a hurry, Juana, to learn everything all at
> once; it's enough that I'm telling you the truth, so sew up your
> mouth. I'll just tell you this, in passing: there's nothing nicer
> in the world for a man than being the honored squire of a
> knight errant seeking adventures." (444)

After having heard Don Quixote expound on the virtues of women
later in the novel, Sancho cites another animal proverb that he relates in a rather negative way to his marriage:

> "What are you mumbling about, Sancho?"
>
> "I'm not saying anything, and I'm not mumbling any-
> thing," responded Sancho. "I was just saying to myself that I
> wish I'd heard what your grace [Don Quixote] said here be-
> fore I married; maybe then I'd be saying now: 'The ox who's
> free can lick where he pleases.'" (598)

At least Sancho does not apply the proverb "Let each whore tend to her spinning" to his wife, and when he utters it in front of Don Quixote, he is immediately rebuked for his foul language:

> "I'm saying this, Señor, because if after having traveled so many highways and byways, and gone through so many bad nights and worse days, the fruit of our labors is being plucked by someone taking his ease in this inn, then there's no reason for me to hurry and saddle Rocinante, and harness the donkey, and prepare the palfrey, because we'd be better off sitting still and doing nothing: let each whore tend to her spinning, and we'll eat."
>
> Oh, Lord save me, but what age overcame Don Quixote when he heard his squire's discourteous words! It was so great, I say, that with precipitate voice and stumbling tongue and fire blazing from his eyes, he said:
>
> "Oh, base, lowborn, wretched, rude, ignorant, foul-mouthed, ill-spoken, slanderous, insolent varlet! You have dared to speak such words in my presence and in the presence of these distinguished ladies, dared to fill your befuddled imagination with such vileness and effrontery? Leave my presence, unholy monster, repository of lies, stronghold of falsehoods, storehouse of deceits, inventor of iniquities, promulgator of insolence, enemy of the decorum owed to these royal persons. Go, do not appear before me under pain of my wrath!" (401)

That is quite a dressing down of his loyal servant for this one proverbial infraction, and perhaps this overkill of invectives was part of what resulted in *"Don Quixote's* original reception as a work of humor, whether that mode of expression be construed as parody, irony, wit, burlesque, satire, or even slapstick" (Martín 2002: 161-162). It is to be assumed that Sancho's use of the widely disseminated wellerism "'I see,' said the blind man, as he picked up his hammer and saw" with its numerous variants (Mieder and Kingsbury 1994: 113-117) added to the humorous intent of the novel. And the reference to his corpulence is certainly funny even today:

> "I don't know about these philosophies," responded Sancho Panza, "all I know is that as soon as I have the countship I'll know how to govern it; I have as much soul as any other man, and as much body as the biggest of them, and I'll be as much a king of my estate as any other is of his; and this being true,

I'll do what I want, and doing what I want, I'll do what I like, and doing what I like, I'll be happy, and when a man is happy he doesn't wish for anything else, and not wishing for anything else, that'll be the end of it, so bring on my estate, and God willing we'll see, as one blind man said to the other." (431)

To be sure, as is so often the case with Sancho's proverbial language, there is a deeper meaning to this wellerism variant since, after all, the two blind men are in fact Don Quixote and Sancho Panza, who both are still fumbling on their road to self-recognition.

And as the two seemingly so different companions travel on, Don Quixote has no choice but to acknowledge that Sancho has "too much mother wit to be considered a perfect fool" (Nabokov 1951-1952: 20). The following dialogue with Sancho citing the proverb "Being a good preacher means living a good life" and Don Quixote bringing the proverb "The fear of God is the beginning of wisdom" into play makes clear that not only is the squire not an imbecile but the knight errant is aware of his native intelligence:

> "Enough, Sancho," said Don Quixote at this point. "Stop now before you fall, for the truth is that what you have said about death, in your rustic terms, is what a good preacher might say. I tell you, Sancho, with your natural wit and intelligence, you could mount a pulpit and go around preaching some very nice things."
>
> "Being a good preacher means living a good life," responded Sancho, "and I don't know any other theologies."
>
> "You do not need them," said Don Quixote, "but I cannot understand or comprehend how, since the beginning of wisdom is the fear of God, you, who fear a lizard more than you fear Him, can know so much." (590)

Not quite ten pages later Cervantes adds a fascinating monologue by Sancho in which he reflects equally positively on the knowledge of his master:

> Sancho said to himself: "This master of mine, when I talk about things of pith and substance, usually says that I could take a pulpit in hand and go through the world preaching fine

sermons; and I say of him that when he begins to string together judgments and to give advice, he could not only take a pulpit in hand but hang two on each finger, and go through the squares and say exactly the right thing. What a devil of a knight errant you are, and what a lot of things you know! I thought in my heart that he would only know things that had to do with his chivalry, but there's nothing he doesn't pick at or poke his spoon into." (598)

Ending his thoughts with the proverbial expression "to poke one's spoon into something" is in many ways a fitting colloquial description of Don Quixote's undertakings, showing once again that such folk metaphors have their bearing on the plot and meaning of this literary masterpiece.

But speaking of knowledge, here is yet another understatement by Sancho regarding his mental abilities and other weakness. The proverb "To err is human, to forgive divine" is a perfect argument to ask for his master's understanding who acknowledges the proverb's message:

> "Señor, I confess that for me to be a complete jackass, all that's missing is my tail; if your grace wants to put one on me, I'll consider it well-placed, and I'll serve you like a donkey for the rest of my days. Your grace should forgive me, and take pity on my lack of experience, and remember that I know very little, and if I talk too much, it comes more from weakness than from malice, and to err is human, to forgive, divine."
>
> "I would be amazed, Sancho, if you did not mix some little proverb into your talk. Well, then, I forgive you as long as you mend your ways and from now on do not show so much interest in your own gain, but attempt to take heart, and have the courage and valor to wait for my promises to be fulfilled, for although it may take some time, it is in no way impossible." (646)

As can be seen, Don Quixote is quite willing to accept a singular proverb since, after all, he also cites a proverb from time to time. It is only the amassment of them that vexes him, as anything that is overstated becomes tedious if not mindless. While it is true that Sancho's "salty language, bursting with life and filled with refrains and sayings that express a wealth of popular knowledge"

(Llosa 2005: 67) appears throughout the novel, their presence is by means superfluous as for the most part the proverbs and proverbial expressions are integral parts of the whole narrative. In other words, the proverbs as used in isolated dialogues by both Don Quixote and Sancho Panza make sense, and they show that Sancho is by no means a simpleton but rather a wise fool with traditional wisdom on his side.

9. Sancho Panza's Bottomless Sack of Proverbs

It is almost surprising that Don Quixote's characterization of Sancho Panza as someone who strings proverbs together has not become proverbial in its own right. Anybody who has ever read the *Don Quixote* novel will remember the bottomless sack of proverbs that contains the squire's folk wisdom that he amasses several times into proverbial cannonades. Doubtlessly Cervantes enjoyed assembling these mini-collections of proverbs just as other authors did in Spain and elsewhere in Europe. In fact there is a definite literary tradition of plays and poems that consist of basically nothing but proverbs strung together. Connecting traditionally cited proverbs or varied anti-proverbs, such texts can make perfect sense or they are intentionally created to be perceived as nonsense (Mieder and Bryan 1996, Sobieski and Mieder 2005). While Cervantes is part of this *tour de force* phenomenon, he most likely also wanted to pay tribute to the incredible paremiographical work that Erasmus of Rotterdam and other humanists were undertaking that resulted in monumental proverb collections, including the early Spanish collections by Pedro Vallés (1549), Hernán Nuñez (1555), and Juan de Mal Lara (1568) from the sixteenth century. There is no indication that he intended to parody this worthwhile activity that showed "the triumph of rustic wisdom" (Iventosch 1980: 22). The reason for Cervantes's or better Sancho's obsession with proverbs must be that they made the perfect linguistic and stylistic tool or signature for Sancho the peasant who, by amassing the proverbs *ad infinitum*, becomes a figure of ridicule and at times humor. But there is a twist to this perception, for this alleged simpleton is actually quite wise or at least a wise fool, and even though he strings proverbs together, what most normal people wouldn't do, he actually makes sense of what some readers might perceive as nonsense.

As would be expected, numerous scholars have expressed their thoughts on Sancho Panza "the conjuror of words [and proverbs]" (Stavans 2015: 69). But they have concluded too quickly or superficially that these strings of proverbs are humor-

ous and show Sancho's foolishness. This misses the point, particularly because strings of proverbs that Sancho ties together are
usually related in meaning without being contradictory or nonsensical as has been suggested. There might be humor and even
satire in running of the mouth with proverbs, but that does not
automatically mean foolishness or stupidity. But here is a list of
what scholars have said about Sancho's proverb salvos in chronological order:

> [...] gluttonous, brutal, and clownish to the point of not even
> understanding the proverbs which he [Sancho] piles up in a
> jumbled manner. (Menéndez-Pidal 1947: 50)

> Sancho's cracks and proverbs are not very mirth provoking
> either in themselves or in their repetitious accumulation. [...]
> Sancho Panza's main characteristic is that he is a sackful of
> proverbs, a sack of half-truths that rattle in him like pebbles.
> (Nabokov 1951-1952: 13 and 24)

> Sancho's shallow and artificial application of these tradition-
> al, stereotyped "truths" [...] reveals Sancho's character. He
> strung these ritualistic phrases into conversation – often as
> malapropisms and traditional truths without organic coordi-
> nation. (Raymond 1951: 134)

> Specifically, I refer to his [Sancho's] abuse of proverbs and
> Don Quixote's criticism of this. [...] Sancho has the inborn
> wit and wisdom of the peasant but lacks formal education. A
> symptom of the former is his remarkable facility in proverbs,
> while his ill-judged use of them reflects the latter. (Riley
> 1962: 69)

> Sancho could be said to display jester's wit – his knowledge
> of proverbs. His diffuse and inconsequential recitals of them
> – such torture to Don Quixote's educated mind – are pri-
> marily an aspect of his comic artlessness. Nonetheless, he
> claims that his memory for proverbs is his one intellectual
> resource. [...] Sancho can cite proverbs both as a form of
> verbal foolery and in order to substantiate his judicious re-
> flections. (Close 1973: 350)

> Sancho's use of proverbs is a burlesque derivative of a Re-
> naissance appreciation for the oral vox populi. [...] Sancho's

proverbs are sometimes mechanically linked in irrelevant concatenations. On these occasions, purely verbal associations control discourse, regardless of the topic presumably under discussion. (Rivers 1984: 116-117 and 118)

There is even the view that Cervantes had a low opinion of "Spain's oral tradition, such as Sancho's proverbs. That is to say, he perceived them as just as ridiculous and grotesque a falsification of history" (Gilman 1989: 93). But these views that include such descriptors for Sancho's strings of proverbs as "jumbled", "half-truths", "ill-judged", "inconsequential", and "irrelevant" simply miss the point. There is definitely a method to Sancho's proverb obsession and it is by way of his folk language that he defines himself as an individual just as Don Quixote and other characters do through their verbal communication (MacKey 1974: 51). And there can be no doubt that R.M. Flores is correct with this enlightening statement:

> Sancho's use of proverbs has come to be regarded as the quintessential characteristic of his personality. The widespread belief, however, that he continually misuses them is quite mistaken. If one follows Sancho's train of thought, one soon sees that any one of the proverbs or sayings of a particular series is perfectly appropriate to convey Sancho's reaction and answer to whatever has provoked it. (1982a: 117-118, see also Finello 1994: 87))

More recently Thomas Hart came to the somewhat more guarded conclusion that "when Sancho cites several proverbs in rapid succession, most though usually not all of them emphasize the point he wants to make" and also draws attention to the important fact that "it is Sancho's ability to use proverbs effectively to support his argument that Don Quixote admires and envies" (2002: 46 and 47). But it should be added that it takes Don Quixote considerable time until he learns to appreciate Sancho's lists of proverbs which is clearly a folkloric sign of his becoming "sanchified" as the novel progresses to the end. It is true that "on several occasions, Don Quijote points out that Sancho is using proverbial language indiscriminately and out of context", but Frank Nuessel goes too far in stating that "the appropriate application of proverbial language in the second book of the *Quijote* is one of the ways in which Cervantes signals the *Quijotización* of Sancho" (1999: 260). After all, Sancho's proverb applications whether citing one, two, three or many more proverbs in succession are for all general purposes correct throughout. And, as will be shown by the following interpretations of the most pertinent proverb strings, Don Quixote is as wrong as modern scholars when he considers Sancho's proverbs inappropriate or indiscriminate. That these proverb accumulations can to some degree be considered humorous in the context of other verbal and gesticular communication by Sancho might well be the case, but there is sense in the nonsense of formulating such proverb strings. After all, it is not customary to speak in proverbs to that degree, unless, of course, one would want to compete with the great proverb stringer Sancho Panza.

The first part of the *Don Quixote* contains just four relatively short proverb strings, but already the first one sets the tone for the frequent misinterpretation of them by scholars. Don Quixote, who at this early stage has absolutely no appreciation for Sancho's folk wisdom, and who refers to it as foolish and incongruous to the subject under discussion, leading readers and interpreters to the false conclusion that the four proverbs "If you buy and lie, your purse wants to know why", "Naked I was born, and naked I die", "To think there's bacon when there's not even a hook to hang it on", and "You can't put doors on a field" and to a lesser extent the three proverbial expressions "to eat something with one's bread", "to be someone's own business", and "to stick one's nose into something" don't add up to making sense. But upon closer inspection they do, supporting Sancho's claim that he doesn't care about the talk circulating about Queen Madásima, that there might be nothing to it, and that it can't be stopped in any case:

> "I don't say it and I don't think it [what people say about Queen Madásima' virtue]," responded Sancho. "It's their affair and let them eat it with their bread; whether or not they were lovers, they've already made their accounting with God; I tend to my vines, it's their business, not mine; I don't stick my nose in; if you buy and lie, your purse wants to know why. Besides, naked I was born, and naked I'll die: I don't lose or gain a thing; whatever they were, it's all the same to me. And many folks think there's bacon when

there's not even a hook to hang it on. But who can put doors on a field? Let them say what they please, 1 don't care."

"Lord save me!" said Don Quixote. "What a lot of foolish things you put on the same thread, Sancho! What does the subject of our conversation have to do with the proverbs you string together like beads? If you value your life, Sancho, be quiet, and from now on tend to spurring your donkey and leave matters alone that do not concern you. And know with all five of your senses that everything I have done, am doing, and shall do follows the dictates of reason and the laws of chivalry, which I know better than all the knights in the world who have ever professed them." (191-192)

The actual problem is that Don Quixote does not understand the proverbial metaphors that lead him to brush Sancho's remarks aside as nonsense. He also does not realize that there is a bit of ironic ambiguity in Sancho's speech (Flores 1982a: 118, Gorfkle 1993: 149-151, Flores 2002: 51). That is not to say that the loquacious Sancho would not have done better by curbing his proverb string somewhat. As it is, the bit of humor in all of this stems from the overdose of the proverbial language but not from its incongruity.

The second string of proverbs appears in an exchange between Don Quixote and Sancho Panza, with the former actually starting the proverb duel. And now there is considerable humor here by Sancho responding to his master's proverb "First impulses are not in the hands of men" with the self-characterization that his first impulse is always to talk. Yet, he does not employ a proverb, and instead it is Don Quixote who cites the medieval Latin proverb "The jug (pitcher) goes to the fountain (well) so long until at last it breaks" that has been loan translated into the European languages (Paczolay 1997: 287-291). But notice, he only quotes the first half, attesting to the general knowledge of the proverb by all strata of society. Of course Sancho understands its message as it relates to the danger of talking too much. But in ever so shrewd a proverbial way he leaves the judgment of his loquaciousness up to God by combing the two proverbs "God is in heaven and judges men's hearts" and "God sees all the snares" to "God's in His heaven, and He sees all the snare"– a perfect proverbial defense:

"I mean I didn't look at her [Dulcinea] so carefully," said Sancho, "that I could notice her beauty in particular and her good features point by point, but on the whole, she seemed fine to me."

"Now I forgive you," said Don Quixote, "and you must pardon the anger I have shown you; for first impulses are not in the hands of men." "I can see that," responded Sancho, "just like in me a desire to talk is always my first impulse, and I can never help saying, not even once, what's on my tongue."

"Even so," said Don Quixote, "think about what you say, Sancho, because you can carry the jug to the fountain only so many times... and I shall say no more."

"Well," responded Sancho, "God's in His heaven, and He sees all the snares, and He'll be the judge of who does worse: me in not saying the right thing or your grace in not doing it." (256)

It is important to recognize here that Don Quixote knows and uses proverbs, that he is the one who initiates them in this instance, and that he obviously appreciates their communicative value, especially in his conversations with his peasant squire.

Sancho's proverb strings are not all directed at Don Quixote, as can be seen from his comments to a priest in which he first connects the proverbs "Where envy rules, virtue cannot survive" and "Generosity cannot live with miserliness" to expose the lies of this man of the church. And then, effectively leading into them with the introductory formula "what they say is true", he cites the proverbs "The wheel of fortune turns faster than a water wheel" and "Those who only yesterday were on top of the world today are down on the ground". There could hardly be a better way to tell the priest that his fortune in the world might very quickly change, hopefully for the worse:

"Ah Señor Priest, Señor Priest! Did your grace think I didn't know you? Can you think I don't understand and guess where these new enchantments are heading? Well, you should know that I recognize you no matter how you cover your face and understand you no matter how you hide your lies. In short, where envy rules, virtue cannot survive, and generosity cannot live with miserliness. Devil confound it, if it wasn't for your reverence, my master would be married by now to Princess Micomicona and I'd be a count at least, because I expected nothing less from the goodness of my master, the Knight of the Sorrowful Face, and from the greatness of my services! But now I see that what they say is true: the wheel of fortune turns faster than a water wheel, and those who only yesterday were on top of the world today are down on the ground." (410)

The four proverbs in double sequences are absolutely appropriate and doubling them up does not appear too much of an overkill in this situation with Sancho wanting to put the priest, quite courageously actually, into his place. This is solid proverbial rhetoric without any pun or wordplay, and there is also nothing particularly comical about it all.

The fourth and final accumulation of proverbs in the first part of the novel follows the previous set of proverbs with only one paragraph in between. Having been accused by the barber (a companion of the priest) of being "pregnant" with the lunacy and madness of his master Don Quixote, Sancho begins his response with the claim that he is not pregnant by anybody, This little absurd play with the "pregnant" word still appears quite funny to readers today. But the humor, perhaps also a bit sexual, gets lost once Sancho starts his proverb bombardment of the poor barber. He begins with the proverb "Each man is the child of his actions", thereby echoing Don Quixote's use of the variant "Each man is the child of his deeds" (37) very early in the novel. Whether Cervantes put this proverb into the mouths of both his major characters intentionally would be impossible to ascertain, but the fact remains that the knight errant and the squire both realize that they are the makers of their own fate and that they are responsible for their undertakings. Then Sancho couples the proverbs "There is more to life than trimming beards" and "There's some difference between one Pedro and the other" to point out that there are many different aspects to life and that all people are simply not alike. Next comes the proverbial expression "to throw crooked dice" with which Sancho accuses the barber of trying to convince him of the madness of his master. It might have been smart to stop here, because by adding the proverb "God knows the truth" he appears to be willing to accept the idea that Don Quixote might just be a lunatic. And he still does not cease the floor, closing his tirade with the proverb "Things get worse when you stir them" that also leaves the possibility of his master's madness wide open:

> "I'm not pregnant by anybody," responded Sancho, "and I'm not a man who'd let himself get pregnant even by the king, and though I'm poor I'm an Old Christian, and I don't owe anything to anybody, and if I want ínsulas, other people want things that are worse; each man is the child of his actions, and because I'm a man I could be a pope, let alone the governor of an ínsula, especially since my master could win so many he might not have enough people to give them to. Your grace should be careful what you say, Señor Barber, because there's more to life than trimming beards, and there's some difference between one Pedro and the other. I say this because we all know one another, and you can't throw crooked dice with me. As for the enchantment of my master, only God knows the truth, and let's leave it at that, because things get worse when you stir them." (411)

It is almost surprising that Sancho does not conclude his deliberations with the proverb "Let sleeping dogs lie" that he knew very well, as can be seen from his statement "enough said, we'll let sleeping dogs lie" (532) in another situation later on. In any case, there is danger in getting carried away with strings of proverbs, but they are certainly not inconsequential or nonsensical.

The numerous discussions between Sancho Panza and Don Quixote of the second part of the novel begin with the seventh chapter in which they talk about how Sancho would be paid for his renewed services as squire. Cleary his wife Teresa wanted to make certain of such payment as well, having told her husband proverbially to keep an eye on his master and then adding a string of three proverbs to it to underscore her advice. That makes plenty of sense, as Sancho recalls it to Don Quixote, but when he then states that "A woman's advice is no jewel, and the man who doesn't take it is a fool" the sense is utterly lost. No wonder that Don Quixote is enjoying all of this, since obviously he is glad that Sancho with his anti-feministic proverb appears to speak against his wife's counsel:

> "Teresa says," said Sancho, "that I should keep a sharp eye on you, and there's no arguing against written proof, because

> if you cut the deck you don't deal, and a bird in hand is
> worth two in the bush. And I say that a woman's advice is no
> jewel, and the man who doesn't take it is a fool."
>
> "And I say that as well," responded Don Quixote. "Con-
> tinue, Sancho my friend, go on, for today you are speaking
> pearls." (498)

There is plenty of irony or humor here, since if a woman's advice is no good, then why should someone who doesn't take it be
a fool? Calling all of this "pearls" is also quite humorous, although Sancho does not recognize it at all. Instead, he reminds
Don Quixote with the proverbs "Here today and gone tomorrow", "The lamb goes as quickly as the sheep", and "Death is
silent" that death could come to him at any time, leaving his poor
squire without any financial means. He is making good use of
the "distancing property of proverbs" (Hart 2002: 50) here by
avoiding to tell Don Quixote that he is afraid that his master
might die before him:

> "The fact is," responded Sancho, "that as your grace knows
> very well, we're all subject to death, here today and gone
> tomorrow, and the lamb goes as quickly as the sheep, and
> nobody can promise himself more hours of life in this world
> than the ones God wants to give him, because death is silent,
> and when she comes knocking at the door of our life, she's
> always in a hurry, and nothing will stop her, not prayers or
> struggles or scepters or miters, and that's something that
> everybody hears, something they tell us from the pulpit."
>
> "All of that is true," said Don Quixote, "but I do not
> know where it is taking you." (498)

No wonder that Don Quixote is perplexed, getting Sancho to become a bit more direct with his argument for payment assurances
without wanting to come across like a proverbial pennypincher.
His three proverbs "A hen sits on her eggs", "A lot of littles
make a lot" and "As long as you're earning you don't lose a
thing" clarify matters:

> "It's taking me to this," said Sancho. "Your grace should tell
> me exactly what salary you'll give me for each month I serve
> you, and this salary should be paid to me from your estate; I
> don't want to depend on anybody's favors, which come late,

or badly, or never; may God help me to tend to my own business. The point is, I want to know what I'm earning, whether it's a lot or a little; a hen sits on her egg, and a lot of littles make a lot, and as long as you're earning you don't lose a thing. And if it should happen, and I don't believe or expect that it will, that your grace gives me the ínsula you promised, I'm not such an ingrate, and not such a penny-pincher, that I won't want the rent from the ínsula to be added up and deducted from my salary pro rat." (498-499)

Finally, Don Quixote understands what Sancho is driving at with his "countless arrows of proverbs", and then, quite unexpectedly, he tries himself at a string of three proverbs that include "If the pigeon coop has plenty of feed, it will have plenty of pigeons", "Fine hopes are better than miserable possessions", and "A good lawsuit is better than a bad payment":

"And [I] understood you so well," responded Don Quixote, "that I have penetrated to your most hidden thoughts, and I know the target you are trying to hit with the countless arrows of your proverbs. Look, Sancho: I certainly should have specified a salary for you if I had found in any of the histories of the knights errant an example that would have revealed to me and shown me, by means of the smallest sign, what wages were for a month, or a year, but I have read all or most of their histories, and I do not recall reading that any knight errant ever specified a fixed salary for his squire. I know only that all of them served without pay, and when they least expected it, if things had gone well for their masters, they found themselves rewarded with an ínsula or something comparable; at the very least, they received a title and nobility. If, with these expectations and addenda, you, Sancho, would like to serve me again, then welcome, but if you think I am going to force the ancient usage of knight errantry beyond its limits and boundaries, then you are sadly mistaken. Therefore, my dear Sancho, return to your house and tell your Teresa my intention, and if it pleases her and you to serve me without wages, *bene quidem*, and if not, we shall still be friends, for if the pigeon coop has plenty of feed, it will have plenty of pigeons. And remember, Sancho, that fine hopes are better than miserable possessions, and a good lawsuit [is] better than a bad payment. I am speaking in this manner, Sancho, so you may understand that, like you, I too know how to pour down rainstorms of proverbs. And, finally, I want to tell you, and I do tell you, that if you do not wish to accompany me without pay, and take the same risks I do, then God be with you and turn you into a saint, for I shall have no lack of squires more obedient, more solicitous, less uncouth, and less talkative than you." (499-500)

Sure, Don Quixote claims that he is employing these proverbs only so that Sancho could understand him better, but his statement "I too know how to pour down rainstorms of proverbs" cannot hide the fact that he is enjoying this proverbial contest with his squire. Being part of the Spanish culture of his time, he is obviously as aware of its proverb lore as anybody else (Raymond 1951:118-131).

Sancho, however, is so full of proverbs that he even speaks to himself in proverbs as in this soliloquy:

"Well now: everything has a remedy except death, under whose yoke we all have to pass, even if we don't want to, when our life ends. I've seen a thousand signs in this master of mine that he's crazy enough to be tied up, and I'm not far behind, I'm as much a fool as he is because I follow and serve him, if that old saying is true: 'Tell me who your friends are and I'll tell you who you are,' and that other one that says, 'Birds of a feather flock together.' Then, being crazy, which is what he is, with the kind of craziness that most of the time takes one thing for another, and thinks white is black and black is white, like the time he said that the windmills were giants, and the friars' mules dromedaries, and the flocks of sheep enemy armies, and many other things of that nature." (515-516)

The proverb "Everything has a remedy except death" expresses Sancho's optimism of looking for Dulcinea and the following two proverbs are metaphorical expressions for the friendship relationship of Don Quixote and Sancho. Sancho even admits that he must share in some of the craziness of his master who proverbially speaking "thinks white is black and black is white". But the three proverbs cited by Sancho make eminent sense and are used in serious reflection without any humor intended.

This is definitely also the case in the following sequence of proverbs where Sancho deals with the upcoming wedding of Quiteria and Camacho and the hope that things might still turn out well for Camacho's rival Basilio. After all "God gives the malady and also the remedy", "Nobody knows the future", "There are a lot of hours until tomorrow", and "In a moment a house can fall". He also makes good use of the widely disseminated proverbial expression "to rain while the sun shines" (Kuusi 1957) and the proverbial phrase "to drive a nail into fortune's wheel" to indicate that things might well change for the better. Love will eventually win out, as Sancho declares at the end of his comforting comments: "Love looks through spectacles that make copper look like gold, poverty like riches, and dried rheum like pearls".

> "God will find the cure," said Sancho, "for God gives the malady and also the remedy; nobody knows the future: there's a lot of hours until tomorrow, and in one of them, and even in a moment, the house can fall; I've seen it rain at the same time the sun is shining; a man goes to bed healthy and can't move the next day. And tell me, is there anybody who can boast that he's driven a nail into Fortune's wheel? No, of course not, and I wouldn't dare put the point of a pin between a woman's yes and no, because it wouldn't fit. Tell me that Quiteria loves Basilio with all her heart and all her soul, and I'll give him a sack of good fortune, because I've heard that love looks through spectacles that make copper look like gold, poverty like riches, and dried rheum like pearls." (579)

Don Quixote's negative response to Sancho "string[ing] together proverbs" is unwarranted and unfair, since Sancho expresses them with kindness and compassion:

> "Damn you, Sancho, where will you stop?" said Don Quixote. "When you begin to string together proverbs and stories, nobody can endure it but Judas himself, and may Judas himself take you. Tell me, you brute, what do you know of nails, or wheels, or anything else?"

And then comes Sancho's most telling reaction, claiming that it isn't his fault that people don't understand his proverbs that ought to make perfect sense since there is no foolishness in them. Of course, Don Quixote insists on having the last word, but it is nitpicking and does not earn him favor with the reader:

> "Oh, well, if none of you understand me," responded Sancho, "it's no wonder my sayings are taken for nonsense. But it doesn't matter: I understand what I'm saying, and I know there's not much foolishness in what I said, but your grace is always sentencing what I say, and even what I do."
>
> "*Censuring* is what you should say," said Don Quixote, "and not sentencing, you corrupter of good language, may God confound you!" (579)

Scholars have looked at this particular proverb string quite positively, with R.M. Flores speaking of "the good sense ensconced in Sancho's string of proverbs" and justifiably pointing out that "Sancho's retort to this [Don Quixote's statement] goes straight to the point, and also stands as an answer to the general misconception that holds that Sancho often does not know what he is talking about and misapplies his sayings" (1982a: 119 and 120). On a more philosophical level, Laura Gorfkle has stated that in this case "Sancho's speech, more than the construction of a single argument or point of view, is an exploration of the problem of fortune, and of the manners in which good and bad fortune can combine and alternate" (1993: 147-148, see also Hart 2002: 46-47).

This is not to say that Sancho never cites a proverb the wrong way, as when he changes the proverbs "Wisdom is better than wealth" and "A saddled horse is better than an ass covered in gold" to their opposites. But upon close reading it becomes clear that he does so with the definite purpose of showing how things are out of kilter. The two preceding proverbs about the worth of a person and the haves and have-nots are, on the other hand, are rendered in their normal wording:

> "You're worth what you have, and what you have is what you're worth. There are only two lineages in the world, as my grandmother used to say, and that's the haves and the have-nots, though she was on the side of having; nowadays, Señor Don Quixote, wealth is better than wisdom: an ass covered in gold seems better than a saddled horse. [...]

"Have you finished your harangue, Sancho?" said Don
Quixote.

"I must have," responded Sancho, "because I see that
your grace is bothered by it; if you hadn't cut this one short,
I could have gone on for another three days." (589)

Once again it is Don Quixote here who reacts so negatively to
Sancho's proverbial loquaciousness, when there would actually
be no reason for him not to agree with what Sancho has just said.

It is at times surprising that Sancho remains loyal to his master who has so little understanding for his mouth running over
with proverbs. One wonders how he would have reacted to this
self-characterization of Sancho via three proverbs that is so very
complimentary:

"I'm the one who deserves it [an ínsula] as much as anybody
else; I'm a 'Stay close to a good man and become one'; and
I'm a 'Birds of a feather flock together'; and a 'Lean against
a sturdy trunk if you want good shade.' I have leaned against
a good master, and traveled with him for many months, and
I'll become just like him, God willing; long life to him and
to me, and there'll be no lack of empires for him to rule or
ínsulas for me to govern." (666-667)

And what insight once again by Sancho in saying that he is ever
more becoming like Don Quixote. What the latter is not realizing
yet is that he is also becoming more like Sancho, and that even in
his increased use of proverbs that he appears to despise so much.

Talking about insight, here is a string of eight proverbs that
Sancho introduces with "I may be a fool, but I understand the
proverb that says, 'it did him harm when the ant grew wings'".
With this he begins his thoughts that it might perhaps be best if
he were never to get his governorship, with one proverb after
another stating that things are just fine and a change might not be
good. And not to forget the wisdom of the last proverb that "All
that glitters is not gold":

"If I were a clever man, I would have left my master days
ago. But this is my fate and this is my misfortune; I can't
help it; I have to follow him: we're from the same village,
I've eaten his bread, I love him dearly, he's a grateful man,
he gave me his donkeys, and more than anything else, I'm

faithful; and so it's impossible for anything to separate us except the man with the pick and shovel [an allusion to death]. And if your highness doesn't want me to have the governorship I've been promised, God made me without it, and maybe not giving it to me will be for the good of my conscience; I may be a fool, but I understand the proverb that says, 'It did him harm when the ant grew wings,' and it might even be that Sancho the squire will enter heaven more easily than Sancho the governor. The bread they bake here is as good as in France, and at night every cat is gray, and the person who hasn't eaten by two in the afternoon has more than enough misfortune, and no stomach's so much bigger than any other that it can't be filled, as they say, with straw and hay [the actual proverb is "Straw and hay and hunger's away"], and the little birds of the field have God to protect and provide for them, and four *varas* of flannel from Cuenca will warm you more than four of *limiste* [a very fine cloth] from Segovia, and when we leave this world and go into the ground, the path of the prince is as narrow as the laborer's, and the pope's body doesn't need more room underground than the sacristan's, even if one is higher than the other, because when we're in the grave we all have to adjust and shrink or they make us adjust and shrink, whether we want to or not, and that's the end of it. And I say again that if your ladyship doesn't want to give me the ínsula because I'm a fool, I'll be smart enough not to care at all; I've heard that the devil hides behind the cross, and that all that glitters isn't gold, and that from his oxen, plows, and yokes they took the peasant Wamba to be king of Spain, and from his brocades, entertainments, and riches they took Rodrigo to be eaten by snakes, if the lines from the old ballads don't lie." (678-679)

And the duchess, to whom Sancho addresses these remarks, could not "help but marvel at Sancho's words and proverbs" (680), indicating that they made good sense to her. And when she instructs him to govern the vassals of his *ínsula* well, good Sancho cannot resist from adding a few more proverbs and proverbial expressions:

"As for governing them well," responded Sancho, "there's no need to charge me with it, because I'm charitable by nature and have compassion for the poor; and if he kneads and bakes, you can't steal his cakes; by my faith, they won't throw me any crooked dice; I'm an old dog and understand every here, boy [the proverb says: "You don't need here, boy, here, boy, with an old dog"], and I know how to wake up at the right time, and I don't allow cobwebs in front of my eyes, because I know if the shoe fits: I say this because with me good men will have my hand and a place in my house [the phrase means "trust and confidence"], and bad men won't get a foot or permission to enter. And it seems to me that in this business of governorships it's all a matter of starting, and it may be that after two weeks of being a governor I'll be licking my lips over the work and know more about it than working in the fields, which is what I've grown up doing." (680)

Even though Don Quixote was not witness to these proverb strings, he has heard his share of them. Matters come to a breaking point in the forty-third chapter when he instructs Sancho to refrain from using them once and for all when taking over his governorship. While poor Sancho agrees to do so, he cannot help himself and immediately strings four proverbs together (Madariaga 1934: 181-183). Despairing at such verbal behavior, Don Quixote admits to Sancho that one proverb at a time is perfectly fine but that it is the absurd accumulation of them that he objects to so vehemently:

> "Sancho, you also should not mix into your speech the host of proverbs that you customarily use, for although proverbs are short maxims, the ones you bring in are often so farfetched that they seem more like nonsense than like maxims."
>
> "God can remedy that," responded Sancho, "because I know more proverbs than a book, and so many of them come into my mouth at one time when I talk that they fight with one another to get out, but my tongue tosses out the first ones it finds, even if they're not to the point. But I'll be careful from now on to say the ones that suit the gravity of my position, because in a well-stocked house, supper is soon cooked; and if you cut the cards, you don't deal; and the man

who sounds the alarm is safe; and for giving and keeping, you need some sense."

"Go on, Sancho!" said Don Quixote. "Force the proverbs in, string them together one after another on a thread! No one will stop you! My mother punishes me and I deceive her! I tell you to avoid proverbs, and in an instant you have come out with a litany of them that have as much to do with what we are discussing as the hills of Ubeda. Look, Sancho, I am not saying that an appropriate proverb is wrong, but loading and stringing together proverbs any which way makes your conversation lifeless and lowborn." (734-735)

What is important with the four proverbs "In a well-stocked house supper is soon cooked", "If you cut the cards, you don't deal", "The man who sounds the alarm is safe", and "For giving and keeping, you need some sense" is that they have nothing to do with each other. Here Sancho is really just amassing proverbs at random to vex his master even more and to repay him for his constant complaint against his proverbs. As R.M Flores has observed: "This is the only instance I can find in which Sancho's proverbs are apparently mot suited to the occasion. But in this passage Sancho is purposely misusing his proverbs to provoke and exasperate his master" (1982a: 121). It definitely is true that "Sancho does not generally choose proverbs at random as Don Quijote charges" (Hart 2002: 52) and which scholars have too quickly accepted at face value.

One might have thought that Don Quixote and Sancho Panza would let things rest at this point, but Cervantes as the author goes on to let the two of them converse about paremiological concerns, turning this chapter into a unique meta-proverbial discourse that "is richly laced with proverbs so that the two discursive modes, the proverbs and the meta-proverbial, illuminate each other sapientially as well as ironically" (Hasan-Rokem 2007: 195). Even though the following textual excerpts have been cited before in the chapter on "Cervantes as Paremiographical Paremiologist", it is such an essential part of this discussion on "strings of proverbs" that it is repeated here. Sancho begins with a statement rich in proverbs that is supposed to illustrate that he will make a good governor despite his lack of education. It is truly amazing how he ties the following eight proverbs together: "There is a remedy for everything except death", "When your father is magistrate, you are safe when you go to trial", "To go for wool and come back shorn", "When God loves you, your house knows it", "The rich man's folly passes for good judgment in the world", "Be like honey and the flies will go after you", "You are worth only as much as you have", and "You won't get revenge on a well-established man":

> "I know how to sign my name very well," responded Sancho, "because when I was steward of a brotherhood in my village, I learned to make some letters like the marks on bundles, and they told me that they said my name; better yet, I'll pretend that my right hand has been hurt, and I'll have somebody else sign for me; there's a remedy for everything except death, and since I'll be in charge of everything, I can do whatever I want; then, too, when your father's the magistrate... [you're safe when you go to trial]. And being a governor, which is more than being a magistrate, just let them come and they'll see what happens! No, let them make fun of me and speak ill of me: they'll come for wool and go home shorn; and when God loves you, your house knows it; and the rich man's folly passes for good judgment in the world; and since that's what I'll be, being a governor and a very generous one, which is what I plan to be, nobody will notice any faults in me. No, just be like honey and the flies will go after you; you're only worth as much as you have, my grandmother used to say; and you won't get revenge on a well-established man." (735)

Don Quixote's by now expected negative reaction to this proverb bombardment is swift and cruel, but, whether he notices it or not, he actually admits his inability to cite proverbs like Sancho. In fact, he would have to "labor like a ditchdigger" to come up with but one applicable proverb:

> "O, may you be accursed, Sancho!" said Don Quixote at this point. "May sixty thousand devils take you and your proverbs! For the past hour you have been stringing them together and with each one giving me a cruel taste of torment. I assure you that one day these proverbs will lead you to the gallows; because of them your vassals will take the governorship away from you, or rise up against you. Tell me, where do you find them, you ignorant man, and how do you apply

them, you fool, when to say only one that is really applicable, I have to perspire and labor like a ditchdigger? (735-736)

This triggers the classic response by Sancho in which he argues that his proverbs are his wealth and that four of them that he can right now think of would, proverbially speaking, fit perfectly well "like pears in a wicker basket". And then, subservient as he is to his master, he employs the traditional Spanish proverb "Golden silence is what they call Sancho" that contains his name to announce that he will try to refrain from speaking in proverbs forthwith:

> "By God, my lord and master," replied Sancho, "your grace complains about very small things. Why the devil does it trouble you when I make use of my fortune, when I have no other, and no other wealth except proverbs and more proverbs? And right now four have come to mind that are a perfect fit, like pears in a wicker basket, but I won't say them, because golden silence is what they call Sancho." (736)

Don Quixote – how smart is he really – takes the bait and asks Sancho for the four proverbs, thus actually taking over the role of an enabler by giving Sancho a chance to launch into yet another string of proverbs:

> "That Sancho is not you," said Don Quixote, "because not only are you not golden silence, you are foolish speech and stubborn persistence, but even so I should like to know which four proverbs came to mind just now that were so to the point, because I have been searching my mind, and I have a good one, and I cannot think of a single proverb."
>
> "Which ones could be better," said Sancho, "than 'Never put your thumbs between two wisdom teeth' and 'There's no answer to get out of my house and what do you want with my wife' and 'Whether the pitcher hits the stone or the stone hits the pitcher, it's bad luck for the pitcher'? They're all just fine. Because nobody should take on his governor or the person in authority because he'll come out of it hurt, like the man who puts his finger between two wisdom teeth, and if they're not wisdom teeth but just plain molars, it doesn't matter; and there's no reply to what the governor says, like

the 'Leave my house and what do you want with my wife.'
As for the stone and the pitcher, even a blind man can see
that. So whoever sees the mote in somebody else's eye has
to see the beam in his own, so that nobody can say about
him: 'The dead woman was frightened by the one with her
throat cut.' And your grace knows very well that the fool
knows more in his own house than the wise man does in
somebody else's."

"That is not so, Sancho," responded Don Quixote, "for
the fool knows nothing whether in his own house or in another's, because on a foundation of foolishness no reasonable building can be erected. Enough of this now, Sancho, for
if you govern badly, the fault will be yours and mine the
shame; but it consoles me that I did what I had to do and advised you with all the truth and wisdom of which I am capable: now I am relieved of my obligation and my promise.
May God guide you, Sancho, and govern you in your governorship, and free me of the misgivings I still have that you
will turn the entire ínsula upside down, something I could
avoid by revealing to the duke who you are, and telling him
that this plump little body of yours is nothing but a sack
filled with proverbs and guile." (736)

As can be seen, Sancho takes the opportunity to enumerate three
proverbs and even supplies explanations for them. Perhaps he
forgot the fourth proverb (Hernandez 1984: 220). But not to worry, he throws in the Biblical proverb "See the mote in someone
else's eye but not the beam in one's own" (Matthew 7:3) and
adds the proverbs "The dead woman was frightened by the one
with her throat cut" and "The fool knows more in his own house
than the wise man does in somebody else's" for good measure.
And it all fits! It's just that Don Quixote misses the points of the
last three proverbs. He sees only Sancho's shortcomings and not
his own, he is perhaps threatened by Sancho's proverb mastery,
and certainly Sancho the fool knows more about his "fount of
proverb lore and folk wisdom" (Sullivan 1996: 229) than Don
Quixote. Galit Hasan-Rokem has discovered a definite pattern in
these proverb duels between the knight errant and his squire:
"Don Quijote confronts Sancho with the excess of proverbs and
their inadequate integration in his speech. Sancho on the one
hand insists on his right to use proverbs, on the other swears to

improve the level of integration and thirdly promises to keep altogether quiet, all three positions being equally characteristically inconsistent and intermittent. Sancho's inconsistency is one of his vital, lifelike characteristics, in blatant contrast to the deadening intransience of his master" (2007: 195). What Don Quixote doesn't understand, and here lies much of the irony, is that Sancho, the wise proverb fool, actually turns out the winner in these confrontations. He might be using proverbs a bit too much, but he knows only too well what he is doing with this traditional wisdom.

That can well be seen when Sancho gets carried away as he patrols his ínsula. After a fancy evening meal at a doctor's house, Sancho makes it perfectly clear that he much rather would enjoy a dinner that he was accustomed to from his social background. Here too one word, or better one proverb, gives another, indicating that Don Quixote's advice of not citing them anymore has born no fruit:

> "Look, Señor Doctor, from now on don't bother about giving me delicate or exquisite things to eat, because that will drive my stomach out of its mind: it's used to goat, beef, bacon, dried meat, turnips, and onions, and if by some chance it's given palace dishes, it gets finicky, and sometimes even sick. What the butler can do is bring me what are called *ollas podridas* [traditional Spanish stew], and the more rotten they are, the better they smell, and he can pack them and fill them with anything he likes as long as it's food, and I'll thank him for it and repay him someday; but don't let anybody try to trick me, because we either are or we aren't: let's all live and eat in peace and good friendship, because when God sends the dawn, it's dawn for everybody. I'll govern this ínsula without forsaking the law or taking a bribe, and let everybody keep his eyes open and tend to his own affairs, because I want you to know that the devil makes trouble everywhere, and if you give me a chance, you'll see marvels. And if you turn into honey, the flies will eat you." (773-774)

The proverbs and proverbial expressions "We either are or we aren't", "When God sends the dawn, it is dawn for everybody", "The devil makes trouble everywhere", "to keep one's eyes open", "to look (tend) to one's own affairs", and "Be as honey

and the flies will go after you" all add up to a convincing statement by Sancho concerning his plan to govern his *ínsula* in a
constructive fashion. He does not appear at all as foolish in this
regard as Don Quixote thinks.

Having given up his governorship after but a short time,
Sancho shows himself quite philosophical about the turn of
events, employing such proverbs and proverbial expressions as
"Man proposes, God disposes", "God knows what suits each
man", "Time changes the rhyme", "to be water that someone will
not drink", and "To think there's bacon and not even find a nail"
most effectively to rationalize matters and to deal with the possible fallout:

> "It was eight or ten days ago, Brother Gossip [a student], that
> I came to govern the ínsula that they gave me, and in all that
> time I didn't even have enough bread to eat; I've been perse-
> cuted by doctors and had my bones trampled by enemies,
> and I haven't had time to take any bribes or collect any fees,
> and this being true, which it is, in my opinion I didn't de-
> serve to leave in this way; but man proposes and God dis-
> poses, and God knows what suits each man and what's best
> for him, and time changes the rhyme, and nobody should
> say, 'That's water I won't drink,' because you're in a place
> where you think there's bacon, and you don't even find a
> nail; God understands me, and that's enough, and I'll say no
> more, though I could." (821-822)

This time Don Quixote does not pick on his squire's use of proverbial language and in telling him that he shouldn't worry too
much about slanderous gossip that cannot be stopped in any
case, he calls on the proverb "You cannot put doors on a field" to
underscore his well-intended comment. And he can count on
Sancho's knowledge of the proverb who had used it early in the
novel in a related way: "But who can put doors on a field? Let
them say what they please, I don't care" (192):

> "Do not be angry, Sancho [said Don Quixote], or troubled by
> what you may hear, for there is no end to it: you keep your
> conscience clear, and let them say whatever they wish, for
> trying to restrain the tongues of slanderers is the same as try-
> ing to put doors in [*sic*] a field. If the governor leaves his
> governorship a wealthy man, they say he has been a thief,

and if he leaves it poor, they say he has been a dullard and a fool." (822)

Later on Don Quixote even accepts a short string of proverbs by Sancho that includes the proverbs "Long live the hen, even with the pip", "Today it's your turn and tomorrow it's mine", and "The man who falls today can pick himself up tomorrow". Adding the proverbial expression "to lose heart" to it, this statement serves Sancho's attempt to cheer the battle-weary Don Quixote up very well:

"Enough of that, Señor [Don Quixote]," said Sancho. "Long live the hen, even with the pip; today it's your turn and tomorrow it's mine; these matters of clashes and blows shouldn't be taken too seriously, because the man who falls today can pick himself up tomorrow, unless he decides to stay in bed, I mean if he lets himself lose heart and doesn't find new spirit for new fights. And your grace should get up now to receive Don Gaspar Gregorio, because it seems to me that everybody's in an uproar, and he must be in the house by now." (890)

The "hen" proverb that at least metaphorically reduces the valorous knight errant to a chicken adds plenty of irony or humor to it all, but Don Quixote appears to be too down to reprimand Sancho for his excessive use of proverbial language this time.

Not to worry though! There is yet another proverb string that will give Don Quixote a chance to pick on the proverbial Sancho. Having suggested that they become shepherds, Sancho imagines his daughter bringing them food out in the country. But since Sanchica is a beautiful maiden, he thinks that some shepherd might take advantage of her, bringing to mind the proverbs "To go for wool and come back shorn", "If you take away the cause, you take away the sin", "If your eyes don't see, your heart doesn't break", and "A jump over the thicket is better than the prayers of good men". As the reader contextualizes these proverbs with the young girl meeting a young shepherd in the open, they make good sense and leave the chance of a sexual encounter to the imagination:

"Oh, how polished I'll keep the spoons when I'm a shepherd. What soft bread, what cream, what garlands, what pastoral odds and ends that, if they don't earn me fame as a wise man, can't help but earn me fame as a clever one! Sanchica, my daughter, will bring food up to our flocks. But wait! She's a good-looking girl, and there are shepherds more wicked than simple, and I wouldn't want her to go for wool and come back shorn; love and unchaste desires are as likely in the countryside as in the cities, in shepherd's huts as in royal palaces, and if you take away the cause, you take away the sin, and if your eyes don't see, your heart doesn't break, and a jump over the thicket is better than the prayers of good men." (901)

Don Quixote's negative reaction is quick and to the point, but while he wants "no more proverbs", he is now ready to admit that "any one of those you have said is enough to explain your thoughts". In other words, he is no longer arguing that Sancho's proverb strings make no sense! Relying on the proverbial expression "to preach in the desert" to express his dismay over Sancho's continued use of proverb accumulations after having been told repeatedly not to do so (Raymond 1951: 135), he underscores Sancho's "misbehavior" by way of the proverb "My mother punished me, and I deceive her". Although the metaphor of the proverb seems inappropriate regarding Sancho as a male, there probably is some humor in this feminization of the plump squire. Be that as it may, Sancho takes no offense but rather pulls in the proverb "The pot calls the kettle black" to confront his master with the undeniable fact that he too uses proverbs (Madariaga 1934: 183). That is true, of course, but Sancho overstates matters by claiming that his master "strings them together":

> "No more proverbs, Sancho," said Don Quixote, "for any one of those you have said is enough to explain your thoughts; I have often advised you not to be so prodigal in your proverbs and to restrain yourself from saying them, but it seems that is like preaching in the desert, and 'My mother punishes me, and I deceive her.'"
> "It seems to me," responded Sancho, "that your grace is like the pot calling the kettle black. You reprove me for saying proverbs, and your grace strings them together two at a time." (901-902)

As usual, Don Quixote insists to have the last word before suggesting that they drop the whole matter. He stresses once again that proverbs are fine if they, proverbially speaking, "fit [the context] like the rings on your finger" and are not randomly and *en masse* "dragged in by the hair".

> "Look, Sancho," responded Don Quixote, "I say proverbs when they are appropriate, and when I say them they fit like the rings on your fingers, but you drag them in by the hair, and pull them along, and do not guide them, and if I remember correctly, I have already told you that proverbs are brief maxims derived from the experience and speculation of wise men in the past, and if the proverb is not to the point, it is not a maxim, it is nonsense. But let us leave this for now, and since night is approaching, let us withdraw some distance from the king's highway, and spend the night there, and God alone knows what tomorrow will bring." (902)

Don Quixote will just not let go of his *idée fixe* of Sancho applying proverbs nonsensically. Whether he likes it or not, he is wrong, and the careful reader is catching on, realizing that Sancho is making plenty of sense as the wise fool towards the end of their adventures. And Don Quixote cannot escape this folk wisdom either, as evidenced by the proverbial conclusion "God alone knows what tomorrow will bring" of his statement that is a proverb definition of sorts for his squire. As if Sancho doesn't know what a proverb is!

Relatively close to the end of the *Don Quixote*, one might have thought that Cervantes had enough of these exchanges around proverbs between the knight errant and his squire. But in fact, just a few pages beyond the previous dialogue, he returns to this proverbial theme one more time in the next chapter. Sancho is finally standing up to his master, telling him that he just wants to sleep and be himself. As always, Don Quixote is not pleased, and in his anger scolds his loyal squire by giving him hope for solitude with the personalized medieval Latin proverb "Post tenebras lux (see also Job 17:12): Understandably so, Sancho responds by telling Don Quixote that he does not understand Latin and then goes on quite philosophically about the equality of all people, certainly when they sleep. But that reminds him of yet another proverb that he cites only indirectly, i.e., "Sleep resembles (is the brother of) death":

> "O unfeeling soul! O pitiless squire! O undeserved bread and unthinking favor that I [Don Quixote] have given to you and intend to give to you in the future! Because of me you found yourself a governor, and because of me you have hopes of becoming a count or receiving another equivalent title, and the fulfillment of those hopes will take no longer than the time it takes for this year to pass, for *Post tenebras spero lucem.*"
>
> "I don't understand that," replied Sancho. "I only understand that while I'm sleeping I have no fear, or hope, or trouble, or glory; blessed be whoever invented sleep, the mantle that covers all human thought, the food that satisfies hunger, the water that quenches thirst, the fire that warms the cold, the cold that cools down ardor, and, finally, the general coin with which all things are bought, the scale and balance that make the shepherd equal to the king, and the simple man equal to the wise. There is only one defect in sleep, or so I've heard, and it is that it resembles death, for there is very little difference between a man who is sleeping and a man who is dead." (903-904)

Don Quixote, his anger passed, actually praises Sancho for this philosophical statement and pays him the ultimate compliment by acknowledging the truth of one of his proverbs. In other words, he is starting to talk like his squire and that's a big change indeed. Sancho's response is in typical fashion once again exaggerated. After all, his claim that Don Quixote is now the one who strings proverbs together is not corroborated by his actual statement:

> "I have never heard you speak, Sancho," said Don Quixote, "as elegantly as now, which leads me to recognize the truth of the proverb that you like to quote: 'It is not where you were born but who your friends are now that counts.'"
>
> "Ah, confound it, Señor!" replied Sancho. "Now I'm not the one stringing proverbs together; they also drop two by two from your grace's mouth better than they do from mine, but between my proverbs and yours there must be this dif-

ference: your grace's come at the right time, while mine are
out of place, but in fact they're all proverbs." (904)

Instead of asserting himself as a capable proverbialist, Sancho
back-paddles by declaring that his master uses proverbs correctly
whereas he as the subservient squire does not have this ability.
Don Quixote has succeeded in brainwashing him to this split
viewpoint. At least Sancho winds up his response with the pro-
nouncement that "in fact they're all proverbs!"

And now, very close to the end of the novel, Cervantes gives
both of his heroes one more chance to go for each other proverbially. The reader might well have hoped that Sancho will finally
stand his ground, but instead appears to succumb to the wishes of
his master one last time. Cervantes does not even let him utter
his four proverbs "In delay there is danger", "Pray to God and
use a hammer", "One 'here you are' is worth more than two 'I'll
give it to you'", and "A bird in the hand is worth two in the
bush" directly but only lists them through indirect speech:

> Sancho responded that he would do as his master wished but
> would like to conclude this matter quickly, while his blood
> was hot and the grindstone rough, because in delay there is
> often danger, and pray to God and use the hammer, and one
> "here you are" was worth more than two "I'll give it to you,"
> and a bird in hand was worth two in the bush. (924)

Don Quixote's predictable answer is "no more proverbs", and he
can't resist plugging in a bit of superfluous Latin that he knows
Sancho can't understand. Accusing Sancho of being up to his old
tricks with proverbs is correct, but who is telling whom here to
speak plainly? And, wouldn't the reader know and expect it by
now, Don Quixote winds up by using the proverb "One loaf is
the same as a hundred". The loaf of bread here becomes a metaphor for Sancho's proverbs which, at least to Don Quixote, are
all the same and should most certainly not be amassed.

> "By the one God, Sancho, no more proverbs," said Don
> Quixote. "It seems you are going back to *sicut erat* ["as it
> was before" – that is, "up to your old tricks"]; speak plainly,
> and simply, and without complications, as I have often told
> you, and you will see how one loaf will be the same as a
> hundred for you." (924)

Sancho's timid response – he doesn't even point out that Don Quixote just used a proverb – is perhaps disappointing on first reading:

> "I don't know why I'm so unlucky," responded Sancho, "that I can't say a word without a proverb, and every proverb seems exactly right to me, but I'll change, if I can." (924)

The modern reader might wish that the closing phrase "I'll change, if I can" were not there so that Sancho could insist that proverbs are his life and that it is his right as an individual to use them. But to be sure, nobody has ever argued with Sancho or for that matter Don Quixote that a proverb or two in the right place at the right time is not appropriate. This communication by proverbial "indirection" (Weiger 1985: 22) is certainly an integral part of the novel's complex nature. It is only Sancho's strings of proverbs that are at issue and legitimately questioned. The message of such proverbs as "Moderation in all things" and "Nothing in excess" is absent in Sancho's mind, leaving the door wide open for satire, irony, and humor.

10. Ten Translations of the String of Proverbs in Chapter 43

Following the "string of proverbs" excerpt of chapter 43 of the second part of the *Don Quixote* in its original Spanish, ten English translations from between 1620 and 2009 are presented for the sake of comparison. This single example alone shows the difficulty that the various translators have faced in rendering just these few paragraphs into proverbial English. As was mentioned in the chapter on translations before, it would be a most welcome undertaking if someone were to make a comparative study of most of the proverbial passages to establish which translator has mastered the Spanish proverbs the best. Such a study would also be of much use for the next English translations that will most certainly come along.

The following original Spanish text from 1615 is cited from Miguel de Cervantes Saavedra, *Don Qvixote de la Mancha*. Eds. Rodolfo Schevill and Adolfo Bonilla. Madrid: Gráficas Reunidas, 1948. VI, 57-58 and 60-62.

"Tambien, Sancho, no has de mezclar en tus platicas la muchedumbre de refranes que sueles; que puesto que los refranes son sentencias breues, muchas vezes los traes tan por los cabellos, que mas parecen disparates que sentencias."

"Esso Dios lo puede remediar", respondio Sancho, "porque se mas refranes que vn libro, y vienenseme tantos juntos a la boca quando hablo, que riñen por salir vnos con otros; pero la lengua va arrojando los primeros que encuentra, aunque no vengan a pelo. Mas yo tendre cuenta de aqui adelante de dezir los que conuengan a la grauedad de mi cargo; que en casa llena presto se guisa la cena; y quien destaja no baraja; y a buen saluo está el que repica; y el dar y el tener seso ha menester."

"Esso si, Sancho!", dixo don Quixote. "Encaxa, ensarta, enhila refranes; que nadie te va a la mano! Castigame mi madre, y yo trompogelas. Estoyte diziendo que escuses refranes, y en un instante has echado aqui vna letania dellos, que assi quadran con lo que vamos tratando como por los cerros de Vbeda. Mira, Sancho, no te digo yo que parece mal vn refran traydo a proposito; pero

cargar y ensartar refranes a troche moche haze la platica desmaya-
da y baxa."

[...]

"Bien se firmar mi nombre", respondio Sancho; "que quando
fuy prioste en mi lugar aprendi a hazer vnas letras como de marca
de fardo, que dezian que dezia mi nombre; quanto mas que fingire
que tengo tullida la mano derecha, y hare que firme otro por mi;
que para todo ay remedio, so no es para la muerte; y teniendo yo
el mando y el palo, hare lo que quisiere; quanto mas que el que
tiene el padre alcalde ... Y siendo yo gouernador, que es mas que
ser alcalde, llegaos, que la dexan ver! No sino popen y caloñenme;
que vendran por lana y bolueran trasquilados; y a quien Dios
quiere bien, la casa le sabe; y las necedades del rico por sentencias
passan en el mundo; y siendolo yo, siendo gouernador y juntamen-
te liberal, como lo pienso ser, no aura falta que se me parezca. No
sino hazeos miel, y paparos han moscas; tanto vales quanto tienes,
dezia vna mi aguela; y del hombre arraygado no te veras ven-
igado."

"O, maldito seas de Dios, Sancho!", dixo a esta sazon don
Quixote. "Sesenta mil satanases te lleuen a ti y a tus refranes! Vna
hora ha que los estás ensartando y dandome con cada vno tragos
de tormento. Yo te asseguro que estos refranes te han de lleuar vn
dia a la horca; por ellos te han de quitar el gouierno tus vassallos,
o ha de auer entre ellos comunidades. Dime: dónde los hallas, ig-
norante, o cómo los aplicas, mentecato?; que para dezir yo vno, y
aplicarle bien, sudo y trabajo como si cauasse."

"Por Dios, señor nuestro amo", replicó Sancho, "que vuessa
merced se quexa de bien pocas cosas. A qué diablos se pudre de
que yo me sirua de mi hazienda, que ninguna otra tengo, ni otro
caudal alguno sino refranes y mas refranes? Y aora se me ofrecen
quatro, que venian aqui pintiparados, o como peras en tabaque;
pero no los dire, porque al buen callar llaman Sancho."

"Esse Sancho no eres tu", dixo don Quixote; "porque no solo
no eres buen callar, sino mal hablar y mal porfiar; y, con todo
esso, querria saber qué quatro refranes te ocurrian aora a la memo-
ria, que venian aqui a proposito; que yo ando recorriendo la mia,
que la tengo buena, y ninguno se me ofrece."

"Qué mejores", dixo Sancho, "que 'entre dos muelas cordales
nunca pongas tus pulgares', y 'a ydos de mi casa y qué quereis con
mi muger?, no ay responder', y 'si da el cantaro en la piedra, o la

piedra en el cantaro, mal para el cantaro', todos los quales vienen a pelo? Que nadie se tome con su gouernador, ni con el que le manda, porque saldra lastimado, como el que pone el dedo entre dos muelas cordales, y aunque no sean cordales, como sean muelas no importa; y a lo que dixere el gouernador no ay que replicar, como al 'salios de mi casa, y qué quereis con mi muger?' Pues lo de la piedra en el cantaro, vn ciego lo vera. Assi, que es menester que el que vee la mota en el ojo ageno, vea la viga en el suyo, porque no se diga por el 'espantose la muerta de la degollada'; y vuessa merced sabe bien que mas sabe el necio en su casa que el cuerdo en la agena."

"Esso no, Sancho", respondio don Quixote; "que el necio en su casa ni en la agena sabe nada, a causa que sobre el cimiento de la necedad no assienta ningun discreto edificio. Y dexemos esto aqui, Sancho; que si mal gouernares, tuya sera la culpa, y mia la verguença; mas consuelome que he hecho lo que deuia en aconsejarte con las versa, y con la discrecion a mi possible; con esto salgo de mi obligacion, y de mi promessa. Dios te guie, Sancho, y te gouierne en tu gouierno, y a mi me saque del escrupulo que me queda que has de dar con toda la ínsula patas arriba, cosa que pudiera yo escusar con descubrir al duque quien eres, diziendole que toda essa gordura, y essa personilla que tienes, no es otra cosa que vn costal lleno de refranes y de malicias."

What follows are the ten English translations in chronological order spanning four hundred years:

1. Thomas Shelton, 1620
    Cited from: Miguel des Cervantes, *The History of the Valorous and Witty Knight-Errant Don Quixote of the Mancha*. Translated by Thomas Shelton. Introduction by Royal Cortissoz. 4 vols. New York: Charles Scribner's Sons, 1907. IV, 75-76 and 77-79.

'Likewise, Sancho, you must not intermix your discourse with that multiplicity of proverbs you use; for though proverbs be witty short sentences, yet thou bringest them in so by head and shoulders that they are rather absurdities than sentences.'

'This,' quoth Sancho, 'God Almighty can only help; for I have more proverbs than a book will hold, and when I speak they come so thick to my mouth that they fall out, and strive one with another who shall come out first; but my tongue casts out the first it meets withal, though they be nothing to the purpose; but I will have a care hereafter to speak none but shall be fitting to the gravity of my place; for "Where there is plenty the guests are not empty", and "He that works doth not care for play"; and "He is in safety that stands under the bells"; and "His judgment's rare that can spend and spare."'

'Now, now,' quoth Don Quixote, 'glue, thread, fasten thy proverbs together; nobody comes: the more thou art told a thing, the more thou dost it; I bid thee leave thy proverbs, and in an instant thou hast cast out a litany of them, that are as much to the purpose as To-morrow I found a horse-shoe. Look thee, Sancho, I find not fault with a proverb brought in to some purpose, but to load and heap on proverbs, huddling together, makes a discourse wearisome and base.'

[…]

'I can set to my name,' quoth Sancho, 'for when I was constable of our town I learned to make certain letters, such as are set to mark trusses of stuff, which they said spelt my name: besides now, I'll feign that my right hand is maimed, and so another shall firm for me; for there's a remedy for everything but death, and since I bear sway I'll do what I list; for, according to the proverb, "he that hath the judge to his father," etc., and I am governor, which is more than judge. Ay, ay, let 'em come and play at bo-peep, let 'em back-bite me, let 'em come for wool, and I'll send them back shorn, whom God loves, his house is savoury to him, and every man bears with the rich man's follies; so I being rich, and a governor, and liberal too, as I mean to be, I will be without all faults. No, no, pray be dainty, and see what will become on't; have much, and thou shalt be esteemed much, quoth a grandame of mine; and might overcomes right.'

'Oh, a plague on thee, Sancho!' quoth Don Quixote; 'three-score thousand Satans take thee and thy proverbs; this hour thou hast been stringing them one upon another, and giving me tormenting potions with each of them: I assure thee that one of these days these proverbs will carry thee to the gallows; for them thy vassals will bereave thee of thy government, or there will be a community amongst them. Tell me, ignorant, where dost tough find them all? or how dost thou apply them, ninny-hammer? for, for me to speak one, and apply it well, it makes me sweat and labor, as if I had digged.'

'Assuredly, master mine,' quoth Sancho, 'a small matter makes you angry: why the devil do you pine that I make use of my own goods? for I have no other, nor any other stock but proverbs upon proverbs: and now I have four that fall out jump to the purpose, like pears for a working-basket: but I will say nothing, for now Sancho shall be called Silence.'

'Rather Babbling,' quoth Don Quixote, 'or Obstinacy itself; yet I would fain know what four proverbs they be that came into thy mind so to the purpose; for I think upon none, yet I have a good memory.'

'What better,' said Sancho, 'than "Meddle not with a hollow tooth"; and "Go from my house, What will you have with my wife?" there's no answering; and "If the pot fall upon the stone, or the stone on the pot, ill for the pot, ill for the stone"; all which are much to the purpose. That nobody meddle with their governor, nor with their superior, lest they have the worst, as he that puts his hand to his teeth (so they be not hollow, 'tis no matter if they be teeth). Whatsoever the governor says, there is no replying, as in saying, "Get you from my house," and "What will you have with my wife?" and that of the pot and the stone, a blind man may perceive it: so that he that sees the mote in another man's eye, let him see the beam in his own, that it may not be said by him, The dead was afraid of her that was flayed. And you know, sir, that the fool knows more in his house than the wise man doth in another's.'

'Not so, Sancho,' quoth Don Quixote; 'for the fool, neither in his own house nor another's, knows aught, by reason that no wise edifice is seated upon the increase of his folly: and let us leave this, Sancho, or if thou govern ill thou must bear the fault, and mine must be the shame; but it comforts me that I have done my duty in advising thee truly, and as discreetly as I could, and with this I have accomplished with my obligation; and God speed thee, Sancho, and govern thee in thy government, and bring me out of the scruple I am in, that thou wilt turn thy government with the heels upwards; which I might prevent, by letting the duke know thee better, and telling him, that all that fatness, and little corpse of thine, is nothing but a sack of proverbs and knavery.'

2. Peter Anthony Motteux, 1700
    Cited from: Miguel de Cervantes Saavedra, *The History of the Ingenious Gentleman Don Quixote*. Translated by Peter An-

thony Motteux. 4 vols. Edinburgh: John Grant, 1908. IV, 63-64 and 66-70.

"In the next place, Sancho," said the knight, "do not overlard your common discourse with that glut of proverbs which you mix in it continually; for though proverbs are properly concise and pithy sentences, yet as thou bringest them in, in such a huddle, by the head and shoulders, thou makest them look like so many absurdities."

"Alas! Sir," quoth Sancho, "this is a disease that Heaven alone can cure; for I have more proverbs than will fill a book; and when I talk, they crowd so thick and fast to my mouth, that they quarrel which shall get out first; so that my tongue is forced to let them out as fast, first come first served, though nothing to my purpose. But hence-forwards I will set a watch on my mouth, and let none fly out, but such as shall befit the gravity of my place. For in a rich man's house, the cloth is soon laid: Where there is plenty, the guests cannot be empty. A blot's no blot till it is hit. He is safe who stands under the bells. You cannot eat your cake and have your cake: And store's no sore."

"Go on, go one, friend," said Don Quixote, "thread, tack, stitch on, heap proverb upon proverb, out with them, man, spew them out! There is nobody coming. My mother whips me, and I whip the gigg. I warn thee to forbear foisting in a rope of proverbs everywhere, and thou blunderest out a whole litany of old saws, as much to the purpose as the last year's snow! Observe me, Sancho, I condemn not the use of proverbs: but it is most certain, that such a confusion and hodge-podge of them, as thou throwest out and draggest in by the hair together, makes conversation fulsome and poor."

[...]

"Oh! as for that," quoth Sancho, "I can do well enough: I can set my name: for when I served several offices in our parish, I learned to scrawl a sort of letters, such as they mark bundles of stuff with, which they told me spelt my name. Besides I can pretend my right hand is lame, and so another shall sign for me; for there is a remedy for all things but death. And since I have the power, I will do what I list; for, as the saying is, he whose father is judge, goes safe to his trial. And, as I am governor, I hope I am somewhat higher than a judge. New lords, new laws. Ay, ay, let them come as they will, and play at bo-peep. Let them backbite me to my face, I will bite-back the biters. Let them come for wool, and I will send them home shorn. Whom God loves, his house happy proves. The rich man's follies pass for wise sayings in the world. So I, being rich, do you see, and a governor, and too free-hearted into the bargain, as I intend to be, I shall have no faults at all. It is so, daub yourself with honey, and you will never want flies. What a man has, so much he is sure of, said my old grannam: And who shall hang the bell about the cat's neck?"

"Confound thee," cried Don Quixote, "for an eternal proverb-voiding swagbelly! Threescore thousand Beelzebubs take thee, and thy damned nauseous rubbish! Thou hast been this hour stringing them together, like so many ropes of onions, and poisoning and racking me with them. I dare say, these wicked proverbs will one day bring thee to the gallows; they will provoke thy islanders to pull thee down, or at least make them shun thee like a common nuisance. Tell me, thou essence of ignorance, where dost thou make them up? and who taught thy codshead to apply them? For it makes me sweat, as if I were delving and threshing, to speak but one, and apply it properly."

"Uds [*sic*] precious! my good master," quoth Sancho, "what a small matter puts you in a pelting case! why the devil should you grudge me the use of my own goods and chattels? I have no other estate. Proverbs on proverbs are all my stock. And now I have four ready to pop out, as pat to the purpose as pears to a panier; but mum for that. Now silence is my name."

"No," replied Don Quixote, "rather paste-roast and sauce-box, I should call thee; for thou art all tittle-tattle and obstinacy. Yet, methinks, I would fain hear these four notable proverbs that come so pat to the purpose. I thank heaven I have a pretty good memory, and yet I cannot for my soul call one to mind."

"Why, sir," quoth Sancho, "what proverbs would you have better than these? Between two cheek-teeth never clap thy thumbs. And when a man says get out of my house; what would you have with my wife? there is no answer to be made. And again, whether the pitcher hit the stone, or the stone the pitcher, it is bad for the pitcher. All these fit to a hair, sir; that is, let nobody meddle with his governor, or his betters, or he will rue for it, as sure as a gun; as he must expect who runs his finger between two cheek-teeth, (and though they were not cheek-teeth if they be but teeth that is enough). In the next place, let the governor say what he will, there is no gainsaying him; it is as much as when one says, get out of my house; what would you with my my wife? and as for the stone and the pitcher, a blind man may see through it. And so he that sees a mote in another man's eye, should do well to take the beam out of his own; that people may not say, The pot calls the kettle black a–se, and the dead woman is afraid of her that is flayed. Besides, your worship knows, that a fool knows more in his house, than a wise body in another man's."

"That is a mistake, Sancho," replied Don Quixote, "for the fool knows nothing, neither in his own house, nor in another man's; for no substantial knowledge can be erected on so bad a foundation as folly. But let us break off this discourse: If thou dost not discharge the part of a good governor, thine will be the fault, though the shame and discredit will be mine. However, this is my comfort, I have done my duty in giving thee the best and most wholesome advice I could: And so heaven prosper and direct thee in thy government, and disappoint my fears for thy turning all things upside down in that poor island; which I might indeed prevent, by giving the duke a more perfect insight into thee, and discovering to him, that all that gorbellied paunch-gutted little corpse of thine is nothing but a bundle of proverbs, and sackful of knavery."

3. Charles Jarvis, 1742
    Cited from: Miguel de Cervantes Saavedra, *Don Quixote de la Mancha*. Translated by Charles Jarvis. Edited with an Introduction by E.C. Riley. Oxford: Oxford University Press, 1992. 824-825 and 826-828.

'Likewise, Sancho, intermix not in your discourse that multitude of proverbs you are wont: for, though proverbs are short sentences, you often drag them in so by the head and shoulders, that they seem rather cross purposes, than sentences.'

'God alone can remedy that,' quoth Sancho; 'for I know more proverbs than will fill a book, and, when I talk, they crowd so thick into my mouth, that they jostle which shall get out first: but my tongue tosses out the first it meets, though it be not always very pat. But, for the future, I will take heed to utter such as become the gravity of my place: for, In a plentiful house supper is soon dressed; and, He that cuts does not deal; and, He that has the repique is safe; and, To spend and to spare, require judgement.'

'So, so, Sancho,' quoth Don Quixote; 'thrust in, rank, and string on your proverbs, nobody is going about to hinder you. My mother whips me, and I tear on. I am warning you to abstain from proverbs, and in an instant you pour forth a litany of them, which square with what we are upon as much as, Over the hills and far away. Look you, Sancho, I do not say a proverb is amiss when skillfully applied; but to accumulate, and string them at random, renders a discourse flat and low.'

[...]

'I can sign my name very well,' answered Sancho; 'for, when I was steward of the brotherhood in our village, I learned to make certain characters, like the marks upon a woolpack, which, I was told, spelt my name: but, at the worst, I can pretend my right hand is lame, and make another sign for me: for there is a remedy for everything but death; and I, having the command of the staff, will do what I please. Besides, he whose father is mayor, etc., you know, and I, being a governor, am surely something more than a mayor. Let them come and play at bo-peep. Aye, aye, let them slight and backbite me: They may come for wool, and be sent back shorn; and, Whom God loves, his house smells savoury to him; and, The rich man's blunder pass for maxims in the world; and I, being governor, and consequently rich, and bountiful to boot, as I intend to be, nobody will see my defects. No, no, Get yourself honey, and clowns will have flies. As much as you have, so much you are worth, said my grandam; and, There is no revenging yourself upon a rich man.'

'Oh! God's curse light on you,' cried out Don Quixote at this instant; 'sixty thousand devils take you, and your proverbs! You have been stringing of them this full hour, and putting me to the rack with every one of them. Take my word for it, these proverbs will one day bring you to the gallows: upon their account, your subjects will strip you of your government, or at least conspire against you. Tell me, where find you them, ignorant? or how apply you them, dunce? For my part, to utter but one, and apply it properly, I sweat and labour as if I were digging.'

'Before God, master of mine,' replied Sancho, 'your worship complains of very trifles. Why the devil are you angry, that I make use of my own goods? for I have no other, nor any stock, but proverbs upon proverbs and just now I have four that present themselves pat to the purpose, and sit like pears in a pannier: but I will not produce them; for, "To keep silence well is called San-cho".'

'That you will never do, Sancho,' quoth Don Quixote; 'for you are so far from keeping silence well, that you are an arrant prate-apace, and an eternal babbler. But, for all that, I would fain know what four proverbs occurred to you just now, so pat to the purpose; for I have been running over my own memory, which is a pretty good one, and I can think of none.'

'Can there be better,' quoth Sancho, 'than, Never venture your fingers between two eye-teeth; and to get out of my house, what would you have with my wife? There is no reply; and, Whether the pitcher hits the stone, or the stone hits the pitcher, it is bad for the pitcher: all which fit to a hair. Let no one contest with his governor, or his governor's substitutes; for he will come off by the worst, like him who claps his finger between two eye-teeth: but though they be not eye-teeth, so they be teeth, it matters not. To what a governor says, there is no replying; for it is like, Get you out of my house, what business have you with my wife? Then, as to the stone and the pitcher, a blind man may see into it. So that he who sees a mote in another man's eye, should first look to the beam in his own; that it may not be said of him, The dead woman was afraid of her that was flayed: and your worship knows well, that, The fool knows more in his own house, than the wise in another man's.'

'Not so, Sancho,' answered Don Quixote: 'the fool knows nothing, either in his own house or another's; for knowledge is not a structure to be erected upon so shallow a foundation as folly. And so much for that, Sancho, for if you govern ill, yours will be the fault, but the shame will be mine. But I comfort myself, that I have done my duty in advising you as seriously and as discreetly as I possibly could: and so I am acquitted both of my obligation and my promise. God speed you, Sancho, and govern you in your government, and deliver me from a suspicion I have, that you will turn the whole island topsyturvy: which I might prevent, by letting the duke know what you are, and telling him, that all that paunchgut and little carcass of thine is but a sackful of proverbs and sly remarks.'

4. Tobias Smollett, 1755
    Cited from: Miguel de Cervantes Saavedra, *The History and Adventures of the Renowned Don Quixote*. Translated by To-

bias Smollett. Introduction by Robin Chapman. London: The
Folio Society, 1995. 602 and 603-604.

'Moreover, Sancho, you must not intermingle so many proverbs
with your discourse; for although proverbs are short sentences,
you very often bring them in by the head and shoulders so prepos-
terously, that they look more like the ravings of distraction than a
connected chain of conversation.'

'That defect God himself must remedy,' said Sancho; 'for I
have more proverbs by heart than would be sufficient to fill a large
book; and, when I speak, they crowd together in such a manner as
to quarrel for utterance; so that my tongue discharges them just as
they happen to be in the way, whether they are or are not to the
purpose: but I will take care henceforward, to throw out those only
that may be suitable to the gravity of my office; for Where there's
plenty of meat, the supper will soon be complete; He that shuffles
does not cut. A good hand makes a short game; and, It requires a
good brain, to know when to give and retain.'

'Courage, Sancho,' cried Don Quixote, 'squeeze, tack, and
string your proverbs together; here are none to oppose you. My
mother whips me, and I whip the top. Here am I exhorting thee to
suppress thy proverbs, and in an instant thou hast spewed forth a
whole litany of them, which are as foreign from the subject as an
old ballad. Remember, Sancho, I do not say that a proverb properly applied is amiss; but, to throw in, and string together, old saws
helter-skelter, renders conversation altogether mean and despica-
ble.'

[...]

'I can sign my name very well,' answered Sancho; 'for, during my stewardship of the brotherhood, I learned to make such
letters as are ruddled upon packs, and those they told me stood for
my name: besides, I can feign myself lame of my right hand, and
keep a secretary to sign in my room; so that there is a remedy for
everything but death. And I having the cudgel in my hand, will
make them do as I command; for, He whose father is mayor – you
know – and I shall be a governor which is still better. Let them
come and see, but not throw their squibs or slanders at me: otherwise they may come for wool, and go home shorn. The house itself will tell, if God loves its master well. A rich man's folly is
wisdom in the world's eye: now, I being rich as being governor,
and liberal withal, as I intend to be, nobody will spy my defects.

Make yourself honey, and a clown will have flies. You are worth as much as you have, said my grannam; and, Might overcomes right.'

'O! God's curse light on thee!' cried Don Quixote: 'threescore devils fly away with thee and thy proverbs! A full hour hast thou been stringing them together, and every one has been like a dagger in my soul. Take my word for it, these proverbs will bring thee to the gallows; for these, thy vassals will deprive thee of thy government, or at least enter into associations against thee. Tell me, numskull, where didst thou find this heap of old saws? Or how didst thou learn to apply them, wiseacre? It makes me sweat like a day-labourer, to utter one proverb as it ought to be applied.'

'Fore God, sir master of mine,' replied Sancho, 'your worship complains of mere trifles. Why the devil should you be in dudgeon with me for making use of my own: I have no other fortune or stock, but proverbs upon proverbs, and now there are no less than four at my tongue's end, that come as pat to the purpose as pears in a basket; but, for all that, they shall not come forth; for, sagacious silence is Sancho.'

'That thou art not Sancho,' said the knight, 'far from being sagaciously silent, thou art an obstinate and eternal babbler. Nevertheless, I would fain hear those four proverbs that are so pat to the purpose; for I have been rummaging my whole memory, which I take to be a good one, and not a proverb occurs to my recollection.'

'What can be better than these?' replied the squire: 'Never thrust your thumb between another man's grinders; and to Get out of my house; what would you with my wife? There is no reply: Whether the stone goes to the pitcher, or the pitcher to the stone, 'ware pitcher. Now all these fit to hair. Let no man meddle with a governor or his substitute; otherwise he will suffer, as if he had thrust his finger between two grinders; and even if they should not be grinders, if they are teeth, it makes little difference: then, to what a governor says, there is no reply to be made; no more than to, Get out of my house, what would you with my wife? And as to the stone and the pitcher, a blind man may see the meaning of it: Wherefore, let him who spies a mote in his neighbour's eye, look first to the beam in his own, that people may not say of his, The dead was frightened at the flayed mule: and your worship is very sensible that a fool knows more in his own house than a wise man in that of his neighbour.'

"There, Sancho, you are mistaken,' answered Don Quixote; 'a fool knows nothing either in his own or his neighbour's house; because no edifice of understanding can be raised upon the foundation of folly. But here let the subject rest: if thou shouldst misbehave in thy government, thine will be the fault, and mine the shame: I console myself, however, in reflecting that I have done my duty, in giving thee advice, with all the earnestness and discretion in my power; so that I have acquitted myself in point of promise and obligation. God conduct thee, Sancho, and govern thee in thy government, and deliver me from an apprehension I have, that thou wilt turn the island topsy-turvy; a misfortune which I might prevent, by discovering to the duke what thou art, and telling him all that paunch and corpulency of thine is no other than a bag full of proverbs and impertinence.'

5.   John Ormsby, 1885
     Cited from: Miguel de Cervantes Saavedra, *The Ingenious Gentleman Don Quixote of La Mancha*. Translated by John Ormsby. 4 vols. New York: Macmillan, 1885. IV, 40-41 and 43-45.

'Likewise, Sancho,' said Don Quixote, 'thou must not mingle such a quantity of proverbs in thy discourse as thou dost; for though proverbs are short maxims, thou dost drag them in so often by the head and shoulders that they savour more of nonsense than of maxims.'

'God alone can cure that,' said Sancho; 'for I have more proverbs in me than a book, and when I speak they come so thick together into my mouth that they fall to fighting among themselves to get out; that's why my tongue lets fly the first that come, though they may not be pat to the purpose. But I'll take care henceforward to use such as befit the dignity of my office; for "in a house where there's plenty, supper is soon cooked," and "he who binds does not wrangle," and "the bellringer's in a safe berth," and "giving and keeping require brains."'

'That's it, Sancho!' said Don Quixote; 'pack, tack, string proverbs together; nobody is hindering thee! "My mother beats me, and I go on with my tricks." I am bidding thee avoid proverbs, and here in a second thou hast shot out a whole litany of them, which have as much to do with what we are talking about as "over the hills of Úbeda." Mind, Sancho, I do not say that a proverb aptly brought in is objectionable; but to pile up and string together proverbs at random makes conversation dull and vulgar.

[…]

'I can sign my name well enough,' said Sancho, 'for when I was steward of the brotherhood in my village I learned to make certain letters, like the marks on bales of goods, which they told me made out my name. Besides I can pretend my right hand is disabled and make some one else sign for me, for "there's a remedy for everything except death;" and as I shall be in command and hold the staff, I can do as I like; moreover, "he who has the alcalde for his father –," and I'll be governor, and that's higher than alcalde. Only come and see! Let them make light of me and abuse me; "they'll come for wool and go back shorn;" "whom God loves, his house is sweet to him;" "the silly sayings of the rich pass for the saws in the world;" and as I'll be rich, being a governor, and at the same time generous, as I mean to be, no fault will be seen in me. "Only make yourself honey and the flies will suck you;" "as much as thou hast so much art thou worth," as my grandmother used to say; and "thou canst have no revenge of a man of substance."'

'Oh, God's curse upon thee, Sancho!' here exclaimed Don Quixote; 'sixty thousand devils fly away with thee and thy proverbs! For the last hour thou hast been stringing them together and inflicting the pangs of torture on me with every one of them. Those proverbs will bring thee to the gallows one day, I promise thee; thy subjects will take the government from thee, or there will be revolts among them, all because of them. Tell me, where dost thou pick them up, thou booby? How dost thou apply them, thou blockhead? For with me, to utter one and make it apply properly, I have to sweat and labour as if I were digging.'

'By God, master mine,' said Sancho, 'your worship is making a fuss about very little. Why the devil should you be vexed if I make use of what is my own? And I have got nothing else, nor any other stock in trade except proverbs and more proverbs; and here are three [!] just this instant come into my head, pat to the purpose and like pears in a basket; but I won't repeat them, for "Sage silence is called Sancho."'

'That, Sancho, thou art not,' said Don Quixote; 'for not only art thou not sage silence, but thou art pestilent prate and perversity; still I would like to know what three proverbs have just come into thy memory, for I have been turning over mine own – and it is a good one – and none occur to me.'

'What can be better,' said Sancho, 'than "never put thy thumbs between two back teeth;" and "to '*get out of my house'* and *'what do you want with my wife?'* there is no answer;" and "whether the pitcher hits the stone, or the stone the pitcher, it's bad business for the pitcher;" all which fit to a hair? For no one should quarrel with his governor, or him in authority over him, because he will come off the worst, as he does who puts his finger between two back teeth, and if they are not back teeth it makes no difference, so long as they are teeth; and to whatever the governor may say there's no answer, any more than to "get out of my house" and "what do you want with my wife?" and then, as for that about the stone and the pitcher, a blind man could see that. So that he who sees the mote in another's eye had need to see the beam in his own, that it be not said of himself, 'the dead woman was frightened at the one with her throat cut,' and your worship knows well that the fool knows more in his own house than the wise man in another's.'

'Nay, Sancho,' said Don Quixote, 'the fool knows nothing, either in his own house or in anybody else's, for no wise structure of any sort can stand on a foundation of folly; but let us say no more about it, Sancho, for if thou governest badly, thine will be the fault and mine the shame; but I comfort myself with having done my duty in advising thee as earnestly and as wisely as I could; and thus I am released from my obligations and my promise. God guide thee, Sancho, and govern thee in thy government, and deliver me from the misgiving I have that thou wilt turn the whole island upside down, a thing I might prevent by explaining to the duke what thou art and telling him that all that fat little person of thine is nothing else but a sack full of proverbs and sauciness.'

6. Samuel Putnam, 1949
   Cited from: Miguel de Cervantes Saavedra, *The Ingenious Gentleman Don Quixote de la Mancha*. Translated by Samuel Putnam. New York: The Viking Press, 1949. 784-785 and 786-787.

"Also, Sancho, you must not introduce such a host of proverbs into your conversation; for although proverbs are concise maxims, you very often drag them in by the hair of the head, with the result that they sound more like nonsense than wisdom."

"That is something only God can remedy," said Sancho; "for I know more old sayings than would fill a book, and when I start to speak they all come rushing into my mouth at once, fighting with one another to get out, and so, what happens is, my tongue throws out the first ones it gets hold of, whether or not they are to the point. But I'll remember after this to use the ones that are suited to the dignity of my office; for in the house where there is plenty supper is soon on the table, and he who binds does not wrangle, and the bell-ringer's in a safe place, and keeping and giving call for brains."

"That's it, Sancho!" cried Don Quixote. "Go on threading and stringing and coupling your proverbs, there is no one to stop you! My mother whips me and I keep right on. I have just done telling you that you should avoid proverbs, and here in a moment you have let go with a whole litany of them that, so far as what we are talking about is concerned, are over the hills of Ubeda. Mind you, Sancho, I do not say that a proverb aptly brought in is not all right, but when you overload your speech with them and string them together helter-skelter, it makes your conversation dull and vulgar."

[…]

"I can sign my name well enough," said Sancho. "When I was steward of the confraternity in my village I learned to make certain letters such as they use in marking bundles and which, so they told me, spelled out my name. And, anyway, I can always pretend that my right hand is crippled and have someone else sign for me; for there's a remedy for everything except death, and, seeing that I'm in command and hold the rod, I can do anything I like. 'He whose father is a judge –' you know. And I'll be a governor, which is higher than a judge; so come on and see! Let them make fun of me and slander me; let them come for wool and go back shorn. For whom God loves, his house knows it, and the silly sayings of the rich pass for maxims in this world. Being a governor, I'll be rich, and I mean to be generous at the same time; and that way no one will find any fault with me. Only make yourself some honey and the flies will come to suck you, as much as you have so much are you worth, as my grandmother used to say, and there's no way of getting even with a man of means."

"May God curse you, Sancho!" cried Don Quixote at this point. "May sixty thousand devils carry you off, and your proverbs with you! For an hour now you have been stringing them, and every one is a torture to me. I can assure you that these sayings of yours will one day bring you to the gallows; on account of them your vassals will take the government away from you, or else there will be conspiracies among them. Tell me, where do you find them all, you ignorant lout, or how do you manage to apply them? If I utter one and apply it properly, I have to sweat and labor as if I were digging a ditch."

"In God's name, master," replied Sancho, "you are complaining over very little. Why should you be vexed if I make use of my own property, seeing that I have no other – no other wealth except sayings and more sayings? Here are four that have just popped into my head, as pat to the purpose as could be, or like pears in a basket; but I'm not going to repeat them, for to keep silence well is called *Sancho*."

"That Sancho is not you," said Don Quixote, "for not only do you not know how to keep silent, but you are a mischievous prattler in the bargain. Nevertheless, I am curious to know what the four sayings are that you have just remembered and that fit in so aptly here; for I have been ransacking my own memory – and it is a good one – and none of the sort have occurred to me."

"What better could you ask for," said Sancho, "than these: 'Never put your thumbs between two of your back grinders'; and 'To "Get out of my house" and "What do you want with my wife?" there is no answer'; and 'Whether the pitcher hits the stone or the stone the pitcher, it will be bad for the pitcher,' all of which fit to a hair? Let no one fall out with his governor or with the one who is in command or he will be sorry for it in the end, like him who puts his thumb between his grinders, whether they be back teeth or not, so long as they are grinders that's all that matters. And to whatever the governor may say there's no answer to be made, any more than there is to 'Get out of my house' or 'What do you want with my wife?' As for the stone and the pitcher, a blind man could see that. And so it is that he who sees the mote in another's eye should see the beam in his own, that it may not be said of him, 'The dead woman was frightened at the one with her throat cut'; for your Grace is well aware that the fool knows more in his own house than the wise man in the house of another."

"That is not true, Sancho," said Don Quixote, "for the fool knows nothing, in his own house or in the house of another, for the reason that upon a foundation of folly no edifice of wisdom can be reared. But let us leave the matter there. If you make a bad governor, the fault will be yours and mine will be the shame, but I find consolation in the thought that I have done my duty in thus earnestly advising you, with all the wisdom at my command; in this way am I released from my obligation and my promise. May God guide you, Sancho, and govern you in your government, and may He deliver me from the fear I have that you are going to turn the whole island upside down, a thing that I might prevent by revealing to the duke what you are, telling him that your fat little person is nothing other than a bag stuffed with proverbs and mischief."

7.   Burton Raffel, 1995
     Cited from: Miguel de Cervantes, *Don Quijote*. Translated by
     Burton Raffel. Edited by Diana de Armas Wilson. New York:
     W.W. Norton, 1999. 582-583 and 584-585.

"In addition, Sancho, you shouldn't jumble up your speech with piles of proverbs, as you usually do, because even though proverbs pack a lot of wisdom into a short space, you often drag them in by the hair, so they seem less like sense than nonsense."

"God will have to take care of that," replied Sancho, "because I know more proverbs than any book, and they come jumping into my mouth whenever I open it to say anything, and then they fight with each other to see who can get out first, but my tongue just tosses out the first one it finds, even if it's not right on target. But from now on I'll try to stick to ones better suited to the dignity of my office, because when a house has a well-stocked larder, there's always something cooking, and the man who cuts the cards doesn't shuffle them, and the man who rings the alarm bell doesn't get caught in the fire, and if you're going to be a giver or a keeper, you'd better know what you're doing."

"That's exactly it, Sancho!" said Don Quijote. "Let them roar, let them rip, there's bound to be one that makes a fit – and who's going to stop you from pouring them out! My mother may catch me at it, but I'll keep on fooling her! Here I am, telling you to stay away from proverbs, and quick as a wink you trot out a whole troop of them, all about as relevant to what we're discussing as your great aunt's uncle. Look, Sancho: I'm not telling you there's anything wrong with a proverb, properly used, but to reel off cart-loads of them, all helter-skelter, drains the life out of your speech and makes it worthless."

[...]

"Of course I can sign my name," replied Sancho, "because when I was an usher at union meetings, back home, I learned how to write some of the letters of the alphabet – like the marks they put on bales and barrels – and they said that was how my name was written and, anyway, I can make believe my right hand's par-alyzed, so somebody else has to sign things for me, because there's a way around everything except death, and when I'm in charge and the stick's in my hand I can do whatever I want to, because, you know, when your father's the judge ... And I'll be the governor, which is even better than being a judge – so come on, and we'll see what we'll see! No, let 'em make fun of me and call me names, because they can come after wool and go home fleeced, and when God loves you, He knows where you live, and in this world a rich man's foolishness is called wisdom, and since I'm going to be both a governor and generous (because that's what I'm planning), no one's going to criticize me. No, just make honey and there'll be flies all over, because, as my grandmother used to say, whatever you own, that's what you're worth, and you can't sue city hall."

"Oh in the name of God, Sancho!" said Don Quijote after this outburst. "May sixty thousand demons come and carry off you and your proverbs too! You've been reeling them off for the last hour, and for me every single one of them is sheer torture! They'll bring you to the gallows, some day; on their account, your subjects will drive you out of your governorship, or else you'll start a revolu-tion. Tell me, you jackass: where on earth do you find them, and what do you think you're doing with them, you idiot? For me to say just one, in the right way and at the right time, I have to sweat and struggle like a ditch digger."

"By God, my dear master," answered Sancho, "your grace is making a big fuss about nothing. Why in the name of the devil are you getting mad, just because I use something that belongs to me, since I don't own anything else, not a blessed thing except prov-erbs and more proverbs? Right now I've got four of them, as right to the point as pears in a basket – but I won't say them, because, as Sancho always says, silence is golden."

"That must be some other Sancho," said Don Quijote, "because you not only don't know how to hold your tongue, you also don't know how to use it, and in addition you're as stubborn as a goat – and yet, in spite of everything, I'd like to know which four proverbs your memory just produced, each one of them right to the point, because I've been running through my own memory, which I think a good one, and I can't find a one."

"So what would be better," said Sancho, "than 'never let yourself get between two close relatives'? And there's no answer to 'get out of my house' or 'what do you want from my wife?' And how about 'whether the pitcher whacks the stone, or the stone whacks the pitcher, it's the pitcher that breaks'? That fits just right. Because nobody ought to pick a fight with the governor, or whoever's in charge, because he's sure to lose, just like the man who gets between two close relatives – and even if they're not close, but just relatives, that's good enough – and there's no answering the governor, just as in 'get out of my house' and 'what do you want from my wife?' And even a blind man can see the one about the stone and the pitcher. So what you have to do, to see the mote in someone else's eye, is see the beam in your own, because otherwise it's like the dead woman who was frightened by a corpse – and your grace surely knows that a fool knows more, in his own house, than a wise man knows when he's in someone else's?"

"That one won't work, Sancho," replied Don Quijote, "because a fool doesn't know anything either in his own house or in anyone else's, and you can't build a sensible building on a foolish foundation. But let's leave this where it is, Sancho, because if you govern badly the fault will be yours, but the shame will be mine: I have to take comfort in having done what I ought to do and given you the best, the soundest advice of which I'm capable, which releases me from both my obligation and my vow. May God guide you, Sancho, and may He govern you while you yourself govern, and may He deliver me from my nagging fear that you'll turn the whole island topsy-turvy, which is something I could prevent by telling the duke who and what you really are, explaining to him that, inside that fat and grubby little person, there's only a bag stuffed with proverbs and perversity."

8. Edith Grossman, 2003
    Cited from: Miguel de Cervantes, *Don Quixote*. Translated by
    Edith Grossman. Introduction by Harold Bloom. New York:
    HarperCollins, 2003.733-734 and 735-736.

"Sancho, you also should not mix into your speech the host of
proverbs that you customarily use, for although proverbs are short
maxims, the ones you bring in are often so far-fetched that they
seem more like nonsense than like maxims."

"God can remedy that," responded Sancho, "because I know
more proverbs than a book, and so many of them come into my
mouth at one time when I talk that they fight with one another to
get out, but my tongue tosses out the first ones it finds, even if
they're not to the point. But I'll be careful from now on to say the
ones that suit the gravity of my position, because in a well-stocked
house, supper is soon cooked; and if you cut the cards, you don't
deal; and the man who sounds the alarm is safe; and for giving and
keeping, you need some sense."

"Go on, Sancho!" said Don Quixote. "Force the proverbs in,
string them together one after another on a thread! No one will
stop you! My mother punishes me and I deceive her! I tell you to
avoid proverbs, and in an instant you have come out with a litany
of them that have as much to do with what we are discussing as
the hills of Ubeda. [The next sentence has been cited before]
Look, Sancho, 1 am not saying that an appropriate proverb is
wrong, but loading and stringing together proverbs any which way
makes your conversation lifeless and lowborn."

[...]

"I know how to sign my name very well," responded Sancho,
"because when I was steward of a brotherhood in my village, I
learned to make some letters like the marks on bundles, and they
told me that they said my name; better yet, I'll pretend that my
right hand has been hurt, and I'll have somebody else sign for me;
there's a remedy for everything except death, and since I'll be in
charge of everything, I can do whatever I want; then, too, when
your father's the magistrate... [you're safe when you go to trial].
And being a governor, which is more than being a magistrate, just
let them come and they'll see what happens! No, let them make
fun of me and speak ill of me: they'll come for wool and go home
shorn; and when God loves you, your house knows it; and the rich
man's folly passes for good judgment in the world; and since

that's what I'll be, being a governor and a very generous one, which is what I plan to be, nobody will notice any faults in me. No, just be like honey and the flies will go after you; you're only worth as much as you have, my grandmother used to say; and you won't get revenge on a well-established man."

"O, may you be accursed, Sancho!" said Don Quixote at this point. "May sixty thousand devils take you and your proverbs! For the past hour you have been stringing them together and with each one giving me a cruel taste of torment. I assure you that one day these proverbs will lead you to the gallows; because of them your vassals will take the governorship away from you, or rise up against you. Tell me, where do you find them, you ignorant man, and how do you apply them, you fool, when to say only one that is really applicable, I have to perspire and labor like a ditchdigger?"

"By God, my lord and master," replied Sancho, "your grace complains about very small things. Why the devil does it trouble you when I make use of my fortune, when I have no other, and no other wealth except proverbs and more proverbs? And right now four have come to mind that are a perfect fit, like pears in a wicker basket, but I won't say them, because golden silence is what they call Sancho."

"That Sancho is not you," said Don Quixote, "because not only are you not golden silence, you are foolish speech and stubborn persistence, but even so I should like to know which four proverbs came to mind just now that were so to the point, because I have been searching my mind, and I have a good one, and I cannot think of a single proverb."

"Which ones could be better," said Sancho, "than 'Never put your thumbs between two wisdom teeth' and 'There's no answer to get out of my house and what do you want with my wife' and 'Whether the pitcher hits the stone or the stone hits the pitcher, it's bad luck for the pitcher'? They're all just fine. Because nobody should take on his governor or the person in authority because he'll come out of it hurt, like the man who puts his finger between two wisdom teeth, and if they're not wisdom teeth but just plain molars, it doesn't matter; and there's no reply to what the governor says, like the 'Leave my house and what do you want with my wife.' As for the stone and the pitcher, even a blind man can see that. So whoever sees the mote in somebody else's eye has to see the beam in his own, so that nobody can say about him: 'The dead woman was frightened by the one with her throat cut.' And your grace knows very well that the fool knows more in his own house than the wise man does in somebody else's."

"That is not so, Sancho," responded Don Quixote, "for the fool knows nothing whether in his own house or in another's, because on a foundation of foolishness no reasonable building can be erected. Enough of this now, Sancho, for if you govern badly, the fault will be yours and mine the shame; but it consoles me that I did what I had to do and advised you with all the truth and wisdom of which I am capable: now I am relieved of my obligation and my promise. May God guide you, Sancho, and govern you in your governorship, and free me of the misgivings I still have that you will turn the entire ínsula upside down, something I could avoid by revealing to the duke who you are, and telling him that this plump little body of yours is nothing but a sack filled with proverbs and guile."

9. Tom Lathrop, 2005
    Cited from: Miguel de Cervantes Saavedra, *Don Quixote.* Translated by Tom Lathrop. Newark, Delaware: Lingua Text, 2005. 679 and 680-681.

"Also, Sancho, you must not mix the multitude of proverbs that you know into your conversation as you always do. Although proverbs distill the wisdom of the ages, you often drag them in by their hair and they seem more like foolishness than maxims."

"God will have to provide a remedy for this," responded Sancho, "because I know more proverbs than are in a book and they come to my mouth so jumbled together when I speak they fight with each other to get out. But my tongue throws out the first one it finds, even though it may not fit the situation exactly. I'll be careful from now on to say only those that conform to the gravity of my office, because «in a full house supper is soon cooked» and «the one who shuffles doesn't cut» and «the man who sounds the alarm is safe» and «to give and to retain requires a good brain»."

"That's exactly what I mean," said don Quixote, "you insert, string together, and pile up proverbs. No one can stop you! «My mother punishes me and I make fun of her!» I'm trying to tell you to stop using proverbs and in an instant you've tossed out a long list of them that fit into what we're talking about as well as «over the hills of Úbeda». Look, Sancho, I'm not saying that an appropriate proverb isn't a good thing. But to heap and string proverbs together willy-nilly makes for a dull and coarse conversation."

[...]

"I *can* sign my name," responded Sancho, "because when I was a steward in my town, I learned to make some letters like they use to mark on bales, and they said that it was my name. Besides, I can pretend that my right hand is maimed and I can have someone else sign for me. «There's a remedy for everything except death», and «holding the power and the staff, I'll do whatever I want». And what's more, «he who has a bailiff for a father...» And since I'll be governor, which is higher than bailiff, come on and we'll see what happens! Let them scorn and slander me! «They'll come for wool and go back shorn» and «the lucky man has nothing to worry about». And «the foolish remarks of the rich man pass for wisdom in the world». And being governor and liberal at the same time, as I plan to be, they'll think I'm flawless. «Make yourself into honey and the flies will eat you up». As my grandmother used to say: «you're worth as much as you have». And «you can't take vengeance on the landed gentry»."

"May God curse you, Sancho!" said don Quixote. "May sixty thousand devils haul you and your proverbs off! It's been an hour since you started stringing them together and torturing me with each one. I can assure you that these proverbs will lead you to the gallows one day. Because of them your vassals will take away your government, or it will cause them to revolt against you. Tell me, you ignoramus, where do you find them? or how do you apply them, you idiot? For me to say a single one and apply it well, I sweat and work as if I were digging a ditch."

"Before God, *señor* our master," replied Sancho, "you're complaining about very little. Why the devil do you get angry because I'm using my heritage, since it's all I have? My only wealth is proverbs and more proverbs. And right now four of them come to mind that fit the situation exactly, «like peaches in a basket». But I won't say them, because «good silence is called Sancho»."

"That's not you," said don Quixote, "because not only are you not 'good silence', you're 'bad speech' and obstinate as well. But even so, I'd like to find out which four proverbs just came to you that fit the situation so well. I've been ransacking my brain, and I can't think of a single one that's *à propos*."

"What better ones are there than «never put your thumbs between your wisdom teeth», and «to 'leave my home' and 'what do you want with my wife?' there's nothing to answer», and «if the pitcher hits the stone or the stone hits the pitcher, it's bad for the pitcher»? All of them fit perfectly. No one should take on their governor, nor anyone who's in charge, because he'll come out hurt, just like someone who puts his finger between his wisdom teeth, and even if they're not the wisdom teeth, as long as they're molars it doesn't make any difference. And no matter what the governor asks, there's nothing to say, just like «'leave my house' and 'what do you want with my wife'?» And the one about the pitcher and the rock, a blind man can see it. So, «why do you look at the speck in your brother's eye with never a thought for the plank in your own», lest it be said of him: «the dead woman was frightened to see another with a slit throat». And your grace already knows the one about «the fool knows more in his own house than the wise man in someone else's»."

"Not so, Sancho," responded don Quixote, "for the fool in his own house or in anyone else's doesn't know anything because on the foundation of foolishness you can't build the edifice of intelligence. And let's let it go here, Sancho, because if you govern badly, «yours will be the blame and mine will be the shame». But I can console myself in that I've done what I should by advising you with truths and with whatever discretion I could. With that I'm discharged from my obligation and promise. May God guide you, Sancho, and may He govern you in your government, and take from me the misgiving that I have that you might wind up with the *ínsula* flat on its back, something that I could prevent by revealing to the duke who you are, telling him that the little fat person that you are is nothing more than a sack filled with proverbs and mischief."

10. James H. Montgomery, 2009
    Cited from: Miguel de Cervantes Saavedra, *Don Quixote*. Translated by James H. Montgomery. Introduction by David Quint. Indianapolis, Indiana: Hackett Publishing, 2009. 648 and 649-651.

"Also, Sancho, you are not to lard your conversation with that horde of proverbs of yours, for though proverbs are encapsulated knowledge, you so frequently drag them in by the hair of the head that they sound more like nonsense than knowledge."

"The solution to that is in the hands of God," said Sancho. "I know enough proverbs to fill a book, and so many crowd into my mouth at one time when I speak that they fight among themselves to see which ones get out, and my tongue launches the first one it encounters, even though it may not make sense. But from this moment on I'll be sure to use those appropriate to the high calling of my office, for «when the cupboard is full, the meals come fast», and «the same person should not deal who has cut the cards». Likewise, «the person who tolls the alarm is always safe from harm», and «it takes brains to know when to give and when to keep»."

"There you go," said Don Quixote, "rattle on with your endless string of proverbs, since no one can stop you! To correct a stubborn person is like carrying water in a sieve. Here I am telling you to forsake your proverbs, and a moment later you have reeled off a whole litany that are as appropriate to what we are discussing as is the man in the moon. Mind you, Sancho, I am not saying there is anything wrong with proverbs that are to the point, but to unleash a string of proverbs helter-skelter turns a conversation into something dreary and demeaning."

[...]

"I know how to sign my name," said Sancho, "for when I was a steward in my village, I learned to print a few letters like those big ones on sacks, which, I was told, spelled out my name. Besides, I can always pretend my right hand is crippled and have someone else sign for me, for «there's a remedy for everything except death». And since I'll be in command and will wield the stick, I'll do what I please, especially when «the one whose father is mayor ... ». And once I'm governor, which is greater than being mayor, just let them try something, and they'll be in for a surprise! I'd like to see them try to make a fool of me! «They may come looking for wool but they'll go home shorn». «When God loves someone, He knows which house he's in»; moreover, «a rich man's follies always pass for wisdom», and when I'm rich, as I intend to be, and am not only governor but a generous one at that, no defect of mine will be labeled as such. No, «cover yourself with honey and you'll not want for flies». «You're worth as much as you've got», a grandmother of mine used to say, and «there's no getting revenge on a man of means»."

"Curse your soul, Sancho!" cried Don Quixote at this point, "you and your proverbs can go to blazes! You have been stringing them together for an hour and twisting my soul on the rack with each one. Mark my word, Sancho, those proverbs will get you hanged some day, and because of them your vassals will rise up against you and strip you of your government. But tell me one thing: where does an idiot and simpleton like yourself come up with them and know how to apply them? Why, for me to come up with just one and apply it correctly, I have to sweat and slave like a ditch digger."

"For heaven's sake, my lord and master," said Sancho, "your grace is making a mountain out of a mole hill. Why the dickens should it upset your grace if I make use of my resources, since I have nothing else of value except proverbs and more proverbs? By the way, I've just thought of several others that are simply perfect for the occasion and are sitting there like ducks on a pond, but I won't mention them, for I'm not called Silent Sancho for nothing."

"'Silent Sancho' you are not!" said Don Quixote, "Not only are you not good at keeping silent but you are bad at it, and persistently so. Despite that, though, I should like to know which proverbs you have just thought of that are so apropos. As for myself I have been racking my brain, which is a fairly good one, and have not come up with a single one."

"What better proverbs," said Sancho, "than these: «never stick your finger between anyone's wisdom teeth»; «to the question, 'Have you stopped beating your wife?' what can one answer?»; and «whether the jug hits the stone or the stone the jug, it's bad news for the jug» – all of which fit here like the glove on your hand. No one should pick a fight with his governor or any person in command, for he'll end up on the short end of the stick, like the person who puts his finger between two wisdom teeth; and even if they're not wisdom teeth, so long as they're grinders, it won't matter. Likewise, there's no way to respond to the person who asks if you've stopped beating your wife; and as for the stone's hitting the jug, even a blind man can see through that one. Thus it behooves one who sees a mote in his neighbor's eye to see the beam in his own, or it will be labeled a case of «the pot calling the kettle black». Your grace is certainly aware that «a fool knows more in his own house than a wise man does in someone else's»."

"That is not so, Sancho," said Don Quixote. "A fool knows nothing in his own house or in anyone else's, for no edifice of wisdom can be erected upon a foundation of folly. But let us leave it at that, Sancho, for if you govern badly, the fault will be yours but the shame mine. Still, I take comfort in the fact that I have performed my duty and counseled you with all the earnestness and wisdom of which I am capable, thereby fulfilling my obligation and my vow. May God guide and direct you in your government, Sancho, and may He rid me of the suspicion that you will make a mishmash of the whole island; a circumstance I could prevent by letting the duke know who you are and explaining to him that all that corpulence and pettiness of yours is nothing but a sack full of proverbs and mischief-making."

Index of Proverbs and Proverbial Expressions

All contextualized references are cited from Edith Grossman's translation published as Miguel de Cervantes, *Don Quixote*. Introduction by Harold Bloom (New York: HarperCollins, 2003). The index contains 714 entries (including a number of duplicates): 386 proverbs, 327 proverbial expressions and comparisons, and 1 wellerism. The entries are arranged alphabetically according to keywords. The numbers in parentheses at the end of each entry refer to this translation, of which part I with its 52 chapters comprises pp. 3-449 while part II with 74 chapters covers pp. 451-940. What follows is a list of the page numbers with their corresponding chapter numbers of each part of the long novel:

Part I (pp. 3-449)		182-190	24
3-9	Prologue	190-204	25
11-18	To the Book	205-212	26
19-24	1	212-226	27
24-29	2	227-239	28
29-35	3	239-249	29
35-41	4	249-258	30
41-45	5	258-266	31
45-52	6	266-272	32
53-57	7	272-288	33
58-65	8	289-305	34
65-70	9	305-313	35
70-75	10	313-321	36
75-81	11	321-330	37
81-86	12	330-334	38
86-94	13	334-341	39
94-102	14	341-352	40
102-109	15	352-368	41
109-115	16	368-374	42
116-123	17	374-383	43
124-133	18	383-390	44
134-140	19	391-397	45
141-152	20	398-405	46
152-162	21	405-414	47
163-172	22	414-421	48
173-182	23	421-427	49

428-433   50
433-438   51
438-449   52

Part II (pp. 451-940)   702-704   37
455-458   Prologue   704-710   38
459-468   1   710-712   39
469-473   2   713-718   40
473-480   3   718-727   41
480-485   4   727-732   42
485-490   5   732-737   43
491-495   6   737-746   44
496-502   7   746-752   45
502-509   8   753-757   46
509-512   9   757-765   47
513-521   10   765-772   48
521-526   11   772-782   49
526-532   12   782-790   50
533-538   13   790-797   51
538-548   14   798-804   52
548-550   15   804-809   53
550-558   16   809-816   54
558-567   17   817-823   55
567-575   18   823-827   56
576-582   19   828-832   57
582-591   20   832-842   58
591-596   21   842-849   59
597-604   22   849-861   60
604-614   23   861-863   61
614-619   24   864-875   62
620-628   25   875-883   63
628-636   26   884-887   64
636-642   27   888-892   65
642-646   28   893-897   66
647-652   29   898-902   67
653-657   30   902-907   68
657-665   31   907-912   69
665-677   32   912-918   70
677-683   33   919-924   71
683-690   34   924-928   72
690-696   35   929-933   73
697-702   36   934-940   74

If the **abbot** sings he eats his supper.
"Well, I [Sancho] swear that if they bring me another patient [like Altisidora], before I cure anybody they'll have to grease my palm, because if the abbot sings he eats his supper, and I don't want to believe that heaven gave me this virtue to use for others at no charge." (919)

If the **abbot** sings well, the altar boy is not far behind.
"'We're a talented pair, compadre,' responded the other [man], 'because if the abbot sings well, the altar boy's not far behind.'

And so, disconsolate and hoarse, they returned to their village and told their friends, neighbors, and acquaintances what had happened to them in their search for the donkey, each exaggerating the other's talent for braying, all of which was learned and circulated in nearby towns. And the devil, who never sleeps, and loves to sow and plant quarrels and discord wherever he goes, spreading mischief on the wind and creating disputes out of nothing, ordered and arranged matters so that people from other towns, when they saw someone from our village, would bray." (622-623)

Abundance of things makes people esteem them less.
Cervantes: I do not wish to say more to you except to tell you to consider that this second part of *Don Quixote,* which I offer to you now, is cut by the same artisan and from the same cloth as the first, and in it I give you a somewhat expanded Don Quixote who is, at the end, dead and buried, so that no one will dare tell more tales about him, for the ones told in the past are enough, and it is also enough that an honorable man has recounted his clever follies and does not want to take them up again; for abundance, even of things that are good, makes people esteem them less, and scarcity, even of bad things, lends a certain value. (458)

A woman's **advice** is no jewel.
"Teresa says," said Sancho, "that I should keep a sharp eye on you, and there's no arguing against written proof, because if you cut the deck you don't deal, and a bird in hand is worth two in the bush. And I say that a woman's advice is no jewel, and the man who doesn't take it is a fool." (498)

To look (tend) to one's own **affairs**
"Señor Commissary," the galley slave said, "just take it easy and let's not go around dropping all kinds of names and surnames. My name is Ginés, not Ginesillo, and my family is from Pasamonte, nor Parapilla, as you've said; and if each man looks to his own affairs, he'll have plenty to tend to." "Keep a civil tongue," replied the commissary, "you great thief, unless you want me to shut you up in a way you won't like." "It certainly seems," responded the galley slave, "that man pro-

poses and God disposes, but one day somebody will know whether or not my name is Ginesillo de Parapilla." (168)

Sancho said: "Don't let anybody try to trick me, because we either are or we aren't: let's all live and eat in peace and good friendship, because when God sends the dawn, it's dawn for everybody. I'll govern this ínsula without forsaking the law or taking a bribe, and let everybody keep his eyes open and tend to his own affairs, because I want you to know that the devil makes trouble everywhere, and if you give me a chance, you'll see marvels. And if you turn into honey, the flies will eat you." (773-774)

To put on **airs**.
"Do you hear what you're saying, husband?" responded Teresa. "Well, even so, I'm afraid that if my daughter becomes a countess it will be her ruin. You'll do whatever you want, whether you make her a duchess or a princess, but I can tell you it won't be with my agreement or consent. Sancho, I've always been in favor of equality, and I can't stand to see somebody putting on airs for no reason. They baptized me Teresa, a plain and simple name without any additions or decorations or trimmings of *Dons* or *Doñas;* my father's name was Cascajo, and because I'm your wife, they call me Teresa Panza, though they really ought to call me Teresa Cascajo. But where laws go kings follow [Teresa cites the proverb backward. It actually is "Where kings go laws follow"], and I'm satisfied with this name without anybody adding on a *Doña* that weighs so much I can't carry it, and I don't want to give people who see me walking around dressed in a countish or governorish way a chance to say: 'Look at the airs that sow is putting on! Yesterday she was busy pulling on a tuft of flax for spinning, and she went to Mass and covered her head with her skirts instead of a mantilla, and today she has a hoopskirt and brooches and airs, as if we didn't know who she was.' If God preserves my seven senses, or five, or however many I have, I don't intend to let anybody see me in a spot like that. You, my husband, go and be a governor or an insular and put on all the airs you like; I swear on my mother's life that my daughter and I won't set foot out of our village: to keep her chaste, break her leg and keep her in the house; for a chaste girl, work is her fiesta. You go with your Don Quixote and have your adventures, and leave us with our misfortunes, for God will set them right if we're good; I certainly don't know who gave him [Don Quixote] a *Don,* because his parents and grandparents never had one." (488)

"Now I'll say," replied Sancho, "that you must have an evil spirit in that body of yours. God save you, woman, what a lot of things you've strung together willy-nilly! What do Cascajo, brooches, proverbs, and putting on airs have to do with what I'm saying? Come here, you simple, ignorant woman, and I can call you that because you don't understand my words and try to run away from good luck. If I had said that my daughter ought to throw herself off a tower or go roaming around the way the Infanta Doña Urraca wanted to [allusion to the ballad about Doña Urraca's desire to go wandering], you'd be right not to go along with me; but if in two shakes and in the wink of an eye I dress her in a *Doña* and put a *my lady* on her back for you, and take her out of the dirt and put her under a canopy and up on a pedestal in a drawing room with more velvet cushions than Moors in the line of the Almohadas of Morocco, why won't you consent and want what I want?" (488-489)

Done eris felix, multos nuerabis **amicos**; tempora si fuerint nibila, solus eris.
If the topic is the fickleness of friends, Cato's [actually Ovid] there, ready with his couplet:
> *Done eris felix, multos nuerabis amicos,*
> *Tempora si fuerint nubila, solus eris.*
> [While you are fortunate, you have many friends;
> When times become nebulous, you are alone.]
And with these little Latin phrases and others like them, people will think you are a grammarian; being one is no small honor and advantage these days. (6)

Amicus Plato, sed magis amica veritas.
Letter from Don Quixote to Sancho Panza: *A matter has been presented to me that I believe will discredit me with the duke and duchess, but although it concerns me a great deal, at the same time it does not concern me at all, for, in the end, I must comply with my profession rather than with their desires; as the saying goes: Amicus Plato, sed magis amica veritas ["Be a friend to Plato, but a better friend to the truth"]. I say this to you in Latin because I assume you must have learned it after you became a governor.* (794-795)

[**Amicus**] usque ad aras.
Lotario said: "Good friends may test their friends and make use of them, as a poet [Plutarch attributes the phrase to Pericles] said, [*Amicus*] *usque ad aras* [A friend as far as to the alters = A friend to the end], which means that they must not make use of their friendship in things that go against God." (276)

The **anger** of lovers often ends in curses.
Don Quixote said: "Altisidora, it seems, loved me dearly; she gave me the three nightcaps, which you [Sancho] know about, she wept at my departure, she cursed me, she reviled me, she complained, despite all modesty, publicly; all of these were signs that she adored me, for the anger of lovers often ends in curses." (898-899)

There is no **answer** to get out of my house and what do you want with my wife.

"That Sancho is not you," said Don Quixote, "because not only are you not golden silence, you are foolish speech and stubborn persistence, but even so I should like to know which four proverbs came to mind just now that were so to the point, because I have been searching my mind, and I have a good one, and I cannot think of a single proverb."

"Which ones could be better," said Sancho, "than 'Never put your thumbs between two wisdom teeth' and 'There's no answer to get out of my house and what do you want with my wife' and 'Whether the pitcher hits the stone or the stone hits the pitcher, it's bad luck for the pitcher'? They're all just fine. Because nobody should take on his governor or the person in authority because he'll come out of it hurt, like the man who puts his finger between two wisdom teeth, and if they're not wisdom teeth but just plain molars, it doesn't matter; and there's no reply to what the governor says, like the 'Leave my house and what do you want with my wife.' As for the stone and the pitcher, even a blind man can see that. So whoever sees the mote in somebody else's eye has to see the beam in his own, so that nobody can say about him: 'The dead woman was frightened by the one with her throat cut.' And your grace knows very well that the fool knows more in his own house than the wise man does in somebody else's." (736)

It did him harm when the **ant** grew wings.

"I [Sancho] may be a fool, but I understand the proverb that says, 'It did him harm when the ant grew wings,' and it might even be that Sancho the squire will enter heaven more easily than Sancho the governor. The bread they bake here is as good as in France, and at night every cat is gray, and the person who hasn't eaten by two in the afternoon has more than enough misfortune, and no stomach's so much bigger than any other that it can't be filled, as they say, with straw and hay [the actual proverb is "Straw and hay and hunger's away"], and the little birds of the field have God to protect and provide for them." (679)

To be the **apple** of someone's eye.

Don Quixote responded: "Children, Señor, are the very apple of their parents' eyes, and whether they are good or bad, they are loved as we love the souls that give us life; from the time they are little, it is the obligation of parents to guide them along the paths of virtue, good breeding, and good Christian customs. (555-556)

Knight and squire returned to their animals feeling rather melancholy and out of sorts, especially Sancho, for whom touching their store of money touched his very soul, since it seemed to him that taking anything away from it meant taking away the apple of his eye. (653)

"Well now," said the duchess, "that's enough: Doña Rodríguez, be still, and Señor Panza, calm down, and let me take care of looking after this gray [donkey], for if he is Sancho's jewel, I shall value him more highly than the apple of my eye."

"It's enough if he's in the stable," responded Sancho. As for being valued more highly than the apple of your highness's eye, he and I aren't worthy of that even for an instant, and I would no more agree to it than to being stabbed; though my master says that in courtesies it's better to lose by a card too many than a card too few, as far as donkeys and apples are concerned, you have to go with your compass in hand, and at a measured pace." (682-683)

To compare (mix up) **apples** and oranges. (478)
"I'll bet," replied Sancho, "that the dogson mixed up apples and oranges [in the original: to mix up cabbages with baskets]" (478)

We either **are** or we aren't.
Sancho said: "Don't let anybody try to trick me, because we either are or we aren't: let's all live and eat in peace and good friendship, because when God sends the dawn, it's dawn for everybody. I'll govern this ínsula without forsaking the law or taking a bribe, and let everybody keep his eyes open and tend to his own affairs, because I want you to know that the devil makes trouble everywhere, and if you give me a chance, you'll see marvels. And if you turn into honey, the flies will eat you." (773-774)

There's no **arguing** against written proof.
"Teresa says," said Sancho, "that I should keep a sharp eye on you, and there's no arguing against written proof, because if you cut the deck you don't deal, and a bird in hand is worth two in the bush. And I say that a woman's advice is no jewel, and the man who doesn't take it is a fool." (498)

Aspirations are ruled by good and bad fortune.
"I [Don Quixote], who had set aside a portion of my success as payment for your services, find myself at the very beginning of my advancement, and you [Sancho], before it is time and contrary to the law of reasonable discourse, find yourself rewarded with all your desires. Others bribe, importune, solicit, are early risers, plead, persist, and do not achieve what they long for, and another comes along and without knowing how or why finds himself with the office and position that many others strove for; and here the saying certainly applies and is appropriate: aspirations are ruled by good and bad fortune. You, who in my opinion are undoubtedly a dolt, and who, without rising early or staying up late or making any effort whatsoever, with nothing more than the breath of knight errantry that has touched you, without further

ado find yourself governor of an ínsula as if it were of no consequence." (729-730)

To be an **ass**.
"I say that your grace is correct in everything," responded Sancho, "and that I am an ass. But I don't know why my mouth says ass, when you shouldn't mention the rope in the hanged man's house." (201)

Dubitat Augustinus.
"Señores, all I know," responded the page, "is that I am a true emissary, and Señor Sancho Panza is a real governor, and my master and mistress the duke and duchess can give, and have given him, the governorship, and I've heard that in it Sancho Panza is performing valiantly; whether or not there's enchantment in this is something your graces can argue among yourselves, because I don't know any more than this, and I swear to that on the lives of my parents, who are still living and whom I love and cherish very much."

"That may well be true," replied the bachelor, "but *dubitat Augustinus* ["St. Augustine places that in doubt," a phrase used by students and scholars]." (789)

As innocent as a **baby**.
"Not mine," responded Sancho. "I mean, there's nothing of the scoundrel in him; mine's as innocent as a baby; he doesn't know how to harm anybody, he can only do good to everybody, and there's no malice in him: a child could convince him it's night in the middle of the day, and because he's simple I love him with all my heart and couldn't leave him no matter how many crazy things he does." (536)

To sleep like a **baby**.
"For that," said the Squire of the Wood, "I have just the remedy: before we begin the fight, I'll just come up to your grace and give you three or four slaps in the face that will knock you down, and that'll be enough to wake up your anger even if it's sleeping like a baby." (542)

To talk behind someone's **back**.
Sancho writes to his wife Teresa Panza: *You should know, Teresa, that I've decided you should go around in a carriage, because that's the way it should be; anything else is going around on all fours. You're the wife of a governor, and nobody's going to talk about you behind your back!* (698)

To think there's **bacon** and not even find a nail.
Sancho said: "It was eight or ten days ago, Brother Gossip, that I came to govern the ínsula that they gave me, and in all that time I didn't even have enough bread to eat; I've been persecuted by doctors and had my bones trampled by enemies, and I haven't had time to take any bribes

or collect any fees, and this being true, which it is, in my opinion I didn't deserve to leave in this way; but man proposes and God disposes, and God knows what suits each man and what's best for him, and time changes the rhyme, and nobody should say, 'That's water I won't drink,' because you're in a place where you think there's bacon, and you don't even find a nail; God understands me, and that's enough, and I'll say no more, though I could." (821-822)

To think there's **bacon** when there's not even a hook to hang it on.
"I don't say it and I don't think it," responded Sancho. "It's their affair and let them eat it with their bread; whether or not they were lovers, they've already made their accounting with God; I tend to my vines, it's their business, not mine; I don't stick my nose in; if you buy and lie, your purse wants to know why. Besides, naked I was born, and naked I'll die: I don't lose or gain a thing; whatever they were, it's all the same to me. And many folks think there's bacon when there's not even a hook to hang it on. But who can put doors on a field? Let them say what they please, I don't care." (191-192)

Sancho said: "Señor, your grace should lift up your head and be glad, if you [Don Quixote] can, and give thanks to heaven that even though you were toppled to the ground, you didn't break any ribs; and since you know there are always wins and losses, and you may have the hook but not the bacon, forget about the doctor because you don't need him to be cured of what's ailing you, and let's go back home and stop going around looking for adventures in places and countries we don't know." (889)

"Be quiet, Teresa," responded Sancho, "because often you can have hooks and no bacon [citing this proverb appears to be inappropriate since Sancho means to say that despite his wretched appearance, he has brought home money]; let's go home, and there you will hear wonderful things. I have money, which is what matters, that I earned by my own labor, and with no harm to anybody." (931)

Where there is no **bacon**, there are no stakes.
"I'll go and come back very quickly," said Sancho, "and swell that heart of yours, which can't be any bigger now than a hazelnut, and remember what they say: a good heart beats bad luck, and where there is no bacon, there are no stakes [Sancho misquotes the proverb; actually: "To think there's bacon when there's not even a hook to hang it on"], and they also say that a hare leaps out when you least expect it. I'm saying this because if we didn't find my lady's palaces or castles last night, now that it's day I think I'll find them when I least expect to, and once I've found them, just leave everything to me."

"Well, Sancho," said Don Quixote, "you certainly bring in proverbs that suit our affairs perfectly, and I hope God gives me as much good fortune in my desires." (514)

To go from **bad** to worse.
Sancho said: "And what's clear to me in all this is that in the long run, these adventures we're looking for will bring us so many misadventures that we won't know our right foot from our left. And the better and smarter thing, to the best of my poor understanding, would be for us to go back home now it's harvesttime, and tend to our own affairs, and stop going from pillar to post and from bad to worse, as they say." (125)

To pass through the **banks** of Flanders.
Sancho said: "Nobody can say anything about her [Quiteria] grace and form except to compare her to a swaying palm tree loaded down with dates, which is just what the jewels look like hanging from her hair and throat! I swear she's a fine, rosy-cheeked girl who can pass through the banks of Flanders [that is, she is beautiful enough to pass through any danger]." (591-592)

Let him be **base** who thinks himself base.
"May God grant," replied Don Quixote, "what I desire and what you, Sancho, need, and let him be base who thinks himself base." (161)

They cook **beans** everywhere.
"There's no road so smooth," replied Sancho, "that it doesn't have some obstacle or stumbling block; they cook beans everywhere, but in my house they do it by the potful; craziness must have more companions and friends than wisdom. But if what they say is true, that misery loves company, then I can find comfort with your grace, because you serve a master who's as great a fool as mine."

To not be worth two **beans**.
Sancho responded: "Now, all of you, give me something to eat, otherwise take your governorship back, because an office that doesn't give a man food to eat isn't worth two beans." (760)

By my **beard**.
"Your grace should tell me [Sancho] what we're going to do with this dappled gray horse that looks like a gray donkey and was left behind by that Martino [Mambrino] who was toppled by your grace, because seeing how he took to his heels and ran like Villadiego, he has no intention of ever coming back. By my beard, this dappled gray is a good one!" (156)

Bedbugs are passed from friend to friend.
For this reason [the friendship between the horse Rocinante and San-cho's donkey], it was sung: "Bedbugs are passed from friend to friend." No one should think that the author digressed by comparing the friend-ship of these animals to that of men, for men have learned a great deal from animals and have been taught many important things by them. (529)

Well **begun** is half-done.
"You see now, friend Sancho, the long journey that awaits us; only God knows when we shall return or what facility and opportunity this busi-ness will afford us; therefore, I [Don Quixote] should like you to with-draw now to your room, as if you were going to find something you needed for the journey, and as quickly as you can give yourself a good measure, perhaps even five hundred, of the three thousand and three hundred lashes you are obliged to receive, and once given you will have them, for well begun is half-done." (720)

A full **belly** gives courage.
"I don't deny it," responded Sancho, "and for now give me a piece of bread and about four pounds of grapes, because they really can't be poisoned, and I can't get by without eating, and if we have to be ready for those battles that are threatening us, we'll need to be well-fed, be-cause a full belly gives you courage and not the other way around." (761)

The **belly** leads the feet.
"May it please God, Sancho, because there's many a slip between the cup and the lip, [said the duke]."
    "That may be so," replied Sancho, "but if you pay your debts, you don't worry about guaranties, and it's better to have God's help than to get up early, and your belly leads your feet, not the other way around; I mean, if God helps me, and I do what I ought to with good intentions, I'll be sure to govern in grand style. Just put a finger in my mouth and see if I bite or not!" (686)

A **bird** in the hand is better than a vulture in the air.
"Take my advice, and forgive me, and get married right away in the first town where there's a priest, or else here's our own licentiate, and he'll do a wonderful job. Remember that I'm [Sancho] old enough to give advice, and the advice I'm giving you [Don Quixote] now is ex-actly right, and a bird in the hand is better than a vulture in the air, and if you have something good and choose something evil, you can't complain about the good that happens to you." (262)

A **bird** in (the) hand is worth two in the bush.
"Teresa says," said Sancho, "that I should keep a sharp eye on you, and there's no arguing against written proof, because if you cut the deck you don't deal, and a bird in hand is worth two in the bush. And I say that a woman's advice is no jewel, and the man who doesn't take it is a fool." (498)

Sancho said to his master: "Señor, what a fool I would've been if I'd chosen the spoils of the first adventure your grace completed as my reward instead of your three mares' foals! It's true, it's true: a bird in hand is worth two in the bush." (526-527)

Sancho responded: "Nothing but one insult after another, though she [Dulcinea] must know the proverb that says that a jackass loaded down with gold climbs the mountain fast, and gifts can break boulders, and God helps those who help themselves, and a bird in hand is worth two in the bush. And then my master, who should have coddled me and flattered me so I'd turn as soft as wool and carded cotton, says that if he catches me he'll tie me naked to a tree and double the number of lashes; these noble folk so full of pity should remember that they're not only asking a squire to whip himself, but a governor; like they say, 'That's the finishing touch.' Let them learn, let them learn, damn them, how to beg, and how to ask, and how to have good manners; all times are not the same, and men are not always in a good humor." (694)

Sancho responded that he would do as his master wished but would like to conclude this matter quickly, while his blood was hot and the grindstone rough, because in delay there is often danger, and pray to God and use the hammer, and one "here you are" was worth more than two "I'll give it to you," and a bird in hand was worth two in the bush.
    "By the one God, Sancho, no more proverbs," said Don Quixote. "It seems you are going back to *sicut erat* ["as it was before"]; speak plainly, and simply, and without complications, as I have often told you, and you will see how one loaf will be the same as a hundred for you." (924)

Birds of a feather flock together.
Sancho said to himself: "Well now: everything has a remedy except death, under whose yoke we all have to pass, even if we don't want to, when our life ends. I've seen a thousand signs in this master of mine that he's crazy enough to be tied up, and I'm not far behind, I'm as much a fool as he is because I follow and serve him, if that old saying is true: 'Tell me who your friends are and I'll tell you who you are,' and that other one that says, 'Birds of a feather flock together.' Then, being crazy, which is what he is, with the kind of craziness that most of the time takes one thing for another, and thinks white is black and black

is white, like the time he said that the windmills were giants, and the friars' mules dromedaries, and the flocks of sheep enemy armies, and many other things of that nature." (515-516)

"And by any chance do the enchanted sleep, Señor?" asked Sancho.

"No, certainly not," responded Don Quixote. "At least, in the three days I have been with them not one of them closed an eye, and neither did I."

"Here," said Sancho, "the proverb fits: birds of a feather flock together; your grace flocks with enchanted people who fast and stay awake, so it's no surprise you don't sleep while you're with them." (610)

"I am," responded Sancho, "and I'm the one who deserves it [an ínsula] as much as anybody else; I'm a 'Stay close to a good man and become one'; and I'm a 'Birds of a feather flock together'; and a 'Lean against a sturdy trunk it you want good shade.' I have leaned against a good master, and traveled with him for many months, and I'll become just like him, God willing; long life to him and to me, and there'll be no lack of empires for him to rule or ínsulas for me to govern." (666-667)

The **birds** of the field have God to protect them.

"I [Sancho] may be a fool, but I understand the proverb that says, 'It did him harm when the ant grew wings,' and it might even be that Sancho the squire will enter heaven more easily than Sancho the governor. The bread they bake here is as good as in France, and at night every cat is gray, and the person who hasn't eaten by two in the afternoon has more than enough misfortune, and no stomach's so much bigger than any other that it can't be filled, as they say, with straw and hay [the actual proverb is "Straw and hay and hunger's away"], and the little birds of the field have God to protect and provide for them." (679)

There are no **birds** today in yesterday's nests.

"Señores," said Don Quixote, "let us go slowly, for there are no birds today in yesterday's nests. I was mad, and now I am sane; I was Don Quixote of La Mancha, and now I am, as I have said, Alonso Quixano the Good. May my repentance and sincerity return me to the esteem your graces once had for me." (937)

If the **blind** leads the blind, they will both fall into the ditch. (Matthew 15:14)

"Even so, Señor," said the Squire of the Wood, "if the blind man leads the blind man, they're both in danger of falling into the ditch. Brother, we'd better leave soon and go back where we came from; people who look for adventures don't always find good ones." (536)

To be so **blind** as not to be able to look through a sieve.
"Well, Señor Barber, this is the story," said Don Quixote, "so much to the point that you had to tell it? Ah, Señor Shaver, Señor Shaver, how blind must one be not to see through a sieve? Is it possible your grace does not know that comparisons of intelligence, or valor, or beauty, or lineage are always hateful and badly received? (464)

To throw a **bone** to a dog.
"Throw that bone to another dog!" responded the innkeeper. "As if I didn't know how to add two and three or where my shoe pinches! Your grace [a priest] shouldn't try to treat me like a child, because, by God, I'm not an idiot." (270)

There is no **book** so bad that it does not have something good in it.
"There is no book so bad," said the bachelor, "that it does not have something good in it."
   "There is no doubt about that," replied Don Quixote, "but it often happens that those who had deservedly won and achieved great fame because of their writings lost their fame, or saw it diminished, when they had their works printed." (479)

As soon as Don Quixote heard his name, he stood and listened very carefully to what they were saying about him, and he heard the man called Don Jeronimo respond:
   "Señor Don Juan, why does your grace want us to read this nonsense? Whoever has read the first part of the history of Don Quixote of La Mancha cannot possibly derive any pleasure from reading this second part."
   "Even so," said Don Juan, "it would be nice to read it because there's no book so bad that it doesn't have something good in it. What I dislike the most in this one is that it depicts Don Quixote as having fallen out of love with Dulcinea of Toboso." (845)

The **bread** baked here is as good as in France.
"I [Sancho] may be a fool, but I understand the proverb that says, 'It did him harm when the ant grew wings,' and it might even be that Sancho the squire will enter heaven more easily than Sancho the governor. The bread they bake here is as good as in France, and at night every cat is gray, and the person who hasn't eaten by two in the afternoon has more than enough misfortune, and no stomach's so much bigger than any other that it can't be filled, as they say, with straw and hay [the actual proverb is "Straw and hay and hunger's away"], and the little birds of the field have God to protect and provide for them." (679)

To eat something with one's **bread**
"I don't say it and I don't think it," responded Sancho. "It's their affair and let them eat it with their bread; whether or not they were lovers,

they've already made their accounting with God; I tend to my vines, it's their business, not mine; I don't stick my nose in; if you buy and lie, your purse wants to know why. Besides, naked I was born, and naked I'll die: I don't lose or gain a thing; whatever they were, it's all the same to me. And many folks think there's bacon when there's not even a hook to hang it on. But who can put doors on a field? Let them say what they please, I don't care." (191-192)

To look for **bread** made from something better than wheat.
"Who can doubt it?" said the niece. "But, Señor Uncle [Don Quixote], who has involved your grace in those disputes? Wouldn't it be better to stay peacefully in your house and not wander around the world searching for bread made from something better than wheat, never to think that many people go looking for wool and come back shorn?" (55)

To (not be able to) wait for one's **bread** to bake.
He [a page] took out two letters [from Teresa Panza] and placed them in the hands of the duchess. One of them said in the address: *Letter for my lady the duchess so-and-so of I don't know where,* and the other said: To *my husband, Sancho Panza, governor of the ínsula of Barataria. God keep him more years than me.* The duchess could not wait for her bread to bake, as the saying goes, until she had read her letter, and she opened it and read it to herself. (801)

One should build a silver **bridge** for the enemy who flees.
Don Quixote, stumbling here and falling there, began to run as fast as he could after the herd of bulls, shouting:
"Stop, wait, you villainous rabble! A single knight awaits you, one who does not concur or agree with those who say that one should build a silver bridge for the enemy who flees!"
But not even this could stop the speeding runners, and they paid no more attention to his threats than to the clouds of yesteryear. (841)

To be of three-pile **brocade**.
The duchess said: "Sancho should be of good heart, for when he least expects it he will find himself seated on the throne of his ínsula and of his estate, and he will hold his governorship in his hand and not trade it for another of three-pile brocade [the phrase means "no matter how fine"]. My charge to him is that he attend to how he governs his vassals, knowing that all of them are loyal and wellborn." (680)

The **bulls** are certain.
"Didn't I tell you?" said Sancho when he heard this. "I told you [a priest] I wasn't drunk: now you can see if my master [Don Quixote] hasn't slaughtered and salted that giant! Now it's for sure [the Spanish has *ciertos son los toros* which is equivalent to "the bulls are certain" –

that is, "there's no doubt about the outcome."]: my countship's on the way!" (307)

Let them **bury** me with you.
"Señor," replied Sancho, "I imagine that it's good to command, even if it's only a herd of cattle."
      "Let them bury me with you [a phrase indicating complete agreement with another person's opinions], Sancho, for you know everything," replied the duke, "and I expect you to be the kind of governor your good judgment promises." (728)

To beat around the **bush**.
"That's fine," said Sancho. "You [a farmer] should realize, brother, that now you've painted her [a maiden] from head to toe. What is it that you want? And get to the point without beating around the bush or going around in circles, or taking anything away or adding anything to it." (764)

To beat the **bushes**.
"You'll see, compadre, that when we least expect it, our gentleman will leave again and beat the bushes, putting all the birds to flight."
      "I have no doubt about that," responded the barber, "but I'm not as astounded by the madness of the knight as I am by the simplicity of the squire, who has so much faith in the story of the ínsula that I don't believe all the disappointments imaginable will ever get it out of his head."
      "May God help them," said the priest, "and let us be on the alert: we'll see where all the foolishness in this knight and squire will lead, because it seems as if both were made from the same mold, and that the madness of the master, without the simplicity of the servant, would not be worth anything." (470)

To be someone's own **business**.
"I don't say it and I don't think it," responded Sancho. "It's their affair and let them eat it with their bread; whether or not they were lovers, they've already made their accounting with God; I tend to my vines, it's their business, not mine; I don't stick my nose in; if you buy and lie, your purse wants to know why. Besides, naked I was born, and naked I'll die: I don't lose or gain a thing; whatever they were, it's all the same to me. And many folks think there's bacon when there's not even a hook to hang it on. But who can put doors on a field? Let them say what they please, I don't care." (191-192)

Sancho said: "It won't be good for the priest to have a shepherdess, because he ought to set a good example, but if the bachelor wants to have one, his soul is his own business." (900)

To mind (tend) one's **business**.
"It's taking me to this," said Sancho. "Your grace should tell me ex-actly what salary you'll give me for each month I serve you, and this salary should be paid to me from your estate; I don't want to depend on anybody's favors, which come late, or badly, or never; may God help me to tend to my own business. The point is, I want to know what I'm earning, whether it's a lot or a little; a hen sits on her egg, and a lot of littles make a lot, and as long as you're earning you don't lose a thing. And if it should happen, and I don't believe or expect that it will, that your grace gives me the ínsula you promised, I'm not such an ingrate, and not such a pennypincher, that I won't want the rent from the ínsula to be added up and deducted from my salary pro rat." (498-499)

"Brother [a Castilian]," said Don Antonio, "go on your way, and don't give advice to people who don't ask for it. Señor Don Quixote of La Mancha is a very prudent man, and we who accompany him are not dolts; virtue must be honored wherever it is found; go now, and bad luck to you, and stop minding other people's business." (867)

As soft as **butter**.
"No, of course not," said Sancho, who was close to them, "because my lady is as meek as a lamb: she's as soft as butter." (532)

When they give you a **calf** (heifer), don't forget to bring a rope.
"Sancho I was born, and Sancho I plan to die; but even so, if heaven should be so kind as to offer me, without too much trouble or risk, an ínsula or something else like that, I'm not such a fool that I'd turn it down, because, as they say: 'When they give you a heifer, don't forget to bring a rope,' and 'When good comes along, lock it in your house.'" (483-484)

Sancho said: "Since it's more than three thousand leagues from here to Candaya, if the horse gets tired or the giant gets angry, it'll take us more than half a dozen years to get back, and by then there won't be any ínsulas or ínsulos left in the world that recognize me; and since it's a common saying that danger lies in delay, and when they give you a heifer you'd better hurry over with the rope, may the beards of these ladies forgive me, but St. Peter's fine in Rome; I mean that I'm fine in this house, where I have received so many favors and where I expect a great benefit from its master, which is being a governor." (719)

"O daughter [Sanchica], you certainly are right!" responded Teresa [Panza]. "And all of this good fortune, and some even greater than this, my good Sancho predicted for me, and you'll see, daughter, how he doesn't stop until he makes me a countess; it's all a matter of starting to be lucky; and I've heard your good father say very often – and he loves proverbs as much as he loves you – that when they give you the calf, run over with the rope; when they give you a governorship, take it; when they give you a countship, hold on to it tight, and when they call you over with a nice present, pack it away. Or else just sleep and don't answer when fortune and good luck come knocking at your door!" (788)

Sancho responded: "I'm more clean than gluttonous, and my master, Don Quixote, here before you [Don Antonio], knows very well that we both can go a week on a handful of acorns or nuts. It's true that if somebody happens to give me a calf, I come running with the rope; I mean, I eat what I'm given, and take advantage of the opportunities I find, and anybody who says I'm dirty and stuff myself when I eat doesn't know what he's talking about, and I'd say it another way if I didn't see so many honorable beards at this table." (865)

I **came**, I saw, I conquered.
The Knight of the Wood said: On one occasion she [Casildea of Vandalia] ordered me to challenge the famous giantess of Sevilla called La Giralda, who is as valiant and strong as if she were made of bronze and, without moving from one spot, is the most changeable and fickle woman in the world. I came, I saw, I conquered her, and I made her keep still and to the point, because for more than a week only north winds blew." (539)

Quando **caput** dolet caetera membra dolent.
"That was right and proper," responded Sancho, "because, according to your grace, misfortunes afflict knights errant more than their squires."
　　"You are wrong, Sancho," said Don Quixote. "As the saying goes, *Quando caput dolet – "*
　　"I don't understand any language but my own," responded Sancho.
　　"I mean," said Don Quixote, "that when the head aches, all the other members ache, too; since I am your lord and master, I am your head, and you my part, for you are my servant; for this reason, the evil that touches or may touch me will cause you pain, and yours will do the same to me."
　　"That's how it should be," said Sancho. (470)

It is better to lose with too many **cards** than too few.
Don Quixote said: "It is better to lose with too many cards than too few, because 'This knight is reckless and daring' sounds better to the ear of those who hear it than 'This knight is timid and cowardly.'" (566-567)

"It's enough if he's in the stable," responded Sancho. As for being valued more highly than the apple of your highness's eye, he and I aren't worthy of that even for an instant, and I would no more agree to it than to being stabbed; though my master says that in courtesies it's better to lose by a card too many than a card too few, as far as donkeys and apples are concerned, you have to go with your compass in hand, and at a measured pace." (683)

"I [Sancho] involved myself, and I can involve myself as a squire who had learned the terms of courtesy in the school of your grace, the most courteous and polite knight in all courtliness; in these things, as I have heard your grace say, you can lose as much for a card too many as for a card too few, and a word to the wise is sufficient." (704)

"Be careful, my friend, not to tear yourself to pieces; pause between lashes; do not try to race so quickly that you lose your breath in the middle of the course; I [Don Quixote] mean, you should not hit yourself so hard that you lose your life before you reach the desired number. And to keep you from losing by a card too many or too few, I shall stand to one side and count the lashes you administer on my rosary. May heaven favor you as your good intentions deserve."

   "A man who pays his debts doesn't care about guaranties," responded Sancho. "I plan to lash myself so that it hurts but doesn't kill me: that must be the point of this miracle." (921)

If you cut the **cards**, you don't deal. [see **deck**]
"God can remedy that," responded Sancho, "because I know more proverbs than a book, and so many of them come into my mouth at one time when I talk that they fight with one another to get out, but my tongue tosses out the first ones it finds, even if they're not to the point. But I'll be careful from now on to say the ones that suit the gravity of my position, because in a well-stocked house, supper is soon cooked; and if you cut the cards, you don't deal; and the man who sounds the alarm is safe; and for giving and keeping, you need some sense." (733-734)

At night every **cat** is gray.
"I [Sancho] may be a fool, but I understand the proverb that says, 'It did him harm when the ant grew wings,' and it might even be that Sancho the squire will enter heaven more easily than Sancho the governor. The bread they bake here is as good as in France, and at night every cat is gray, and the person who hasn't eaten by two in the afternoon has more than enough misfortune, and no stomach's so much bigger than any other that it can't be filled, as they say, with straw and hay [the actual proverb is "Straw and hay and hunger's away"], and the little birds of the field have God to protect and provide for them." (679)

Don't go around looking for a three-legged **cat**.
The commissary responded: "He [Don Quixote] wants us to let the king's prisoners go, as if we had the authority to free them or he had the authority to order us to do so! Your grace, Señor, be on your way,

and straighten that basin you're wearing on your head, and don't go
around looking for a three-legged cat [i.e., Don't go looking for trou-
ble]." (170)

If you give the **cat** what you were going to give the mouse, your troubles will be over.
The duke said to Tosilos: "Is it true, O knight, that you declare yourself
defeated, and that pressed by your timorous conscience, you wish to
marry this maiden?"
    "Yes, Señor," responded Tosilos.
    "He's doing the right thing," said Sancho Panza, "because if you
give the cat what you were going to give the mouse, your troubles will
be over." (826)

The **cat** chased the rat, the rat chased the rope, the rope chased the
stick.
Cervantes: And, as the old saying goes, the cat chased the rat, the rat
chased the rope, the rope chased the stick: the muledriver hit Sancho,
Sancho hit the girl, the girl hit Sancho, the innkeeper hit the girl, and all
of them acted so fast and furiously that they did not let up for an instant; then, the best part was that the innkeeper's lamp went out, and
since they were in darkness, everyone hit everyone with so little mercy
that wherever their hands landed they left nothing whole and sound.
(115)

To be a good **catch**.
"Tell me [Sancho] the queen's not a good catch! All the fleas in my
head should be so nice!" (253)

If you take away the **cause**, you take away the sin.
"I [Sancho] am, Señor, so unfortunate, that I fear the day will never
come when I can join this exercise. Oh, how polished I'll keep the
spoons when I'm a shepherd. What soft bread, what cream, what garlands, what pastoral odds and ends that, if they don't earn me fame as a
wise man, can't help but earn me fame as a clever one! Sanchica, my
daughter, will bring food up to our flocks. But wait! She's a good-
looking girl, and there are shepherds more wicked than simple, and I
wouldn't want her to go for wool and come back shorn; love and unchaste desires are as likely in the countryside as in the cities, in shepherd's huts as in royal palaces, and if you take away the cause, you take
away the sin, and if your eyes don't see, your heart doesn't break, and a
jump over the thicket is better than the prayers of good men." (901)

To have a few vacant **chambers** in one's head.
"That sounds to me," responded the goatherd, "like the things one reads
in books about knights errant, who did everything your grace [a barber]
says with regard to this man [Don Quixote], though it seems to me that

either your grace is joking or this gentleman must have a few vacant chambers in his head." (439)

Let the **chicken** live even if she has the pip.
"I'll tell you, Teresa," responded Sancho, "that if I didn't expect to be the governor of an ínsula before too much more time goes by, I'd fall down dead right here."

"Not that, my husband," said Teresa, "let the chicken live even if she has the pip; may you live, and let the devil take all the governorships there are in the world; you came out of your mother's womb without a governorship, and you've lived until now without a governorship, and when it pleases God you'll go, or they'll carry you, to the grave without a governorship. Many people in the world live without a governorship, and that doesn't make them give up or not be counted among the living. The best sauce in the world is hunger, and since poor people have plenty of that, they always eat with great pleasure. But look, Sancho: if you happen to find yourself a governor somewhere, don't forget about me and your children. Remember that Sanchico is already fifteen, and he ought to go to school if his uncle the abbot is going to bring him into the Church. And don't forget that our daughter, Mari Sancha, won't die if we marry her; she keeps dropping hints that she wants a husband as much as you want to be a governor, and when all is said and done, a daughter's better off badly married than happily kept." (486-487)

To treat someone like a **child**.
"Throw that bone to another dog!" responded the innkeeper. "As if I didn't know how to add two and three or where my shoe pinches! Your grace [a priest] shouldn't try to treat me like a child, because, by God, I'm not an idiot." (270)

To be **child's play**.
"Then, there is more?" asked Don Quixote.

"And something much worse," said Sancho. "So far it's been nothing but child's play, but if your grace wants to know all the slander they're saying about you, I'll bring somebody here who will tell you everything and not leave out a crumb." (472)

Sancho was stunned to see so many people undressed, especially when he saw the canopy lowered so quickly it seemed to him that all the devils were working there, but this was mere child's play compared to what I [the author] shall tell you now. (876)

"If I [Don Quixote] could wield my weapons, Sancho, and the promise I gave had not tied my arms, I would deem this group coming toward us as nothing more than mere child's play, but perhaps it is not what we fear." (906)

The **Church**, the sea, or the royal house.

"What I [the father of a captive] have decided is to divide my fortune into four parts: three I will give to you [his three sons], each one receiving exactly the same share, and the fourth I will retain to keep me for the time it pleases heaven to grant me life. But after each of you has his share of the estate, I would like you to follow the path I indicate. There is a proverb in our Spain, one that I think is very true, as they all are, for they are brief maxims taken from long, judicious experience; the one I have in mind says: 'The Church, the sea, or the royal house'; in other words, whoever wishes to be successful and wealthy should enter the Church, or go to sea as a merchant, or enter the service of kings in their courts, for, as they say: 'Better the king's crumbs than the noble lord's favors.' I say this because I would like, and it is my desire, that one of you should pursue letters, another commerce, and the third should serve the king in war, for it is very difficult to enter his service at court, and although war does not provide many riches, it tends to bring great merit and fame." (335)

To go around in **circles**.

"That's fine," said Sancho. "You [a farmer] should realize, brother, that now you've painted her [a maiden] from head to toe. What is it that you want? And get to the point without beating around the bush or going around in circles, or taking anything away or adding anything to it." (764)

To believe that the things of this life will endure forever, unchanged, is to believe the impossible; it seems instead that everything goes around, I mean around in a circle: spring pursues summer, summer pursues *estío*, *estío* pursues autumn, autumn pursues winter, and winter pursues spring, and in this way time turns around a continuous wheel; only human life races to its end more quickly than time, with no hope for renewal except in the next life, which has no boundaries that limit it. (804)

Under a poor **cloak** you can find a good drinker.

"Everything said here by our good Sancho," said the duchess, "are Catonian sentences, or, at least, taken from the very heart of Micael Verino himself, *florentibus occidit annis* ["Dead in the flower of his youth]. Well, well, to say it in his fashion, under a poor cloak you can find a good drinker." (682)

To be cut from the same **cloth**.

Cervantes: I do not wish to say more to you except to tell you to consider that this second part of *Don Quixote,* which I offer to you now, is cut by the same artisan and from the same cloth as the first, and in it I give you a somewhat expanded Don Quixote who is, at the end, dead and buried, so that no one will dare tell more tales about him, for the ones told in the past are enough, and it is also enough that an honorable man has recounted his clever follies and does not want to take them up again; for abundance, even of things that are good, makes people esteem them less, and scarcity, even of bad things, lends a certain value. (458)

"As for governing them well," responded Sancho, "there's no need to charge me with it, because I'm charitable by nature and have compassion for the poor; and if he kneads and bakes, you can't steal his cakes; by my faith, they won't throw me any crooked dice; I'm an old dog and understand every here, boy [the proverb says: "You don't need here, boy, here, boy, with an old dog"], and I know how to wake up at the right time, and I don't allow cobwebs in front of my eyes, because I know if the shoe fits: I say this because with me good men will have my hand and a place in my house [the phrase means "trust and confidence"], and bad men won't get a foot or permission to enter." (680)

To be the **clouds** of yesteryear.
Don Quixote, stumbling here and falling there, began to run as fast as he could after the herd of bulls, shouting:
"Stop, wait, you villainous rabble! A single knight awaits you, one who does not concur or agree with those who say that one should build a silver bridge for the enemy who flees!"
But not even this could stop the speeding runners, and they paid no more attention to his threats than to the clouds of yesteryear. (841)

"Here, Señor, are your omens, broken and wrecked, and as far as I'm concerned, though I [Sancho] may be a fool, they have no more to do with our affairs than the clouds of yesteryear. And if I remember correctly, I've heard the priest in our village say that it isn't right for sensible Christians to heed this kind of nonsense, and even your grace has told me the same thing, letting me know that Christians who paid attention to omens were fools. But there's no need to spend any more time on this; let's go on into our village." (930)

To have **cobwebs** in front of one's eyes.
"As for governing them well," responded Sancho, "there's no need to charge me with it, because I'm charitable by nature and have compassion for the poor; and if he kneads and bakes, you can't steal his cakes; by my faith, they won't throw me any crooked dice; I'm an old dog and understand every here, boy [the proverb says: "You don't need here, boy, here, boy, with an old dog"], and I know how to wake up at the right time, and I don't allow cobwebs in front of my eyes, because I know if the shoe fits: I say this because with me good men will have

my hand and a place in my house [the phrase means "trust and confidence"], and bad men won't get a foot or permission to enter." (680)

To show one's true **colors**.
Don Quixote said: "For the love of God, Sancho, restrain yourself, and do not reveal your true colors lest they [some maidens] realize that the cloth you are made of is coarse and rustic." (660)

Comparisons are odious.
"'Stop right there, Señor Don Montesinos,' I [Don Quixote] said then. 'Your grace should recount this history in the proper manner, for you know that all comparisons are odious, and there is no reason to compare anyone to anyone else. The peerless Dulcinea of Toboso is who she is, and Señora Belerma is who she is, and who she was, and no more should be said about it.'

    To which he responded:

    'Señor Don Quixote, may your grace forgive me, for I confess that I erred and misspoke when I said that Señora Dulcinea would barely be the equal of Señora Belerma, for it was enough for me to have realized, by means of I am not certain what conjectures, that your grace is her knight, and I would rather bite my tongue than compare her to anything but heaven itself.'" (609)

Whoever tries to **conceal** you, reveals you.
"Do you know why, Sancho?" responded Teresa. "Because of the proverb that says: 'Whoever *tries* to conceal you, reveals you!' Nobody does more than glance at the poor, but they look closely at the rich; if a rich man was once poor, that's where the whispers and rumors begin, and the wicked murmurs of gossips who crowd the streets like swarms of bees." (489)

To one's heart's **content**.
"What do you mean?" replied Sancho. "I tell you, Ricote my friend, I left there this morning, and yesterday I was there governing to my heart's content, like an archer; but even so, I left it because the post of governor seems like a dangerous one to me." (815)

De **corde** exeunt cogitationes malae.
If you mention evil thoughts, go to the Gospel: *De corde exeunt cogitationes malae* [For out of the heart proceed evil thoughts; Matthew 15:19]. (6)

Harder than a **cork tree**.
"I'll tell her [Dulcinea] such wonders about the foolish things and the crazy things, because they amount to the same thing, that your grace has done and is still doing that she'll become softer than a glove even if I find her harder than a cork tree." (198)

What **costs** less is valued less.

It happened once, when Camilla found herself alone with her maid, she said:

"I am mortified, my dear Leonela, to see how lightly I valued myself, for I did not even oblige Lotario to pay with time for the complete possession of my desire; I gave it to him so quickly, I fear he will judge only my haste or indiscretion, not taking into account that he urged me so strongly I could no longer resist him."

"Do not be concerned, Señora," responded Leonela. "Giving quickly is of little significance, and no reason to lessen esteem, if, in fact, what one gives is good and in itself worthy of esteem. They even say that by giving quickly, one gives twice."

"They also say," said Camila, "that what costs less is valued less."

"The argument doesn't apply to you," responded Leonela, "because love, I've heard it said, sometimes flies and sometimes walks; it runs with one, and goes slowly with another; it cools some and burns others; some it wounds, and others it kills; it begins the rush of its desires at one point, and at the same point it ends and concludes them; in the morning it lays siege to a fortress, and by nightfall it has broken through, because there is no power that can resist it." (293-294)

Under the **cover** of my cloak I can kill the king.

Cervantes: You know the old saying: under the cover of my cloak I can kill the king. Which exempts and excuses you from all respect and obligation, and you can say anything you desire about this history without fear that you will be reviled for the bad things or rewarded for the good that you might say about it. (3-4)

Craziness has more companions than wisdom.

"There's no road so smooth," replied Sancho, "that it doesn't have some obstacle or stumbling block; they cook beans everywhere, but in my house they do it by the potful; craziness must have more companions and friends than wisdom. But if what they say is true, that misery loves company, then I can find comfort with your grace, because you serve a master who's as great a fool as mine." (535-536)

To go **crazy**.

Letter from Teresa Panza to Sancho Panza: *I received your letter, Sancho of my soul, and I can tell you and swear to you as a Catholic Christian that I practically went crazy with happiness. Just think, my husband: when I heard that you were a governor, I thought I'd fall down dead from sheer joy, because you know, people say that sudden joy can kill just like great sorrow.* (802)

Before one can say **credo**.
"Did I not tell you so?" said Don Quixote. "Wait, Sancho. And I shall do them [crazy things] before you can say Credo." (204)

To be **cries** (a voice crying) in the wilderness. (Matthew 3:3)
Cervantes: Finally, after an entire night spent in wretched complaints and lamentations, day broke, and in its clear, bright light Sancho saw that it was utterly impossible to get out of the pit without help, and he began to lament and cry out, to see if anyone heard him, but all his shouts were cries in the wilderness, because there was no one to hear him anywhere in the vicinity, and then he began to think of himself as dead. (818)

Down to the last **crumb**.
"I [a herder of swine] paid her enough, she [a woman] wasn't satisfied, she caught hold of me and didn't let go until she brought me here. She says I forced her and she lies, by the oath I swear or plan to swear; this is the whole truth, down to the last crumb." (751)

Better the king's **crumbs** than the noble lord's favors.
"What I [the father of a captive] have decided is to divide my fortune into four parts: three I will give to you [his three sons], each one receiving exactly the same share, and the fourth I will retain to keep me for the time it pleases heaven to grant me life. But after each of you has his share of the estate, I would like you to follow the path I indicate. There is a proverb in our Spain, one that I think is very true, as they all are, for they are brief maxims taken from long, judicious experience; the one I have in mind says: 'The Church, the sea, or the royal house'; in other words, whoever wishes to be successful and wealthy should enter the Church, or go to sea as a merchant, or enter the service of kings in their courts, for, as they say: 'Better the king's crumbs than the noble lord's favors.' I say this because I would like, and it is my desire, that one of you should pursue letters, another commerce, and the third should serve the king in war, for it is very difficult to enter his service at court, and although war does not provide many riches, it tends to bring great merit and fame." (335)

Danger lies in delay.
"Thou mayest, Señora, from this day forth, cast off the melancholy that afflicts thee and let thy faint hope take on new vigor and strength; for, with the help of God and this my [Don Quixote] arm, thou wilt soon see thyself restored to thy kingdom and seated on the throne of thy great and ancient state, in spite of and despite the base cowards who wisheth to deny it to thee. And now, to work, for they sayeth that in delay there lies danger." (244-245)

Sancho said: "Since it's more than three thousand leagues from here to Candaya, if the horse gets tired or the giant gets angry, it'll take us more than half a dozen years to get back, and by then there won't be any ínsulas or ínsulos left in the world that recognize me; and since it's a common saying that danger lies in delay, and when they give you a heifer you'd better hurry over with the rope, may the beards of these ladies forgive me, but St. Peter's fine in Rome; I mean that I'm fine in this house, where I have received so many favors and where I expect a great benefit from its master, which is being a governor." (719)

Sancho responded that he would do as his master wished but would like to conclude this matter quickly, while his blood was hot and the grindstone rough, because in delay there is often danger, and pray to God and use the hammer, and one "here you are" was worth more than two "I'll give it to you," and a bird in hand was worth two in the bush.

"By the one God, Sancho, no more proverbs," said Don Quixote. "It seems you are going back to *sicut erat* ["as it was before"]; speak plainly, and simply, and without complications, as I have often told you, and you will see how one loaf will be the same as a hundred for you." (924)

Whoever goes looking for **danger** perishes.
Sancho said: "Señor, I don't know why your grace wants to embark on this fearful adventure; it's night, nobody can see us here, we can turn around and get away from the danger, even if we don't drink anything for three days, and since there's nobody here to see us, there's nobody to call us cowards; besides, I've heard the sermons of our village priest, and your grace knows him very well, and he says that whoever goes looking for danger perishes; so it isn't a good idea to tempt God by undertaking something so terrible that you can't get out of it except through some miracle." (142-143)

A **daughter** is better off badly married than happily kept.
"I'll tell you, Teresa," responded Sancho, "that if I didn't expect to be the governor of an ínsula before too much more time goes by, I'd fall down dead right here."

"Not that, my husband," said Teresa, "let the chicken live even if she has the pip; may you live, and let the devil take all the governorships there are in the world; you came out of your mother's womb without a governorship, and you've lived until now without a governorship, and when it pleases God you'll go, or they'll carry you, to the grave without a governorship. Many people in the world live without a governorship, and that doesn't make them give up or not be counted among the living. The best sauce in the world is hunger, and since poor people have plenty of that, they always eat with great pleasure. But look, Sancho: if you happen to find yourself a governor somewhere, don't forget about me and your children. Remember that Sanchico is already fifteen, and he ought to go to school if his uncle the abbot is going to bring him into the Church. And don't forget that our daughter, Mari Sancha, won't die if we marry her; she keeps dropping hints that she wants a husband as much as you want to be a governor, and when all is said and done, a daughter's better off badly married than happily kept." (486-487)

To be the **day** or reckoning.
"I have already heard of this book [Avellaneda's *Don Quixote*]," said Don Quixote, "and by my conscience, the truth is I thought it had already been burned and turned to ashes for its insolence; but its day of reckoning will come, as it does to every pig [the Spanish phrase is *su San Martín se le llegará, como a cada puerco*, with "Having your St. Martin's Day come" being roughly equivalent to "paying the piper in English; St. Martin's Day also refers to the time when animals were slaughtered], for feigned histories are good and enjoyable the closer they are to the truth or the appearance of truth, and as for true ones, the truer they are, the better." (875)

When you have a good **day**, put it in the house.
Letter from Teresa Panza to the duchess: *Señora of my soul, I've decided, with your grace's permission, to put this good day in my house [the phrase is based on the proverb "When you have a good day, put it in the house," which is somewhat equivalent to "Make hay while the sun shines] by going to court and leaning back in a carriage and making their eyes pop, for there are thousands who are already envious of me; and so I beg Your Excellency to tell my husband to send me some money, and to make it enough, because at court expenses are high: bread sells for a real, and a pound of meat costs thirty maravedís, which is a judgment [a sin, crime], and if he doesn't want me to go, he should let me know soon, because my feet are itching to get started.* (801-802)

Let the **dead** go to the grave and the living to the loaf of bread.
"Señor, your grace has come to the end of this dangerous adventure more safely than all the others I [Sancho] have seen [...]. The donkey is carrying what it should, the mountains are nearby, hunger is pressing, and there's nothing else to do but withdraw as fast as we can and, as they say, let the dead go to the grave and the living to the loaf of bread." (140)

To fall down **dead**.
"I'll tell you, Teresa," responded Sancho, "that if I didn't expect to be the governor of an ínsula before too much more time goes by, I'd fall down dead right here." (486)

Letter from Teresa Panza to Sancho Panza: *I received your letter, Sancho of my soul, and I can tell you and swear to you as a Catholic Christian that I practically went crazy with happiness. Just think, my husband: when I heard that you were a governor, I thought I'd fall down dead from sheer joy, because you know, people say that sudden joy can kill just like great sorrow.* (802)

Death is silent.
"The fact is," responded Sancho, "that as your grace knows very well, we're all subject to death, here today and gone tomorrow, and the lamb goes as quickly as the sheep, and nobody can promise himself more hours of life in this world than the ones God wants to give him, because death is silent, and when she comes knocking at the door of our life, she's always in a hurry, and nothing will stop her, not prayers or struggles or scepters or miters, and that's something that everybody hears, something they tell us from the pulpit." (498)

If you pay your **debts**, you don't worry about guaranties.
"That is true," responded Sancho, "but if you pay your debts, you don't worry about guaranties, and in a prosperous house supper's soon on the stove; I mean that nobody has to tell me things or give me any advice: I'm prepared for anything, and I know something about everything." (654)

"May it please God, Sancho, because there's many a slip between the cup and the lip, [said the duke]."
"That may be so," replied Sancho, "but if you pay your debts, you don't worry about guaranties, and it's better to have God's help than to get up early, and your belly leads your feet, not the other way around; I mean, if God helps me, and I do what I ought to with good intentions, I'll be sure to govern in grand style. Just put a finger in my mouth and see if I bite or not!" (686)

"Who is answering us?" came the response from the next room.
"Who can it be," responded Sancho, "but Don Quixote of La Mancha himself, who'll carry out everything he's said, and even what he might say? For the man who pays his debts doesn't worry about guaranties." (845-846)

"Be careful, my friend, not to tear yourself to pieces; pause between lashes; do not try to race so quickly that you lose your breath in the middle of the course; I [Don Quixote] mean, you should not hit yourself so hard that you lose your life before you reach the desired number. And to keep you from losing by a card too many or too few, I shall stand to one side and count the lashes you administer on my rosary. May heaven favor you as your good intentions deserve."

"A man who pays his debts doesn't care about guaranties," responded Sancho. "I plan to lash myself so that it hurts but doesn't kill me: that must be the point of this miracle." (921)

If you cut the **deck**, you don't deal. [see **cards**]
"Teresa says," said Sancho, "that I should keep a sharp eye on you, and there's no arguing against written proof, because if you cut the deck you don't deal, and a bird in hand is worth two in the bush. And I say that a woman's advice is no jewel, and the man who doesn't take it is a fool." (498)

To run like a **deer**.
The student responded: "He [Basilio] is the most agile youth we know, a great hurler of the bar, an excellent wrestler, a fine pelota player; he runs like a deer, leaps like a goat, and plays bowls as if he were enchanted; he sings like a lark, plays the guitar so well he makes it speak, and, most of all, he can fence with the best of them." (577-578)

A constable said: "Señor Governor, this lad was coming toward us, and as soon as he saw that we were the law, he turned his back and began to run like a deer, a sign that he must be a criminal. I went after him, and if he hadn't tripped and fallen, I never would have caught him." (776)

To preach in the **desert**.
While Sancho Panza and his wife, Teresa Cascajo, were having the incongruous talk that has just been related, Don Quixote's niece and housekeeper were not idle; a thousand indications had led them to infer that their uncle and master wished to leave for the third time and return to the practice of what was, to their minds, his calamitous chivalry, and they attempted by all means possible to dissuade him from so wicked a thought, but it was all preaching in the desert and hammering on cold iron. (491)

"Enough!" Don Quixote said to himself. "It will be preaching in the desert to try to convince this rabble to take any virtuous action." (652)

"No more proverbs, Sancho," said Don Quixote, "for any one of those you have said is enough to explain your thoughts; I have often advised you not to be so prodigal in your proverbs and to restrain yourself from saying them, but it seems that is like preaching in the desert, and 'My mother punishes me, and I deceive her.'"

"It seems to me," responded Sancho, "that your grace is like the pot calling the kettle black. You reprove me for saying proverbs, and your grace strings them together two at a time." (901-902)

If he can, the **devil** will give you a snub-nosed woman rather than one with an aquiline nose.

Don Quixote said to himself: "Who knows if the devil, who is subtle and cunning, wants to deceive me now with a duenna when he has failed with empresses, queens, duchesses, marquises, and countesses? For I have often heard it said by many wise men that, if he can, he will give you a snub-nosed woman rather than one with an aquiline nose. And who knows whether this solitude, this opportunity, this silence, will awaken my sleeping desires and cause me, at this advanced age, to fall where I never have stumbled? In cases like this, it is better to flee than to wait for the battle." (767)

One **devil** looks like another.

"What I can say," said Sancho, "is that I smelled a mannish kind of odor, and it must have been that with all that moving around, she was sweaty and sort of sour."

"That could not be," responded Don Quixote. "You must have had a head cold or else you were smelling yourself, because I know very well the fragrance of that rose among thorns, that lily of the field, that delicate liquid ambergris."

"That may be," responded Sancho, "because very often the same smell comes from me, though at the time I thought it was coming from her grace the lady Dulcinea, but there's no reason to be surprised, since one devil looks like another." (259)

The **devil** can hide (hides) behind the cross.

Another book was opened and they saw that its title was *The Knight of the Cross*. [The priest said:] "Because of the holy name this book bears one might pardon its stupidity, but as the saying goes, 'The devil can hide behind the cross.' Into the fire." (47)

And I [Sancho] say again that if your ladyship doesn't want to give me the ínsula because I'm a fool, I'll be smart enough not to care at all; I've heard that the devil hides behind the cross, and that all that glitters isn't gold, and that from his oxen, plows, and yokes they took the peasant Wamba to be king of Spain, and from his brocades, entertainments, and riches they took Rodrigo to be eaten by snakes, if the lines from the old ballads don't lie." (679)

"It also seems to me," said the butler, "that your grace [Sancho] shouldn't eat anything that is on this table because it was prepared by nuns, and as the saying goes, behind the cross lurks the devil." (761)

The **devil** is sly.

"We have not run across anyone," responded Don Quixote, "but we found a saddle cushion and traveling case not far from here." "I found them, too," responded the goatherd, "but I never wanted to pick them up or go near them because I was afraid there's be trouble and they'd say I stole them; the devil's sly, and he puts things under our feet that make us stumble and fall, and we don't know how or why." "That's just what I say," responded Sancho. "I found them, too, and I didn't want to get within a stone's throw of them: I left them there, and there they remain, just as they were; I don't want a dog with a bell around its neck." (179)

The **devil** makes trouble everywhere.
Sancho said: "Don't let anybody try to trick me, because we either are or we aren't: let's all live and eat in peace and good friendship, because when God sends the dawn, it's dawn for everybody. I'll govern this ínsula without forsaking the law or taking a bribe, and let everybody keep his eyes open and tend to his own affairs, because I want you to know that the devil makes trouble everywhere, and if you give me a chance, you'll see marvels. And if you turn into honey, the flies will eat you." (773-774)

The **devil** never sleeps.
Cervantes: As luck and the devil, who is not always sleeping, would have it, grazing in that valley was a herd of Galician ponies tended by some drovers from Yanguas, whose custom it is to take a siesta with their animals in grassy, well-watered places and sites, and the spot where Don Quixote happened to find himself. (103)

"I didn't know her [Torralba]," responded Sancho. "But the man who told me this story said it was true and correct that I certainly could, when I told it to somebody else, affirm and swear that I had seen it all. And so, as the days came and went, the devil who never sleeps and is always stirring up trouble, turned the love that the goatherd had for the shepherdess into hate and ill will." (145)

Cervantes: At that very moment the devil, who never sleeps, willed the arrival at the inn of the barber from whom Don Quixote had taken the helmet of Mambrino, and Sancho Panza the donkey's gear that he had exchanged for his own. (389)

"'We're a talented pair, compadre,' responded the other [man], 'because if the abbot sings well, the altar boy's not far behind.'
    And so, disconsolate and hoarse, they returned to their village and told their friends, neighbors, and acquaintances what had happened to them in their search for the donkey, each exaggerating the other's talent for braying, all of which was learned and circulated in nearby towns. And the devil, who never sleeps, and loves to sow and plant quarrels and discord wherever he goes, spreading mischief on the wind and creating disputes out of nothing, ordered and arranged matters so that peo-

ple from other towns, when they saw someone from our village, would bray." (622-623)

To go to the **devil**.
"Come now, my good Sancho," said the duchess, "take heart and be grateful to Don Quixote for the bread you have eaten; we all must serve and please him for his virtuous nature and his high acts of chivalry. Say yes, my friend, to this flogging, and let the devil go to the devil and fear to the coward, for a brave heart breaks bad luck, as you know very well." (695)

To know a point or two more than the **devil**.
"Montesinos said: 'This is my friend Durandarte, the flower and model of enamored and valiant knights of his time; here he lies, enchanted, as I and many others are enchanted, by Merlin, the French enchanter who was, people say, the son of the devil; and what I believe is that he was not the son of the devil but knew, as they say, a point or two more than the devil. How and why he enchanted us no one knows, but that will be revealed with the passage of time, and is not too far off now, I imagine.'" (606-607)

To be harder than **diamonds**.
Don Quixote responded: "He [any knight errant] must not be afraid in the slightest, but with a gallant air and an intrepid heart he must charge and attack them [giants] and, if possible, defeat and rout them in an instant, even if they are armed with the shells of a certain fish that are, they say, harder than diamonds, and instead of swords they carry sharp knives." (492)

The **dice** have fallen.
"The dice may fall," said Don Quixote, "so that everything you say turns out to be true; forgive what happened, for you are clever and know that first impulses are not ours to control, but be advised of one thing: from now on you are to refrain and abstain from speaking too much to me, for in all the books of chivalry that I have read, which are infinite in number, I have never found any squire who talks as much with his master as you do with yours. (151)

The throw of the **dice**.
"And is this deed very dangerous?" asked Sancho Panza.
    "No," responded the Knight of the Sorrowful Face, "although depending on luck and the throw of the dice, our fortunes may be either favorable or adverse, but everything will depend on your diligence." (192)

To throw crooked **dice**.

"I'm not pregnant by anybody," responded Sancho, "and I'm not a man who'd let himself get pregnant even by the king, and though I'm poor I'm an Old Christian, and I don't owe anything to anybody, and if I want ínsulas, other people want things that are worse; each man is the child of his actions, and because I'm a man I could be a pope, let alone the governor of an ínsula, especially since my master could win so many he might not have enough people to give them to. Your grace should be careful what you say, Señor Barber, because there's more to life than trimming beards, and there's some difference between one Pedro and the other. I say this because we all know one another, and you can't throw crooked dice with me. As for the enchantment of my master, only God knows the truth, and let's leave it at that, because things get worse when you stir them." (411)

"As for governing them well," responded Sancho, "there's no need to charge me with it, because I'm charitable by nature and have compassion for the poor; and if he kneads and bakes, you can't steal his cakes; by my faith, they won't throw me any crooked dice; I'm an old dog and understand every here, boy [the proverb says: "You don't need here, boy, here, boy, with an old dog"], and I know how to wake up at the right time, and I don't allow cobwebs in front of my eyes, because I know if the shoe fits: I say this because with me good men will have my hand and a place in my house [the phrase means "trust and confidence"], and bad men won't get a foot or permission to enter." (680)

There's some **difference** between one Pedro and the other.

"I'm not pregnant by anybody," responded Sancho, "and I'm not a man who'd let himself get pregnant even by the king, and though I'm poor I'm an Old Christian, and I don't owe anything to anybody, and if I want ínsulas, other people want things that are worse; each man is the child of his actions, and because I'm a man I could be a pope, let alone the governor of an ínsula, especially since my master could win so many he might not have enough people to give them to. Your grace should be careful what you say, Señor Barber, because there's more to life than trimming beards, and there's some difference between one Pedro and the other. I say this because we all know one another, and you can't throw crooked dice with me. As for the enchantment of my master, only God knows the truth, and let's leave it at that, because things get worse when you stir them." (411)

Diligence is the mother of good fortune.

Don Quixote said: "'Tis a common proverb, O beauteous lady, that diligence is the mother of good fortune, and in many grave and serious matters experience hath shown that solicitude canst bring a doubtful matter to a successful conclusion, but nowhere is this truth clearer than in questions of war, in which celerity and speed canst disrupt the ene-my's plans and achieve victory ere the adversary prepareth his defens-es." (399)

Don Quixote said: "When you mount a horse, do not lean your body back over the hind bow of the saddle, or hold your legs stiff and stick-ing out at an angle from the belly of the horse, or ride so carelessly that it looks as if you were riding your donkey, for riding a horse makes gentlemen of some men and stable boys of others. Be moderate in your sleeping, for the man who does not get up with the sun does not possess the day; and remember, Sancho, that diligence is the mother of good fortune, and sloth, her opposite, never reached the conclusion demand-ed by good intentions." (734)

The **discord** in (of) Agramante's camp.
And in the midst of this chaos, this enormous confusion, it passed through the mind of Don Quixote that he had been plunged headlong into the discord in Agramante's camp [The dispute, which became pro-verbial, was described by Ariosto in *Orlando furioso*.]. (394)

"I [Don Quixote] wish you to see with your own eyes what has tran-spired here and how the discord of Agramante's camp has descended upon us. (395)

To labor like a **ditchdigger**.
"O, may you be accursed, Sancho!" said Don Quixote at this point. "May sixty thousand devils take you and your proverbs! For the past hour you have been stringing them together and with each one giving me a cruel taste of torment. I assure you that one day these proverbs will lead you to the gallows; because of them your vassals will take the governorship away from you, or rise up against you. Tell me, where do you find them, you ignorant man, and how do you apply them, you fool, when to say only one that is really applicable, I have to perspire and labor like a ditchdigger?" (736)

The **dog** in linen breeches says how crude, how crude.
"And what difference does it make to me," added Sanchica, "if they say when they see me so proud and haughty: 'The dog in linen breeches ... [says how crude, how crude'; a proverb aimed at the poor who prosper and then scorn their old friends] and all the rest?" (788)

To be a **dog** with a bell around its neck.
"We have not run across anyone," responded Don Quixote, "but we found a saddle cushion and traveling case not far from here." "I found them, too," responded the goatherd, "but I never wanted to pick them up or go near them because I was afraid there's be trouble and they'd say I stole them; the devil's sly, and he puts things under our feet that

make us stumble and fall, and we don't know how or why." "That's just what I say," responded Sancho. "I found them, too, and I didn't want to get within a stone's throw of them: I left them there, and there they remain, just as they were; I don't want a dog with a bell around its neck [i.e., I don't want things that can cause trouble]." (179)

You don't need here, boy, here, boy, with an old **dog**.
"As for governing them well," responded Sancho, "there's no need to charge me with it, because I'm charitable by nature and have compassion for the poor; and if he kneads and bakes, you can't steal his cakes; by my faith, they won't throw me any crooked dice; I'm an old dog and understand every here, boy [the proverb says: "You don't need here, boy, here, boy, with an old dog"], and I know how to wake up at the right time, and I don't allow cobwebs in front of my eyes, because I know if the shoe fits: I say this because with me good men will have my hand and a place in my house [the phrase means "trust and confidence"], and bad men won't get a foot or permission to enter." (680)

Sancho said: "By God, I'm as likely to become a Moor as to let anybody mark my face or slap my nose! By my faith! What does slapping my face have to do with the resurrection of this maiden? The old woman liked the greens so much ... [the second part of the proverb is "that she didn't leave any, green or dry"]. They enchant Dulcinea, and whip me to disenchant her; Altisidora dies of ills that God sent her, and they'll bring her back by slapping me twenty-four times and riddling my body with pinpricks, and pinching my arms black and blue! Try those tricks on your brother-in- law! I'm an old dog, and you don't have to call me twice!" (911)

Let sleeping **dogs** lie.
"I have never seen a squire," replied the Knight of the Wood, "who would dare speak when his master was speaking: at least, there stands mine, as big as his father, and no one can prove he has even moved his lips while I am speaking."
  "Well, by my faith," said Sancho, "I have spoken, and can speak, in front of any ... enough said, we'll let sleeping dogs lie." (532)

What is **done** is done.
"I [Don Quixote] have always heard, Sancho, that doing good to the lowborn is throwing water into the sea. If I had believed what you told me, I should have avoided this grief, but what is done is done, and so patience, and let it be a lesson for the future." (173)

The **donkey** will endure the load, but not an extra load.
Don Quixote said: "On your life, friend [Sancho], let the matter stop here, for this remedy seems very harsh to me, and it would be a good idea to take more time: Zamora was not won in an hour. You have giv-

en yourself more than a thousand lashes, if I have counted correctly: that is enough for now, for the donkey, speaking coarsely, will endure the load, but not an extra load." (922)

To look for the **donkey** one is riding on.
"I want you to hear only one more word of mine, O valiant Don Quixote!" said Altisidora. "I beg your pardon for saying you stole my garters, because by God and my soul, I am wearing them, and I have fallen into the careless error of the man who went looking for the donkey he was riding on." (831)

To run like a **donkey** with quicksilver in its ear.
"That must be it," said Sancho, "because, by my faith, Rocinante was galloping like a Gypsy's donkey with quicksilver in its ear [a ruse allegedly used by Roma to make their animals run faster]" (261)

One **door** closes and another opens.
"It seems to me, Sancho, that there is no proverb that is not true, because all of them are judgments based on experience, the mother of all knowledge, in particular the one that says: 'One door closes and another opens.' I [Don Quixote] say this because if last night fortune closed the door on what we were seeking, deceiving us with fulling hammers, now she opens wide another that will lead to a better and truer adventure; if I do not succeed in going through this door, the fault will be mine, and I shall not be able to blame my ignorance of fulling hammers or the dark of the night." (153)

To shut the **door** in someone's face.
"Come here, you imbecile, you troublemaker," replied Sancho. "Why do you [Teresa] want to stop me now, and for no good reason, from marrying my daughter to somebody who'll give me grandchildren they'll call *Lord* and *Lady*? Look, Teresa: I've always heard the old folks say that if you don't know how to enjoy good luck when it comes, you shouldn't complain if it passes you by. It wouldn't be a good idea, now that it's come knocking, to shut the door in its face; we should let the favorable wind that's blowing carry us along." (487)

You cannot put **doors** on a field.
"I don't say it and I don't think it," responded Sancho. "It's their affair and let them eat it with their bread; whether or not they were lovers, they've already made their accounting with God; I tend to my vines, it's their business, not mine; I don't stick my nose in; if you buy and lie, your purse wants to know why. Besides, naked I was born, and naked I'll die: I don't lose or gain a thing; whatever they were, it's all the same to me. And many folks think there's bacon when there's not even a hook to hang it on. But who can put doors on a field? Let them say what they please, I don't care." (191-192)

"Do not be angry, Sancho [said Don Quixote], or troubled by what you may hear, for there is no end to it: you keep your conscience clear, and let them say whatever they wish, for trying to restrain the tongues of slanderers is the same as trying to put doors in [*sic*] a field. If the governor leaves his governorship a wealthy man, they say he has been a thief, and if he leaves it poor, they say he has been a dullard and a fool." (822)

As long as you are **earning** you don't lose a thing.
"It's taking me to this," said Sancho. "Your grace should tell me exactly what salary you'll give me for each month I serve you, and this salary should be paid to me from your estate; I don't want to depend on anybody's favors, which come late, or badly, or never; may God help me to tend to my own business. The point is, I want to know what I'm earning, whether it's a lot or a little; a hen sits on her egg, and a lot of littles make a lot, and as long as you're earning you don't lose a thing. And if it should happen, and I don't believe or expect that it will, that your grace gives me the ínsula you promised, I'm not such an ingrate, and not such a pennypincher, that I won't want the rent from the ínsula to be added up and deducted from my salary pro rat." (498-499)

One **egg** resembles another.
"To that we respond," said the Knight of the Mirrors, "that you resemble the knight I vanquished as much as one egg resembles another; but since you say that enchanters pursue him, I do not dare to state whether you are the aforementioned or not." (544)

To be in one's **element**.
When Don Quixote saw himself in the open countryside, free and clear of Altisidora's wooing, it seemed to him that he had returned to his own element, that his spirits had revived and were ready to resume his chivalric pursuits. (832)

To ask the **elm tree** for pears.
"Id' like to see him [a horse]," responded Sancho, "but thinking that I'll climb up on him, either in the saddle or on his hindquarters, is asking the elm tree for pears. I can barely stay on my donkey, and that's on a packsaddle softer than silk, and now they want me to sit on the hindquarters made of wood, without even a pillow or cushion!" (716)

Doña Rodríguez said: "I recounted to you the injustice and treachery committed by a wicked farmer against my dearly loved daughter, this unfortunate woman here present, and you promised to defend her, righting the wrong that has been done to her, and now it has come to my attention that you wish to leave this castle to wander in search of good fortune, and may God grant that to you; but before you slip away down those roads I would like you to challenge this uncouth rustic and force him to marry my daughter and fulfill the promise he made to be her husband before and prior to his lying with her, because to think that my lord the duke will execute justice is to ask the elm tree for pears." (799)

It all comes out in the **end**.
"At least," responded Sancho, "your grace knew how to place the lance, aiming for my head and hitting me on the back, thanks be to God and the care I took to move to the side. Well, well, it all comes out in the end, for I've heard people say: 'The one who hurts you is the one who loves you,' and I've also heard that great gentlemen, after speaking harshly to a servant, give him breeches, though I don't know what they give after beating him with a lance, unless knights errant give ínsulas after a beating, or kingdoms on dry land." (151)

Where **envy** rules, virtue cannot survive.
"Ah Señor Priest, Señor Priest! Did your grace think I [Sancho] didn't know you? Can you think I don't understand and guess where these new enchantments are heading? Well, you should know that I recognize you no matter how you cover your face and understand you no matter how you hide your lies. In short, where envy rules, virtue cannot survive, and generosity cannot live with miserliness. Devil confound it, if it wasn't for your reverence, my master would be married by now to Princess Micomicona and I'd be a count at least, because I expected nothing less from the goodness of my master, the Knight of the Sorrowful Face, and from the greatness of my services! But now I see that what they say is true: the wheel of fortune turns faster than a water wheel, and those who only yesterday were on top of the world today are down on the ground." (410)

To **err** is human, to forgive divine.
"Señor, I [Sancho] confess that for me to be a complete jackass, all that's missing is my tail; if your grace wants to put one on me, I'll consider it well-placed, and I'll serve you like a donkey for the rest of my days. Your grace should forgive me, and take pity on my lack of experience, and remember that I know very little, and if I talk too much, it comes more from weakness than from malice, and to err is human, to forgive, divine."
"I would be amazed, Sancho, if you did not mix some little proverb into your talk. Well, then, I forgive you as long as you mend your ways and from now on do not show so much interest in your own gain, but attempt to take heart, and have the courage and valor to wait for my promises to be fulfilled, for although it may take some time, it is in no way impossible." (646)

Everything is possible.

"Everything's possible," responded Sancho, "because I was as upset by her beauty as your grace was by her ugliness. But let us leave everything to God, for He knows the things that will happen in this vale of tears, this evil world of ours, where hardly anything's untouched by wickedness, lies, and deception." (522)

"Everything is possible," responded Don Quixote, "but I shall do as you advise, although I still have certain scruples in that regard." (627)

Evil to him who seeks it.

"Your grace should pay careful attention, because here I [Sancho] go. 'Once upon a time, and may good come to all and evil to him who seeks it ...' And, Señor, your grace should notice that the beginnings the ancients gave to their tales didn't come out of nowhere; this was a maxim of the Roman Cato Nonsensor, and it says: 'Evil to him who seeks it,' which fits here like the ring on your finger and means that your grace should stay put and not go looking for evil anywhere, and we should take another route, nobody's forcing us to continue on this one with so many frightening things to scare us." [Sancho is alluding to Cato Censor, who was popularly considered to be the source of proverbs and saying.] (144-145)

If you choose something **evil**, you can't complain about the evil that happens to you.

"Take my advice, and forgive me, and get married right away in the first town where there's a priest, or else here's our own licentiate, and he'll do a wonderful job. Remember that I'm [Sancho] old enough to give advice, and the advice I'm giving you [Don Quixote] now is exactly right, and a bird in the hand is better than a vulture in the air, and if you have something good and choose something evil, you can't complain about the good that happens to you." (262)

Experience is the mother of all knowledge.

"It seems to me, Sancho, that there is no proverb that is not true, because all of them are judgments based on experience, the mother of all knowledge, in particular the one that says: 'One door closes and another opens.' I [Don Quixote] say this because if last night fortune closed the door on what we were seeking, deceiving us with fulling hammers, now she opens wide another that will lead to a better and truer adventure; if I do not succeed in going through this door, the fault will be mine, and I shall not be able to blame my ignorance of fulling hammers or the dark of the night." (153)

In the blink of an **eye**.

Don Quixote said to Don Lorenzo: "You need do nothing else but leave the narrow path of poetry and follow the even narrower one of knight errantry, which will suffice to make you an emperor in the blink of an eye." (575)

Sancho said: "It seems to me I can pass judgment on this case in the blink of an eye, and it's this: the man swears he's going to die on the gallows, and if he dies there, his oath was true and by law he deserves to be free and cross over the bridge; and if they don't hang him, his oath was false, and by the same law he deserves to be hanged." (792)

In the wink of an **eye**.
"Do not be distressed, my friend," said Don Quixote, "for I shall now prepare the precious balm with which we shall be healed in the wink of an eye." (117)

"Who says I [Don Quixote] don't have the wit or ability to arrange things and sell thirty or ten thousand vassals in the wink of an eye?" (245)

If I had said that my daughter ought to throw herself off a tower or go roaming around the way the Infanta Doña Urraca wanted to, you'd be right not to go along with me; but if in two shakes and in the wink of an eye I dress her in a *Doña* and put a *my lady on* her back for you, and take her out of the dirt and put her under a canopy and up on a pedestal in a drawing room with more velvet cushions than Moors in the line of the Almohadas of Morocco, why won't you consent ad want what I want?" (489)

Sancho responded; "These things are better left to my master, Don Quixote, who in the wink of an eye would dispatch and see to them [arms]. But I, sinner that I am, I don't know anything about this kind of battle." (805)

"If your grace [Roque] wishes to save time and put yourself without difficulty on the road to salvation, come with me, and I [Don Quixote] shall teach you how to be a knight errant, a profession in which one undergoes so many trials and misfortunes that, if deemed to be penance, they would bring you to heaven in the wink of an eye." (858)

A peasant said: "If the servant is this intelligent, what must the master be like! I'll bet if they went to study in Salamanca, in the wink of an eye they'd be magistrates; everything's deceit except studying and more studying, and having favor and good luck; when a man least expects it, he finds himself with a staff in his hand or a mitre on his head." (896)

To keep an **eye** on someone.
"Teresa says," said Sancho, "that I should keep a sharp eye on you, and there's no arguing against written proof, because if you cut the deck you

don't deal, and a bird in hand is worth two in the bush. And I say that a woman's advice is no jewel, and the man who doesn't take it is a fool." (498)

If your **eyes** don't see, your heart doesn't break.
"I [Sancho] am, Señor, so unfortunate, that I fear the day will never come when I can join this exercise. Oh, how polished I'll keep the spoons when I'm a shepherd. What soft bread, what cream, what garlands, what pastoral odds and ends that, if they don't earn me fame as a wise man, can't help but earn me fame as a clever one! Sanchica, my daughter, will bring food up to our flocks. But wait! She's a good-looking girl, and there are shepherds more wicked than simple, and I wouldn't want her to go for wool and come back shorn; love and unchaste desires are as likely in the countryside as in the cities, in shepherd's huts as in royal palaces, and if you take away the cause, you take away the sin, and if your eyes don't see, your heart doesn't break, and a jump over the thicket is better than the prayers of good men." (901)

To have **eyes** as wide open as a hare.
Sancho was already poultice and in his bed, and although he tried to sleep, the pain in his ribs would not allow him, and Don Quixote's ribs hurt so much that his eyes were as wide open as a hare's. (112)

To keep one's **eyes** open.
Sancho said: "Don't let anybody try to trick me, because we either are or we aren't: let's all live and eat in peace and good friendship, because when God sends the dawn, it's dawn for everybody. I'll govern this ínsula without forsaking the law or taking a bribe, and let everybody keep his eyes open and tend to his own affairs, because I want you to know that the devil makes trouble everywhere, and if you give me a chance, you'll see marvels. And if you turn into honey, the flies will eat you." (773-774)

To make someone's **eyes** pop.
Letter from Teresa Panza to the duchess: *Señora of my soul, I've decided, with your grace's permission, to put this good day in my house [the phrase is based on the proverb "When you have a good day, put it in the house," which is somewhat equivalent to "Make hay while the sun shines] by going to court and leaning back in a carriage and making their eyes pop, for there are thousands who are already envious of me; and so I beg Your Excellency to tell my husband to send me some money, and to make it enough, because at court expenses are high: bread sells for a real, and a pound of meat costs thirty maravedís, which is a judgment [a sin, crime], and if he doesn't want me to go, he should let me know soon, because my feet are itching to get started.* (801-802)

To see something with one's own **eyes**.
"That could be true, Sancho," replied Don Quixote, "but it is not, because what I have recounted I saw with my own eyes and touched with
my own hands." (611)

"Well, of course they are!" said another [man]. "They [wooden images
carved in relief] cost enough: the truth is that every one of them costs
more than fifty *ducados*; so that your grace [Don Quixote] can see the
truth of this, just wait, and your grace will see with your own eyes."
(833)

With one's **eyes** blazing.
And after dismounting Rocinante and grasping his lance, he [Don
Quixote] stood in the middle of the road, at the same time that the li-
centiate, with spirited grace and measured steps, was advancing on
Corchuelo, who came toward him, his eyes, as the saying goes, blazing.
The two peasants who had accompanied them did not dismount their
donkeys, but served as spectators to the mortal tragedy. (581)

To hit someone right in the **face**.
"That," responded the Squire of the Wood, "is why they say that it's
greed that tears the sack, and if we're going to talk about madmen,
there's nobody in the world crazier than my master, because he's one
of those who say: 'Other people's troubles kill the donkey,' and to help
another knight find the wits he's lost, he pretends to be crazy and goes
around looking for something that I think will hit him right in the face
when he finds it." (535)

To be as true as a **fairy tale**.
Sancho said: "The first thing I'll say is that I believe my master, Don
Quixote, is completely crazy, even though sometimes he says things
that in my opinion, and in the opinion of everybody who hears him, are
so intelligent and well-reasoned that Satan himself couldn't say them
better; but even so, truly and without any scruples, it's clear to me that
he's a fool. And because I have this idea in mind, I can dare to make
him believe anything, even if it makes no sense, like that reply to his
letter, or something that happened six or eight days ago that isn't in the
history yet, I mean the enchantment of Señora Doña Dulcinea, because
I've made him think she's enchanted, and that's as true as a fairy tale."
(678)

Faster than a **falcon**.
Sancho said: "By St. Roque, our mistress is faster than a falcon, and
she could teach the most skilled Cordoban or Mexican how to ride! She
was over the hind bow of the saddle in one jump, and without any spurs
she makes that palfrey run like a zebra. And her damsels are not far
behind; they're all running like the wind." (519)

When your **father** is the magistrate, you are safe when you go to trial.
"I know how to sign my name very well," responded Sancho, "because
when I was steward of a brotherhood in my village, I learned to make
some letters like the marks on bundles, and they told me that they said
my name; better yet, I'll pretend that my right hand has been hurt, and
I'll have somebody else sign for me; there's a remedy for everything
except death, and since I'll be in charge of everything, I can do whatever I want; then, too, when your father's the magistrate... [you're safe
when you go to trial]. And being a governor, which is more than being
a magistrate, just let them come and they'll see what happens! No, let
them make fun of me and speak ill of me: they'll come for wool and go
home shorn; and when God loves you, your house knows it; and the
rich man's folly passes for good judgment in the world; and since that's
what I'll be, being a governor and a very generous one, which is what I
plan to be, nobody will notice any faults in me. No, just be like honey
and the flies will go after you; you're only worth as much as you have,
my grandmother used to say; and you won't get revenge on a well-
established man." (735)

Don't ask as a **favor** what you can take by force.
"And that's where something else comes in, too," said Sancho, "because some wicked people say: 'Don't ask as a favor what you can take
by force,' though what fits even better is: 'Escaping punishment is
worth more than the pleading of a good men.' I say this because if my
lord the king, your grace's father-in-law, does not agree to giving you
my lady the princess, there's nothing else to do, like your grace says,
but abduct her and hide her away." (161)

Fear has many eyes.
"That's true," said Sancho, but fear has many eyes and can see things
under the ground, let alone high in the sky; even so, it stands to reason
that it won't be long until daylight." (143)

The **fear** of God is the beginning of wisdom.
"Enough, Sancho," said Don Quixote at this point. "Stop now before
you fall, for the truth is that what you have said about death, in your
rustic terms, is what a good preacher might say. I tell you, Sancho, with
your natural wit and intelligence, you could mount a pulpit and go
around preaching some very nice things."

   "Being a good preacher means living a good life," responded Sancho, "and I don't know any other theologies."

   "You do not need them," said Don Quixote, "but I cannot understand or comprehend how, since the beginning of wisdom is the fear of
God, you, who fear a lizard more than you fear Him, can know so
much." (590)

To keep one's **feet** on the ground.
The housekeeper said: "The truth is, Señor, that if your grace doesn't keep your feet firmly on the ground, and stay quietly in your house, and stop wandering around the mountains and the valleys like a soul in torment looking for things that are called adventures but that I call misfortunes, then I'll have to cry and complain to God and the king and ask them for a remedy." (491)

Riper than a soft **fig**.
"Well, the truth is, Sancho my friend," said the duke, "that if you don't become softer than a ripe fig, you won't lay hands on the governorship. It would be a fine thing if I sent my islanders a cruel governor with a heart of flint who does not bow to the tears of damsels in distress or the entreaties of wise, proud, and ancient enchanters and sages! In short, Sancho, either you lash yourself, or let someone else lash you, or you won't be governor." (694-695)

To give (show) someone the **fig**.
"Brother, if you're a jester," replied the duenna, "then keep your jokes for people who like them and pay you for them; you won't get anything but a fig [a proverbial expression based on a gesture of contempt made by placing the thumb between the forefinger and middle finger or under the upper front teeth; see Leite de Vasconcellos 1925, Rettenbeck 1953] from me."
      "That's fine," responded Sancho, "as long as it's nice and ripe, because your grace won't lose the hand if you count years as points."
      "Whoreson," said the duenna, in a rage, "if I'm old or not is God's business, not yours, you garlic-stuffed scoundrel!" (659)

To not give (care) a **fig** for someone or something.
"Be quiet, Señor, because if you [a priest] heard this, you'd go mad with pleasure. I [an innkeeper] don't give two figs for the Great Captain or that Diego García!" (270)

Sancho responded: "Ever since I've felt the pride of being a governor I've lost the foolish ideas of a squire, and I don't care a fig for all the duennas in the world." (703)

Fire cannot be hidden.
"That is so, Señor Don Quixote," responded Don Antonio, "for just as fire cannot be hidden and enclosed, virtue cannot fail to be recognized, and that which is achieved through the profession of arms exceeds and outshines all others." (867)

Fire shows the worth of gold.
"The desire that plagues me [Anselmo] is my wondering if Camila, my wife, is as good and perfect as I think she is, and I cannot learn the truth

except by testing her so that the rest reveals the worth of her virtue, as fire shows the worth of gold." (275)

To add **flames** to the fire.
"We matured, as did our love, until it seemed to Luscinda's father that, in deference to public opinion, he was obliged to deny me [Cardenio] entrance to his house, almost imitating in this regard the parents of that same Thisbe praised so often by poets. And this denial added more flames to the fire and more ardor to our desire, because, although it silenced our tongues, it could not silence our pens." (184)

To be made of **flesh** and blood.
"I [Leonela] know this very well, more from experience than from hearsay, and one day I'll tell you about it, Señora [Camila], for I'm also young and made of flesh and blood." (294)

"It's strange," said Sancho, "about these petitioners. Is it possible they're so foolish they can't see that this isn't the right time of day to come with their petitions? By some chance aren't those of us who are governors and judges men of flesh and blood, too, and don't we need to have time to rest, or do they think we're made of marble? By God and my conscience, if my governorship lasts (and I have an idea it won't), I'll get these petitioners under control." (761-762)

To be like **flies** around honey.
If many thoughts had troubled Don Quixote before his fall, many more troubled him after he was toppled. As has been said, he was in the shade of the tree, and there, like flies swarming around honey, thought came to him and stung him. (898)

As hard as **flint**.
Don Quixote said: "Remember, all you enamored ladies, that for Dulcinea alone I am as soft as sugar paste, and for all the rest I am as hard as flint; for her I am honey, and for you, bitter aloe; for me only Dulcinea is beautiful, wise, modest, gallant, and wellborn, and the rest are ugly, foolish, licentious, and of the worst lineage; to be hers alone, and no other's, nature cast me into the world." (746)

As far as you can shoot a **flintlock**.
"You [Sancho] will look fine," said Don Quixote, "but it will be necessary for you to shave your beard often; yours is so heavy, tangled, and unkempt that unless you shave with a razor at least every other day, people will see what you are from as far away as you can shoot a flintlock." (161)

To be a **fly** in the honey (ointment).
"There can be no doubt that he [a brave man] was out of his mind, or as great a villain as they [four highwaymen], or a man without soul or

conscience, for he wanted to set the wolf loose in the midst of the sheep, the fox in the midst of the chickens, the fly in the midst of the honey: he wanted to defraud justice and oppose his king and natural lord, for he opposed his just commands." (240)

The rich man's **folly** passes for good judgment in the world.
"I know how to sign my name very well," responded Sancho, "because when I was steward of a brotherhood in my village, I learned to make some letters like the marks on bundles, and they told me that they said my name; better yet, I'll pretend that my right hand has been hurt, and I'll have somebody else sign for me; there's a remedy for everything except death, and since I'll be in charge of everything, I can do whatever I want; then, too, when your father's the magistrate... [you're safe when you go to trial]. And being a governor, which is more than being a magistrate, just let them come and they'll see what happens! No, let them make fun of me and speak ill of me: they'll come for wool and go home shorn; and when God loves you, your house knows it; and the rich man's folly passes for good judgment in the world; and since that's what I'll be, being a governor and a very generous one, which is what I plan to be, nobody will notice any faults in me. No, just be like honey and the flies will go after you; you're only worth as much as you have, my grandmother used to say; and you won't get revenge on a well-established man." (735)

The **fool** knows more in his own house than the wise man does in somebody else's.
Sancho said: "So whoever sees the mote in somebody else's eye has to see the beam in his own, so that nobody can say about him: 'The dead woman was frightened by the one with her throat cut.' And your grace knows very well that the fool knows more in his own house than the wise man does in somebody else's." (736)

To get a **foot** in the door.
"As for governing them well," responded Sancho, "there's no need to charge me with it, because I'm charitable by nature and have compassion for the poor; and if he kneads and bakes, you can't steal his cakes; by my faith, they won't throw me any crooked dice; I'm an old dog and understand every here, boy [the proverb says: "You don't need here, boy, here, boy, with an old dog"], and I know how to wake up at the right time, and I don't allow cobwebs in front of my eyes, because I know if the shoe fits: I say this because with me good men will have my hand and a place in my house [the phrase means "trust and confidence"], and bad men won't get a foot or permission to enter." (680)

To not know one's right **foot** from the left.
Sancho said: "And what's clear to me in all this is that in the long run, these adventures we're looking for will bring us so many misadventures that we won't know our right foot from our left. And the better and smarter thing, to the best of my poor understanding, would be for us to go back home now it's harvesttime, and tend to our own affairs, and stop going from pillar to post and from bad to worse, as they say." (125)

To nail something to one's **forehead**.
Sancho said: "The enemy that I've conquered I want you to nail to my forehead [this phrase indicates that what has just been said is either impossible or untrue]. I don't want to divide the enemy's spoils, but I beg and implore some friend, if I have any, to give me a drink of wine and wipe away and dry this sweat, because I'm turning into water." (807)

Forewarned is forearmed.
The gentleman responded: "Forewarned is forearmed: nothing is lost by cautioning me, although I know from experience that I have visible and invisible enemies, and I do not know when, or where, or how, or in what guise they will attack me." (559)

Fortune always leaves a door open.
"Fortune always leaves a door open in adversity so that it can be remedied," said Don Quixote. "I say this because the beast [a donkey] can make up for the lack of Rocinante and carry me from here to some castle where my wounds can be cured." (107-108)

Fortune changes.
"Be still, my friend," said the priest, "for it is God's will that fortune changes, and that what is lost today is won tomorrow; your grace should tend to your health now, for it seems to me your grace must be fatigued, if not badly wounded." (53)

Fortune is fickle.
"Señor, it is as fitting for valiant hearts to endure misfortune as it is for them to rejoice in prosperity; and I [Sancho] judge this on the basis of my own experience, for if I was happy when I was governor, now that I'm a squire on foot, I'm not sad, because I've heard that the woman they call Fortune is drunken, and fickle, and most of all blind, so she doesn't see what she's doing and doesn't know who she's throwing down or raising up." (893)

To have **fortune** come knock on the door.
"O daughter [Sanchica], you certainly are right!" responded Teresa [Panza]. "And all of this good fortune, and some even greater than this,

my good Sancho predicted for me, and you'll see, daughter, how he doesn't stop until he makes me a countess; it's all a matter of starting to be lucky; and I've heard your good father say very often – and he loves proverbs as much as he loves you – that when they give you the calf, run over with the rope; when they give you a governorship, take it; when they give you a countship, hold on to it tight, and when they call you over with a nice present, pack it away. Or else just sleep and don't answer when fortune and good luck come knocking at your door!" (788)

To let the **fox** loose among the chickens.
"There can be no doubt that he [a brave man] was out of his mind, or as great a villain as they [four highwaymen], or a man without soul or conscience, for he wanted to set the wolf loose in the midst of the sheep, the fox in the midst of the chickens, the fly in the midst of the honey: he wanted to defraud justice and oppose his king and natural lord, for he opposed his just commands." (240)

It is not where you were born but who your **friends** are now that counts.
"I have never heard you speak, Sancho," said Don Quixote, "as elegantly as now, which leads me to recognize the truth of the proverb that you like to quote: 'It is not where you were born but who your friends are now that counts.'"

    "Ah, confound it, Señor!" replied Sancho. "Now I'm not the one stringing proverbs together; they also drop two by two from your grace's mouth better than they do from mine, but between my proverbs and yours there must be this difference: your grace's come at the right time, while mine are out of place, but in fact they're all proverbs." (904)

Tell me who your **friends** are and I'll tell you who you are.
Sancho said to himself: "Well now: everything has a remedy except death, under whose yoke we all have to pass, even if we don't want to, when our life ends. I've seen a thousand signs in this master of mine that he's crazy enough to be tied up, and I'm not far behind, I'm as much a fool as he is because I follow and serve him, if that old saying is true: 'Tell me who your friends are and I'll tell you who you are,' and that other one that says, 'Birds of a feather flock together.' Then, being crazy, which is what he is, with the kind of craziness that most of the time takes one thing for another, and thinks white is black and black is white, like the time he said that the windmills were giants, and the friars' mules dromedaries, and the flocks of sheep enemy armies, and many other things of that nature." (515-516)

To earn the **fruit** of one's labors.
Sancho continued: "I'm saying this, Señor, because if after having traveled so many highways and byways, and gone through so many bad nights and worse days, the fruit of our labors is being plucked by someone taking his ease in this inn, then there's no reason for me to hurry and saddle Rocinante, and harness the donkey, and prepare the palfrey, because we'd be better off sitting still and doing nothing: let each whore tend to her spinning, and we'll eat."

Oh, Lord save me, but what age overcame Don Quixote when he heard his squire's discourteous words! It was so great, I say, that with precipitate voice and stumbling tongue and fire blazing from his eyes, he said:

"Oh, base, lowborn, wretched, rude, ignorant, foul-mouthed, ill-spoken, slanderous, insolent varlet!" (401)

Nobody knows the **future**.
"God will find the cure," said Sancho, "for God gives the malady and also the remedy; nobody knows the future: there's a lot of hours until tomorrow, and in one of them, and even in a moment, the house can fall; I've seen it rain at the same time the sun is shining; a man goes to bed healthy and can't move the next day. And tell me, is there anybody who can boast that he's driven a nail into Fortune's wheel? No, of course not, and I wouldn't dare put the point of a pin between a woman's yes and no, because it wouldn't fit. Tell me that Quiteria loves Basilio with all her heart and all her soul, and I'll give him a sack of good fortune, because I've heard that love looks through spectacles that make copper look like gold, poverty like riches, and dried rheum like pearls." (579)

Gains can be lost.
"I already told you, Ricote," replied Sancho, "that I don't want to; be satisfied that I won't betray you, and go on your way in peace, and let me continue on mine: I know that well-gotten gains can be lost, and ill-gotten ones can be lost, too, along with their owner." (815)

To play **games**.
Don Quixote replied: "Señores, I feel that I am dying very rapidly; let us put all jokes aside, and bring me a confessor to hear my confession, and a scribe to write my will, for at critical moments like these a man cannot play games with his soul; and so, while the priest hears my confession, I beg you to bring the scribe." (936)

Generosity cannot live with miserliness.
"Ah Señor Priest, Señor Priest! Did your grace think I [Sancho] didn't know you? Can you think I don't understand and guess where these new enchantments are heading? Well, you should know that I recog-

nize you no matter how you cover your face and understand you no matter how you hide your lies. In short, where envy rules, virtue cannot survive, and generosity cannot live with miserliness. Devil confound it, if it wasn't for your reverence, my master would be married by now to Princess Micomicona and I'd be a count at least, because I expected nothing less from the goodness of my master, the Knight of the Sorrowful Face, and from the greatness of my services! But now I see that what they say is true: the wheel of fortune turns faster than a water wheel, and those who only yesterday were on top of the world today are down on the ground." (410)

To give up the **ghost**.
In brief, Don Quixote's end came after he had received all the sacraments and had execrated books of chivalry with many effective words. The scribe happened to be present, and he had said he had never read in any book of chivalry of a knight errant dying in his bed in so tranquil and Christian manner as Don Quixote, who, surrounded by the sympathy and tears of those present, gave up the ghost, I mean to say, he died. (938)

Gifts can break boulders.
Sancho responded: "Nothing but one insult after another, though she [Dulcinea] must know the proverb that says that a jackass loaded down with gold climbs the mountain fast, and gifts can break boulders, and God helps those who help themselves, and a bird in hand is worth two in the bush. And then my master, who should have coddled me and flattered me so I'd turn as soft as wool and carded cotton, says that if he catches me he'll tie me naked to a tree and double the number of lashes; these noble folk so full of pity should remember that they're not only asking a squire to whip himself, but a governor; like they say, 'That's the finishing touch.' Let them learn, let them learn, damn them, how to beg, and how to ask, and how to have good manners; all times are not the same, and men are not always in a good humor." (694)

For a chaste **girl**, work is her fiesta.
"If God preserves my seven senses, or five, or however many I [Teresa Panza] have, I don't intend to let anybody see me in a spot like that. You, my husband, go and be a governor or an insular and put on all the airs you like; I swear on my mother's life that my daughter and I won't set foot out of our village: to keep her chaste, break her leg and keep her in the house; for a chaste girl, work is her fiesta. You go with your Don Quixote and have your adventures, and leave us with our misfortunes, for God will set them right if we're good; I certainly don't know who gave him [Don Quixote] a *Don,* because his parents and grandparents never had one." (488)

By **giving** quickly, one gives twice.
It happened once, when Camilla found herself alone with her maid, she said:

"I am mortified, my dear Leonela, to see how lightly I valued myself, for I did not even oblige Lotario to pay with time for the complete possession of my desire; I gave it to him so quickly, I fear he will judge only my haste or indiscretion, not taking into account that he urged me so strongly I could no longer resist him."

"Do not be concerned, Señora," responded Leonela. "Giving quickly is of little significance, and no reason to lessen esteem, if, in fact, what one gives is good and in itself worthy of esteem. They even say that by giving quickly, one gives twice." [see Erler 1986].

"They also say," said Camila, "that what costs less is valued less."

"The argument doesn't apply to you," responded Leonela, "because love, I've heard it said, sometimes flies and sometimes walks; it runs with one, and goes slowly with another; it cools some and burns others; some it wounds, and others it kills; it begins the rush of its desires at one point, and at the same point it ends and concludes them; in the morning it lays siege to a fortress, and by nightfall it has broken through, because there is no power that can resist it." (293-294)

For **giving** and keeping, you need some sense (brains).
"God can remedy that," responded Sancho, "because I know more proverbs than a book, and so many of them come into my mouth at one time when I talk that they fight with one another to get out, but my tongue tosses out the first ones it finds, even if they're not to the point. But I'll be careful from now on to say the ones that suit the gravity of my position, because in a well-stocked house, supper is soon cooked; and if you cut the cards, you don't deal; and the man who sounds the alarm is safe; and for giving and keeping, you need some sense." (733-734)

The man uncovered it [a wooden image carved in relief], and it seemed to be St. Martin astride a horse as he divided his cape with the poor man; and as soon as he saw it, Don Quixote said:

"This knight was another Christian seeker of adventures, and I believe he was more generous than brave, as you can see, Sancho, for he is dividing his cape with the poor man and giving him half, and no doubt it must have been winter then; otherwise, he was so charitable he would have given him the entire cape."

"That couldn't have been the reason," said Sancho, "but he must have been paying attention to the proverb that says: 'For giving and keeping you need some brains.'" (833)

People who live in **glass houses** should not throw stones.
Be careful: it is impru-

if your walls are made of crys-
to pick up stones and peb-
and throw them at your neigh-. (13)

Softer than a **glove**.
"I'll tell her [Dulcinea] such wonders about the foolish things and the crazy things, because they amount to the same thing, that your grace has done and is still doing that she'll become softer than a glove even if I find her harder than a cork tree." (198)

To fit like a **glove**.
He [Don Quixote] would buy enough sheep and livestock to give them the name of shepherds; and he told them [the priest and the bachelor] that the most important part of the business had already been taken care of, because he had given them [the sheep] names that would fit them like a glove. (931)

As annoying as **gnats**.
"I [Sancho] imagine that on this ínsula there must be more Dons than stones, but that's enough of that: God understands me, and it may be that if my governorship lasts a few days, I'll weed out these Dons, because there's so many of them they must be as annoying as gnats." (748)

To leap like a **goat**.
The student responded: "He [Basilio] is the most agile youth we know, a great hurler of the bar, an excellent wrestler, a fine pelota player; he runs like a deer, leaps like a goat, and plays bowls as if he were enchanted; he sings like a lark, plays the guitar so well he makes it speak, and, most of all, he can fence with the best of them."(577-578)

God alone knows what tomorrow will bring.
Don Quixote responded: "But let us leave this for now, and since night is approaching, let us withdraw some distance from the king's highway, and spend the night there, and God alone knows what tomorrow will bring." (902)

God brings his children to heaven by many paths.
"All of that is true," responded Don Quixote, "but we cannot all be friars, and God brings His children to heaven by many paths: chivalry is a religion, and there are sainted knights in Glory." (508)

God endures the wicked, but not forever.
"Well now, Señora Rodríguez," said Don Quixote, "and Señora Trifaldi and company, I trust that heaven will look with kindly eyes upon your afflictions; Sancho will do what I tell him to do, whether Clavileño comes or whether I find myself in combat with Malambruno, for I know there is no razor that could shave your graces more easily

than my sword could shave Malambruno's head from his shoulders; God endures the wicked, but not forever." (717)

God gives the malady and also the remedy.
"God will find the cure," said Sancho, "for God gives the malady and also the remedy; nobody knows the future: there's a lot of hours until tomorrow, and in one of them, and even in a moment, the house can fall; I've seen it rain at the same time the sun is shining; a man goes to bed healthy and can't move the next day. And tell me, is there anybody who can boast that he's driven a nail into Fortune's wheel? No, of course not, and I wouldn't dare put the point of a pin between a woman's yes and no, because it wouldn't fit. Tell me that Quiteria loves Basilio with all her heart and all her soul, and I'll give him a sack of good fortune, because I've heard that love looks through spectacles that make copper look like gold, poverty like riches, and dried rheum like pearls." (579)

God grant that it is oregano and not caraway.
"I'll be sure to move aside," replied Sancho, "but may it please God," he continued, "that it turns out to be oregano and not fulling hammers." [The actual proverb warns against fool's gold with oregano being considered more valuable than caraway.] (153)

Sancho said: "There are two things in which the good governor is slightly mistaken: one, when he says or implies that this governorship has been given to him in exchange for the lashes that he'll give himself, when he knows and cannot deny that when my lord the duke promised it to him, nobody even dreamed there were lashes in the world; the other is that he shows himself to be very greedy, and I wouldn't want it to be oregano; greed rips the sack, and a greedy governor dispenses unjust justice." (699)

God helps those who help themselves.
Sancho responded: "Nothing but one insult after another, though she [Dulcinea] must know the proverb that says that a jackass loaded down with gold climbs the mountain fast, and gifts can break boulders, and God helps those who help themselves, and a bird in hand is worth two in the bush. And then my master, who should have coddled me and flattered me so I'd turn as soft as wool and carded cotton, says that if he catches me he'll tie me naked to a tree and double the number of lashes; these noble folk so full of pity should remember that they're not only asking a squire to whip himself, but a governor; like they say, 'That's the finishing touch.' Let them learn, let them learn, damn them, how to beg, and how to ask, and how to have good manners; all times are not the same, and men are not always in a good humor." (694)

God is in heaven and judges men's hearts.
"I [Sancho] made it up to avoid a scolding from my master, Don Quixote, not to offend him, and if it's turned out wrong, God's in heaven and judges men's hearts." (681)

God knows the truth.
"I'm not pregnant by anybody," responded Sancho, "and I'm not a man who'd let himself get pregnant even by the king, and though I'm poor I'm an Old Christian, and I don't owe anything to anybody, and if I want ínsulas, other people want things that are worse; each man is the child of his actions, and because I'm a man I could be a pope, let alone the governor of an ínsula, especially since my master could win so many he might not have enough people to give them to. Your grace should be careful what you say, Señor Barber, because there's more to life than trimming beards, and there's some difference between one Pedro and the other. I say this because we all know one another, and you can't throw crooked dice with me. As for the enchantment of my master, only God knows the truth, and let's leave it at that, because things get worse when you stir them." (411)

Don Quixote said: "But despite this I am comforted, because in the end, regardless of his shape and appearance, I have conquered my enemy."
   "God knows the truth of all things," responded Sancho. (551)

"Say what you wish, Your Excellency [the duchess]," said Doña Rodríguez, "for God knows the truth of everything, and whether or not we duennas are good or bad, bearded or hairless, our mothers bore us just like all other women, and since God put us into the world, He knows the reason, and I rely on His mercy and not on anybody's beard." (717)

God knows what suits each man.
Sancho said: "It was eight or ten days ago, Brother Gossip, that I came to govern the ínsula that they gave me, and in all that time I didn't even have enough bread to eat; I've been persecuted by doctors and had my bones trampled by enemies, and I haven't had time to take any bribes or collect any fees, and this being true, which it is, in my opinion I didn't deserve to leave in this way; but man proposes and God disposes, and God knows what suits each man and what's best for him, and time changes the rhyme, and nobody should say, 'That's water I won't drink,' because you're in a place where you think there's bacon, and you don't even find a nail; God understands me, and that's enough, and I'll say no more, though I could." (821-822)

God looks after his own.
Don Quixote said: "God will look after His people and provide one [a knight arrant] who, if not as excellent as the knights errant of old, at

least will not be inferior to them in courage; God understands me, and I shall say no more." (461)

God provides all things.
Don Quixote responded: "But be that as it may, mount your donkey, my good Sancho, and follow me, for God, who provides all things, will not fail us, especially since we are so much in His service, when He does not fail the gnats in the air, or the grubs in the earth, or the tadpoles in the water. He is so merciful that He makes His sun to shine on the good and the evil and His rain to fall on the just and the unjust." (132)

God remedies everything.
"Well, then, God will remedy everything," said Don Quixote. "Give me my clothes and let me go there, for I wish to see the changes and transformations you [Sancho] have mentioned." (322)

God sees all the snares.
"I mean I didn't look at her [Dulcinea] so carefully," said Sancho, "that I could notice her beauty in particular and her good features point by point, but on the whole, she seemed fine to me."

    "Now I forgive you," said Don Quixote, "and you must pardon the anger I have shown you; for first impulses are not in the hands of men."

    "I can see that," responded Sancho, "just like in me a desire to talk is always my first impulse, and I can never help saying, not even once, what's on my tongue."

    "Even so," said Don Quixote, "think about what you say, Sancho, because you can carry the jug to the fountain only so many times ... and I shall say no more."

    "Well," responded Sancho, "God's in His heaven, and He sees all the snares, and He'll be the judge of who does worse: me in not saying the right thing or your grace in not doing it." (256)

God understands all things.
"It's enough if God understands me, my wife," responded Sancho, "for He understands all things, and say no more about it for now; you should know, Teresa, that you have to take special care of the donkey for the next three days, so that he's ready to carry weapons: double his feed and look over the packsaddle and the rest of the trappings; we're not going to a wedding but to travel the world and have our battles with giants, dragons, and monsters, and hear their hisses, roars, bellows, and shrieks." (486)

God willing we'll see, as one blind man said to the other.
"I don't know about these philosophies," responded Sancho Panza, "all I know is that as soon as I have the countship I'll know how to govern it; I have as much soul as any other man, and as much body as the big-

gest of them, and I'll be as much a king of my estate as any other is of his; and this being true, I'll do what I want, and doing what I want, I'll do what I like, and doing what I like, I'll be happy, and when a man is happy he doesn't wish for anything else, and not wishing for anything else, that'll be the end of it, so bring on my estate, and God willing we'll see, as one blind man said to the other." (431)

Pray to **God** and use a hammer.
Sancho responded that he would do as his master wished but would like to conclude this matter quickly, while his blood was hot and the grindstone rough, because in delay there is often danger, and pray to God and use the hammer, and one "here you are" was worth more than two "I'll give it to you," and a bird in hand was worth two in the bush.

    "By the one God, Sancho, no more proverbs," said Don Quixote. "It seems you are going back to *sicut erat* ["as it was before"]; speak plainly, and simply, and without complications, as I have often told you, and you will see how one loaf will be the same as a hundred for you." (924)

When **God** loves you, your house knows it.
"I know how to sign my name very well," responded Sancho, "because when I was steward of a brotherhood in my village, I learned to make some letters like the marks on bundles, and they told me that they said my name; better yet, I'll pretend that my right hand has been hurt, and I'll have somebody else sign for me; there's a remedy for everything except death, and since I'll be in charge of everything, I can do whatever I want; then, too, when your father's the magistrate... [you're safe when you go to trial]. And being a governor, which is more than being a magistrate, just let them come and they'll see what happens! No, let them make fun of me and speak ill of me: they'll come for wool and go home shorn; and when God loves you, your house knows it; and the rich man's folly passes for good judgment in the world; and since that's what I'll be, being a governor and a very generous one, which is what I plan to be, nobody will notice any faults in me. No, just be like honey and the flies will go after you; you're only worth as much as you have, my grandmother used to say; and you won't get revenge on a well-established man." (735)

When **God** sends the dawn, it is dawn for everybody.
Sancho said: "Don't let anybody try to trick me, because we either are or we aren't: let's all live and eat in peace and good friendship, because when God sends the dawn, it's dawn for everybody. I'll govern this ínsula without forsaking the law or taking a bribe, and let everybody keep his eyes open and tend to his own affairs, because I want you to know that the devil makes trouble everywhere, and if you give me a

chance, you'll see marvels. And if you turn into honey, the flies will eat you." (773-774)

All that glitters is not **gold**.
And I [Sancho] say again that if your ladyship doesn't want to give me the ínsula because I'm a fool, I'll be smart enough not to care at all; I've heard that the devil hides behind the cross, and that all that glitters isn't gold, and that from his oxen, plows, and yokes they took the peasant Wamba to be king of Spain, and from his brocades, entertainments, and riches they took Rodrigo to be eaten by snakes, if the lines from the old ballads don't lie." (679)

Doña Rodríguez said: "Your grace [Don Quixote] should keep in mind that my daughter is an orphan, and well-bred, and young, and possessed of all those gifts that I have mentioned to you, for by God and my conscience, of all the maidens that my mistress has, there is none that can even touch the sole of her shoe, and the one they call Altisidora, the one they consider the most elegant and spirited, can't come within two leagues of my daughter. Because I want your grace to know, Señor, that all that glitters is not gold; this little Altisidora has more vanity than beauty, and more spirit than modesty, and besides, she's not very healthy: she has breath so foul that you can't bear to be near her even for a moment. And then, my lady the duchess ... But I'd better be quiet, because they say that the walls have ears." (771)

To glitter like **gold**.
And he [Don Quixote] stood up, stopped eating, and went to remove the covering of the first image [a wooden image carved in relief], which turned out to be St. George mounted on a horse, a serpent lying coiled at his feet, its mouth run through by a lance, all of it depicted with the customary ferocity. The entire image seemed to glitter like gold, as they say. (833)

When **good** comes along, lock it in your house.
"Sancho I was born, and Sancho I plan to die; but even so, if heaven should be so kind as to offer me, without too much trouble or risk, an ínsula or something else like that, I'm not such a fool that I'd turn it down, because, as they say: 'When they give you a heifer, don't forget to bring a rope,' and 'When good comes along, lock it in your house.'" (483-484)

To swim like a **goose**.
The millers pushed against the boat with their poles and stopped it but could not keep it from capsizing and throwing Don Quixote and Sancho into the water; it was fortunate for Don Quixote that he knew how to swim like a goose, although the weight of his armor mad him sink

twice, and if it had not been for the millers, who jumped into the water and pulled them out, it would have been the end of them both. (651)

To be a **Gordian knot**.
Don Quixote said: "The companionship of one's own wife is not merchandise that, once purchased, can be returned, or exchanged, or altered; it is an irrevocable circumstance that lasts as long as one lives: it is a rope that, if put around one's neck, turns into the Gordian knot, and if the scythe of Death does not cut it, there is no way to untie it." (578)

Don Quixote reasoned: "If Alexander the Great cut the Gordian knot, saying: 'It does not matter if it is cut or untied,' and that did not keep him from being the universal lord of all Asia, then in the disenchantment of Dulcinea it might not matter if I whip Sancho against his will, for if the condition of this remedy is that Sancho receive some three thousand lashes, what difference does it make to me if he administers them himself or if another does, since the essence of the matter is that he receive them regardless of where they come from." (850)

All are equal in the **grave**.
Don Quixote said: "Well, the same thing happens in the drama and business of this world, where some play emperors, others pontiffs, in short, all the figures that can be presented in a play, but at the end, which is when life is over, death removes all the clothing that differentiated them, and all are equal in the grave." (527)

Greed makes the sack burst.
I [Sancho] left my home and my children and my wife to serve your grace, thinking I would be better off, not worse; but just as greed makes the sack burst, it has torn my hopes apart when they were brightest for getting that wretched, ill-starred ínsula your grace has promised me so often. (143)

Greed tears (rips) the sack.
"That," responded the Squire of the Wood, "is why they say that it's greed that tears the sack, and if we're going to talk about madmen, there's nobody in the world crazier than my master, because he's one of those who say: 'Other people's troubles kill the donkey,' and to help another knight find the wits he's lost, he pretends to be crazy and goes around looking for something that I think will hit him right in the face when he finds it." (535)

Sancho said: "There are two things in which the good governor is slightly mistaken: one, when he says or implies that this governorship has been given to him in exchange for the lashes that he'll give himself, when he knows and cannot deny that when my lord the duke promised it to him, nobody even dreamed there were lashes in the world; the oth-

er is that he shows himself to be very greedy, and I wouldn't want it to
be oregano; greed rips the sack, and a greedy governor dispenses unjust
justice." (699)

Griefs are better with bread.
The gray [the donkey] was lying on his back, and Sancho Panza moved
him around until he had him on his feet, though he could barely stand;
he took a piece of bread out of the saddlebags, which had experienced
the same unfortunate fall, and gave it to his donkey, who thought it did
not taste bad, and Sancho said to him, as if he could understand:
    "Griefs are better with bread." (818)

To get gray **hair**.
"During the harvest, many of the harvesters gather here [with the inn-
keeper] during their time off, and there's always a few who know how
to read, and one of them takes down one of those books, and more than
thirty of us sit around him and listen to him and read with so much
pleasure that it saves us a thousand gray hairs." (267)

To have one's **hair** stand on end.
At this everyone certainly was stunned; at this everyone's hair certainly
stood on end from sheer terror! (869)

To pull in by the **hair**.
"Look, Sancho," responded Don Quixote, "I say proverbs when they
are appropriate, and when I say them they fit like the rings on your fingers, but you drag them in by the hair, and pull them along, and do not
guide them, and if I remember correctly, I have already told you that
proverbs are brief maxims derived from the experience and speculation
of wise men in the past, and if the proverb is not to the point, it is not a
maxim, it is nonsense." (902)

To be one's better **half**.
Sancho added: "I've never seen in all my life a lace- maker who's died
for love; maidens who are occupied think more about finishing their
tasks than about love. At least that's true for me, because when I'm
busy digging I never think about my better half, I mean my Teresa Panza, and I love her more than my eyelashes." (918)

To have a **hand** and a place in one's house.
"As for governing them well," responded Sancho, "there's no need to
charge me with it, because I'm charitable by nature and have compassion for the poor; and if he kneads and bakes, you can't steal his cakes;
by my faith, they won't throw me any crooked dice; I'm an old dog and
understand every here, boy [the proverb says: "You don't need here,
boy, here, boy, with an old dog"], and I know how to wake up at the
right time, and I don't allow cobwebs in front of my eyes, because I

know if the shoe fits: I say this because with me good men will have my hand and a place in my house [the phrase means "trust and confidence"], and bad men won't get a foot or permission to enter." (680)

To know something like the back of one's **hand**.
Sancho said: "My master, Don Quixote of La Mancha, who was once called *The Knight of the Sorrowful Face* and is now called *The Knight of the Lions,* is a very prudent gentleman who knows Latin and Spanish like a bachelor, and in all his dealings and advice he proceeds like a very good soldier, and he knows all the laws and rules about what is called dueling like the back of his hand, and so there's nothing else to do but listen to what he says, and if you're wrong, let it be on my head, especially since they say that it's foolish to lose your temper just because you hear somebody bray." (641)

To put one's **hand** over one's own heart.
Sancho said: "Let each man put his hand over his own heart and not start judging white as black and black as white; each of us is as God made him, and often much worse." (481-482)

To be in God's **hands**.
"Well, well, then it's in God's hands," said Sancho. "I consent to my bad fortune; I say that I accept the penance, with the conditions that have been stated." (696)

"Continue, Sancho my friend, and do not lose heart," said Don Quixote, "for I shall double the stakes on the price."
    "In that case," said Sancho, "let it be in God's hands, and rain down the lashes!" (921)

A **hare** leaps out (up) when you least expect it.
"I'll go and come back very quickly," said Sancho, "and swell that heart of yours, which can't be any bigger now than a hazelnut, and remember what they say: a good heart beats bad luck, and where there is no bacon, there are no stakes [Sancho misquotes the proverb], and they also say that a hare leaps out when you least expect it [that is, Life is full of surprises.]. I'm saying this because if we didn't find my lady's palaces or castles last night, now that it's day I think I'll find them when I least expect to, and once I've found them, just leave everything to me."
    "Well, Sancho," said Don Quixote, "you certainly bring in proverbs that suit our affairs perfectly, and I hope God gives me as much good fortune in my desires." (514)

Sancho said: "It can't be denied but must be affirmed that my lady Dulcinea of Toboso is very beautiful, but the hare leaps up when you least expect it; I've heard that this thing they call nature is like a potter who makes clay bowls, and if he makes a beautiful bowl, he can also make two, or three, or a hundred: I say this because, by my faith, my lady the duchess is as good-looking as my mistress the lady Dulcinea of Toboso." (656)

As agile as a **hawk**.
When the saddle had been put in place, and Don Quixote tried to lift his enchanted lady in his arms and put her back on the donkey, the lady got up from the ground and saved him the trouble, because she moved back, ran a short distance, and, placing both hands on the donkey's rump, jumped right into the saddle, as agile as a hawk and sitting astride as if she were a man. (519)

As brown as a **hazelnut**.
At her call, Teresa Panza, her mother, came pout, spinning a bunch of flax and wearing a dun-colored skirt so short it looked as if it had been cut to shame her, a bodice that was also dun colored, and a chemise. She was not very old, although she looked over forty, but she was strong, hard, vigorous, and as brown as a hazelnut. (783-784)

From **head** to foot.
The gentleman said: "What can this be, Sancho? It seems as if my head is softening, or my brains are melting, or that I am bathed in perspiration from head to foot. And if I am perspiring, the truth is that it is not because of fear, although I undoubtedly must believe that the adventure about to befall me will be a terrible one. Give me something, if you have it, that I can use to wipe away this copious perspiration, for it is blinding me." (559)

He [Don Quixote] saw instead a most reverend duenna wearing white veils so long and intricate that they covered an enshrouded her from head to foot. (766)

From **head** to toe.
When Don Quixote saw this he fell silent and sat as if paralyzed from head to toe. Sancho looked at him and saw that his head hung down toward his chest, indicating that he was mortified. (150)

"That's fine," said Sancho. "You [a farmer] should realize, brother, that now you've painted her [a maiden] from head to toe. What is it that you want? And get to the point without beating around the bush or going around in circles, or taking anything away or adding anything to it." (764)

They [two constables] looked at her [a woman] from head to toe and saw that she was wearing stockings of scarlet silk, with garters of white taffeta edged in gold and seed pearls; her breeches were green, made of cloth of gold, as was her jacket or loose coat, and her men's shoes were white. (778)

Suddenly there came through the door of the great room two women, as they subsequently proved to be, covered in mourning from head to toe, and one of them came up to Don Quixote and threw herself on the floor before him. (798)

Head over heels.
He [Sancho] told them of the state in which he had left him [Don Quixote], and the adventures that had befallen him, and how he was carrying a letter to the lady Dulcinea of Toboso, who was the daughter of Lorenzo Corchuelo and the one with whom his master was head over heels in love. (209)

To get something out of one's **head**.
Letter from Teresa Panza to Sancho Panza: The priest, the barber, the bachelor, and even the sacristan can't believe you're a governor; they say it's all a fraud, or a question of enchantment, like everything that has to do with your master Don Quixote; Sansón says he'll go to look for you and get the governorship out of your head and Don Quixote's craziness out of his skull; I don't do anything but laugh, and look at my necklace, and plan the dress I'll make for our daughter out of your outfit. (803)

The beginning of **health** lies in knowing the disease.
Don Quixote responded: "Señor Roque, the beginning of health lies in knowing the disease, and in the patient's willingness to take the medicines the doctor prescribes; your grace is ill, you know your ailment, and heaven, or I should say God, who is our physician, will treat you with the medicines that will cure you, and which tend to cure gradually, not suddenly and miraculously." (858)

A good **heart** beats bad luck.
"I'll go and come back very quickly," said Sancho, "and swell that heart of yours, which can't be any bigger now than a hazelnut, and remember what they say: a good heart beats bad luck, and where there is no bacon, there are no stakes [Sancho misquotes the proverb], and they also say that a hare leaps out when you least expect it. I'm saying this because if we didn't find my lady's palaces or castles last night, now that it's day I think I'll find them when I least expect to, and once I've found them, just leave everything to me."
    "Well, Sancho," said Don Quixote, "you certainly bring in proverbs that suit our affairs perfectly, and I hope God gives me as much good fortune in my desires." (514)

Nobody knows another man's **heart**.
Sancho responded: Let each man look out for himself, though the best thing would be to let everybody's anger stay asleep; nobody knows another man's heart, and many who come for wool go home clipped and shorn, and God blessed peace and cursed fights, because if a cat that's hunted and locked up and treated badly turns into a lion, then since I'm a man, God knows what I could turn into, and so from now on I'm letting your grace know, Señor Squire, that all the harm and damage that result from our quarrel will be on your head." (542-543)

To be of good **heart**.
The duchess said: "Sancho should be of good heart, for when he least expects it he will find himself seated on the throne of his ínsula and of his estate, and he will hold his governorship in his hand and not trade it for another of three-pile brocade [the phrase means "no matter how fine"]. My charge to him is that he attend to how he governs his vassals, knowing that all of them are loyal and wellborn." (680)

To break someone's **heart**.
Sancho said: "Don't cry, Master Pedro, and don't wail, or you'll break my heart, and let me tell you that my master, Don Quixote, is so Catholic and scrupulous a Christian that if he realizes he's done you any harm, he'll tell you so and want to pay and satisfy you, and with interest." (634)

To go to the **heart** of the matter.
"I [Sancho] say that I'm sure of my master's good ness and truthfulness, and so I'll ask something that goes right to the heart of the matter; speaking with respect, since your grace has been locked in the cage, enchanted, in your opinion, have you had the desire and will to pass what they call major and minor waters?"

"I do not understand what you mean by *passing waters*, Sancho; speak more clearly if you want me to respond in a straightforward way."

"Is it possible that your grace doesn't understand what it means to pass minor or major waters? Even schoolboys know that. Well, what I mean is, have you had the desire to do the thing nobody else can do for you?"

"Ah, now I understand you, Sancho! Yes, I have, quite often. And even do now. Save me from this danger, for not everything is absolutely pristine!" (420-421)

To have a **heart** of flint.
"Well, the truth is, Sancho my friend," said the duke, "that if you don't become softer than a ripe fig, you won't lay hands on the governorship. It would be a fine thing if I sent my islanders a cruel governor with a

heart of flint who does not bow to the tears of damsels in distress or the entreaties of wise, proud, and ancient enchanters and sages! In short, Sancho, either you lash yourself, or let someone else lash you, or you won't be governor." (694-695)

To have a **heart** of marble.
"What notable cruelty!" said Sancho. "What glaring ingratitude! For me, I can say that at her [Altisidora] smallest word of love I'd surrender and submit. Whoreson, what a heart of marble you have, and a will of bronze, and a soul of mortar!" (836)

To lose **heart**.
"Enough of that, Señor [Don Quixote]," said Sancho. "Long live the hen, even with the pip; today it's your turn and tomorrow it's mine; these matters of clashes and blows shouldn't be taken too seriously, because the man who falls today can pick himself up tomorrow, unless he decides to stay in bed, I mean if he lets himself lose heart and doesn't find new spirit for new fights. And your grace should get up now to receive Don Gaspar Gregorio, because it seems to me that everybody's in an uproar, and he must be in the house by now." (890)

"Continue, Sancho my friend, and do not lose heart," said Don Quixote, "for I shall double the stakes on the price."
"In that case," said Sancho, "let it be in God's hands, and rain down the lashes!" (921)

With **heart** and soul.
Ah!" said Sancho. "I've got you there: that's what I wanted to know with all my heart and soul. Come, Señor, can you deny what people usually say when a person's not feeling well." (421)

Heaven is just.
"But, as they say, one ill leads to another, and the end of one misfortune tends to be the beginning of another even greater, and that is what happened to me [Dorotea]; my good servant, faithful and trustworthy until then, saw me in this desolate place, and inflamed by his own depravity rather than my beauty, attempted to take advantage of the opportunity which, to his mind, this setting offered him; with little shame and less fear of God or respect for me, he tried to persuade me to make love to him, and seeing that I responded with words of censure and rebuke to his outrageous proposals, he set aside the entreaties that he thought at first would succeed and began to use force. But heaven is just, rarely or never failing to regard and favor righteous intentions, and it favored mine, so that with my scant strength, and not too much effort, I pushed him over a precipice, where I left him, not knowing if he was dead or alive." (238)

Hell is filled with the ungrateful.

Don Quixote said: "Although some say pride is the greatest sin men commit, I say it is ingratitude, for I am guided by the adage that says hell is filled with the ungrateful. This sin is one I have attempted to flee, as much as it was possible for me to do so, since I first reached the age of reason; if I cannot repay the good deeds done for me with other deeds, in their place I put the desire I have to perform them, and if that is not enough, I proclaim those good deeds far and wide, because the person who tells about and proclaims the good deeds that have been performed on his behalf would also recompense them with other deeds if he could, because most of the time those who receive are subordinate to those who give." (839)

It is better to have God's **help** than to get up early.

"May it please God, Sancho, because there's many a slip between the cup and the lip, [said the duke]."

"That may be so," replied Sancho, "but if you pay your debts, you don't worry about guaranties, and it's better to have God's help than to get up early, and your belly leads your feet, not the other way around; I mean, if God helps me, and I do what I ought to with good intentions, I'll be sure to govern in grand style. Just put a finger in my mouth and see if I bite or not!" (686)

A **hen** sits on her eggs.

"It's taking me to this," said Sancho. "Your grace should tell me exactly what salary you'll give me for each month I serve you, and this salary should be paid to me from your estate; I don't want to depend on anybody's favors, which come late, or badly, or never; may God help me to tend to my own business. The point is, I want to know what I'm earning, whether it's a lot or a little; a hen sits on her egg, and a lot of littles make a lot, and as long as you're earning you don't lose a thing. And if it should happen, and I don't believe or expect that it will, that your grace gives me the ínsula you promised, I'm not such an ingrate, and not such a pennypincher, that I won't want the rent from the ínsula to be added up and deducted from my salary pro rat." (498-499)

Long live the **hen**, even with the pip.

"Enough of that, Señor [Don Quixote]," said Sancho. "Long live the hen, even with the pip; today it's your turn and tomorrow it's mine; these matters of clashes and blows shouldn't be taken too seriously, because the man who falls today can pick himself up tomorrow, unless he decides to stay in bed, I mean if he lets himself lose heart and doesn't find new spirit for new fights. And your grace should get up now to receive Don Gaspar Gregorio, because it seems to me that everybody's in an uproar, and he must be in the house by now." (890)

One "**here** you are" is worth more than two "I'll give it to you".
Sancho responded that he would do as his master wished but would
like to conclude this matter quickly, while his blood was hot and the
grindstone rough, because in delay there is often danger, and pray to
God and use the hammer, and one "here you are" was worth more than
two "I'll give it to you," and a bird in hand was worth two in the bush.
   "By the one God, Sancho, no more proverbs," said Don Quixote.
"It seems you are going back to *sicut erat* ["as it was before"]; speak
plainly, and simply, and without complications, as I have often told
you, and you will see how one loaf will be the same as a hundred for
you." (924)

Aliquando bonus dormitat **Homerus**.
"All this is true, Señor Don Quixote," said Carrasco, "but I should like
those censurers to be more merciful and less severe and not pay so
much attention to the motes in the bright sun of the work they criticize,
for if *aliquando bonus dormitat Homerus* [a line from Horace's *Ars
poetica*: "From time to time even Homer nods."], they should consider
how often he was awake to give a brilliant light to his work with the
least amount of shadow possible; and it well may be that what seem
defects to them are birthmarks that often increase the beauty of the face
where they appear; and so I say that whoever prints a book exposes
himself to great danger, since it is utterly impossible to write in a way
that will satisfy and please everyone who reads it." (479)

As sweet as **honey**.
"That's true," said Maritornes, "and by my faith, I really like to hear
those things, too, they're very pretty, especially when they tell about a
lady under some orange trees in the arms of a knight, and a duenna's
their lookout, and she's dying of envy and scared to death. I think all
that's as sweet as honey." (268)

Be as **honey** and the flies will go after you.
"I know how to sign my name very well," responded Sancho, "because
when I was steward of a brotherhood in my village, I learned to make
some letters like the marks on bundles, and they told me that they said
my name; better yet, I'll pretend that my right hand has been hurt, and
I'll have somebody else sign for me; there's a remedy for everything
except death, and since I'll be in charge of everything, I can do whatever I want; then, too, when your father's the magistrate... [you're safe
when you go to trial]. And being a governor, which is more than being
a magistrate, just let them come and they'll see what happens! No, let
them make fun of me and speak ill of me: they'll come for wool and go
home shorn; and when God loves you, your house knows it; and the
rich man's folly passes for good judgment in the world; and since that's
what I'll be, being a governor and a very generous one, which is what I

plan to be, nobody will notice any faults in me. No, just be like honey and the flies will go after you; you're only worth as much as you have, my grandmother used to say; and you won't get revenge on a well-established man." (735)

Sancho said: "Don't let anybody try to trick me, because we either are or we aren't: let's all live and eat in peace and good friendship, because when God sends the dawn, it's dawn for everybody. I'll govern this ínsula without forsaking the law or taking a bribe, and let everybody keep his eyes open and tend to his own affairs, because I want you to know that the devil makes trouble everywhere, and if you give me a chance, you'll see marvels. And if you turn into honey, the flies will eat you." (773-774)

Honey is not for the donkey's mouth.
"I'll show them to you at home," said Panza, "and for now be happy, because if it's God's will that we go out again in search of adventures, in no time you'll see me made a count, or the governor of an ínsula, and not any of the ones around here, but the best that can be found."

"May it please God, my husband, because we surely need it. But tell me, what's all this about ínsulas? I don't understand."

"Honey's not for the donkey's mouth," responded Sancho. "In time you will, dear wife, and even be amazed to hear yourself called ladyship by all your vassals."

"What are you saying, Sancho, about ladyships, ínsulas, and vassals?" responded Juana Panza, which was the name of Sancho's wife; they were not kin, but in La Mancha wives usually take their husbands' family name.

"Don't be in such a hurry, Juana, to learn everything all at once; it's enough that I'm telling you the truth, so sew up your mouth. I'll just tell you this, in passing: there's nothing nicer in the world for a man than being the honored squire of a knight errant seeking adventures." (444)

There is no **honey** without gall.
"Now, when I [Don Quixote] intended to place you [Sancho] in a position where, despite your wife, you would be called Señor, now you take your leave? Now you go, when I had the firm and binding intention of making you lord of the best ínsula in the world? In short, as you have said on other occasions, there is no honey ... [Nothing is perfect]. You are a jackass, and must be a jackass, and will end your days as a jackass, for in my opinion, your life will run its course before you accept and realize that you are an animal." (646)

To be **honey** on hotcakes.
Sancho responded: "This seems like one dirty trick on top of another, and not honey on hotcakes. How nice it would be after pinches, slaps, and pinpricks to have a few lashes. Why not just take a big stone and tie it around my neck and put me in a well, and I won't mind it too much since I have to be a laughingstock in order to solve other people's problems. Let me alone; if not, I swear I'll knock down and destroy everything, and I don't care what happens." (911)

Hope is born at the same time as love.
Cervantes: But not even this brusque behavior could weaken Loratio's hope, for hope is always born at the same time as love; instead, he held Camila in even higher esteem. (288)

Fine **hopes** are better than miserable possessions.
Therefore, my dear Sancho, return to your house and tell your Teresa my intention, and if it pleases her and you to serve me without wages, *bene quidem*, and if not, we shall still be friends, for if the pigeon coop has plenty of feed, it will have plenty of pigeons. And remember, Sancho, that fine hopes are better than miserable possessions, and a good lawsuit [is] better than a bad payment. I [Don Quixote] am speaking in this manner, Sancho, so you may understand that, like you, I too know how to pour down rainstorms of proverbs. And, finally, I want to tell you, and I do tell you, that if you do not wish to accompany me without pay, and take the same risks I do, then God be with you and turn you into a saint, for I shall have no lack of squires more obedient, more solicitous, less uncouth, and less talkative than you." (499-500)

"When I [Sancho] gave up the governorship I also gave up any desire to be a governor again, but I didn't give up wanting to be a count, which will never happen if your grace gives up being a king by giving up the practice of your chivalry, which means all my hopes going up in smoke."
    "Be quiet, Sancho, for my retirement and withdrawal do not need to last longer than a year, and then I [Don Quixote] shall return to my honorable practice, and there will be no lack of kingdoms for me to win and countships to give to you."
    "May God hear you," said Sancho, "and sin be deaf, for I've always heard that virtuous hope is better than wicked possession." (890)

A saddled **horse** is better than an ass covered in gold.
Sancho said: "To hell with Basilio's talents! You're worth what you have, and what you have is what you're worth. There are only two lineages in the world, as my grandmother used to say, and that's the haves and the have-nots, though she was on the side of having; nowadays, Señor Don Quixote, wealth is better than wisdom: an ass covered in

gold seems better than a saddled horse. And so I say again that I'm on the side of Camacho, whose pots are overflowing with geese and chickens, hares and rabbits, while Basilio's, if they ever show up, and even if they don't, won't hold anything but watered wine." (589)

Sturdy as a **horse**.
"I [Sancho] can say that she [Dulcinea] can throw a metal bar just as well as the brawniest lad in the village. Praise our Maker, she's a fine girl in every way, sturdy as a horse, and just the one to pull any knight errant or about to be an errant, who has her for his lady, right out of a mudhole he's fallen into!" (199)

There are a lot of **hours** until tomorrow.
"God will find the cure," said Sancho, "for God gives the malady and also the remedy; nobody knows the future: there's a lot of hours until tomorrow, and in one of them, and even in a moment, the house can fall; I've seen it rain at the same time the sun is shining; a man goes to bed healthy and can't move the next day. And tell me, is there anybody who can boast that he's driven a nail into Fortune's wheel? No, of course not, and I wouldn't dare put the point of a pin between a woman's yes and no, because it wouldn't fit. Tell me that Quiteria loves Basilio with all her heart and all her soul, and I'll give him a sack of good fortune, because I've heard that love looks through spectacles that make copper look like gold, poverty like riches, and dried rheum like pearls." (579)

To sleep more than six **hours** at a stretch.
It was the physician's opinion that melancholy and low spirits were bringing his life to an end. Don Quixote asked to be left alone because he wanted to sleep for a while. They did as he asked, and he slept more than six hours at a stretch, as they say, so long that his housekeeper and his niece thought he would never open his eyes again. (935)

In a moment the **house** can fall.
"God will find the cure," said Sancho, "for God gives the malady and also the remedy; nobody knows the future: there's a lot of hours until tomorrow, and in one of them, and even in a moment, the house can fall; I've seen it rain at the same time the sun is shining; a man goes to bed healthy and can't move the next day. And tell me, is there anybody who can boast that he's driven a nail into Fortune's wheel? No, of course not, and I wouldn't dare put the point of a pin between a woman's yes and no, because it wouldn't fit. Tell me that Quiteria lves Basilio with all her heart and all her soul, and I'll give him a sack of good fortune, because I've heard that love looks through spectacles that make copper look like gold, poverty like riches, and dried rheum like pearls." (579)

Hunger is the best sauce.
Cervantes: After riding a short while between two hills, they found themselves in a broad, secluded valley, where they dismounted, and Sancho lightened the donkey's load, and they stretched out on the green grass, and with hunger as their sauce, they had breakfast, lunch, dinner, and supper all at once, satisfying their stomachs. (140)

"I'll tell you, Teresa," responded Sancho, "that if I didn't expect to be the governor of an ínsula before too much more time goes by, I'd fall down dead right here."
"Not that, my husband," said Teresa, "let the chicken live even if she has the pip; may you live, and let the devil take all the governorships there are in the world; you came out of your mother's womb without a governorship, and you've lived until now without a governorship, and when it pleases God you'll go, or they'll carry you, to the grave without a governorship. Many people in the world live without a governorship, and that doesn't make them give up or not be counted among the living. The best sauce in the world is hunger, and since poor people have plenty of that, they always eat with great pleasure. But look, Sancho: if you happen to find yourself a governor somewhere, don't forget about me and your children. Remember that Sanchico is already fifteen, and he ought to go to school if his uncle the abbot is going to bring him into the Church. And don't forget that our daughter, Mari Sancha, won't die if we marry her; she keeps dropping hints that she wants a husband as much as you want to be a governor, and when all is said and done, a daughter's better off badly married than happily kept." (486-487)

The one who **hurts** you is the one who loves you.
"At least," responded Sancho, "your grace knew how to place the lance, aiming for my head and hitting me on the back, thanks be to God and the care I took to move to the side. Well, well, it all comes out in the end, for I've heard people say: 'The one who hurts you is the one who loves you,' and I've also heard that great gentlemen, after speaking harshly to a servant, give him breeches, though I don't know what they give after beating him with a lance, unless knights errant give ínsulas after a beating, or kingdoms on dry land." (151)

As cold as **ice**.
Altisidora said:
> As for your squire named Sancho,
> may his heart be as hard as stone,
> as cold as ice: then Dulcinea
> will ne'er be freed of enchantment. (830)

One **ill** leads to another.

"But, as they say, one ill leads to another, and the end of one misfortune tends to be the beginning of another even greater, and that is what happened to me [Dorotea]; my good servant, faithful and trustworthy until then, saw me in this desolate place, and inflamed by his own depravity rather than my beauty, attempted to take advantage of the opportunity which, to his mind, this setting offered him; with little shame and less fear of God or respect for me, he tried to persuade me to make love to him, and seeing that I responded with words of censure and rebuke to his outrageous proposals, he set aside the entreaties that he thought at first would succeed and began to use force. But heaven is just, rarely or never failing to regard and favor righteous intentions, and it favored mine, so that with my scant strength, and not too much effort, I pushed him over a precipice, where I left him, not knowing if he was dead or alive." (238)

First **impulses** are not in the hands of men.

"I mean I didn't look at her [Dulcinea] so carefully," said Sancho, "that I could notice her beauty in particular and her good features point by point, but on the whole, she seemed fine to me."

"Now I forgive you," said Don Quixote, "and you must pardon the anger I have shown you; for first impulses are not in the hands of men."

"I can see that," responded Sancho, "just like in me a desire to talk is always my first impulse, and I can never help saying, not even once, what's on my tongue."

"Even so," said Don Quixote, "think about what you say, Sancho, because you can carry the jug to the fountain only so many times ... and I shall say no more."

"Well," responded Sancho, "God's in His heaven, and He sees all the snares, and He'll be the judge of who does worse: me in not saying the right thing or your grace in not doing it." (256)

Ingratitude is the daughter of pride.

Letter from Don Quixote to Sancho Panza: *Write to your lord and lady and show them that you are grateful, for ingratitude is the daughter of pride and one of the greatest sins we know, while the person who is grateful to those who have granted him benefits indicates that he will also be grateful to God, who has granted and continues to grant him so many.* (794)

Ego autem dico vobis: diligite **inimicos** vestros.

If it's the friendship and love that God commands us to have for our enemies, you turn right to Holy Scripture, which you can do with a minimum of effort, and say the words of God Himself: *Ego autem dico vobis: diligite inimicos vestros* ["But I say unto you, Love your enemies", Matthew 1:4]. (6)

The one who says **insults** is close to forgiving.
"That seems to me," said the duke, "like the old saying:
   Because the one who says insults,
   is very close to forgiving."
Altisidora made a show of drying her tears with a handkerchief, and after curtsying to her master and mistress, she left the room. (918)

To hammer on cold **iron**.
While Sancho Panza and his wife, Teresa Cascajo, were having the incongruous talk that has just been related, Don Quixote's niece and housekeeper were not idle; a thousand indications had led them to infer that their uncle and master wished to leave for the third time and return to the practice of what was, to their minds, his calamitous chivalry, and they attempted by all means possible to dissuade him from so wicked a thought, but it was all preaching in the desert and hammering on cold iron. (491)

A **jackass** loaded down with gold climbs the mountain fast.
Sancho responded: "Nothing but one insult after another, though she [Dulcinea] must know the proverb that says that a jackass loaded down with gold climbs the mountain fast, and gifts can break boulders, and God helps those who help themselves, and a bird in hand is worth two in the bush. And then my master, who should have coddled me and flattered me so I'd turn as soft as wool and carded cotton, says that if he catches me he'll tie me naked to a tree and double the number of lashes; these noble folk so full of pity should remember that they're not only asking a squire to whip himself, but a governor; like they say, 'That's the finishing touch.' Let them learn, let them learn, damn them, how to beg, and how to ask, and how to have good manners; all times are not the same, and men are not always in a good humor." (694)

To be as foolish as a **jackass**.
Don Quixote and Sancho went back to their animals, and to being as foolish as jackasses and so ended the adventure of the enchanted boat. (652)

Jests that cause pain are not jests.
Cervantes: Don Antonio Moreno was the name of Don Quixote's host, a wealthy and discerning gentleman, very fond of seemly and benign amusements, who, finding Don Quixote in his house, sought ways to make his madness public without harming him; for jests that cause pain are not jests, and entertainments are not worthwhile if they injure another. (864)

Sudden **joy** can kill just like great sorrow.
Letter from Teresa Panza to Sancho Panza: *I received your letter, Sancho of my soul, and I can tell you and swear to you as a Catholic*

Christian that I practically went crazy with happiness. Just think, my husband: when I heard that you were a governor, I thought I'd fall down dead from sheer joy, because you know, people say that sudden joy can kill just like great sorrow. (802)

The **jug** (pitcher) goes to the fountain so long until at last it breaks.

"I mean I didn't look at her [Dulcinea] so carefully," said Sancho, "that I could notice her beauty in particular and her good features point by point, but on the whole, she seemed fine to me."

"Now I forgive you," said Don Quixote, "and you must pardon the anger I have shown you; for first impulses are not in the hands of men."

"I can see that," responded Sancho, "just like in me a desire to talk is always my first impulse, and I can never help saying, not even once, what's on my tongue."

"Even so," said Don Quixote, "think about what you say, Sancho, because you can carry the jug to the fountain only so many times ... and I shall say no more."

"Well," responded Sancho, "God's in His heaven, and He sees all the snares, and He'll be the judge of who does worse: me in not saying the right thing or your grace in not doing it." (256)

A **jump** over the thicket is better than the prayers of good men.

"I [Sancho] am, Señor, so unfortunate, that I fear the day will never come when I can join this exercise. Oh, how polished I'll keep the spoons when I'm a shepherd. What soft bread, what cream, what garlands, what pastoral odds and ends that, if they don't earn me fame as a wise man, can't help but earn me fame as a clever one! Sanchica, my daughter, will bring food up to our flocks. But wait! She's a good-looking girl, and there are shepherds more wicked than simple, and I wouldn't want her to go for wool and come back shorn; love and unchaste desires are as likely in the countryside as in the cities, in shepherd's huts as in royal palaces, and if you take away the cause, you take away the sin, and if your eyes don't see, your heart doesn't break, and a jump over the thicket is better than the prayers of good men." (901)

Where **kings** go laws follow.

"They baptized me Teresa, a plain and simple name without any additions or decorations or trimmings of *Dons* or *Doñas;* my father's name was Cascajo, and because I'm your wife, they call me Teresa Panza, though they really ought to call me Teresa Cascajo. But where laws go kings follow [Teresa cites the proverb backward. It actually is "Where kings go laws follow"], and I'm satisfied with this name without anybody adding on a *Doña* that weighs so much I can't carry it, and I don't want to give people who see me walking around dressed in a countish or governorish way a chance to say: 'Look at the airs that sow is putting on! Yesterday she was busy pulling on a tuft of flax for spinning, and she went to Mass and covered her head with her skirts instead of a mantilla, and today she has a hoopskirt and brooches and airs, as if we didn't know who she was."' (488)

A **knight** (man) without a lady-love (woman) is like tree without leaves.
Cervantes: Having cleaned his armor and made a full helmet out of a simple headpiece, and having given a name to his horse and decided on one for himself, he [Don Quixote] realized that the only thing left for him to do was to find a lady to love; for the knight without a lady-love was a tree without leaves or fruit, a body without a soul. (23)

"I [Don Quixote] have said it many times before, and now I say it again: the knight errant without a lady is like a tree without leaves, a building without a foundation, a shadow without a body to cast it." (671)

As strong as a **laborer**.
"And how old is this lady who's being brought up to be a countess?" asked the Squire of the Wood.
    "Fifteen, give or take a couple of years," responded Sancho, "but she's as tall as a lance, and as fresh as a morning in April, and as strong as a laborer." (534)

From great **ladies**, great favors are expected.
"From great ladies, great favors are expected; the one your grace has granted me today cannot be repaid unless it is with my desire to see myself dubbed a knight errant so that I can spend all the days of my life serving so high a lady. I am a peasant, my name is Sancho Panza, I am married, I have children, and I serve as a squire; if with any of these things I can be of service to your highness, I will take less time to obey than your ladyship will to command." (676)

As meek as a **lamb**.
"No, of course not," said Sancho, who was close to them, "because my lady is as meek as a lamb: she's as soft as butter." (532)

As tall as a **lance**.
"And how old is this lady who's being brought up to be a countess?" asked the Squire of the Wood.
    "Fifteen, give or take a couple of years," responded Sancho, "but she's as tall as a lance, and as fresh as a morning in April, and as strong as a laborer." (534)

To sing like a **lark**.
The student responded: "He [Basilio] is the most agile youth we know, a great hurler of the bar, an excellent wrestler, a fine pelota player; he runs like a deer, leaps like a goat, and plays bowls as if he were en-

chanted; he sings like a lark, plays the guitar so well he makes it speak, and, most of all, he can fence with the best of them." (577-578)

The **laws** go where the kings command.

Doña Rodríguez responded: "My lady the duchess has duennas in her service who could be countesses if fortune so desired, but laws go where kings command; let no one speak ill of duennas, in particular those who are old and maidens, for although I am not one of those, I clearly understand and grasp the advantage a maiden duenna has over one who is widowed; and the person who cut us down to size still has the scissors in his hand."

    "All the same," replied Sancho, "there's so much to cut in duennas, according to my barber, that it would be better not to stir the rice even if it sticks." (703)

A good **lawsuit** is better than a bad payment.

Therefore, my dear Sancho, return to your house and tell your Teresa my intention, and if it pleases her and you to serve me without wages, *bene quidem*, and if not, we shall still be friends, for if the pigeon coop has plenty of feed, it will have plenty of pigeons. And remember, Sancho, that fine hopes are better than miserable possessions, and a good lawsuit [is] better than a bad payment. I [Don Quixote] am speaking in this manner, Sancho, so you may understand that, like you, I too know how to pour down rainstorms of proverbs. And, finally, I want to tell you, and I do tell you, that if you do not wish to accompany me without pay, and take the same risks I do, then God be with you and turn you into a saint, for I shall have no lack of squires more obedient, more solicitous, less uncouth, and less talkative than you." (499-500)

No **leaf** quivers on a tree unless God wills it.

"Trust in God, Sancho," said Don Quixote, "that everything will turn out well and perhaps even better than you expect; not a leaf quivers on a tree unless God wills it." (477)

To not come within two **leagues** of someone.

Doña Rodríguez said: "Your grace [Don Quixote] should keep in mind that my daughter is an orphan, and well-bred, and young, and possessed of all those gifts that I have mentioned to you, for by God and my conscience, of all the maidens that my mistress has, there is none that can even touch the sole of her shoe, and the one they call Altisidora, the one they consider the most elegant and spirited, can't come within two leagues of my daughter. Because I want your grace to know, Señor, that all that glitters is not gold; this little Altisidora has more vanity than beauty, and more spirit than modesty, and besides, she's not very healthy: she has breath so foul that you can't bear to be near her even for a moment. And then, my lady the duchess ... But I'd better be quiet, because they say that the walls have ears." (771)

To follow (obey) to the **letter**.
Don Quixote, at that very moment, without regard for the time or the hour, withdrew with the bachelor and the priest, and when they were alone he told them briefly about his defeat and the obligation he was under not to leave his village for a year, which he intended to obey to the letter and not violate in the slightest, as befitted a knight errant bound by the order and demands of knight errantry, and that he had thought of becoming a shepherd for the year and spending his time in the solitude of the countryside. (931)

Non bene pro toto **libertas** venditur auro.
As for citing in the margins the books and authors that were the source of the sayings and maxims you put into your history, all you have to do is insert some appropriate maxims or phrases in Latin, ones that you know by heart, or, at least, that won't cost you too much trouble to look up, so that if you speak of freedom and captivity, you can say:
Non bene pro toto libertas venditur auro
[Liberty cannot be bought for gold; from Aesop's fables]. (6)

If you have a long **life**, you go through a lot of bad times.
"I'm saying, Señora [a duchess]," he [Sancho] responded, "that in the courts of other princes I've heard that when the tables are cleared they pour water over your hands, but not lather on your bread; and that's why it's good to live a long time, because then you see a lot; though they also say that if you have a long life, you go through a lot of bad times, though going through one of these washings is more pleasure than trouble." (670)

Nothing in **life** is certain.
"Your grace, see if you can stand up, and we'll help Rocinante, though he doesn't deserve it, because he's the main reason for this beating. I [Sancho] never would have believed it of Rocinante; I always thought he was a person as chaste and peaceable as I am. Well, like they say, you need a long time to know a person, and nothing in this life is certain." (105-106)

There's more to **life** than trimming beards.
"I'm not pregnant by anybody," responded Sancho, "and I'm not a man who'd let himself get pregnant even by the king, and though I'm poor I'm an Old Christian, and I don't owe anything to anybody, and if I want ínsulas, other people want things that are worse; each man is the child of his actions, and because I'm a man I could be a pope, let alone the governor of an ínsula, especially since my master could win so many he might not have enough people to give them to. Your grace

should be careful what you say, Señor Barber, because there's more to life than trimming beards, and there's some difference between one Pedro and the other. I say this because we all know one another, and you can't throw crooked dice with me. As for the enchantment of my master, only God knows the truth, and let's leave it at that, because things get worse when you stir them." (411)

To get away with one's **life**.
Letter from Sancho Panza to Don Quixote: *And with this, may God free your grace from the evil intentions of enchanters, and take me from this governorship safe and sound, which I doubt, because according to how Dr. Pedro Recio treats me, I don't think I'll get away with more than my life.* (797)

Where there's **life** there's hope.
"The case was proved, nobody showed me favor, I [a prisoner] had no money, I almost had my gullet in a noose, they sentenced me to six years in the galleys, and I agreed: it's a punishment for my crime; I'm young; just let me stay alive, because where there's life there's hope." (167)

Not in someone's **lifetime**.
"Be content with your station," responded Teresa, "and don't try to go to a higher one; remember the proverb that says: 'Take your neighbor's son, wipe his nose, and bring him into your house.' Sure, it would be very nice to marry our María to some wretch of a count or gentleman who might take a notion to insult her and call her lowborn, the daughter of peasants and spinners! Not in my lifetime, my husband! I didn't bring up my daughter for that!" (487)

Like begets like.
Cervantes: But I have not been able to contravene the natural order; in it, like begets like. And so what could my barren and poorly cultivated wits beget but a history of a child who is dry, withered, capricious, and filled with inconstant thoughts never imagined by anyone else? (3)

Like goes to like.
"Try telling that to my wife!" said Sancho Panza, who so far had been listening in silence. "The only thing she wants is for everybody to marry their equal, following the proverb that says 'Like goes to like.' What I'd like is for this good Basilio, and I'm growing very fond of him, to marry Señora Quiteria; people who keep people who love each other from marrying should rest in peace, world without end, and I was going to say the opposite." (578)

To have a sounding **line** in one's hand.
"Señor Don Quixote," said the duchess, "I say that in everything your grace says you proceed with great caution and, as they say, with the sounding line in your hand." (672)

There are only two **lineages** in the world: the haves and the have-nots.
Sancho said: "To hell with Basilio's talents! You're worth what you have, and what you have is what you're worth. There are only two lineages in the world, as my grandmother used to say, and that's the haves and the have-nots, though she was on the side of having; nowadays, Señor Don Quixote, wealth is better than wisdom: an ass covered in gold seems better than a saddled horse. And so I say again that I'm on the side of Camacho, whose pots are overflowing with geese and chickens, hares and rabbits, while Basilio's, if they ever show up, and even if they don't, won't hold anything but watered wine." (589)

To lick one's **lips**.
"And it seems to me [Sancho] that in this business of governorships it's all a matter of starting, and it may be that after two weeks of being a governor I'll be licking my lips over the work and know more about it than working in the fields, which is what I've grown up doing." (680)

A lot of **littles** make a lot.
"It's taking me to this," said Sancho. "Your grace should tell me exactly what salary you'll give me for each month I serve you, and this salary should be paid to me from your estate; I don't want to depend on anybody's favors, which come late, or badly, or never; may God help me to tend to my own business. The point is, I want to know what I'm earning, whether it's a lot or a little; a hen sits on her egg, and a lot of littles make a lot, and as long as you're earning you don't lose a thing. And if it should happen, and I don't believe or expect that it will, that your grace gives me the ínsula you promised, I'm not such an ingrate, and not such a pennypincher, that I won't want the rent from the ínsula to be added up and deducted from my salary pro rat." (498-499)

You have to **live** a lot to see a lot.
"I'm saying, Señora [a duchess]," he [Sancho] responded, "that in the courts of other princes I've heard that when the tables are cleared they pour water over your hands, but not lather on your bread; and that's why it's good to live a long time, because then you see a lot; though they also say that if you have a long life, you go through a lot of bad times, though going through one of these washings is more pleasure than trouble." (670)

Letter from Teresa Panza to Sancho Panza: *And you know, dear husband, my mother used to say you had to live a lot to see a lot: I say this because I plan to see more if I live more, because I don't plan to stop until I see you as a landlord or a tax collector, for these are trades, after all, in which you always have and handle money, though the devil carries off anyone who misuses them.* (802-803)

One **loaf** is the same as a hundred.
Sancho responded that he would do as his master wished but would like to conclude this matter quickly, while his blood was hot and the grindstone rough, because in delay there is often danger, and pray to God and use the hammer, and one "here you are" was worth more than two "I'll give it to you," and a bird in hand was worth two in the bush.
    "By the one God, Sancho, no more proverbs," said Don Quixote. "It seems you are going back to *sicut erat* ["as it was before"]; speak plainly, and simply, and without complications, as I have often told you, and you will see how one loaf will be the same as a hundred for you." (924)

No **lock** protects a maiden better than her own virtue.
The goatherd said: "Her father [a farmer] watched over her [his daughter], and she watched over herself, for there are no locks or bars or bolts that protect a maiden better than her own modesty and virtue." (434)

To sleep like a **log**.
It was on the stroke of midnight, more or less, when Don Quixote and Sancho left the countryside and entered Toboso. The town lay in peaceful silence, because all the residents were in their beds and sleeping like logs, as the saying goes. (509)

What is **lost** today is won tomorrow.
"Be still, my friend," said the priest, "for it is God's will that fortune changes, and that what is lost today is won tomorrow; your grace should tend to your health now, for it seems to me your grace must be fatigued, if not badly wounded." (53)

Love and finery always walk hand in hand.
[Antonio sings]
    For love and finery
    always walk hand in hand,
    and in your eyes I wish
    always to seem gallant. (79)

Love and war are the same.
Don Quixote shouted: "Hold, Señores, hold, for it is not right to take revenge for the offenses that love commits; you should know that love and war are the same, and just as in war it is legitimate and customary to make use of tricks and stratagems to conquer the enemy, so in the contests and rivalries of love the lies and falsehoods used to achieve a de-

sired end are considered fair, as long as they do not discredit or dishonor the beloved." (595)

Love blinds the eyes (is blind).
"If all people who love each other were to marry," said Don Quixote, "it would deprive parents of the right and privilege to marry their children to the person and at the time they ought to marry; if daughters were entitled to choose their own husbands, one would choose her father's servant, and another a man she saw walking on the street, who seemed to her proud and gallant, although he might be a debauchee and a braggart; for love and affection easily blind the eyes of the understanding, which are so necessary for choosing one's estate, and the estate of matrimony is at particular risk of error, and great caution is required, and the particular favor of heaven, in order to choose correctly." (578)

Love looks through spectacles that make copper look like gold, poverty like riches, and dried rheum like pearls.
"God will find the cure," said Sancho, "for God gives the malady and also the remedy; nobody knows the future: there's a lot of hours until tomorrow, and in one of them, and even in a moment, the house can fall; I've seen it rain at the same time the sun is shining; a man goes to bed healthy and can't move the next day. And tell me, is there anybody who can boast that he's driven a nail into Fortune's wheel? No, of course not, and I wouldn't dare put the point of a pin between a woman's yes and no, because it wouldn't fit. Tell me that Quiteria loves Basilio with all her heart and all her soul, and I'll give him a sack of good fortune, because I've heard that love looks through spectacles that make copper look like gold, poverty like riches, and dried rheum like pearls." (579)

Love makes all things equal.
"So that you may see, Sancho, the virtue contained in knight errantry, and how those who practice any portion of it always tend to be honored and esteemed in the world, I [Don Quixote] want you to sit here at my side and in the company of these good people, and be the same as I, who am your natural lord and master; eat from my plate and drink where I drink, for one may say of knight errantry what is said of love: it makes all things equal." (75)

Love shows no restraint.
"You should know, Sancho," said Don Quixote, "that love shows no restraint, and does not keep within the bounds of reason as it proceeds, and has the same character as death: it attacks the noble palaces of kings as well as the poor huts of shepherds, and when it takes full pos-

session of a heart, the first thing it does is to take away fear and shame." (836)

Love sometimes flies and sometimes walks.

It happened once, when Camilla found herself alone with her maid, she said:

"I am mortified, my dear Leonela, to see how lightly I valued myself, for I did not even oblige Lotario to pay with time for the complete possession of my desire; I gave it to him so quickly, I fear he will judge only my haste or indiscretion, not taking into account that he urged me so strongly I could no longer resist him."

"Do not be concerned, Señora," responded Leonela. "Giving quickly is of little significance, and no reason to lessen esteem, if, in fact, what one gives is good and in itself worthy of esteem. They even say that by giving quickly, one gives twice."

"They also say," said Camila, "that what costs less is valued less."

"The argument doesn't apply to you," responded Leonela, "because love, I've heard it said, sometimes flies and sometimes walks; it runs with one, and goes slowly with another; it cools some and burns others; some it wounds, and others it kills; it begins the rush of its desires at one point, and at the same point it ends and concludes them; in the morning it lays siege to a fortress, and by nightfall it has broken through, because there is no power that can resist it." (293-294)

To die of **love**.
[Grisóstomo's Song]
  And the three-faced guardian of the gates
  of hell, chimeras, monsters by the thousands,
  let them intone the dolorous counterpoint;
  for there can be no better funeral rite
  than this, I think, for one to die of love. (97)

True **love** is not divided and must be voluntary.
"According to what I [Marcela] have heard, true love is not divided and must be voluntary, not forced. If this is true, as I believe it is, why do you want to force me to surrender my will, obliged to do so simply because you say you love me? But if this is not true, then tell me: if the heaven that made me beautiful had made me ugly instead, would it be fair for me to complain that none of you loved me?" (99)

Good **lovers** need to have the four Ss.
"Besides, Señora Camila, [said Leonela], you would not have given yourself or surrendered so quickly if you had not first seen in Lotario's eyes, words, sighs, promises, and gifts all his soul, or not seen in it and its virtues how worthy Lotario was of being loved. If this is true, do not allow those qualms and second thoughts to assault your imagination,

but be assured that Lotario esteems you as you esteem him, and live contented and satisfied that although you were caught in the snare of love, it is he who tightens it around you with his admiration and esteem. He not only has the four Ss that people say good lovers need to have, but a whole alphabet as well. [The four Ss that a lover needed to be were *sabio* ("wise"), *solo* ("alone"), *solicito* ("solicitous"), and *secreto* ("secretive")]. (294)

If **luck** comes knocking, don't shut the door in its face.
"Come here, you imbecile, you troublemaker," replied Sancho. "Why do you [Teresa] want to stop me now, and for no good reason, from marrying my daughter to somebody who'll give me grandchildren they'll call *Lord* and *Lady*? Look, Teresa: I've always heard the old folks say that if you don't know how to enjoy good luck when it comes, you shouldn't complain if it passes you by. It wouldn't be a good idea, now that it's come knocking, to shut the door in its face; we should let the favorable wind that's blowing carry us along." (487)

If you don't know how to enjoy good **luck** when it comes, you shouldn't complain if it passes you by.
"Come here, you imbecile, you troublemaker," replied Sancho. "Why do you [Teresa] want to stop me now, and for no good reason, from marrying my daughter to somebody who'll give me grandchildren they'll call *Lord* and *Lady*? Look, Teresa: I've always heard the old folks say that if you don't know how to enjoy good luck when it comes, you shouldn't complain if it passes you by. It wouldn't be a good idea, now that it's come knocking, to shut the door in its face; we should let the favorable wind that's blowing carry us along." (487)

As sharp-eyed as **lynxes**.
The priest and the bachelor recognized them [Don Quixote and Sancho Panza] immediately and came toward them with open arms. Don Quixote dismounted and embraced them warmly, and some boys, who are as sharp-eyed as lynxes, caught sight of the donkey's hat and hurried over to see it. (930)

A **man** must be a man, and a woman a woman.
"If I [Sancho] tried to work out exactly how much my salary would be, it was to please my wife; when she puts her hand to convincing you of something, no mallet can press down the hoops of a barrel the way she can press you to do what she wants, but the truth is, a man must be a man, and a woman a woman, and since I'm a man everywhere, which I cannot deny, I also want to be a man in my own house, no matter who's inside; and so, there's nothing more to do except for your grace to prepare your will and its codicil so it can't be resoaked [*sic*], and for us to be on our way soon." (501)

A poor **man** may have honor, but not a villain.
Cervantes: A poor man may have honor, but not a villain; need may cloud nobility, but not hide it completely; if virtue sheds her light, even along the crags and cracks of poverty, it will be esteemed by high, noble spirits, and so be favored. (458)

Each **man** is the architect of his own fortune.
"You sound very philosophical, Sancho," responded Don Quixote, "and you speak very wisely; I do not know who taught that to you. What I can say is that there is no fortune in the world, and the things that happen in it, whether good or bad, do not happen by chance but by the particular providence of heaven, which is why people say that each man is the architect of his own fortune." (893)

Each **man** is the child of his actions.
"I'm not pregnant by anybody," responded Sancho, "and I'm not a man who'd let himself get pregnant even by the king, and though I'm poor I'm an Old Christian, and I don't owe anything to anybody, and if I want ínsulas, other people want things that are worse; each man is the child of his actions, and because I'm a man I could be a pope, let alone the governor of an ínsula, especially since my master could win so many he might not have enough people to give them to. Your grace should be careful what you say, Señor Barber, because there's more to life than trimming beards, and there's some difference between one Pedro and the other. I say this because we all know one another, and you can't throw crooked dice with me. As for the enchantment of my master, only God knows the truth, and let's leave it at that, because things get worse when you stir them." (411)

Each **man** is the child of his deeds.
"That is of no importance," replied Don Quixote. "For there can be knights among Haldudos, especially since each man is the child of his deeds." (37)

Let each **man** look out for himself.
Sancho responded: Let each man look out for himself, though the best thing would be to let everybody's anger stay asleep; nobody knows another man's heart, and many who come for wool go home clipped and shorn, and God blessed peace and cursed fights, because if a cat that's hunted and locked up and treated badly turns into a lion, then since I'm a man, God knows what I could turn into, and so from now on I'm letting your grace know, Señor Squire, that all the harm and damage that result from our quarrel will be on your head." (542-543)

Let no **man** stretch his leg farther than the length of the sheet.
Sancho said: "I'll go back to walking on my feet on level ground, and if they're not adorned with cutout shoes of Cordoban leather, they won't

lack for sandals made of hemp. Every sheep with its mate, and let no man stretch his leg farther than the length of the sheet, and now let me pass, it's getting late." (808-809).

Man proposes, God disposes.
"Señor Commissary," the galley slave said, "just take it easy and let's not go around dropping all kinds of names and surnames. My name is Ginés, not Ginesillo, and my family is from Pasamonte, nor Parapilla, as you've said; and if each man looks to his own affairs, he'll have plenty to tend to." "Keep a civil tongue," replied the commissary, "you great thief, unless you want me to shut you up in a way you won't like." "It certainly seems," responded the galley slave, "that man proposes and God disposes, but one day somebody will know whether or not my name is Ginesillo de Parapilla." (168)

Sancho said: "It was eight or ten days ago, Brother Gossip, that I came to govern the ínsula that they gave me, and in all that time I didn't even have enough bread to eat; I've been persecuted by doctors and had my bones trampled by enemies, and I haven't had time to take any bribes or collect any fees, and this being true, which it is, in my opinion I didn't deserve to leave in this way; but man proposes and God disposes, and God knows what suits each man and what's best for him, and time changes the rhyme, and nobody should say, 'That's water I won't drink,' because you're in a place where you think there's bacon, and you don't even find a nail; God understands me, and that's enough, and I'll say no more, though I could." (821-822)

Stay close to a good **man** and become one.
"I am," responded Sancho, "and I'm the one who deserves it [an ínsula] as much as anybody else; I'm a 'Stay close to a good man and become one'; and I'm a 'Birds of a feather flock together'; and a 'Lean against a sturdy trunk if you want good shade.' I have leaned against a good master, and traveled with him for many months, and I'll become just like him, God willing; long life to him and to me, and there'll be no lack of empires for him to rule or ínsulas for me to govern." (666-667)

The **man** who does not get up with the sun does not possess the day.
Don Quixote said: "When you mount a horse, do not lean your body back over the hind bow of the saddle, or hold your legs stiff and sticking out at an angle from the belly of the horse, or ride so carelessly that it looks as if you were riding your donkey, for riding a horse makes gentlemen of some men and stable boys of others. Be moderate in your sleeping, for the man who does not get up with the sun does not possess the day; and remember, Sancho, that diligence is the mother of good fortune, and sloth, her opposite, never reached the conclusion demanded by good intentions." (734)

The **man** who falls today can pick himself up tomorrow.
"Enough of that, Señor [Don Quixote]," said Sancho. "Long live the hen, even with the pip; today it's your turn and tomorrow it's mine; these matters of clashes and blows shouldn't be taken too seriously, because the man who falls today can pick himself up tomorrow, unless he decides to stay in bed, I mean if he lets himself lose heart and doesn't find new spirit for new fights. And your grace should get up now to receive Don Gaspar Gregorio, because it seems to me that everybody's in an uproar, and he must be in the house by now." (890)

The **man** who sounds the alarm is safe.
Sancho writes to his wife Teresa Panza: *The man who sounds the alarm is safe, and it'll all come out in the wash of the governorship; what does make me very sad is that they've told me that if I try to take something away from it, I'll go hungry afterwards, and if that's true it won't be very cheap for me, though the maimed and wounded already have their soft job in the alms they beg; so one way or another, you'll be rich and have good luck.* (699)

"God can remedy that," responded Sancho, "because I know more proverbs than a book, and so many of them come into my mouth at one time when I talk that they fight with one another to get out, but my tongue tosses out the first ones it finds, even if they're not to the point. But I'll be careful from now on to say the ones that suit the gravity of my position, because in a well-stocked house, supper is soon cooked; and if you cut the cards, you don't deal; and the man who sounds the alarm is safe; and for giving and keeping, you need some sense." (733-734)

When a **man** least expects it, he finds himself with a staff in his hand or a mitre on his head.
A peasant said: "If the servant is this intelligent, what must the master be like! I'll bet if they went to study in Salamanca, in the wink of an eye they'd be magistrates; everything's deceit except studying and more studying, and having favor and good luck; when a man least expects it, he finds himself with a staff in his hand or a mitre on his head." (896)

When the brave **man** flees, trickery is revealed, and the prudent man waits for a better opportunity.
Cervantes: When the brave man flees, trickery is revealed, and the prudent man waits for a better opportunity. This truth was proved in Don Quixote, who yielded to the fury of the village and the evil intent of the enraged squadron and fled, not thinking of Sancho or the danger in which he left him, and rode the distance he thought sufficient to ensure his safety.. Sancho followed, lying across his donkey. (642)

Nothing costs less or is cheaper than good **manners**.

Sancho writes to his wife Teresa Panza: *My lady the duchess kisses your hands a thousand times; send her back two thousand, because there's nothing that costs less or is cheaper, as my master says, than good manners.* (699)

As hard as (harder than) **marble**.

Then they all turned to Quiteria, and some with pleas, and others with tears, and still others with persuasive arguments, urged her to give her hand to poor Basilio; she, as hard as marble and as motionless as a statue, showed that she could not and would not and did not wish to say a word, and she would not have responded at all if the priest had not told her to decide quickly what she was going to do, because Basilio's soul was between his teeth, and there was no time for her to be irresolute or indecisive. (594)

Altisidora said: "For two days, on account of the harshness with which you have treated me, O unfeeling knight, – Oh, harder than marble to my complaints! [the line is by Garcilaso]– I was indeed dead, or, at least, judged to be so by those who saw me; and if it had not been that Love took pity on me and placed the remedy in the sufferings of this good squire, I would have remained in the next world." (815)

To be off the **mark**.

He [Sancho] had been heard to say whenever he stumbled or fell that he would have been happy if he had never left his house, because the only thing one got from stumbling or falling was a torn shoe or broken ribs, and though he was a fool, in this he was not far off the mark. (503)
Sancho responded: "But the truth is that this time they're far off the mark, for I trust in the good sense of my master, who will consider that I don't have any curds, or milk, or anything else along those lines, and if I did, I'd put them in my stomach and not in your sallet helmet." (559)

To hit the **mark**.

"By Almighty God," said Don Quixote, "I swear that your highness has hit the mark, and that some evil illusion appeared before this sinner Sancho, making him see what it would have been impossible to see except by way of enchantment." (402)

Let **Marta** die but keep her belly full.

"That means," said Sancho, not stopping his rapid chewing, "that your grace doesn't agree with the proverb that says, 'Let Marta die but keep her belly full.' I, at least, don't plan to kill myself; instead, I plan to do what the shoemaker does when he pulls on the leather with his teeth and stretches it until it reaches as far as he wants: I'll stretch my life by eating until it reaches the end that heaven has arranged for it; you should know, Señor, that there's no greater madness than wanting to despair, the way your grace does; believe me, after you eat something, you should sleep a little on the green featherbed of this grass, and you'll see that when you wake up you'll feel much relieved." (843)

Do what your **master** tells you and sit with him at the table.
"Well, if that's true," responded Sancho, "and your grace at every step insists on finding nonsensical things, or whatever you call them, there's nothing I can do but obey, and bow my head, and follow the proverb that says, 'Do what your master tells you and sit with him at the table.'" (648)

What can be done by good **means** should not be done by bad.
"But, because I [Don Quixote] know that one of the rules of prudence is what can be done by good means should not be done by bad, I want to ask these gentlemen, the guards and the commissary, to be so good as to unchain you [gulley slaves] and let you go in peace." (170)

To do something for good **measure**.
The large grunting herd came running in great haste and confusion, and without showing respect for the authority of either Don Quixote or Sancho, they ran over them both, destroying Sancho's stockade and knocking down not only Don Quixote but Rocinante for good measure. (904)

There is no **memory** that time does not erase.
"Even though, I want you to know, brother Sancho," replied Don Quixote, "that there is no memory that time does not erase, no pain not ended by death." (107)

Wise **men** know to save something for tomorrow and not risk everything in a single day.
"Señor," responded Sancho, "withdrawing is not running away, and waiting is not sensible when danger outweighs hope, and wise men know to save something for tomorrow and not risk everything in a single day. And you should know that even though I'm rough and low-born, I still know something about what people call proper behavior." (174)

To be as old as **Methuselah**.
"By God, Señor," said Sancho, "the island that I can't govern at the age I am now I won't be able to govern if I get to be as old as Methuselah. The trouble is that this ínsula is hidden someplace, I don't know where, it's not that I don't have the good sense to govern it." (477)

To live as long as (longer than) **Methuselah**.
"And I want to tell you now who this girl is, because you ought to know; maybe, and maybe there's no maybe about it, you won't hear

anything like it in all your born days, even if you live to be as old as my mouth sores." "You mean *Methuselah* [Genesis 5:27], replied Don Quixote, unable to tolerate the goatherd's [Pedro] confusion of words. "My mouth sores last a good long time," Pedro responded, "and if, Señor, you keep correcting every word I say, we won't finish in a year." (83)

"By God, your grace [Don Antonio] is right," responded the Castilian. "Giving this good man [Don Quixote] advice is like kicking at thorns; even so, it makes me very sad that the good sense everyone says this fool has in other matters should run out into the gutter of his knight errantry; as for the bad luck your grace mentioned, let it be for me and all my descendants if after today, though I live longer than Methuselah, I ever give advice to anybody again, even if he asks for it." (867)

Choose the **middle** between two extremes.
Letter from Don Quixote to Sancho Panza: *Be a father to virtues and a stepfather to vices. Do not always be severe, or always mild, but choose the middle way between those two extremes; this is the object of wisdom. Visit the prisons, the slaughterhouses, and the market squares, for the presence of the governor in these places is of great importance: it consoles the prisoners, who can hope for a quick release; it frightens the butchers, who then make their weights honest; it terrifies the mar-ketwomen, and for the same reason.* (794)

To be out of one's **mind**.
"My God!" said Sancho. "Your grace must be out of your mind! Like people say: 'You see I'm in a hurry and you demand virginity!' Now that I have to sit on a bare board, your grace wants me to flog my bottom? Really and truly, your grace is wrong. Let's go now and shave those duennas, and when we get back I promise your grace, like the man I am, to fulfill my obligation so fast it will make your grace happy, and that's all I have to say." (720)

To drive out of one's **mind**.
Sancho said: "Look, Señor Doctor, from now on don't bother about giving me delicate or exquisite things to eat, because that will drive my stomach out of its mind: it's used to goat, beef, bacon, dried meat, tur-nips, and onions, and if by some chance it's given palace dishes, it gets finicky, and sometimes even sick." (773)

Misery loves company.
"There's no road so smooth," replied Sancho, "that it doesn't have some obstacle or stumbling block; they cook beans everywhere, but in my house they do it by the potful; craziness must have more compan-ions and friends than wisdom. But if what they say is true, that misery

loves company, then I can find comfort with your grace, because you serve a master who's as great a fool as mine." (535-536)

Misfortunes always pursue the villains.
"You seem clever," said Don Quixote. And unfortunate," responded Ginés, "because misfortunes always pursue the talented." "They pursue villains," said the commissary. (169)

To be made from the same **mold**.
"You'll see, compadre, that when we least expect it, our gentleman will leave again and beat the bushes, putting all the birds to flight."
    "I have no doubt about that," responded the barber, "but I'm not as astounded by the madness of the knight as I am by the simplicity of the squire, who has so much faith in the story of the ínsula that I don't believe all the disappointments imaginable will ever get it out of his head."
    "May God help them," said the priest, "and let us be on the alert: we'll see where all the foolishness in this knight and squire will lead, because it seems as if both were made from the same mold, and that the madness of the master, without the simplicity of the servant, would not be worth anything." (470)

To ask for the **moon**.
"Is my lady Dulcinea, by some chance, more beautiful? No, certainly not, not even by half, and I'd [Sancho] go so far as to say she can't even touch the shoes of the lady [Dorotea] we have before us. So woe is me, I'll never get the rank I'm hoping for if your grace goes around asking for the moon. Marry, marry right now." (254)

"By my faith, Señor [Don Quixote], I think a poor man should be content with whatever he finds and not go asking for the moon." (583)

As fresh as a **morning** in April.
"And how old is this lady who's being brought up to be a countess?" asked the Squire of the Wood.
    "Fifteen, give or take a couple of years," responded Sancho, "but she's as tall as a lance, and as fresh as a morning in April, and as strong as a laborer." (534)

Pallida **mors** aequo pulsat pede pauperum tabernas, regumque turres.
And then, in the margin, you cite Horace or whoever it was who said it. If the subject if the power of death, you can use:
    Pallida mors aequo pulsat pede pauperum tabernas,
    Regumque turres.
    [Pale death comes both to the hovel of the poor wretch
    and the palace of the mighty king; from Horace]. (6)

You can see a **mote** in another's eye but cannot see a beam in your own. (Matthew 7:3)
Sancho said: "So whoever sees the mote in somebody else's eye has to see the beam in his own, so that nobody can say about him: 'The dead woman was frightened by the one with her throat cut.' And your grace knows very well that the fool knows more in his own house than the wise man does in somebody else's." (736)

My **mother** punishes me, and I deceive her.
"No more proverbs, Sancho," said Don Quixote, "for any one of those you have said is enough to explain your thoughts; I have often advised you not to be so prodigal in your proverbs and to restrain yourself from saying them, but it seems that is like preaching in the desert, and 'My mother punishes me, and I deceive her.'"
"It seems to me," responded Sancho, "that your grace is like the pot calling the kettle black. You reprove me for saying proverbs, and your grace strings them together two at a time." (901-902)

A **mouth** without molars is like a mill without a millstone.
"I [Don Quixote] should rather have lost an arm, as long as it was not the one that wields my sword. For I must tell you, Sancho, that a mouth without molars is like a mill without a millstone, and dentation is to be valued much more than diamonds." (133)

To be like the inside of a wolf's **mouth**.
As soon as Don Quixote had finished saying this, the doors of his room banged open, and Doña Rodríguez was so startled that the candle dropped from her hand, and the room was left like the inside of a wolf's mouth, as the saying goes. (771-772)

To sew up one's **mouth**.
"I'll show them to you at home," said Panza, "and for now be happy, because if it's God's will that we go out again in search of adventures, in no time you'll see me made a count, or the governor of an ínsula, and not any of the ones around here, but the best that can be found."
"May it please God, my husband, because we surely need it. But tell me, what's all this about ínsulas? I don't understand."
"Honey's not for the donkey's mouth," responded Sancho. "In time you will, dear wife, and even be amazed to hear yourself called ladyship by all your vassals."
"What are you saying, Sancho, about ladyships, ínsulas, and vassals?" responded Juana Panza, which was the name of Sancho's wife; they were not kin, but in La Mancha wives usually take their husbands' family name.
"Don't be in such a hurry, Juana, to learn everything all at once; it's enough that I'm telling you the truth, so sew up your mouth. I'll

just tell you this, in passing: there's nothing nicer in the world for a man than being the honored squire of a knight errant seeking adventures." (444)

Sancho promised very earnestly that he would sew up his mouth or bite his tongue before speaking a word that was not fitting and carefully considered, just as his master had ordered, and Don Quixote did not need to worry about that anymore, for never through him would it be discovered who they really were. (661)

Where there is **music**, there can be nothing bad (no harm).
Then something else was heard, not a noise, but the sound made by soft and harmonious music, which made Sancho very happy, and which he took as a good omen; and so, he said to the duchess, from whose side he had moved not one iota:
    "Señora, where there is music, there can be nothing bad." (689-690)

You shouldn't play **music** unless you know how.
"May God forgive him [Avellaneda, the author of another *Don Quixote*]," said Sancho. "He should have left me in my corner and forgotten about me, because you shouldn't play music unless you know how, and St. Peter's just fine in Rome." (847)

To drive a **nail** into fortune's wheel.
"God will find the cure," said Sancho, "for God gives the malady and also the remedy; nobody knows the future: there's a lot of hours until tomorrow, and in one of them, and even in a moment, the house can fall; I've seen it rain at the same time the sun is shining; a man goes to bed healthy and can't move the next day. And tell me, is there anybody who can boast that he's driven a nail into Fortune's wheel? No, of course not, and I wouldn't dare put the point of a pin between a woman's yes and no, because it wouldn't fit. Tell me that Quiteria loves Basilio with all her heart and all her soul, and I'll give him a sack of good fortune, because I've heard that love looks through spectacles that make copper look like gold, poverty like riches, and dried rheum like pearls." (579)

As **naked** as the day one was born.
"I shall take you [Sancho]," said Don Quixote, "Don Peasant, you churl stuffed with garlic, and I shall tie you to a tree as naked as the day you were born, and I shall give you not three thousand and three hundred, but six thousand and six hundred lashes, and they will go so deep that they will not come off even if you pull them three thousand and three hundred times. And if you say a word to me, I shall tear out your soul." (692)

Naked I was born, and naked I'll die.
"I don't say it and I don't think it," responded Sancho. "It's their affair and let them eat it with their bread; whether or not they were lovers, they've already made their accounting with God; I tend to my vines, it's their business, not mine; I don't stick my nose in; if you buy and lie, your purse wants to know why. Besides, naked I was born, and naked I'll die: I don't lose or gain a thing; whatever they were, it's all the same to me. And many folks think there's bacon when there's not even a hook to hang it on. But who can put doors on a field? Let them say what they please, I don't care." (191-192)

Sancho said: "In fact, I came into the governorship naked, and I left it naked, and so I can say with a clear conscience, which is no small thing: 'Naked I was born, and I'm naked now: I haven't lost or gained a thing.'" (828)

A good **name** is worth more than great wealth.
"So nobody should blame me, and since I [Sancho] have a good reputation, and I've heard my master say that a good name's worth more than great wealth, just let them pass this governorship on to me and they'll see marvels, because whoever's been a good squire will be a good governor." (682)

To drag one's **name** through the streets.
Sancho responded: "My good name must be turned upside down and dragged helter-skelter and hither and yon, as they say, through the streets." (504)

To drop **names**.
"Señor Commissary," the galley slave said, "just take it easy and let's not go around dropping all kinds of names and surnames. My name is Ginés, not Ginesillo, and my family is from Pasamonte, nor Parapilla, as you've said; and if each man looks to his own affairs, he'll have plenty to tend to." "Keep a civil tongue," replied the commissary, "you great thief, unless you want me to shut you up in a way you won't like." "It certainly seems," responded the galley slave, "that man proposes and God disposes, but one day somebody will know whether or not my name is Ginesillo de Parapilla." (168)

Need may cloud nobility, but not hide it completely.
Cervantes: A poor man may have honor, but not a villain; need may cloud nobility, but not hide it completely; if virtue sheds her light, even along the crags and cracks of poverty, it will be esteemed by high, noble spirits, and so be favored. (458)

To stick one's **nose** into something.
"I don't say it and I don't think it," responded Sancho. "It's their affair
and let them eat it with their bread; whether or not they were lovers,
they've already made their accounting with God; I tend to my vines,
it's their business, not mine; I don't stick my nose in; if you buy and
lie, your purse wants to know why. Besides, naked I was born, and naked I'll die: I don't lose or gain a thing; whatever they were, it's all the
same to me. And many folks think there's bacon when there's not even
a hook to hang it on. But who can put doors on a field? Let them say
what they please, I don't care." (191-192)

As hard as an **oak**.
"This wicked man seized me in the middle of a field, and used my body
like a dirty old rag, and, oh woe is me, he took what I [a woman] had
safeguarded for more than twenty-three years, defending it against
Moors and Christians, Spaniards and foreigners, and I, always as hard
as an oak, kept myself pure like the salamander in the fire, or wool in
the brambles, just so this good man would come along now and put his
clean hands all over me." (751)

Offices alter behavior.
"You, brother Sancho," said Carrasco, "have spoken like a university
professor, but still, trust in God and in Señor Don Quixote, who will
give you a kingdom, not merely an ínsula."
    "Whatever it is, it's all the same to me," responded Sancho,
"though I can tell Señor Carrasco that my master won't be tossing that
kingdom into a sack with holes in it; I've taken my own pulse and I'm
healthy enough to rule kingdoms and govern ínsulas, and this is something I've already told my master."
    "Be careful, Sancho," said Sansón, "for offices can alter behavior,
and it might be that when you are governor you won't know the mother
who bore you." (484)

Oil rises above water.
"That may well be true," replied the bachelor, "but *dubitat Augustinus*."
    "No matter who doubts it," responded the page, "the truth is what I
have said, and truth will always rise above a lie, as oil rises above water." (789)

To seize **opportunity** by the forelock.
"It is, therefore, easier for me [Don Quixote] to imitate him in this fashion than by cleaving giants in two, beheading serpents, slaying dragons,
routing armies, thwarting armadas, and undoing enchantments. And
since this terrain is so appropriate for achieving that end, there is no
reason not to seize Opportunity by the forelock when it is convenient to
do so." (193)

Doubtful **outcomes** should make men bold.
The admiral general asked: "Tell me, ill-advised dog, who urged you [a young captain] to kill my soldiers when you saw it was impossible to escape? Is that the respect you show to flagships? Don't you know that temerity is not valor? Doubtful outcomes should make men bold, not rash." (879)

The **ox** who is free can lick where he pleases.
"What are you mumbling about, Sancho?"
"I'm not saying anything, and I'm not mumbling anything," responded Sancho. "I was just saying to myself that I wish I'd heard what your grace [Don Quixote] said here before I married; maybe then I'd be saying now: 'The ox who's free can lick where he pleases.'" (598)

You should not blame the **packsaddle** for the donkey's mistake.
"Your grace [Don Quixote] is right," responded Sancho, "because according to wise men, you shouldn't blame the packsaddle for the donkey's mistake, and since your grace is to blame for what happened, you should punish yourself and not turn your anger against your battered and bloody arms, or the gentle Rocinante, or my tender feet by wanting them to walk more than is fair." (894)

There is no **pain** that death does not end.
"Even though, I want you to know, brother Sancho," replied Don Quixote, "that there is no memory that time does not erase, no pain not ended by death." (107)

To grease someone's **palm**.
"Well, I [Sancho] swear that if they bring me another patient [like Altisidora], before I cure anybody they'll have to grease my palm, because if the abbot sings he eats his supper, and I don't want to believe that heaven gave me this virtue to use for others at no charge." (918)

The **path** of virtue is narrow, and the road of wickedness is broad.
Don Quixote responded: "I know that the path of virtue is very narrow, and the road of wickedness is broad and spacious; I know that their endings and conclusions are different, because the expansive, spacious road of wickedness ends in death, and the road of virtue, so narrow and difficult, ends in life, not the life that ends, but life everlasting." (495)

Have **patience** and shuffle the deck.
"'And if this is not the case,' responded the mournful Durandarte in a low, faint voice, 'if this is not the case, dear cousin, I say have patience and shuffle the deck.'" (608)

"Durandarte said: 'Have patience and shuffle the deck.' And these words and manner of speaking he could not have learned while he was enchanted but when he was not." (615)

As splendid as **pearls**.
He [Sancho] was so disgusted by this that his stomach turned over and he vomited his innards all over his master, and the two of them were left as splendid as pearls. (131)

To be like **pearls** in the dungheap.
The gentleman responded: "I would like him [his son] to be the crown of his lineage, for we live in a time when our kings richly reward the good, virtuous letters, for letters without virtue are pearls in the dungheap." (555)

To be like asking **pears** of an elm tree.
I [Ginés de Pasamonte] mean to say, that we will take up our chain and set out for Toboso, is to think that night has fallen now when it is not yet ten in the morning; asking that of us is like asking pears of an elm tree." "Well, then, I do swear," said Don Quixote, his wrath rising, "Don Whoreson, Don Ginesillo de Paropilla, or whatever your name is, that you will go alone, your tail between your legs, and the entire chain on your back!" (171-172)

To fit like **pears** in a wicker basket.
"By God, my lord and master," replied Sancho, "your grace complains about very small things. Why the devil does it trouble you when I make use of my fortune, when I have no other, and no other wealth except proverbs and more proverbs? And right now four have come to mind that are a perfect fit, like pears in a wicker basket, but I won't say them, because golden silence is what they call Sancho." (736)

To be like two **peas** in a pod.
"The devil take me," said Sancho to himself, "if this master of mine isn't a theologian, and if he isn't, then he's as much like one as two peas in a pod." (641)

Tantum **pellis** et ossa fuit.
Then he [Don Quixote] went to look at his nag, and though its hooves had more cracks than his master's pate and it showed more flaws than Gonnella's horse, that *tantum pellis et ossa fuit* [was nothing but skin and bones], it seemed to him that Alexander's Bucephalus and El Cid's Babieca were not its equal. (22)

To be a pennypincher.
"It's taking me to this," said Sancho. "Your grace should tell me exactly what salary you'll give me for each month I serve you, and this salary should be paid to me from your estate; I don't want to depend on anybody's favors, which come late, or badly, or never; may God help me to tend to my own business. The point is, I want to know what I'm earning, whether it's a lot or a little; a hen sits on her egg, and a lot of

littles make a lot, and as long as you're earning you don't lose a thing. And if it should happen, and I don't believe or expect that it will, that your grace gives me the ínsula you promised, I'm not such an ingrate, and not such a pennypincher, that I won't want the rent from the ínsula to be added up and deducted from my salary pro rat." (498-499)

The **person** who gives you a bone doesn't want to see you dead.
Sancho's letter to his wife said: *I am sending you, my dear, a string of corals with gold beads; I'd be happy if they were Oriental pearls, but the person who gives you a bone doesn't want to see you dead [the meaning* "A person cannot do more than give you what he has"]; *one day we shall meet and communicate with each other, God knows when that will be. Remember me to your daughter, Sanchica, and tell her for me that she should get ready, because I plan to arrange an excellent marriage for her when she least expects it.* (785)

The **person** who has not eaten by two in the afternoon has more than enough misfortune.
"I [Sancho] may be a fool, but I understand the proverb that says, 'It did him harm when the ant grew wings,' and it might even be that Sancho the squire will enter heaven more easily than Sancho the governor. The bread they bake here is as good as in France, and at night every cat is gray, and the person who hasn't eaten by two in the afternoon has more than enough misfortune, and no stomach's so much bigger than any other that it can't be filled, as they say, with straw and hay [the actual proverb is "Straw and hay and hunger's away"], and the little birds of the field have God to protect and provide for them." (679)

Che **pesce** pigliamo?
Don Quixote asked: "Señor Soothsayer, can your grace tell me *che pesce pigliamo* [what fish are we catching, that is, what are we up to, what are we doing?]? What will become of us?" (624)

To paint a **picture**.
"There is a remedy for everything except death," responded Don Quixote, "for if we have a ship along the coast, we can embark on that even if the whole world attempts to prevent it."
 "Your grace paints a very nice picture and makes it seem very easy," said Sancho, "but there's many a slip 'tween cup and lip, and I'll depend on the renegade, who looks to me like an honest and good-hearted man." (884)

To tear oneself to **pieces**.
"Be careful, my friend, not to tear yourself to pieces; pause between lashes; do not try to race so quickly that you lose your breath in the middle of the course; I [Don Quixote] mean, you should not hit yourself so hard that you lose your life before you reach the desired number.

And to keep you from losing by a card too many or too few, I shall stand to one side and count the lashes you administer on my rosary. May heaven favor you as your good intentions deserve."

"A man who pays his debts doesn't care about guaranties," responded Sancho. "I plan to lash myself so that it hurts but doesn't kill me: that must be the point of this miracle." (921)

If the **pigeon coop** has plenty of feed, it will have plenty of pigeons.
"Therefore, my dear Sancho, return to your house and tell your Teresa my intention, and if it pleases her and you to serve me without wages, *bene quidem*, and if not, we shall still be friends, for if the pigeon coop has plenty of feed, it will have plenty of pigeons. And remember, Sancho, that fine hopes are better than miserable possessions, and a good lawsuit [is] better than a bad payment. I [Don Quixote] am speaking in this manner, Sancho, so you may understand that, like you, I too know how to pour down rainstorms of proverbs. And, finally, I want to tell you, and I do tell you, that if you do not wish to accompany me without pay, and take the same risks I do, then God be with you and turn you into a saint, for I shall have no lack of squires more obedient, more solicitous, less uncouth, and less talkative than you." (499-500)

To go from **pillar** to post.
Sancho said: "And what's clear to me in all this is that in the long run, these adventures we're looking for will bring us so many misadventures that we won't know our right foot from our left. And the better and smarter thing, to the best of my poor understanding, would be for us to go back home now it's harvesttime, and tend to our own affairs, and stop going from pillar to post and from bad to worse, as they say." (125)

To be on **pins** and needles.
Don Quixote was on pins and needles, as the saying goes, until he could hear and learn about the marvels promised by the man carrying the weapons. (620)

Harder than the **pit** of a date.
Altisidora said: "Good Lord! Don Codfish [Don Quixote], with a soul of metal, like the pit of a date harder and more stubborn that a peasant when he has his mind set on something, if I get near you I'll scratch out your eyes!" (916)

It doesn't matter if the **pitcher** hits the stone or the stone hits the pitcher: it will be bad for the pitcher.
"Therefore, from this day forward, we must treat each other with more respect and refrain from mockery, because no matter why I [Don Quixote] lose my temper with you, it will be bad for the pitcher. The rewards and benefits that I have promised you will come in time, and if

they do not, your wages, at least, will not be lost, as I have already told you." (151-152)

"That Sancho is not you," said Don Quixote, "because not only are you not golden silence, you are foolish speech and stubborn persistence, but even so I should like to know which four proverbs came to mind just now that were so to the point, because I have been searching my mind, and I have a good one, and I cannot think of a single proverb."

"Which ones could be better," said Sancho, "than 'Never put your thumbs between two wisdom teeth' and 'There's no answer to get out of my house and what do you want with my wife' and 'Whether the pitcher hits the stone or the stone hits the pitcher, it's bad luck for the pitcher'? They're all just fine. Because nobody should take on his governor or the person in authority because he'll come out of it hurt, like the man who puts his finger between two wisdom teeth, and if they're not wisdom teeth but just plain molars, it doesn't matter; and there's no reply to what the governor says, like the 'Leave my house and what do you want with my wife.' As for the stone and the pitcher, even a blind man can see that. So whoever sees the mote in somebody else's eye has to see the beam in his own, so that nobody can say about him: 'The dead woman was frightened by the one with her throat cut.' And your grace knows very well that the fool knows more in his own house than the wise man does in somebody else's." (736)

Each **place** has its ways.
"Señor," responded Sancho, "each place has its ways: maybe here in Toboso the custom is to build palaces and large buildings in lanes, and so I beg your grace to let me look along these streets and lanes that I see here; maybe at some corner I'll run into that castle." (510)

To put someone in one's **place**.
Teresa Panza said: "By my faith, we're not poor relations anymore! We have a nice little governorship! And if the proudest of the gentlewomen tries to snub me now, I'll know how to put her in her place!" (786)

To bring (hand) on a silver **platter**.
Sancho responded: "I say again that your grace can stop if you want to, because even if she's [a mare] is brought to him [a horse] on a silver platter, I'm sure our horse won't even look your mare in the face." (552)

Sancho said: "By God, I'm as likely to stay here, or accept another governorship, even if they handed it to me on a platter, as I am to fly up to heaven without wings." (808)

To be to the **point**.

Sancho said: "Good: your [a young man] answers are right to the point! You're clever, boy, but you should know that I'm the air, and I'm blowing at your back and sending you to prison. You there, seize him and take him away, and I'll make him sleep without any air tonight!" (777)

The priest said: "I can't help thinking that everyone in the Panza family was born with a sack of proverbs inside; I've never seen one of them who isn't always scattering proverbs around in every conversation they have."

"That's true," said the page, "for Señor Governor Sancho says them all the time, and even though many are not to the point, they still give pleasure, and my lady the duchess and my lord the duke praise them a good deal." (788-789)

"Look, Sancho," responded Don Quixote, "I say proverbs when they are appropriate, and when I say them they fit like the rings on your fingers, but you drag them in by the hair, and pull them along, and do not guide them, and if I remember correctly, I have already told you that proverbs are brief maxims derived from the experience and speculation of wise men in the past, and if the proverb is not to the point, it is not a maxim, it is nonsense." (902)

To get (come) to the **point**.

"That's fine," said Sancho. "You [a farmer] should realize, brother, that now you've painted her [a maiden] from head to toe. What is it that you want? And get to the point without beating around the bush or going around in circles, or taking anything away or adding anything to it." (764)

"Now, Señor Governor [Sancho]," the young man responded with great charm, "let's use our reason and come to the point. Suppose, your grace, that you order me taken to prison, and there I'm put in irons and chains, and placed in a cell, and the warden will suffer great penalties if he lets me out, and he obeys every order you give him; even so, if I don't want to sleep, and stay awake the whole night without closing my eyes, is all your grace's power enough to make me sleep if I don't want to?" (777)

With **pomp** and circumstance.

"Indeed, good squire," responded the lady, "you have delivered your message with all the pomp and circumstance that such messages demand. Rise up from the ground; it is not right for the squire of so great a knight as the Knight of the Sorrowful Face, about whom we have heard so much, to remain on his knees: arise, friend, and tell your master that he is very welcome to serve me and my husband, the duke, on a country estate we have nearby." (654)

If the **poor** kneads and bakes, you can't steal his cakes.
"As for governing them well," responded Sancho, "there's no need to charge me with it, because I'm charitable by nature and have compassion for the poor; and if he kneads and bakes, you can't steal his cakes; by my faith, they won't throw me any crooked dice; I'm an old dog and understand every here, boy [the proverb says: "You don't need here, boy, here, boy, with an old dog"], and I know how to wake up at the right time, and I don't allow cobwebs in front of my eyes, because I know if the shoe fits: I say this because with me good men will have my hand and a place in my house [the phrase means "trust and confidence"], and bad men won't get a foot or permission to enter." (680)

The **pot** calls the kettle black.
"No more proverbs, Sancho," said Don Quixote, "for any one of those you have said is enough to explain your thoughts; I have often advised you not to be so prodigal in your proverbs and to restrain yourself from saying them, but it seems that is like preaching in the desert, and 'My mother punishes me, and I deceive her.'"

"It seems to me," responded Sancho, "that your grace is like the pot calling the kettle black. You reprove me for saying proverbs, and your grace strings them together two at a time." (901-902)

To sing someone's **praises**.
"I am Don Quixote of La Mancha, also known as the Knight of the Sorrowful Face, and although praising oneself is vile, I am obliged perhaps to sing my own praises, which is understandable since there is no one present to do it for me; and so, Señor, neither this horse nor this lance, this shield nor this squire, nor all of my armor, nor my sallow face and extreme thinness: none of this should surprise you now, for I have told you who I am and the profession I follow." (553)

Being a good **preacher** means a good life.
"Enough, Sancho," said Don Quixote at this point. "Stop now before you fall, for the truth is that what you have said about death, in your rustic terms, is what a good preacher might say. I tell you, Sancho, with your natural wit and intelligence, you could mount a pulpit and go around preaching some very nice things."

"Being a good preacher means living a good life," responded Sancho, "and I don't know any other theologies."

"You do not need them," said Don Quixote, "but I cannot understand or comprehend how, since the beginning of wisdom is the fear of God, you, who fear a lizard more than you fear Him, can know so much." (590)

To sit **pretty**.
"If the master is as clever as his servant," responded the duenna, "then we're certainly sitting pretty! Go on, brother, and may bad luck follow you and whoever brought you here, and take care of your jackass yourself; the duennas in this house are not accustomed to duties of that nature." (659)

Pride is the greatest sin.
Don Quixote said: "Although some say pride is the greatest sin men commit, I say it is ingratitude, for I am guided by the adage that says hell is filled with the ungrateful. This sin is one I have attempted to flee, as much as it was possible for me to do so, since I first reached the age of reason; if I cannot repay the good deeds done for me with other deeds, in their place I put the desire I have to perform them, and if that is not enough, I proclaim those good deeds far and wide, because the person who tells about and proclaims the good deeds that have been performed on his behalf would also recompense them with other deeds if he could, because most of the time those who receive are subordinate to those who give." (839)

Promises are simple to make and difficult to keep.
Don Quixote responded: ""Good duenna [Doña Rodríguez], moderate your tears, or, I should say, dry them, and hold back your sighs, for I take it as my responsibility to assist your daughter, who should not have been so ready to believe lovers' promises, which are simple to make and very difficult to keep; and so, with the permission of my lord the duke, I shall leave immediately to look for this heartless young man, and I shall find him, and challenge him, and kill him if and when he refuses to keep the promise he made, for the principal intention of my profession is to forgive the humble and punish the proud, I mean to say, to assist the unfortunate and destroy the cruel." (799)

The **proof** is in the pudding.
Sancho responded: "As for the giant's head, or, I should say, the slashed wineskins, and the blood being red wine, by God I'm not mistaken, because the wounded wineskins are there, at the head of your grace's bed, and the red wine has formed a lake in the room; if you don't believe me, the proof is in the pudding [variant of the longer proverb "The proof of the pudding is in the eating"], I mean, you'll have your proof when his grace the innkeeper asks you to pay damages for everything." (325)

Escaping **punishment** is worth more than the pleading of good men.
"And that's where something else comes in, too," said Sancho, "because some wicked people say: 'Don't ask as a favor what you can take by force,' though what fits even better is: 'Escaping punishment is

worth more than the pleading of a good men.' I say this because if my lord the king, your grace's father-in-law, does not agree to giving you my lady the princess, there's nothing else to do, like your grace says, but abduct her and hide her away." (161)

If you buy and lie, your **purse** wants to know why.
"I don't say it and I don't think it," responded Sancho. "It's their affair and let them eat it with their bread; whether or not they were lovers, they've already made their accounting with God; I tend to my vines, it's their business, not mine; I don't stick my nose in; if you buy and lie, your purse wants to know why. Besides, naked I was born, and naked I'll die: I don't lose or gain a thing; whatever they were, it's all the same to me. And many folks think there's bacon when there's not even a hook to hang it on. But who can put doors on a field? Let them say what they please, I don't care." (191-192)

Rain falls alike on the just and unjust.
Don Quixote responded: "But be that as it may, mount your donkey, my good Sancho, and follow me, for God, who provides all things, will not fail us, especially since we are so much in His service, when He does not fail the gnats in the air, or the grubs in the earth, or the tadpoles in the water. He is so merciful that He makes His sun to shine on the good and the evil and His rain to fall on the just and the unjust." (132)

To look for a María in **Ravenna**.
"Don't rely on that Sancho, because Manchegans are as quick-tempered as they are honorable, and they don't put up with anything from anybody. By God, if they suspect what you're up to, then I predict bad luck for you." "Get out, you dumb bastard! Let the lighting strike somebody else! Not me, I'm not going to look for trouble to please somebody else! Besides, looking for Dulcinea in Toboso will be like looking for a María in Ravenna or a bachelor in Salamanca. The devil, the devil and nobody else has gotten me into this!"
Sancho held this soliloquy with himself. (515)

There is a **remedy** for everything except death.
Sancho said to himself: "Well now: everything has a remedy except death, under whose yoke we all have to pass, even if we don't want to, when our life ends. I've seen a thousand signs in this master of mine that he's crazy enough to be tied up, and I'm not far behind, I'm as much a fool as he is because I follow and serve him, if that old saying is true: 'Tell me who your friends are and I'll tell you who you are,' and that other one that says, 'Birds of a feather flock together.' Then, being crazy, which is what he is, with the kind of craziness that most of the time takes one thing for another, and thinks white is black and black

is white, like the time he said that the windmills were giants, and the friars' mules dromedaries, and the flocks of sheep enemy armies, and many other things of that nature." (515-516)

"I know how to sign my name very well," responded Sancho, "because when I was steward of a brotherhood in my village, I learned to make some letters like the marks on bundles, and they told me that they said my name; better yet, I'll pretend that my right hand has been hurt, and I'll have somebody else sign for me; there's a remedy for everything except death, and since I'll be in charge of everything, I can do whatever I want; then, too, when your father's the magistrate... [you're safe when you go to trial]. And being a governor, which is more than being a magistrate, just let them come and they'll see what happens! No, let them make fun of me and speak ill of me: they'll come for wool and go home shorn; and when God loves you, your house knows it; and the rich man's folly passes for good judgment in the world; and since that's what I'll be, being a governor and a very generous one, which is what I plan to be, nobody will notice any faults in me. No, just be like honey and the flies will go after you; you're only worth as much as you have, my grandmother used to say; and you won't get revenge on a well-established man." (735)

"There is a remedy for everything except death," responded Don Quixote, "for if we have a ship along the coast, we can embark on that even if the whole world attempts to prevent it."

"Your grace paints a very nice picture and makes it seem very easy," said Sancho, "but there's many a slip 'tween cup and lip, and I'll depend on the renegade, who looks to me like an honest and good-hearted man." (884)

You won't get **revenge** on a well-established man.
"I know how to sign my name very well," responded Sancho, "because when I was steward of a brotherhood in my village, I learned to make some letters like the marks on bundles, and they told me that they said my name; better yet, I'll pretend that my right hand has been hurt, and I'll have somebody else sign for me; there's a remedy for everything except death, and since I'll be in charge of everything, I can do whatever I want; then, too, when your father's the magistrate... [you're safe when you go to trial]. And being a governor, which is more than being a magistrate, just let them come and they'll see what happens! No, let them make fun of me and speak ill of me: they'll come for wool and go home shorn; and when God loves you, your house knows it; and the rich man's folly passes for good judgment in the world; and since that's what I'll be, being a governor and a very generous one, which is what I plan to be, nobody will notice any faults in me. No, just be like honey and the flies will go after you; you're only worth as much as you have,

my grandmother used to say; and you won't get revenge on a well-established man." (735)

Without **rhyme** or reason.
Sancho replied: "Because how can anybody stand for a knight errant as famous as your grace to go crazy, without rhyme or reason, for the sake of a …? (203)

The canon replied: "The plays that are popular now, imaginative works as well as historical ones, are known to be nonsense and without rhyme and reason." (415)

"Now I say," said Don Quixote, "that the author of my history was no wise man but an ignorant gossip-monger who, without rhyme or reason, began to write, not caring how it turned out." (478)

Stir the **rice** when it sticks.
Doña Rodríguez responded: "My lady the duchess has duennas in her service who could be countesses if fortune so desired, but laws go where kings command; let no one speak ill of duennas, in particular those who are old and maidens, for although I am not one of those, I clearly understand and grasp the advantage a maiden duenna has over one who is widowed; and the person who cut us down to size still has the scissors in his hand."
     "All the same," replied Sancho, "there's so much to cut in duennas, according to my barber, that it would be better not to stir the rice even if it sticks." (703)

To fit like a **ring** on one's finger.
"Your grace should pay careful attention, because here I [Sancho] go. 'Once upon a time, and may good come to all and evil to him who seeks it …' And, Señor, your grace should notice that the beginnings the ancients gave to their tales didn't come out of nowhere; this was a maxim of the Roman Cato Nonsensor, and it says: 'Evil to him who seeks it,' which fits here like the ring on your finger and means that your grace should stay put and not go looking for evil anywhere, and we should take another route, nobody's forcing us to continue on this one with so many frightening things to scare us." [Sancho is alluding to Cato Censor, who was popularly considered to be the source of proverbs and saying.] (144-145)

"Look, Sancho," responded Don Quixote, "I say proverbs when they are appropriate, and when I say them they fit like the rings on your fingers, but you drag them in by the hair, and pull them along, and do not guide them, and if I remember correctly, I have already told you that proverbs are brief maxims derived from the experience and speculation of wise men in the past, and if the proverb is not to the point, it is not a maxim, it is nonsense." (902)

To seize the **road** with both hands.
Andrés took the bread and the cheese, and seeing that no one gave him anything else, he lowered his head and, as they say, seized the road with both hands. (266)

There is no **road** so smooth that it doesn't have a stumbling block.
"There's no road so smooth," replied Sancho, "that it doesn't have some obstacle or stumbling block; they cook beans everywhere, but in my house they do it by the potful; craziness must have more companions and friends than wisdom. But if what they say is true, that misery loves company, then I can find comfort with your grace, because you serve a master who's as great a fool as mine." (535-536)

To fiddle [like Nero] while **Rome** is burning.
"Do you [Marcela] come, O savage basilisk of these mountains, to see if with your presence blood spurts from the wounds of this wretched man whose life was taken by your cruelty? Or do you come to gloat over the cruelties of your nature, or to watch from the height, like another heartless Nero, the flames of burning Rome, or, in your arrogance, to tread on this unfortunate corpse? (98)

When in **Rome**, do as the Romans do.
Cervantes: All at the same time, they [pilgrims] raised their arms and the wineskins into the air, their mouths pressed against the mouths of the wineskins and their eyes fixed on heaven, as if they were taking aim; they stayed this way for a long time, emptying the innermost contents of the skins into their stomachs, and moving their heads from one side to the other, signs that attested to the pleasure they were receiving.
    Sancho watched everything, and not one thing caused him sorrow; rather, in order to comply with a proverb that he knew very well – "When in Rome, do as the Romans do" – he asked Ricote for his wineskin and took aim along with the rest and with no less pleasure than they enjoyed. (812)

Never mention (talk of) a **rope** in the house of a man who has been hanged.
"I say that your grace is correct in everything," responded Sancho, "and that I am an ass. But I don't know why my mouth says ass, when you shouldn't mention the rope in the hanged man's house." (201)

Don Quixote said: "It was an evil hour when you learned how to bray, Sancho! And when did you decide it would be a good idea to mention rope in the house of the hanged man? When braying is the music, what counterpoint can there be except a beating?" (643)

To be a **rose** among thorns.
"What I can say," said Sancho, "is that I smelled a mannish kind of odor, and it must have been that with all that moving around, she was sweaty and sort of sour."

"That could not be," responded Don Quixote. "You must have had a head cold or else you were smelling yourself, because I know very well the fragrance of that rose among thorns, that lily of the field, that delicate liquid ambergris."

"That may be," responded Sancho, "because very often the same smell comes from me, though at the time I thought it was coming from her grace the lady Dulcinea, but there's no reason to be surprised, since one devil looks like another." (259)

Every **rule** has its exception.
"This humility does not seem a bad thing to me," responded Don Quixote, "because there is no poet who is not arrogant and does not think himself the greatest poet in the world."

"Every rule has its exception," responded Don Lorenzo, "and there must be some who are great and do not think so." (569)

To be the **run** of the mill.
"Well, what did you think?" responded the other man [Squire of the Wood]. "Am I by any chance a run-of-the-mill squire? I carry better provisions on my horse's rump than a general does when he goes marching." (536)

To be a **sack** with holes in it.
"You, brother Sancho," said Carrasco, "have spoken like a university professor, but still, trust in God and in Señor Don Quixote, who will give you a kingdom, not merely an ínsula."

"Whatever it is, it's all the same to me," responded Sancho, "though I can tell Señor Carrasco that my master won't be tossing that kingdom into a sack with holes in it; I've taken my own pulse and I'm healthy enough to rule kingdoms and govern ínsulas, and this is something I've already told my master."

"Be careful, Sancho," said Sansón, "for offices can alter behavior, and it might be that when you are governor you won't know the mother who bore you." (484)

To be **safe** and sound.
Letter from Sancho Panza to Don Quixote: *And with this, may God free your grace from the evil intentions of enchanters, and take me from this governorship safe and sound, which I doubt, because according to how Dr. Pedro Recio treats me, I don't think I'll get away with more than my life.* (797)

He [Sancho] felt his body and took a deep breath to see if he was whole or had been punctured anywhere; and seeing that he was safe and sound and in perfect health, he could not give enough thanks to Our Lord God for the mercy He had shown him, for he no doubt thought he had broken into a thousand pieces. (817)

The less **said** the better.
"I'll wager," replied Sancho, "that your grace thinks I've done something with my person I shouldn't have." "The less said the better, Sancho my friend," responded Don Quixote. (148)

When all is **said** and done.
"But look, Sancho: if you happen to find yourself a governor somewhere, don't forget about me [Teresa Panza] and your children. Remember that Sanchico is already fifteen, and he ought to go to school if his uncle the abbot is going to bring him into the Church. And don't forget that our daughter, Mari Sancha, won't die if we marry her; she keeps dropping hints that she wants a husband as much as you want to be a governor, and when all is said and done, a daughter's better off badly married than happily kept." (486-487)

To look for a bachelor (student) in **Salamanca**.
"Don't rely on that Sancho, because Manchegans are as quick-tempered as they are honorable, and they don't put up with anything from anybody. By God, if they suspect what you're up to, then I predict bad luck for you." "Get out, you dumb bastard! Let the lighting strike somebody else! Not me, I'm not going to look for trouble to please somebody else! Besides, looking for Dulcinea in Toboso will be like looking for a María in Ravenna or a bachelor in Salamanca. The devil, the devil and nobody else has gotten me into this!"
    Sancho held this soliloquy with himself. (515)

To be pure like the **salamander** in the fire.
A woman cried out: "This wicked man seized me in the middle of a field, and used my body like a dirty old rag, and, oh woe is me, he took what I [a woman] had safeguarded for more than twenty-three years, defending it against Moors and Christians, Spaniards and foreigners, and I, always as hard as an oak, kept myself pure like the salamander in the fire, or wool in the brambles, just so this good man would come along now and put his clean hands all over me." (751)

*Omnis **saturatio** mala, perdicis autem pessima.*
The physician responded: "Because our master Hippocrates, the polestar and light of medicine, says in one of his aphorisms: *Omnis saturatio mala, perdicis autem pessima.* Which means: 'A full stomach is bad, but a stomach full of partridges is very bad' [parody of the Latin text with "bread" instead of "partridges"]." (758)

Scarcity of things lends a certain value.
Cervantes: I do not wish to say more to you except to tell you to consider that this second part of *Don Quixote,* which I offer to you now, is cut by the same artisan and from the same cloth as the first, and in it I give you a somewhat expanded Don Quixote who is, at the end, dead and buried, so that no one will dare tell more tales about him, for the ones told in the past are enough, and it is also enough that an honorable man has recounted his clever follies and does not want to take them up again; for abundance, even of things that are good, makes people esteem them less, and scarcity, even of bad things, lends a certain value. (458)

To be (get) between **Scylla** and Charybdis.
Don Quixote went on, saying: "They [students] stumble and fall, pick themselves up and fall again, until they reach the academic title they desire; once this is acquired and they have passed through these shoals, these Scyllas and Charybdises, as if carried on the wings of good fortune, we have seen many who command and govern the world from a chair, their hunger turned into a full belly, their cold into comfort, their nakedness into finery, and their straw mat into linen and damask sheets, the just reward for their virtue. But their hardships, measured against and compared to those of a soldier and warrior, fall far behind." (330)

There are no **secrets** between friends.
"Now, since there are no secrets between friends, and the preference shown by Don Fernando was no longer preference but friendship, he told me [Cardenio] all his thoughts, especially one, having to do with love, which was causing him some concern." (186)

Self-praise is self-debasement.
"Believe me, beauteous lady, thou canst call thyself fortunate of having welcomed into this thy castle my person, which I [Don Quixote] do not praise because, as it is said, self-praise is self-debasement, but my squire wilt tell thee who I am. I say only that I shall keep eternally written in my memory the service that thou hast rendered me, so that I may thank thee for it as long as I shall live." (111)

Every **sheep** with its mate.
Sancho said: "I'll go back to walking on my feet on level ground, and if they're not adorned with cutout shoes of Cordoban leather, they won't lack for sandals made of hemp. Every sheep with its mate, and let no man stretch his leg farther than the length of the sheet, and now let me pass, it's getting late." (808-809).

If the **shoe** fits, wear it.
"As for governing them well," responded Sancho, "there's no need to charge me with it, because I'm charitable by nature and have compas-

sion for the poor; and if he kneads and bakes, you can't steal his cakes; by my faith, they won't throw me any crooked dice; I'm an old dog and understand every here, boy [the proverb says: "You don't need here, boy, here, boy, with an old dog"], and I know how to wake up at the right time, and I don't allow cobwebs in front of my eyes, because I know if the shoe fits: I say this because with me good men will have my hand and a place in my house [the phrase means "trust and confidence"], and bad men won't get a foot or permission to enter." (680)

To know where the **shoe** pinches.
"Throw that bone to another dog!" responded the innkeeper. "As if I didn't know how to add two and three or where my shoe pinches! Your grace [a priest] shouldn't try to treat me like a child, because, by God, I'm not an idiot." (270)

To try to **shoe** someone.
"No doubt about it, the good man must think we're asleep here; well, just let him try to shoe us, and he'll know if we're lame or not. What I [Sancho] can say is that if my master would take my advice, we'd already be out in those fields righting wrongs and undoing injustices, which is the habit and custom of good knights errant." (482)

To wait for someone like the **showers** of May.
Sanchica embraced her father [Sancho] and asked if he had brought her any- thing, for she had been waiting for him like the showers of May, and she held him on one side by his belt; and with his wife holding his hand and his daughter leading the gray, they went to their house, leaving Don Quixote in his, in the hands of his niece and his housekeeper, and in the company of the priest and the bachelor. (931)

To split one's **sides** laughing.
When his armor had been removed, Don Quixote was left in his narrow breeches and chamois doublet – dry, tall, thin, his jaws kissing each other inside his mouth – and if the maidens who were serving him had not been charged with hiding their laughter, for this was one of the precise orders their mistress and master had given them, they would have split their sides laughing. (660)

Golden **silence** is what they call Sancho.
"By God, my lord and master," replied Sancho, "your grace complains about very small things. Why the devil does it trouble you when I make use of my fortune, when I have no other, and no other wealth except proverbs and more proverbs? And right now four have come to mind that are a perfect fit, like pears in a wicker basket, but I won't say them, because golden silence is what they call Sancho."

"That Sancho is not you," said Don Quixote, "because not only are you not golden silence, you are foolish speech and stubborn persistence." (736)

Softer than **silk**.
"Id' like to see him [a horse]," responded Sancho, "but thinking that I'll climb up on him, either in the saddle or on his hindquarters, is asking the elm tree for pears. I can barely stay on my donkey, and that's on a packsaddle softer than silk, and now they want me to sit on the hindquarters made of wood, without even a pillow or cushion!" (716)

A new **sin** demands a new penance.
"As you value your life, Sancho, do not speak of this [Sancho's earlier comment about Dulcinea] again," said Don Quixote, "for it brings me grief; I forgave you then, and you know what they say: a new sin demands a new penance." (257)

To roll the stone of **Sisyphus**.
[Grisóstomo's Song]
    Come, it is time for Tantalus to rise
    with all his thirst from the abysmal deeps;
    let Sisyphus come, bearing the awful weight
    of that dread stone. (97)

To cut someone down to **size**.
Doña Rodríguez responded: "My lady the duchess has duennas in her service who could be countesses if fortune so desired, but laws go where kings command; let no one speak ill of duennas, in particular those who are old and maidens, for although I am not one of those, I clearly understand and grasp the advantage a maiden duenna has over one who is widowed; and the person who cut us down to size still has the scissors in his hand."
"All the same," replied Sancho, "there's so much to cut in duennas, according to my barber, that it would be better not to stir the rice even if it sticks." (703)

To praise to the **skies**.
"He must have been some peasant," said Doña Rodríguez the duenna, "because if he were noble and wellborn, he would have praised them [ladies] to the skies." (682)

To be nothing but **skin** and bone(s).
"I, Señor Sansón, am in no condition now to give accounts or accountings; my stomach has begun to flag, and if I don't restore it with a couple of swallows of mellow wine, I'll be nothing but skin and bone." (480)

Letter from Sancho Panza to Don Quixote: *And this doctor says about himself that he doesn't cure diseases when they've arrived but prevents them so they won't come, and the medicines he uses are diet and more diet and the person's nothing but skin and bones, as if being skinny weren't a worse ailment than having a fever.* (795)

To **skin** someone alive.
A scribe said: "Your grace [Sancho] can show your power against other gambling dens of less distinction, which are the ones that do more harm and harbor more outrages; in the houses of highborn gentlemen and nobles, the notorious cheats don't dare to use their tricks, and since the vice of gambling has become so widespread, it's better to gamble in distinguished houses than in those of workmen, where they keep a poor wretch for half the night and skin him alive." (776)

Sleep resembles (is the brother of) death.
"I don't understand that," replied Sancho. "I only understand that while I'm sleeping I have no fear, or hope, or trouble, or glory; blessed be whoever invented sleep, the mantle that covers all human thought, the food that satisfies hunger, the water that quenches thirst, the fire that warms the cold, the cold that cools down ardor, and, finally, the general coin with which all things are bought, the scale and balance that make the shepherd equal to the king, and the simple man equal to the wise. There is only one defect in sleep, or so I've heard, and it is that it resembles death, for there is very little difference between a man who is sleeping and a man who is dead." (903-904)

There's many a **slip** between the cup and the lip.
"By my faith, Señor, hunting and those pastimes are more for idlers than for governors. What I plan to amuse myself with is playing *triunfo envidado* [a card game] on feast days and ninepins on Sundays and holidays; all this hunting and hollering doesn't go well with my nature and doesn't sit well with my conscience."
     "May it please God, Sancho, because there's many a slip between the cup and the lip, [said the duke]." (686)

"There is a remedy for everything except death," responded Don Quixote, "for if we have a ship along the coast, we can embark on that even if the whole world attempts to prevent it."
     "Your grace paints a very nice picture and makes it seem very easy," said Sancho, "but there's many a slip 'tween cup and lip, and I'll depend on the renegade, who looks to me like an honest and good-hearted man." (884)

To go up in **smoke**.
Sancho listened to all of this with a very sorrowful spirit, for he saw that his hopes for a noble title were disappearing and going up in smoke. (321)

"When I [Sancho] gave up the governorship I also gave up any desire to be a governor again, but I didn't give up wanting to be a count, which will never happen if your grace gives up being a king by giving up the practice of your chivalry, which means all my hopes going up in smoke." (890)

As cool as **snow**.
"I say this, Sancho, because you have clearly seen the luxury and abundance we have enjoyed in this castle that we are leaving, but in the midst of those flavorful banquets and those drinks as cool as snow, it seemed as if I were suffering the pangs of hunger because I could not enjoy them with the freedom I would have had if they had been mine; the obligations to repay the benefits and kindnesses we have received are bonds that hobble a free spirit. Fortunate is the man to whom heaven has given a piece of bread with no obligation to thank anyone but heaven itself!" (832)

As white as **snow**.
The cart was two or even three times larger than the previous ones, and the sides and front were occupied by twelve other penitents as white as snow, all with their burning torches, a sight that caused both wonder and terror; on a raised throne sat a nymph draped in a thousand veils of silver cloth, and on all of them infinite numbers of gold sequins were sparkling, making her seem if not richly, then at least colorfully dressed. (690)

Whiter than **snow**.
Lotario continued, saying: "The honest and chaste woman is the ermine, and the purity of her virtue is whiter and cleaner than snow." (280)

It is better for a **soldier** to be dead in combat than safe in flight.
If my wounds do not shine in the eyes of those who see them, they are, at least, esteemed by those who know where they were acquired; it seems better for a soldier to be dead in combat than safe in flight, and I [Cervantes as author] believe this so firmly that even if I could achieve the impossible now, I would rather have taken part in that prodigious battle than to be free of wounds and not to have been there. [Cervantes is referring to the battle of Lepanto, where he was wounded.]. (454)

To not come up to (touch) the **sole** of someone's shoe.
"I have seen some governors," said Sancho, "who, in my opinion, don't come up to the sole of my shoe, and even so they're called lordship and are served their food on silver." (477)

Doña Rodríguez said: "Your grace [Don Quixote] should keep in mind that my daughter is an orphan, and well-bred, and young, and possessed of all those gifts that I have mentioned to you, for by God and my conscience, of all the maidens that my mistress has, there is none that can even touch the sole of her shoe, and the one they call Altisidora, the one they consider the most elegant and spirited, can't come within two leagues of my daughter. Because I want your grace to know, Señor, that all that glitters is not gold; this little Altisidora has more vanity than beauty, and more spirit than modesty, and besides, she's not very healthy: she has breath so foul that you can't bear to be near her even for a moment. And then, my lady the duchess ... But I'd better be quiet, because they say that the walls have ears." (771)

Take your neighbor's **son**, wipe his nose, and bring him into your house.
"Be content with your station," responded Teresa, "and don't try to go to a higher one; remember the proverb that says: 'Take your neighbor's son, wipe his nose, and bring him into your house.' Sure, it would be very nice to marry our María to some wretch of a count or gentleman who might take a notion to insult her and call her lowborn, the daughter of peasants and spinners! Not in my lifetime, my husband! I didn't bring up my daughter for that!" (487)

To feel out of **sorts**.
Knight and squire returned to their animals feeling rather melancholy and out of sorts, especially Sancho, for whom touching their store of money touched his very soul, since it seemed to him that taking anything away from it meant taking away the apple of his eye. (653)

To have one's **soul** between one's teeth.
Then they all turned to Quiteria, and some with pleas, and others with tears, and still others with persuasive arguments, urged her to give her hand to poor Basilio; she, as hard as marble and as motionless as a statue, showed that she could not and would not and did not wish to say a word, and she would not have responded at all if the priest had not told her to decide quickly what she was going to do, because Basilio's soul was between his teeth, and there was no time for her to be irresolute or indecisive. (594)

To touch one's very **soul**.
Knight and squire returned to their animals feeling rather melancholy and out of sorts, especially Sancho, for whom touching their store of

money touched his very soul, since it seemed to him that taking anything away from it meant taking away the apple of his eye. (653)

To go for **soup**.
Don Quixote went on, saying: "This poverty is suffered in its various forms, in hunger, cold, and nakedness, and sometimes all of them together; even so, his poverty is not so great that he [a student] does not eat, although the meal may be a little later than usual, or may be the leftovers of the rich, and his greatest misery is what students call among themselves *going for soup* [the phrase refers to going to convents and monasteries for the soup that is distributed to the poor]; and they do not lack someone else's brazier or hearth, and if it does not warm them, at least it lessens the cold, and at night they sleep under a blanket." (330)

No **speech** is pleasing if it is long.
Sancho said to his master: "Señor, does your grace wish to give me leave to talk a little? After you gave me that harsh order of silence, more than a few things have been spoiling in my stomach, and one that I have now on the tip of my tongue I wouldn't want to go to waste." "Say it," Don Quixote said, "and be brief, for no speech is pleasing if it is long." (157)

To poke one's **spoon** into something.
Sancho said to himself: "This master of mine, when I talk about things of pith and substance, usually says that I could take a pulpit in hand and go through the world preaching fine sermons; and I say of him that when he begins to string together judgments and to give advice, he could not only take a pulpit in hand but hang two on each finger, and go through the squares and say exactly the right thing. What a devil of a knight errant you are, and what a lot of things you know! I thought in my heart that he would only know things that had to do with his chivalry, but there's nothing he doesn't pick at or poke his spoon into." (598)

St. Peter is fine in Rome.
Sancho said: "Since it's more than three thousand leagues from here to Candaya, if the horse gets tired or the giant gets angry, it'll take us more than half a dozen years to get back, and by then there won't be any ínsulas or ínsulos left in the world that recognize me; and since it's a common saying that danger lies in delay, and when they give you a heifer you'd better hurry over with the rope, may the beards of these ladies forgive me, but St. Peter's fine in Rome; I mean that I'm fine in this house, where I have received so many favors and where I expect a great benefit from its master, which is being a governor." (719)

Sancho said: ""Make way, Señores, and let me return to my old liberty; let me go and find my past life, so that I can come back from this present death. I was not born to be a governor, or to defend ínsulas or cities from enemies who want to attack them. I have a better understanding of plowing and digging, of pruning and layering the vines, than of making laws or defending provinces and kingdoms. St. Peter's fine in Rome: I mean, each man is fine doing the work he was born for. I'm better off with a scythe in my hand than a governor's scepter; I'd rather eat my fill of gazpacho than suffer the misery of a brazen doctor who starves me to death, and I'd rather lie down in the shade of an oak tree in summer and wrap myself in an old bald sheepskin in winter, in freedom, than lie between linen sheets and wear sables, subject to a governorship." (808)

"May God forgive him [Avellaneda, the author of another *Don Quixote*]," said Sancho. "He should have left me in my corner and forgotten about me, because you shouldn't play music unless you know how, and St. Peter's just fine in Rome." (847)

Be content with your **station**.
"Be content with your station," responded Teresa, "and don't try to go to a higher one; remember the proverb that says: 'Take your neighbor's son, wipe his nose, and bring him into your house.' Sure, it would be very nice to marry our María to some wretch of a count or gentleman who might take a notion to insult her and call her lowborn, the daughter of peasants and spinners! Not in my lifetime, my husband! I didn't bring up my daughter for that!" (487)

As motionless as a **statue**.
Then they all turned to Quiteria, and some with pleas, and others with tears, and still others with persuasive arguments, urged her to give her hand to poor Basilio; she, as hard as marble and as motionless as a statue, showed that she could not and would not and did not wish to say a word, and she would not have responded at all if the priest had not told her to decide quickly what she was going to do, because Basilio's soul was between his teeth, and there was no time for her to be irresolute or indecisive. (594)

The **stem** is too hard for making flutes.
His niece said: "What is this, Uncle [Don Quixote]? We thought your grace would stay at home again and lead a quiet and honorable life, and now you want to go into new labyrinths and become
    Little shepherd, now you're coming,
    little shepherd, now you're going?
Well, the truth is that the stem's too hard for making flutes [the origin of the proverb was the tradition of forming flutes or pipes out of green barley stems; it is used when a mature and sensible person does not wish to engage in childish activities]." (932-933)

A neatly dressed **stick** does not seem to be a stick at all.
Letter from Don Quixote to Sancho Panza: *Dress well, for a neatly decorated stick does not seem to be a stick at all. I do not say that you should wear jewels and finery, or, being a judge, that you should dress as a soldier, but only that you should wear the clothing your office requires, as long as it is clean and neat.* (793)

A full **stomach** is bad, but a stomach full of partridges is very bad.
The physician responded: "Because our master Hippocrates, the polestar and light of medicine, says in one of his aphorisms: *Omnis saturatio mala, perdicis autem pessima.* Which means: 'A full stomach is bad, but a stomach full of partridges is very bad' [parody of the Latin text with "bread" instead of "partridges"]." (758)

No **stomach** is so large that it can't be filled.
"I [Sancho] may be a fool, but I understand the proverb that says, 'It did him harm when the ant grew wings,' and it might even be that Sancho the squire will enter heaven more easily than Sancho the governor. The bread they bake here is as good as in France, and at night every cat is gray, and the person who hasn't eaten by two in the afternoon has more than enough misfortune, and no stomach's so much bigger than any other that it can't be filled, as they say, with straw and hay [the actual proverb is "Straw and hay and hunger's away"], and the little birds of the field have God to protect and provide for them." (679)

To be hard to **stomach**.
Sancho asked: "Is he [Knight of the Wood] in love, by any chance?"
"Yes," said the Squire of the Wood, "with a certain Casildea of Vandalia, the crudest lady in the world, and the hardest to stomach, but indigestibility isn't her greatest fault; her other deceits are growling in his belly, and they'll make themselves heard before too many hours have gone by." (535)

As hard as **stone**.
Altisidora said:
> As for your squire named Sancho,
> may his heart be as hard as stone,
> as cold as ice: then Dulcinea
> will ne'er be freed of enchantment. (830)

To be (amount to) more than **stones**.
"I [Sancho] imagine that on this ínsula there must be more Dons than stones, but that's enough of that: God understands me, and it may be that if my governorship lasts a few days, I'll weed out these Dons, because there's so many of them they must be as annoying as gnats." (748)

To have something in **store**.
But fate, having something else in store, ordained that when the flagship had come so close that those on the brigantine could hear the voices telling them to surrender, two drunken *Toraquis*, which is to say, two Turks out of the fourteen on board the brigantine, fired their muskets and killed two soldiers who were on the foredecks. (878)

To be a long **story**.
The man said: "Your graces should know that in a town four and a half leagues from this inn, a councilman lost a donkey through the deceitful efforts of one of his servant girls, but that's a long story, and though the councilman made every effort to find the animal, he could not." (620)

To make a long **story** short.
"To make the story of my misfortune short, I [Claudia Jerónima] shall tell you [Roque Guinart] briefly the grief he [Don Vicente Torrellas] has caused me." (853)

Straw and hay and hunger is away.
"I [Sancho] may be a fool, but I understand the proverb that says, 'It did him harm when the ant grew wings,' and it might even be that Sancho the squire will enter heaven more easily than Sancho the governor. The bread they bake here is as good as in France, and at night every cat is gray, and the person who hasn't eaten by two in the afternoon has more than enough misfortune, and no stomach's so much bigger than any other that it can't be filled, as they say, with straw and hay [the actual proverb is "Straw and hay and hunger's away"], and the little birds of the field have God to protect and provide for them." (679)

Straw or hay, it's the same either way.
"Writing in any other fashion," said Don Quixote, "would mean not writing truths, but lies, and historians who make use of lies ought to be burned, like those who make counterfeit money; I do not know what moved the author to resort to other people's novels and stories when there was so much to write about mine: no doubt he must have been guided by the proverb that says: 'Straw or hay, it's the same either way.' For the truth is that if he had concerned himself only with my thoughts, my sighs, my tears, my virtuous desires, and my brave deeds, he could have had a volume larger than, or just as large as, the collected works of El Tostado [Alonso de Madrigal, a prolific writer of the fifteenth century]." (478)

To be a **stroke** of luck.
"That's a stroke of luck," responded the man with the patch. "I'll lower the price, and consider myself well-paid if I cover my costs." (623)

Stultorum infinitus est numerus.
"The one that tells about me," said Don Quixote, "must have pleased very few."

"Just the opposite is true [said Carrasco]; since *stultorum infinitus est numerus* ["The number of fools is infinite."], an infinite number of people have enjoyed the history, though some have found fault and failure in the author's memory, because he forgets to tell who the thief was who stole Sancho's donkey." (479-480)

As soft as **sugar paste**.
Don Quixote said: "Remember, all you enamored ladies, that for Dulcinea alone I am as soft as sugar paste, and for all the rest I am as hard as flint; for her I am honey, and for you, bitter aloe; for me only Dulcinea is beautiful, wise, modest, gallant, and wellborn, and the rest are ugly, foolish, licentious, and of the worst lineage; to be hers alone, and no other's, nature cast me into the world." (746)

The **sun** shines on the evil as well as the good.
Don Quixote responded: "But be that as it may, mount your donkey, my good Sancho, and follow me, for God, who provides all things, will not fail us, especially since we are so much in His service, when He does not fail the gnats in the air, or the grubs in the earth, or the tadpoles in the water. He is so merciful that He makes His sun to shine on the good and the evil and His rain to fall on the just and the unjust." (132)

To rain while the **sun** shines.
"God will find the cure," said Sancho, "for God gives the malady and also the remedy; nobody knows the future: there's a lot of hours until tomorrow, and in one of them, and even in a moment, the house can fall; I've seen it rain at the same time the sun is shining [see Kuusi 1957]; a man goes to bed healthy and can't move the next day. And tell me, is there anybody who can boast that he's driven a nail into Fortune's wheel? No, of course not, and I wouldn't dare put the point of a pin between a woman's yes and no, because it wouldn't fit. Tell me that Quiteria loves Basilio with all her heart and all her soul, and I'll give him a sack of good fortune, because I've heard that love looks through spectacles that make copper look like gold, poverty like riches, and dried rheum like pearls." (579)

In a prosperous (well-stocked) house **supper** is soon on the stove (cooked).

"That is true," responded Sancho, "but if you pay your debts, you don't worry about guaranties, and in a prosperous house supper's soon on the stove; I mean that nobody has to tell me things or give me any advice: I'm prepared for anything, and I know something about everything." (654)

"God can remedy that," responded Sancho, "because I know more proverbs than a book, and so many of them come into my mouth at one time when I talk that they fight with one another to get out, but my tongue tosses out the first ones it finds, even if they're not to the point. But I'll be careful from now on to say the ones that suit the gravity of my position, because in a well-stocked house, supper is soon cooked; and if you cut the cards, you don't deal; and the man who sounds the alarm is safe; and for giving and keeping, you need some sense." (733-734)

One **swallow** does not a summer make.

"Even so," said the traveler, "it seems to me that if I remember correctly, I have read that Don Galaor, brother of the valorous Amadis of Gaul, never had a specific lady to whom he could commend himself, and despite this he was not held in any less esteem, and was a very valiant and famous knight." To which Don Quixote responded: "Señor, one swallow does not a summer make. Furthermore, I happen to know that this knight was secretly very much in love, even though his courting all the lovely ladies he found attractive was a natural inclination that he could not resist. However, it is clearly demonstrated that there was one lady whom he had made mistress of his will, and to her he commended himself very frequently and very secretly, because he prided himself on being a secretive knight." (90)

In the **sweat** of thy face (brow) shalt thou eat bread. (Genesis 3:19)

Chapter LII: Regarding the quarrel that Don Quixote had with the goatherd, as well as the strange adventure of the penitents, which he brought to a successful conclusion by the sweat of his brow. (438)

The Squire of the Wood said: "We have a difficult life, Señor, those of us who are squires to knights errant: the truth is we eat our bread by the sweat of our brows, which is one of God's curses on our first parents."

"You could also say," added Sancho, "that we eat it in the icy cold of our bodies, because who suffers more heat and cold than we wretched squires of knight errantry? If we ate, it would be easier because sorrows fade with a little bread, but sometimes we can go a day or two with nothing for our breakfast but the wind that blows." (533)

Once you learn how to **swim** you will never forget it.
Sancho said: "I remember, when I was boy, I used to bray whenever I felt like it, and nobody held me back, and I did it so well and so perfectly that when I brayed all the donkeys in the village brayed, but that didn't stop me from being my parents' son, and they were very honorable people, and even though this talent of mine was envied by more than a few of the conceited boys in my village, I didn't care at all. And so that you can see that I'm telling the truth, wait and listen, because if you know this, it's like knowing how to swim: once you've learned you never forget." (641)

To have one's **tail** between one's legs.
I [Ginés de Pasamonte] mean to say, that we will take up our chain and set out for Toboso, is to think that night has fallen now when it is not yet ten in the morning; asking that of us is like asking pears of an elm tree." "Well, then, I do swear," said Don Quixote, his wrath rising, "Don Whoreson, Don Ginesillo de Paropilla, or whatever your name is, that you will go alone, your tail between your legs, and the entire chain on your back!" (171-172)

The **tailor** wasn't paid and had to supply his own braid.
Señor Canon replied: "Since, as far as the authors and actors are concerned, it is better to earn a living with the crowd than a reputation with the elite, this is what would happen to my book after I had singed my eyebrows trying to keep the precepts I have mentioned and had become the tailor who wasn't paid" [The actual proverb "The tailor wasn't paid and had to supply his own braid" means that one can lose twice by not being paid a fee and by not being reimbursed for expenses incurred in performing the service.]. (415)

To tell **tales**.
Sansón said: "Señor Don Quixote, you say this now, when we have news of the disenchantment of Señora Dulcinea? And now that we are on the point of becoming shepherds and spending our lives in song, like princes, now your grace wishes to be a hermit? For God's sake, be quiet, come to your senses, and tell us no more tales." (936)

To have the **tambourine** in the right hands.
A guide said: "I beg your grace, Señor Don Quixote, that you observe carefully and scrutinize with a thousand eyes what you find inside [in an abyss]: perhaps there are things I can put in my book *Transformations*."
"The tambourine's in just the right hands [things are handled in a competent manner]," responded Sancho Panza. (602)

To suffer the pains of **Tantalus**.
[Grisóstomo's Song]

Come, it is time for Tantalus to rise
with all his thirst from the abysmal deeps;
let Sisyphus come, bearing the awful weight
of that dread stone. (97)

A good **teacher** never spares the rod.
"That," replied the duchess, "is more like slapping than flogging. It
seems to me that the wise Merlin will not be satisfied with so much
gentleness, and that it will be necessary for our good Sancho to use a
whip with metal points or a cat-o'-nine-tails, something he can feel,
because a good teacher never spares the rod, and the freedom of so
great a lady as Dulcinea cannot be gotten cheaply and at so little cost;
and be advised, Sancho, that works of charity performed in a lukewarm
and halfhearted way have no merit and are worth nothing." (697)

To be like pulling **teeth**.
Master Pedro said: "Now I am desolate and dejected, impoverished and
a beggar, and worst of all, without my monkey, and by my faith, it will
be like pulling teeth to get him back again, and all because of the ill-
considered rage of this knight." (633)

To lie through one's **teeth**.
Two days later, the duke told Don Quixote that in four days his opponent would come to present himself in the field, armed as a knight, to
maintain that the maiden was lying through some, if not all, of her teeth
[the Spanish phase is: "to lie through half of one's (one's whole)
beard"] if she affirmed he had given her a promise of marriage. (810)

It is foolish to lose one's **temper** just because one hears somebody
bray.
"My master, Don Quixote of La Mancha, who was once called *The
Knight of the Sorrowful Face* and is now called *The Knight of the Lions,* is a very prudent gentleman who knows Latin and Spanish like a
bachelor, and in all his dealings and advice he proceeds like a very
good soldier, and he knows all the laws and rules about what is called
dueling like the back of his hand, and so there's nothing else to do but
listen to what he says, and if you're wrong, let it be on my head, especially since they say that it's foolish to lose your temper just because
you hear somebody bray." (641)

Post **tenebras** spero lucem.
"O unfeeling soul! O pitiless squire! O undeserved bread and unthink-
ing favor that I [Don Quixote] have given to you and intend to give to
you in the future! Because of me you found yourself a governor, and
because of me you have hopes of becoming a count or receiving another equivalent title, and the fulfillment of those hopes will take no longer
than the time it takes for this year to pass, for *Post tenebras spero*

lucem [see Job 17:12; the phrase was the motto of the printer Juan de la Cuesta and therefore appears on the frontispiece of the earliest editions of both parts of *Don Quixote*]." (903)

To do the **thing** that nobody else can do for oneself.
"I [Sancho] say that I'm sure of my master's good ness and truthfulness, and so I'll ask something that goes right to the heart of the matter; speaking with respect, since your grace has been locked in the cage, enchanted, in your opinion, have you had the desire and will to pass what they call major and minor waters?"

"I do not understand what you mean by *passing waters*, Sancho; speak more clearly if you want me to respond in a straightforward way."

"Is it possible that your grace doesn't understand what it means to pass minor or major waters? Even schoolboys know that. Well, what I mean is, have you had the desire to do the thing nobody else can do for you?"

"Ah, now I understand you, Sancho! Yes, I have, quite often. And even do now. Save me from this danger, for not everything is absolutely pristine!" (420-421)

All **things** are possible.
"All things are possible," said Don Quixote.
And the gentleman observed all of this, and all of it amazed him, especially when Don Quixote, after carefully cleaning his head, face, beard, and sallet, steadied his feet in the stirrups, called for his sword, [and] grasped his lance. (559-560)

All **things** pass.
"I'll explain later," responded Don Lorenzo, "nut for now your grace should listen to the glossed verses and to the gloss, which read like this:
Gloss
At last, since all things pass,
the good that Fortune gave me
passed too, though once o'erflowing,
and never to me returned
neither scant nor in abundance. (572)

Things get worse when you stir them.
"I'm not pregnant by anybody," responded Sancho, "and I'm not a man who'd let himself get pregnant even by the king, and though I'm poor I'm an Old Christian, and I don't owe anything to anybody, and if I want ínsulas, other people want things that are worse; each man is the child of his actions, and because I'm a man I could be a pope, let alone the governor of an ínsula, especially since my master could win so many he might not have enough people to give them to. Your grace

should be careful what you say, Señor Barber, because there's more to life than trimming beards, and there's some difference between one Pedro and the other. I say this because we all know one another, and you can't throw crooked dice with me. As for the enchantment of my master, only God knows the truth, and let's leave it at that, because things get worse when you stir them." (411)

To kick at **thorns**.
Sancho Panza said: "Oh, Señor, heaven, moved by my tears and prayers, has willed Rocinante not to move, and if you persist, and spur and urge him on, that will anger Fortune, and it will be, as they say, like kicking at thorns." (144)

"By God, your grace [Don Antonio] is right," responded the Castilian. "Giving this good man [Don Quixote] advice is like kicking at thorns; even so, it makes me very sad that the good sense everyone says this fool has in other matters should run out into the gutter of his knight errantry; as for the bad luck your grace mentioned, let it be for me and all my descendants if after today, though I live longer than Methuselah, I ever give advice to anybody again, even if he asks for it." (867)

To be a stone's **throw** away.
"We have not run across anyone," responded Don Quixote, "but we found a saddle cushion and traveling case not far from here." "I found them, too," responded the goatherd, "but I never wanted to pick them up or go near them because I was afraid there'be trouble and they'd say I stole them; the devil's sly, and he puts things under our feet that make us stumble and fall, and we don't know how or why." "That's just what I say," responded Sancho. "I found them, too, and I didn't want to get within a stone's throw of them: I left them there, and there they remain, just as they were; I don't want a dog with a bell around its neck." (179)

Never put your **thumbs** between two wisdom teeth.
"That Sancho is not you," said Don Quixote, "because not only are you not golden silence, you are foolish speech and stubborn persistence, but even so I should like to know which four proverbs came to mind just now that were so to the point, because I have been searching my mind, and I have a good one, and I cannot think of a single proverb."

"Which ones could be better," said Sancho, "than 'Never put your thumbs between two wisdom teeth' and 'There's no answer to get out of my house and what do you want with my wife' and 'Whether the pitcher hits the stone or the stone hits the pitcher, it's bad luck for the pitcher'? They're all just fine. Because nobody should take on his governor or the person in authority because he'll come out of it hurt, like the man who puts his finger between two wisdom teeth, and if they're not wisdom teeth but just plain molars, it doesn't matter; and there's no reply to what the governor says, like the 'Leave my house and what do you want with my wife.' As for the stone and the pitcher, even a blind man can see that. So whoever sees the mote in somebody else's eye has to see the beam in his own, so that nobody can say about him: 'The dead woman was frightened by the one with her throat cut.' And your grace knows very well that the fool knows more in his own house than the wise man does in somebody else's." (736)

To run at full **tilt**.
"Even so," replied the traveler, "I still have a misgiving, and it is that I have often read that words are exchanged between two knights errant, and one word leads to another, their anger rises, they turn their horses and ride off a good distance to the far ends of the field, and then, without further ado, they ride at full tilt toward each other, and in the middle of the charge they commend themselves to their ladies, and what usually happens after their encounter is that one falls from his horse, run through by his opponent's lance, and the same thing happens to the other as well, for unless he holds on to his horse's mane, he cannot help but fall to the ground, too." (89-90)

It is never the wrong **time** for a gift.
"She [Dulcinea] is liberal to the extreme," said Don Quixote, "and if she did not present you with a jewel of gold, no doubt it was because she did not have one near at hand, but it is never the wrong time for a gift: I shall see her and you [Sancho] will have your reward." (260)

It takes a long **time** to know a person.
"Your grace, see if you can stand up, and we'll help Rocinante, though he doesn't deserve it, because he's the main reason for this beating. I [Sancho] never would have believed it of Rocinante; I always thought he was a person as chaste and peaceable as I am. Well, like they say, you need a long time to know a person, and nothing in this life is certain." (105-106)

Time changes the rhyme.
"Be quiet, girl," said Teresa [Panza]. "You don't know what you're saying, and this gentleman is right; time changes the rhyme: when it's Sancho, it's Sancha, and when it's governor, it's Señora, and I don't know if I'm saying something or not." (789-790)

Sancho said: "It was eight or ten days ago, Brother Gossip, that I came to govern the ínsula that they gave me, and in all that time I didn't even have enough bread to eat; I've been persecuted by doctors and had my bones trampled by enemies, and I haven't had time to take any bribes or collect any fees, and this being true, which it is, in my opinion I didn't deserve to leave in this way; but man proposes and God disposes, and God knows what suits each man and what's best for him, and time changes the rhyme, and nobody should say, 'That's water I won't drink,' because you're in a place where you think there's bacon, and you don't even find a nail; God understands me, and that's enough, and I'll say no more, though I could." (821-822)

Time flies.
> *Gloss*
> What I ask is the impossible,
> for there is no force on earth
> that has the power to turn
> back time that has passed us by,
> to bring back what once was ours.
> Time races, it flies, it charges
> past, and will never return,
> and only a fool would beg
> a halt, or if the time would pass,
> *or if at last the time would come.* (572-573)

Time is swift.
Cervantes: But since time is swift and there is no obstacle that can stop it, the hours raced by and morning soon arrived. Seeing which Don Quixote left the soft featherbed, and, by no means slothful, dressed in his chamois outfit and put on the traveling boots in order to hide the misfortune of his stocking. (753)

Time reveals all things.
"I [Don Quixote] prefer to remain silent, because I do not wish anyone to say that I am lying, but Time, which reveals all things, will disclose the truth to us when we least expect it." (323-324)

"Events will tell the truth of things, Sancho," responded Don Quixote, "for time, which reveals all things, brings everything into the light of day even if it is hidden in the bowels of the earth." (627-628)

Time will tell.
The barber recounted: "'You, cured?' said the madman. 'Well, well, time will tell; go with God, but I vow by Jupiter, whose majesty I represent on earth, that on account of the sin that Sevilla commits today by taking you out of this madhouse and calling you sane, I must inflict on her a punishment so severe that its memory will endure for all eternity, amen.'" (464)

All **times** are not the same.
Sancho responded: "Nothing but one insult after another, though she [Dulcinea] must know the proverb that says that a jackass loaded down with gold climbs the mountain fast, and gifts can break boulders, and

God helps those who help themselves, and a bird in hand is worth two in the bush. And then my master, who should have coddled me and flattered me so I'd turn as soft as wool and carded cotton, says that if he catches me he'll tie me naked to a tree and double the number of lashes; these noble folk so full of pity should remember that they're not only asking a squire to whip himself, but a governor; like they say, 'That's the finishing touch.' Let them learn, let them learn, damn them, how to beg, and how to ask, and how to have good manners; all times are not the same, and men are not always in a good humor." (694)

"What you say is correct, Sancho," said Don Quixote, "but you must realize that not all times are the same, nor do they always follow the same course, and what common people generally call omens, which are not founded on any natural cause, the wise man must consider and judge to be happy events." (835)

Here **today** and gone tomorrow.
"The fact is," responded Sancho, "that as your grace knows very well, we're all subject to death, here today and gone tomorrow, and the lamb goes as quickly as the sheep, and nobody can promise himself more hours of life in this world than the ones God wants to give him, because death is silent, and when she comes knocking at the door of our life, she's always in a hurry, and nothing will stop her, not prayers or struggles or scepters or miters, and that's something that everybody hears, something they tell us from the pulpit." (498)

Today it's your turn and tomorrow it's mine.
"Enough of that, Señor [Don Quixote]," said Sancho. "Long live the hen, even with the pip; today it's your turn and tomorrow it's mine; these matters of clashes and blows shouldn't be taken too seriously, because the man who falls today can pick himself up tomorrow, unless he decides to stay in bed, I mean if he lets himself lose heart and doesn't find new spirit for new fights. And your grace should get up now to receive Don Gaspar Gregorio, because it seems to me that everybody's in an uproar, and he must be in the house by now." (890)

To bite one's **tongue**.
"'Stop right there, Señor Don Montesinos,' I [Don Quixote] said then. 'Your grace should recount this history in the proper manner, for you know that all comparisons are odious, and there is no reason to compare anyone to anyone else. The peerless Dulcinea of Toboso is who she is, and Señora Belerma is who she is, and who she was, and no more should be said about it.'
    To which he responded:
    'Señor Don Quixote, may your grace forgive me, for I confess that I erred and misspoke when I said that Señora Dulcinea would barely be

the equal of Señora Belerma, for it was enough for me to have realized, by means of I am not certain what conjectures, that your grace is her knight, and I would rather bite my tongue than compare her to anything but heaven itself.'" (609)

Sancho promised very earnestly that he would sew up his mouth or bite his tongue before speaking a word that was not fitting and carefully considered, just as his master had ordered, and Don Quixote did not need to worry about that anymore, for never through him would it be discovered who they really were. (661)

To have on the tip of the **tongue**.
"Señor, does your grace wish to give me leave to talk a little? After you gave me that harsh order of silence, more than a few things have been spoiling in my stomach, and one that I have now on the tip of my tongue I wouldn't want to go to waste." "Say it," Don Quixote said, "and be brief, for no speech is pleasing if it is long." (157)

"I mean I didn't look at her [Dulcinea] so carefully," said Sancho, "that I could notice her beauty in particular and her good features point by point, but on the whole, she seemed fine to me."

"Now I forgive you," said Don Quixote, "and you must pardon the anger I have shown you; for first impulses are not in the hands of men."

"I can see that," responded Sancho, "just like in me a desire to talk is always my first impulse, and I can never help saying, not even once, what's on my tongue."

"Even so," said Don Quixote, "think about what you say, Sancho, because you can carry the jug to the fountain only so many times ... and I shall say no more."

"Well," responded Sancho, "God's in His heaven, and He sees all the snares, and He'll be the judge of who does worse: me in not saying the right thing or your grace in not doing it." (256)

To watch one's **tongue**.
"As far as I am concerned," replied Don Quixote, "you can lie, Sancho, as much as you wish, and I shall not stop you, but watch your tongue." (662)

Not to be able to **touch** someone or something.
"Is my lady Dulcinea, by some chance, more beautiful? No, certainly not, not even by half, and I'd [Sancho] go so far as to say she can't even touch the shoes of the lady [Dorotea] we have before us. So woe is me, I'll never get the rank I'm hoping for if your grace goes around asking for the moon. Marry, marry right now." (254)

To be the finishing **touch**.
Sancho responded: "Nothing but one insult after another, though she [Dulcinea] must know the proverb that says that a jackass loaded down with gold climbs the mountain fast, and gifts can break boulders, and God helps those who help themselves, and a bird in hand is worth two in the bush. And then my master, who should have coddled me and flattered me so I'd turn as soft as wool and carded cotton, says that if he catches me he'll tie me naked to a tree and double the number of lashes; these noble folk so full of pity should remember that they're not only asking a squire to whip himself, but a governor; like they say, 'That's the finishing touch.' Let them learn, let them learn, damn them, how to beg, and how to ask, and how to have good manners; all times are not the same, and men are not always in a good humor." (694)

For the **treason** we are grateful, though we find the traitor hateful.
The captive recounts: "These Arabs cut off his head and took it to the commander of the Turkish fleet, who confirmed for them our Spanish proverb: 'For the treason we are grateful, though we find the traitor hateful.' And so, they say, the commander ordered the two who brought him the present to be hanged because they did not bring the man to him alive." (340)

To be a goblin's **treasure**.
"I [Don Quixote] had no hopes to offer her [Altisidora] or treasures to present to her, because all of mine I have given to Dulcinea, and the treasures of knights errant are, like those of goblins [it was believed that goblins turned buried treasure into coal, thus leading to the phrase *tesoro de duende* ("goblin's treasure") to describe wealth that has been squandered], apparent and false, and I can give her only the innocent memories I have of her." (899)

To be a dirty **trick**.
Sancho responded: "This seems like one dirty trick on top of another, and not honey on hotcakes. How nice it would be after pinches, slaps, and pinpricks to have a few lashes. Why not just take a big stone and tie it around my neck and put me in a well, and I won't mind it too much since I have to be a laughingstock in order to solve other people's problems. Let me alone; if not, I swear I'll knock down and destroy everything, and I don't care what happens." (911)

Other people's **troubles** kill the donkey.
"That," responded the Squire of the Wood, "is why they say that it's greed that tears the sack, and if we're going to talk about madmen, there's nobody in the world crazier than my master, because he's one of those who say: 'Other people's troubles kill the donkey,' and to help another knight find the wits he's lost, he pretends to be crazy and goes

around looking for something that I think will hit him right in the face when he finds it." (535)

Troubles take wing for the man who can sing.
"What?" Don Quixote repeated, "Men also go to the galleys for being musicians and singers?" "Yes, Señor," responded the galley slave, "because there's nothing worse than singing when you're in difficulty." "But I have heard it said," said Don Quixote, "that troubles take wing for the man who can sing." "Here just the opposite is true," said the galley slave. "Warble once, and you weep the rest of your days." (165)

Trout are not caught with a bare line.
Sancho responded: "It comes to a total of eight hundred twenty-five *reales*. I'll take that out of your grace's [Don Quixote's] money, and I'll walk into my house a rich and happy man, though badly whipped; because trout aren't caught … [with a bare line], and that's all I'll say." (920)

Lean against a sturdy **trunk** if you want good shade.
"I am," responded Sancho, "and I'm the one who deserves it [an ínsula] as much as anybody else; I'm a 'Stay close to a good man and become one'; and I'm a 'Birds of a feather flock together'; and a 'Lean against a sturdy trunk it you want good shade.' I have leaned against a good master, and traveled with him for many months, and I'll become just like him, God willing; long life to him and to me, and there'll be no lack of empires for him to rule or ínusulas for me to govern." (666-667)

To be the naked **truth**.
"I want you to know, Sancho, that if the naked truth, bare of flattery, were to reach the ears of princes, the times would be different and other ages would be deemed to be of iron when compared to our own, which, I believe, would be considered golden. Heed this warning, Sancho, and with good sense and intentions bring to my ears the truth of what you know in response to what I have asked you."
    "I will do that very gladly, Señor," responded Sancho, "on the condition that your grace will not be angry at what I say, since you want me to tell the naked truth and not dress it in any clothes except the ones it was wearing when I heard it." (471)

Truth rises above a lie.
"That may well be true," replied the bachelor, "but *dubitat Augustinus*."
    "No matter who doubts it," responded the page, "the truth is what I have said, and truth will always rise above a lie, as oil rises above water." (789)

To sing a different **tune**.
"Go in peace," said Sancho, "poor maiden [Altisidora], go in peace, I mean, you have bad luck because you fell in love with a soul of esparto grass and a heart of oak. By my faith, if you'd fallen in love with me, you'd be singing a different tune!" (918)

To know how to add **two** and three.
"Throw that bone to another dog!" responded the innkeeper. "As if I didn't know how to add two and three or where my shoe pinches! Your grace [a priest] shouldn't try to treat me like a child, because, by God, I'm not an idiot." (270)

To have its **ups** and downs.
"It seems to me," said Don Quixote, "there is no human history in the world that does not have its ups and downs, especially those that deal with chivalry; they cannot be filled with nothing but successful exploits." (476)

To run like **Villadiego**.
"Your grace should tell me [Sancho] what we're going to do with this dappled gray horse that looks like a gray donkey and was left behind by that Martino [Mambrino] who was toppled by your grace, because seeing how he took to his heels and ran like Villadiego [i.e., to flee an unexpected danger], he has no intention of ever coming back. By my beard, this dappled gray is a good one!" (156)

You see I'm in a hurry and you demand **virginity**.
"My God!" said Sancho. "Your grace must be out of your mind! Like people say: 'You see I'm in a hurry and you demand virginity!' Now that I have to sit on a bare board, your grace wants me to flog my bottom? Really and truly, your grace is wrong. Let's go now and shave those duennas, and when we get back I promise your grace, like the man I am, to fulfill my obligation so fast it will make your grace happy, and that's all I have to say." (720)

Virtue must be honored.
"Brother [a Castilian]," said Don Antonio, "go on your way, and don't give advice to people who don't ask for it. Señor Don Quixote of La Mancha is a very prudent man, and we who accompany him are not dolts; virtue must be honored wherever it is found; go now, and bad luck to you, and stop minding other people's business." (867)

Virtue will be recognized.
"That is so, Señor Don Quixote," responded Don Antonio, "for just as fire cannot be hidden and enclosed, virtue cannot fail to be recognized, and that which is achieved through the profession of arms exceeds and outshines all others." (867)

Waiting is not sensible when danger outweighs hope.

"Señor," responded Sancho, "withdrawing is not running away, and waiting is not sensible when danger outweighs hope, and wise men know to save something for tomorrow and not risk everything in a single day. And you should know that even though I'm rough and lowborn, I still know something about what people call proper behavior." (174)

Walls have ears.

Doña Rodríguez said: "Your grace [Don Quixote] should keep in mind that my daughter is an orphan, and well-bred, and young, and possessed of all those gifts that I have mentioned to you, for by God and my conscience, of all the maidens that my mistress has, there is none that can even touch the sole of her shoe, and the one they call Altisidora, the one they consider the most elegant and spirited, can't come within two leagues of my daughter. Because I want your grace to know, Señor, that all that glitters is not gold; this little Altisidora has more vanity than beauty, and more spirit than modesty, and besides, she's not very healthy: she has breath so foul that you can't bear to be near her even for a moment. And then, my lady the duchess ... But I'd better be quiet, because they say that the walls have ears." (771)

Warble once, and you weep the rest of your days.

"What?" Don Quixote repeated, "Men also go to the galleys for being musicians and singers?" "Yes, Señor," responded the galley slave, "because there's nothing worse than singing when you're in difficulty." "But I have heard it said," said Don Quixote, "that troubles take wing for the man who can sing." "Here just the opposite is true," said the galley slave. "Warble once, and you weep the rest of your days." (165)

To come out in the **wash**.

Sancho writes to his wife Teresa Panza: *The man who sounds the alarm is safe, and it'll all come out in the wash of the governorship; what does make me very sad is that they've told me that if I try to take something away from it, I'll go hungry afterwards, and if that's true it won't be very cheap for me, though the maimed and wounded already have their soft job in the alms they beg; so one way or another, you'll be rich and have good luck.* (699)

To be **water** that someone will not drink.

Sancho said: "It was eight or ten days ago, Brother Gossip, that I came to govern the ínsula that they gave me, and in all that time I didn't even have enough bread to eat; I've been persecuted by doctors and had my bones trampled by enemies, and I haven't had time to take any bribes or collect any fees, and this being true, which it is, in my opinion I didn't deserve to leave in this way; but man proposes and God disposes, and God knows what suits each man and what's best for him, and time changes the rhyme, and nobody should say, 'That's water I won't drink,' because you're in a place where you think there's bacon, and you don't even find a nail; God understands me, and that's enough, and I'll say no more, though I could." (821-822)

To throw **water** into the sea.
"I [Don Quixote] have always heard, Sancho, that doing good to the lowborn is throwing water into the sea. If I had believed what you told me, I should have avoided this grief, but what is done is done, and so patience, and let it be a lesson for the future." (173)

To pass minor and major **waters**.
"I [Sancho] say that I'm sure of my master's good ness and truthfulness, and so I'll ask something that goes right to the heart of the matter; speaking with respect, since your grace has been locked in the cage, enchanted, in your opinion, have you had the desire and will to pass what they call major and minor waters?"
"I do not understand what you mean by *passing waters*, Sancho; speak more clearly if you want me to respond in a straightforward way."
"Is it possible that your grace doesn't understand what it means to pass minor or major waters? Even schoolboys know that. Well, what I mean is, have you had the desire to do the thing nobody else can do for you?"
"Ah, now I understand you, Sancho! Yes, I have, quite often. And even do now. Save me from this danger, for not everything is absolutely pristine!" (420-421)

Wealth has the power to mend a good many cracks.
"No," responded the student, "not a prince, but the richest farmer in this entire land, and the most beautiful farmgirl men have ever seen. The preparations for the wedding celebration are extraordinary and remarkable, because it will be held in a meadow near the bride's village; she is always called fair Quiteria, and the groom is called rich Camacho; she is eighteen and he is twenty-two; they are equals, though certain inquisitive people who have the lineages of the entire world memorized claim that fair Quiteria's is superior to Camacho's, but nobody thinks about that nowadays: wealth has the power to mend a good many cracks." (577)

The **wheel** of fortune turns faster than a water wheel.
"Ah Señor Priest, Señor Priest! Did your grace think I [Sancho] didn't know you? Can you think I don't understand and guess where these new enchantments are heading? Well, you should know that I recognize you no matter how you cover your face and understand you no

matter how you hide your lies. In short, where envy rules, virtue cannot survive, and generosity cannot live with miserliness. Devil confound it, if it wasn't for your reverence, my master would be married by now to Princess Micomicona and I'd be a count at least, because I expected nothing less from the goodness of my master, the Knight of the Sorrowful Face, and from the greatness of my services! But now I see that what they say is true: the wheel of fortune turns faster than a water wheel, and those who only yesterday were on top of the world today are down on the ground." (410)

To turn the **wheel** of fortune.
"Señores, if fortune turns her wheel so that my master decides not to be an emperor but an archbishop, I'd [Sancho] like to know how: what do archbishops errant usually give their squires?" (211)

This deception lasted some months until Fortune spun her wheel, the wickedness they had concealed with so much skill was made public, and Anselmo's reckless curiosity cost him his life. (305)

To judge **white** as black and black as white.
Sancho said: "Let each man put his hand over his own heart and not start judging white as black and black as white; each of us is as God made him, and often much worse." (481-482)

To say it is **white** or it is black.
Sancho writes to his wife Teresa Panza: *Don't tell anybody about this, because if you tell your business in public, some will say it's white, and others that it's black. In a few days I'll leave for the governorship, and I'm going there with a real desire to make money because I've been told that all new governors have this same desire.* (699)

To think **white** is black and black is white.
Sancho said to himself: "Well now: everything has a remedy except death, under whose yoke we all have to pass, even if we don't want to, when our life ends. I've seen a thousand signs in this master of mine that he's crazy enough to be tied up, and I'm not far behind, I'm as much a fool as he is because I follow and serve him, if that old saying is true: 'Tell me who your friends are and I'll tell you who you are,' and that other one that says, 'Birds of a feather flock together.' Then, being crazy, which is what he is, with the kind of craziness that most of the time takes one thing for another, and thinks white is black and black is white, like the time he said that the windmills were giants, and the friars' mules dromedaries, and the flocks of sheep enemy armies, and many other things of that nature." (515-516)

Let each **whore** tend to her spinning.
Sancho continued: "I'm saying this, Señor, because if after having traveled so many highways and byways, and gone through so many bad nights and worse days, the fruit of our labors is being plucked by someone taking his ease in this inn, then there's no reason for me to hurry and saddle Rocinante, and harness the donkey, and prepare the palfrey, because we'd be better off sitting still and doing nothing: let each whore tend to her spinning, and we'll eat."

Oh, Lord save me, but what age overcame Don Quixote when he heard his squire's discourteous words! It was so great, I say, that with precipitate voice and stumbling tongue and fire blazing from his eyes, he said:

"Oh, base, lowborn, wretched, rude, ignorant, foul-mouthed, ill-spoken, slanderous, insolent varlet!" (401)

To be a finger's **width**.
"When I [Sancho] leave your grace I'm filled with fear that plagues me with a thousand different kinds of sudden frights and visions. And I just want to let you know this, so that from now on I won't have to move a finger's width from your presence." (178)

Willy-nilly.
"Miracles or no miracles," said Sancho, "each man should be careful how he talks or writes about people and not put down willy-nilly the first thing that comes into his head." (477)

"Now I'll say," replied Sancho, "that you [Teresa Panza] must have an evil spirit in that body of yours. God save you, woman, what a lot of things you've strung together willy-nilly! What do Cascajo, brooches, proverbs, and putting on airs have to do with what I'm saying? Come here, you simple, ignorant woman, and I can call you that because you don't understand my words and try to run away from good luck." (488-489)

Don Quixote said: "Or is it enough for clerics simply to enter other people's houses willy-nilly to guide the owners, even though some have been brought up in the narrow confines of a boarding school and never have seen more of the world than the twenty or thirty leagues of their district, and then suddenly decide to dictate laws to chivalry and make judgments concerning knights errant?" (666)

Sancho said: "No, let them come and mock the bumpkin, and I'll put up with that the way it's nighttime now! Bring a comb here, or whatever you want, and curry this beard, and if you find anything there that offends cleanliness, then you can shear me willy-nilly." (676)

To be a favorable **wind**.

"Come here, you imbecile, you troublemaker," replied Sancho. "Why do you want to stop me now, and for no good reason, from marrying my daughter to somebody who'll give me grandchildren they'll call *Lord* and *Lady*? Look, Teresa: I've always heard the old folks say that if you don't know how to enjoy good luck when it comes, you shouldn't complain if it passes you by. It wouldn't be a good idea, now that it's come knocking, to shut the door in its face; we should let the favorable wind that's blowing carry us along." (487)

To be an ill **wind**.

Sancho said to himself: "They [men on horseback] call us tortoise-tykes? Barbers and ant puffs? Pollies that can be called like pissants? I don't like these names at all; it's an ill wind blowing on this pile of grain; all this wickedness comes down on us at once, like blows on a dog, and may it please God that what this misadventurous adventure threatens goes no further than blows!" (906-907)

To run like the **wind**.

Sancho said: "By St. Roque, our mistress is faster than a falcon, and she could teach the most skilled Cordoban or Mexican how to ride! She was over the hind bow of the saddle in one jump, and without any spurs she makes that palfrey run like a zebra. And her damsels are not far behind; they're all running like the wind." (519)

To catch forty **winks**.

Don Quixote said: "No longer does anyone, with his feet still in the stirrups and leaning on his lance, catch forty winks, as they say, as the knights errant used to do." (465)

There are always **wins** and losses.

Sancho said: "Señor, your grace should lift up your head and be glad, if you [Don Quixote] can, and give thanks to heaven that even though you were toppled to the ground, you didn't break any ribs; and since you know there are always wins and losses, and you may have the hook but not the bacon, forget about the doctor because you don't need him to be cured of what's ailing you, and let's go back home and stop going around looking for adventures in places and countries we don't know." (889)

Wisdom is better than wealth.

Sancho said: "To hell with Basilio's talents! You're worth what you have, and what you have is what you're worth. There are only two lineages in the world, as my grandmother used to say, and that's the haves and the have-nots, though she was on the side of having; nowadays, Señor Don Quixote, wealth is better than wisdom: an ass covered in gold seems better than a saddled horse. And so I say again that I'm on the side of Camacho, whose pots are overflowing with geese and chickens, hares and rabbits, while Basilio's, if they ever show up, and even if they don't, won't hold anything but watered wine." (589)

Wit and humor do not reside in slow minds.
The duchess responded: "That our good Sancho is comical is something I esteem greatly, because it is a sign of his cleverness; for wit and humor, Señor Don Quixote, as your grace well knows, do not reside in slow minds, and since our good Sancho is comical and witty, from this moment on I declare him a clever man." (656)

Withdrawing is not running away.
"Señor," responded Sancho, "withdrawing is not running away, and waiting is not sensible when danger outweighs hope, and wise men know to save something for tomorrow and not risk everything in a single day. And you should know that even though I'm rough and low-born, I still know something about what people call proper behavior." (174)

To set the **wolf** loose among the sheep.
"There can be no doubt that he [a brave man] was out of his mind, or as great a villain as they [four highwaymen], or a man without soul or conscience, for he wanted to set the wolf loose in the midst of the sheep, the fox in the midst of the chickens, the fly in the midst of the honey: he wanted to defraud justice and oppose his king and natural lord, for he opposed his just commands." (240)

A good **woman** and a broken leg stay at home (To keep a woman honorable break her leg and keep her in the house).
"If God preserves my seven senses, or five, or however many I [Teresa Panza] have, I don't intend to let anybody see me in a spot like that. You, my husband, go and be a governor or an insular and put on all the airs you like; I swear on my mother's life that my daughter and I won't set foot out of our village: to keep her chaste, break her leg and keep her in the house; for a chaste girl, work is her fiesta. You go with your Don Quixote and have your adventures, and leave us with our misfortunes, for God will set them right if we're good; I certainly don't know who gave him [Don Quixote] a *Don*, because his parents and grandparents never had one." (488)

"No," responded Sancho, "a good governor and a broken leg stay at home [variation of the proverb "A good woman and a broken leg stay at home."]. How nice if weary merchants came to see him and he was in the woods enjoying himself! What a misfortune for the governorship!" (686)

"Nothing's been lost," responded Sancho. "Let's go, and we'll leave your graces [a young maiden and her brother] at your father's house; maybe he hasn't missed you [a maiden]. And from now on don't be so childish, or so eager to see the world; an honorable maiden and a broken leg stay in the house; and a woman and a hen are soon lost when they wander; and a woman who wants to see also wants to be seen. That's all I'll say." (781)

A **woman** and a hen are soon lost when they wander.
"Nothing's been lost," responded Sancho. "Let's go, and we'll leave your graces [a young maiden and her brother] at your father's house; maybe he hasn't missed you [a maiden]. And from now on don't be so childish, or so eager to see the world; an honorable maiden and a broken leg stay in the house; and a woman and a hen are soon lost when they wander; and a woman who wants to see also wants to be seen. That's all I'll say." (781)

A **woman** who wants to see also wants to be seen.
"Nothing's been lost," responded Sancho. "Let's go, and we'll leave your graces [a young maiden and her brother] at your father's house; maybe he hasn't missed you [a maiden]. And from now on don't be so childish, or so eager to see the world; an honorable maiden and a broken leg stay in the house; and a woman and a hen are soon lost when they wander; and a woman who wants to see also wants to be seen. That's all I'll say." (781)

The dead **woman** was frightened by the one with her throat cut.
Sancho said: "So whoever sees the mote in somebody else's eye has to see the beam in his own, so that nobody can say about him: 'The dead woman was frightened by the one with her throat cut.' And your grace knows very well that the fool knows more in his own house than the wise man does in somebody else's." (736)

The old **woman** liked the greens so much that she didn't leave any, green or dry.
Sancho said: "By God, I'm as likely to become a Moor as to let anybody mark my face or slap my nose! By my faith! What does slapping my face have to do with the resurrection of this maiden? The old woman liked the greens so much ... [the second part of the proverb is "that she didn't leave any, green or dry"]. They enchant Dulcinea, and whip me to disenchant her; Altisidora dies of ills that God sent her, and they'll bring her back by slapping me twenty-four times and riddling my body with pinpricks, and pinching my arms black and blue! Try those tricks on your brother-in- law! I'm an old dog, and you don't have to call me twice!" (910)

Women reject the man who loves them and love the man who despises them.
"Torralba, when she found herself rejected by Lope, began to love him dearly, though she had never loved him before." "That is the nature of women," said Don Quixote. "They reject the man who loves them and love the man who despises them. Go on, Sancho." (145-146)

As soft as **wool**.
Sancho responded: "Nothing but one insult after another, though she [Dulcinea] must know the proverb that says that a jackass loaded down with gold climbs the mountain fast, and gifts can break boulders, and God helps those who help themselves, and a bird in hand is worth two in the bush. And then my master, who should have coddled me and flattered me so I'd turn as soft as wool and carded cotton, says that if he catches me he'll tie me naked to a tree and double the number of lashes; these noble folk so full of pity should remember that they're not only asking a squire to whip himself, but a governor; like they say, 'That's the finishing touch.' Let them learn, let them learn, damn them, how to beg, and how to ask, and how to have good manners; all times are not the same, and men are not always in a good humor." (694)

To be pure like **wool** in the brambles.
"This wicked man seized me in the middle of a field, and used my body like a dirty old rag, and, oh woe is me, he took what I [a woman] had safeguarded for more than twenty-three years, defending it against Moors and Christians, Spaniards and foreigners, and I, always as hard as an oak, kept myself pure like the salamander in the fire, or wool in the brambles, just so this good man would come along now and put his clean hands all over me." (751)

To look (come) for **wool** and come back shorn.
"Who can doubt it?" said the niece. "But, Señor Uncle [Don Quixote], who has involved your grace in those disputes? Wouldn't it be better to stay peacefully in your house and not wander around the world searching for bread made from something better than wheat, never to think that many people go looking for wool and come back shorn?" (55)

Sancho responded: Let each man look out for himself, though the best thing would be to let everybody's anger stay asleep; nobody knows another man's heart, and many who come for wool go home clipped and shorn, and God blessed peace and cursed fights, because if a cat that's hunted and locked up and treated badly turns into a lion, then since I'm a man, God knows what I could turn into, and so from now on I'm letting your grace know, Señor Squire, that all the harm and damage that result from our quarrel will be on your head." (542-543)

"I know how to sign my name very well," responded Sancho, "because when I was steward of a brotherhood in my village, I learned to make some letters like the marks on bundles, and they told me that they said my name; better yet, I'll pretend that my right hand has been hurt, and I'll have somebody else sign for me; there's a remedy for everything except death, and since I'll be in charge of everything, I can do whatever I want; then, too, when your father's the magistrate... [you're safe when you go to trial]. And being a governor, which is more than being a magistrate, just let them come and they'll see what happens! No, let them make fun of me and speak ill of me: they'll come for wool and go home shorn; and when God loves you, your house knows it; and the rich man's folly passes for good judgment in the world; and since that's what I'll be, being a governor and a very generous one, which is what I plan to be, nobody will notice any faults in me. No, just be like honey and the flies will go after you; you're only worth as much as you have, my grandmother used to say; and you won't get revenge on a well-established man." (735)

"I [Sancho] am, Señor, so unfortunate, that I fear the day will never come when I can join this exercise. Oh, how polished I'll keep the spoons when I'm a shepherd. What soft bread, what cream, what garlands, what pastoral odds and ends that, if they don't earn me fame as a wise man, can't help but earn me fame as a clever one! Sanchica, my daughter, will bring food up to our flocks. But wait! She's a good-looking girl, and there are shepherds more wicked than simple, and I wouldn't want her to go for wool and come back shorn; love and unchaste desires are as likely in the countryside as in the cities, in shepherd's huts as in royal palaces, and if you take away the cause, you take away the sin, and if your eyes don't see, your heart doesn't break, and a jump over the thicket is better than the prayers of good men." (901)

A **word** to the wise is sufficient.

"I [Sancho] involved myself, and I can involve myself as a squire who had learned the terms of courtesy in the school of your grace, the most courteous and polite knight in all courtliness; in these things, as I have heard your grace say, you can lose as much for a card too many as for a card too few, and a word to the wise is sufficient." (704)

One **word** leads to another.

"Even so," replied the traveler, "I still have a misgiving, and it is that I have often read that words are exchanged between two knights errant, and one word leads to another, their anger rises, they turn their horses and ride off a good distance to the far ends of the field, and then, without further ado, they ride at full tilt toward each other, and in the middle of the charge they commend themselves to their ladies, and what usually happens after their encounter is that one falls from his horse, run through by his opponent's lance, and the same thing happens to the other as well, for unless he holds on to his horse's mane, he cannot help but fall to the ground, too." (89-90)

To hang on someone's every **word**.
Cervantes: Sancho made so many comical remarks that all the servants in the house, and everyone else who heard him, hung on his every word. (864)

To say the **word**.
Sancho's letter to his wife said: *I am told that there are fat acorns in your village: send me about two dozen, and I shall esteem them greatly because they come from your hand; write me a long letter informing me of your health and well-being; if you happen to need anything, you only have to say the word, and your word will be heeded.* (785)

To turn the **world** upside down.
Don Quixote responded: "May God guide you, Sancho, and govern you in your governorship, and free me of the misgivings I still have that you will turn the entire ínsula upside down, something I could avoid by revealing to the duke who you are, and telling him that this plump little body of yours is nothing but a sack filled with proverbs and guile." (736)

You are **worth** what you have, and what you have is what you are worth.
Sancho said: "To hell with Basilio's talents! You're worth what you have, and what you have is what you're worth. There are only two lineages in the world, as my grandmother used to say, and that's the haves and the have-nots, though she was on the side of having; nowadays, Señor Don Quixote, wealth is better than wisdom: an ass covered in gold seems better than a saddled horse. And so I say again that I'm on the side of Camacho, whose pots are overflowing with geese and chickens, hares and rabbits, while Basilio's, if they ever show up, and even if they don't, won't hold anything but watered wine." (589)

"I know how to sign my name very well," responded Sancho, "because when I was steward of a brotherhood in my village, I learned to make some letters like the marks on bundles, and they told me that they said my name; better yet, I'll pretend that my right hand has been hurt, and I'll have somebody else sign for me; there's a remedy for everything except death, and since I'll be in charge of everything, I can do whatever I want; then, too, when your father's the magistrate... [you're safe when you go to trial]. And being a governor, which is more than being a magistrate, just let them come and they'll see what happens! No, let them make fun of me and speak ill of me: they'll come for wool and go home shorn; and when God loves you, your house knows it; and the rich man's folly passes for good judgment in the world; and since that's what I'll be, being a governor and a very generous one, which is what I plan to be, nobody will notice any faults in me. No, just be like honey and the flies will go after you; you're only worth as much as you have, my grandmother used to say; and you won't get revenge on a well-established man." (735)

To look like an **X**.
Sancho finished eating, and leaving the innkeeper looking like an X [the idiom (*hecho equis*) means "staggering drunk" and is based on the image of the shape an inebriated person's legs assume when trying to keep the balance], he went to the room where his master was having supper. (847)

Those who only **yesterday** were on top of the world today are down on the ground.
"Ah Señor Priest, Señor Priest! Did your grace think I didn't know you? Can you think I don't understand and guess where these new enchantments are heading? Well, you should know that I recognize you no matter how you cover your face and understand you no matter how you hide your lies. In short, where envy rules, virtue cannot survive, and generosity cannot live with miserliness. Devil confound it, if it wasn't for your reverence, my master would be married by now to Princess Micomicona and I'd be a count at least, because I expected nothing less from the goodness of my master, the Knight of the Sorrowful Face, and from the greatness of my services! But now I see that what they say is true: the wheel of fortune turns faster than a water wheel, and those who only yesterday were on top of the world today are down on the ground." (410)

Zamora was not won in an hour.
Don Quixote said: "On your life, friend [Sancho], let the matter stop here, for this remedy seems very harsh to me, and it would be a good idea to take more time: Zamora was not won in an hour. You have given yourself more than a thousand lashes, if I have counted correctly: that is enough for now, for the donkey, speaking coarsely, will endure the load, but not an extra load." (922)

Bibliography

Spanish Edition:

Miguel de Cervantes Saavedra, *Don Qvixote de la Mancha*. Eds. Rodolfo Schevill and Adolfo Bonilla. 10 vols. Madrid: Gráficas Reunidas, 1947-1949.

Translations:

1612/1620. Thomas Shelton
Miguel des Cervantes, *The History of the Valorous and Witty Knight-Errant Don Quixote of the Mancha*. Translated by Thomas Shelton. Introduction by Royal Cortissoz. 4 vols. New York: Charles Scribner's Sons, 1907.

1700. Peter Anthony Motteux
Miguel de Cervantes Saavedra, *The History of the Ingenious Gentleman Don Quixote*. Translated by Peter Anthony Motteux. 4 vols. Edinburgh: John Grant, 1908.

1742. Charles Jarvis
Miguel de Cervantes Saavedra, *Don Quixote de la Mancha*. Translated by Charles Jarvis. Edited with an Introduction by E.C. Riley. Oxford: Oxford University Press, 1992.

1755. Tobias Smollett
Miguel de Cervantes Saavedra, *The History and Adventures of the Renowned Don Quixote*. Translated by Tobias Smollett. Introduction by Robin Chapman. London: The Folio Society, 1995

1885. John Ormsby
Miguel de Cervantes Saavedra, *The Ingenious Gentleman Don Quixote of La Mancha*. Translated by John Ormsby. 4 vols. New York: Macmillan, 1885

1949. Samuel Putnam
Miguel de Cervantes Saavedra, *The Ingenious Gentleman Don Quixote de la Mancha*. Translated by Samuel Putnam. New York: The Viking Press, 1949.

1995. Burton Raffel
Miguel de Cervantes, *Don Quijote*. Translated by Burton Raffel. Edited by Diana de Armas Wilson. New York: W.W. Norton, 1999.

2003. Edith Grossman
Miguel de Cervantes, *Don Quixote*. Translated by Edith Grossman. Introduction by Harold Bloom. New York: HarperCollins, 2003.

2005. Tom Lathrop
Miguel de Cervantes Saavedra, *Don Quixote*. Translated by Tom Lathrop. Newark, Delaware: Lingua Text, 2005.

2009. James H. Montgomery
Miguel de Cervantes Saavedra, *Don Quixote*. Translated by James H. Montgomery. Introduction by David Quint. Indianapolis, Indiana: Hackett Publishing, 2009.

References Cited:

Abrahams, Roger D., and Barbara A. Babcock. 1977 (1994). "The Literary Use of Proverbs." *Journal of American Folklore*, 90: 414-429. Also in *Wise Words: Essays on the Proverb*. Ed. Wolfgang Mieder. New York: Garland Publishing, 1994; rpt. London: Routledge, 2015. 415-437.

Allen, John J. 1979. *Don Quixote: Hero or Fool?* Gainesville, Florida: University Presses of Florida.

Alonso, Amado. 1948. "Las prevaricaciones idiomáticas de Sancho." *Nueva Revista de Filología Hispánica*, 2: 1-20.

Álvarez Curiel, Francisco J. 1999. "'Al revés lo habéis, necio, de decir...' o los refranes en *El Quijote* apócrifo." *Paremia*, 8: 13-17.

Álvarez Díaz, Juan José. 2009. "Las armas y las letras en el refranero. El pleito que inspiró a Cervantes." *Paremia*, 18: 77-85.

Armas, Frederick A. de. 2015. "Windmills of the Mind: The Devilish Devices of *Don Quixote*, Part I, Chapter 8." *Approaches to Teaching Cervantes's "Don Quixote"*. Eds. James A. Parr and Lisa Vollendorf. New York: Modern Language Association of America. 112-118.

Aulnaye, M. de. 1821. "Proverbes et sentences tirés de l'*Histoire de Don Quixote*." In M. de Aulnaye. *L'Ingénieux Chevalier Don Quixote de la Manche*. Paris: Th. Desoer. IV, 401-440.

Avalle-Arce, Juan Bautista. 1984. "Background Material on *Don Quixote*." *Approaches to Teaching Cervantes' "Don Quixote"*. Ed. Richard Bjornson. New York: Modern Language Association of America. 127-135.

Axnick, Margarete. 1984. *Probleme der deutschen Sprichwortübersetzungen aus Miguel de Cervantes' "Don Quijote" – eine vergleichende sprachliche und literarische Untersuchung*. M.A. Thesis University of Bonn.

Ayala Mejíra, Róbinson. 2007. *Ecos de "Don Quijote" en el habla moderna de El Salvador: Los refranes españoles y su transmisión oral*. M.A. Thesis University of Calgary (chronological list of 318 proverbs from *Don Quixote* on pp. 140-154, alphabetical list on pp. 155-169).

Bañeza Román, Celso. 1989. "Refranes de origen bíblico en Cervantes." *Anales Cervantinos*, 27: 45-77.

Barbadillo de la Fuente, María Teresa. 2006. "Presupuestos didácticos para la enseñanza de los refranes a través de *El Quijote*." *Paremia*, 15: 141-150.

Barsanti Vigo, María Jesús. 2003. *Estudio paremiológico contrastivo de la traducción de "El Quijote" de Ludwig Tieck*. Salamanca: Ediciones Universidad de Salamanca.

Barsanti Vigo, María Jesús. 2006. "Cinco refranes retóricos de Sancho en *El Quijote* de Ludwig Tieck." *Paremia*, 15: 179-186.

Barsanti Vigo, María Jesús. 2010. "Las paremias de *El Quijote* en alemán y español. Delimitación de una investigación." *Estudios Filológicos Alemanes*, 21: 285-305.

Bizzarri, Hugo O. 2003. "Los refranes en Cervantes." *Boletín Hispánico Helvético*, 2: 25-49.

Bizzarri, Hugo O. 2011. "Apuntes para la realización de un 'diccionario de refranes, frases proverbiales y sentencias cervantinas'." *Crisol*, no volume given, no. 14: 117-129.

Bizzarri, Hugo O. 2015. *Diccionario de paremias cervantinas*. Alcalá de Henares: Universidad de Alcalá.

Bjornson, Richard, ed. 1984a. *Approaches to Teaching Cervantes' "Don Quixote"*. New York: Modern Language Association of America.

Bjornson, Richard. 1984b. "Editions." *Approaches to Teaching Cervantes' "Don Quixote"*. Ed. Richard Bjornson. New York: Modern Language Association of America. 3-14.

Bloom, Harold. 1994 (2001). "Cervantes: The Play of the World." *Cervantes's "Don Quixote"*. Ed. Harold Bloom. Philadelphia: Chelsea House. 145-160.

Bloom, Harold, ed. 2001. *Cervantes's "Don Quixote"*. Philadelphia: Chelsea House.

Bloom, Harold, ed. 2005. *Miguel de Cervantes*. Philadelphia: Chelsea House.

Bloom, Harold, ed. 2010. *Miguel de Cervantes's "Don Quixote". New Edition*. New York: Bloom's Literary Criticism.

Burke, Ulick Ralph. 1872 (1877, 1977). *Sancho Panza's Proverbs, and Others which Occur in "Don Quixote"; with Literal English Translation, Notes and Introduction*. London: Basil M. Pickering, 1872. Later edition: *Spanish Salt. A Collection of all the Proverbs which are to be Found in Don Quixote*. London: Pickering, 1877; rpt. Philadelphia: R.West, 1977.

Cantera Ortiz de Urbina, Jesús, Julia Sevilla Muñoz, and Manuel Sevilla Muñoz. 2005. *Refranes, otras paremias y fraseologismos en*

"Don Quijote de la Mancha". Ed. Wolfgang Mieder. Burlington, Vermont: The University of Vermont.

Cárcer y de Sobíes, Enrique de. 1916. *Las frases del "Quijote". Su exposición, ordenación y comentarios, y su versión á las lenguas francesa, portugesa, italiana, catalana, inglesa y alemana.* Lérida: Artes Gráficas de Sol y Benet.

Carnes, Pack. 1988. *Proverbia in Fabula. Essays on the Relationship of the Fable and the Proverb.* Bern: Peter Lang.

Casalduero, Joaquín. 1947. "The Composition of *Don Quixote.*" *Cervantes Across the Centuries.* Eds. Angel Flores and M.J. Benardete. New York: Dryden Press. 56-93.

Cascardi, Anthony J. 2002a. "*Don Quixote* and the Invention of the Novel." *The Cambridge Companion to Cervantes.* Ed. Anthony J. Cascardi. Cambridge: Cambridge University Press. 58-79.

Cascardi, Anthony J. ed. 2002b. *The Cambridge Companion to Cervantes.* Cambridge: Cambridge University Press.

Cassou, Jean. 1947. "An Introduction to Cervantes." *Cervantes Across the Centuries.* Eds. Angel Flores and M.J. Benardete. New York: Dryden Press. 3-31.

Castillo de Lucas, Antonio. 1943 (1996). "Refranes de aplicación médica en *El Quijote.*" *Paremia*, 5: 43-48 (published lecture from the year 1943).

Castillo de Lucas, Antonio. 1947. "Paremiología médica cervantina." *El siglo médico*, 115 (May 10): 577-582.

Castro, Américo. 1925. "Refranes." In A. Castro. *El pensamiento de Cervantes.* Madrid: Casa Editorial Hernando. 190-195.

Chevalier, Maxime. 1993. "Conte, proverbe, romance: Trois formes traditionelles en question au siècle d'or." *Bulletin Hispanique*, 95: 237-264.

Ciallella, Louise. 2003. "Teresa Panza's Character Zone and [Proverbial] Discourse of Domesticity in *Don Quijote.*" *Cervantes: Bulletin of the Cervantes Society of America*, 23: 275-296.

Ciallella, Louise. 2007. "Quixotic Antecedents and Zones of Proverbial Tactics." In L. Ciallella. *Quixotic Modernists. Reading Gender in "Tristana," Trigo, and Martínez Sierra.* Lewisburg, Pennsylvania: Bucknell University Press. 24-30.

Close, A.J. 1973. "Sancho Panza: Wise Fool." *Modern Language Review*, 68: 344-357.

Cobelo, Silvia. 2009. *Historiografia das traduções do "Quixote" publicadas no Brasil – Provérbios do Sancho Panza.* Diss. Universidade de São Paulo.

Coll y Vehí, José. 1874. *Los refranes del "Quijote" ordenados por materias y glosados.* Barcelona: Diario de Barcelona.

Colombi, María Cecilia. 1988. *Los refranes en "Don Quijote"*. Diss. University of California at Santa Barbara.

Colombi, María Cecilia. 1989a. "'Al buen callar llaman Sancho'." *Speculum historiographiae linguisticae*. Ed. Klaus D. Dutz. Münster: Modus Publikationen. 243-252.

Colombi, María Cecilia. 1989b. *Los refranes en el "Quijote": texto y contexto*. Potomac, Maryland: Scripta Humanistica.

Colombi, María Cecilia. 1990. "Los refranes en el *Quijote*: Discurso autoritario y des-autor-itario [*sic*]." *Proverbium*, 7: 37-55.

Combet, Louis. 1997. "La fonction occulte des proverbes dans le *Don Quichotte*." *Paremia*, 6: 173-178.

Combet, Louis. 1998, "Les refranes dans le *Quichotte* d'Avellaneda." *Paremia*, 7: 35-42.

Correas, Gonzalo de. 1627 (1906, 1967). *Vocabulario de refranes y frases proverbiales*. Madrid: Ratés; rpt. ed Louis Combet. Lyon: Institute d'Étude Ibériques et Ibéro-Américaines de l'Université de Bordeaux, 1967.

Corley, Ames Haven. 1917. *Word-Play in the "Don Quixote"*. New York: Bailly-Baillière. Also in *Revista Hispánica*, 40: 543-591.

Cull, John T. 2014. "Nunca mucho costó poco. Una vez más sobre las paremias del *Quijote*." *Paremia*, 23: 147-161.

Denis, Ferdinand. 1834. "Les proverbes, essai sur la philosophie de Sancho." In F. Denis. *Le Brahme Voyageur, ou la sagesse populaire de toutes les nations*. Paris: Librairie d'Abel Ledoux. 1-45.

Diaz Isaacs, Gloria. 1974. "Los Refranes del *Quijote*." *Loteria* (Panama), no. 220: 20-38.

Dundes, Alan. 1965. "The Study of Folklore in Literature and Culture: Identification and Interpretation." *Journal of American Folklore*, 78: 136-142.

Dunn, Peter. 1984. "Getting Started: *Don Quixote* and the Reader's Response." *Approaches to Teaching Cervantes' "Don Quixote"*. Ed. Richard Bjornson. New York: Modern Language Association of America. 77-86.

Durán, Manuel. 1974. *Cervantes*. New York: Twayne Publishers.

Durán, Manuel, and Ray R. Rogg. 2006 (2010). "Constructing *Don Quixote*." *Miguel d Cervantes's "Don Quixote". New Edition*. Ed. Harold Bloom. New York: Bloom's Literary Criticism. 91-107.

Eisenberg, Daniel. 1984. "Teaching *Don Quixote* as a Funny Book." *Approaches to Teaching Cervantes' "Don Quixote"*. Ed. Richard Bjornson. New York: Modern Language Association of America. 62-68.

Eisenberg, Daniel. 2006. "The Text of *Don Quixote* as Seen by its Modern English Translators." *Cervantes*, 26: 103-126.

El Saffar, Ruth. 1975. *Distance and Control in "Don Quixote". A Study in Narrative Technique.* Chapel Hill, North Carolina: University of North Carolina Department of Romance Languages.

Erler, Anette. 1986. "Zur Geschichte des Spruches 'Bis dat, qui cito dat." *Philologus*, 130: 210-220.

Estévez Molinero, Ángel. 1999. "Paremias de Sancho, parénesis de Don Quijote y algunos entretenidos razonamientos." *Paremia*, 8: 155-160.

Finello, Dominick. 1994. *Pastoral Themes and Forms in Cervantes's Fiction.* Lewisburg, Pennsylvania: Bucknell University Press.

Flores, Angel, and M.J. Benardete, eds. 1947. *Cervantes Across the Centuries.* New York: Dryden Press.

Flores, R.M. 1982a. *Sancho Panza Through Three Hundred Seventy-Five Years of Continuations, Imitations, and Criticism, 1605-1980.* Newark, Delaware: Juan de la Cuesta.

Flores, R.M. 1982b. "Sayings and Proverbs [in Spanish]." In R.M. Flores. *Sancho Panza Through Three Hundred Seventy-Five Years of Continuations, Imitations, and Criticism, 1605-1980.* Newark, Delaware: Juan de la Cuesta. 215-222.

Fournet-Pérot, Sonia. 2009. "Les proverbes dans *'El ingenioso hidalgo' don Quijote de la Mancha*: des stéréotypes linguistiques et culturels révélateurs de la complexité du message cervantin." *Cahiers de Narratologie*, 17: 16 pp. (electronic journal).

Gates, Steven H. 1973. "Cervantes' Influence on Dickens, with Comparative Emphasis on *Don Quijote* and P*ickwick Papers.*" *Anales Cervantinos*, 12: 135-156.

Gerhard, Sandra Forbes. 1982. *"Don Quixote" and the Shelton Translation. A Stylistic Analysis.* Potomac, Maryland: Studia Humanitatis.

Gilman, Stephen. 1989. *The Novel According to Cervantes.* Berkeley, California: University of California Press.

González Echevarría, Roberto. 2001 (2005). "Introduction to *Don Quixote.*" *Miguel de Cervantes.* Ed. Harold Bloom. Philadelphia: Chelsea House. 263-276.

González Echevarría, Roberto, ed. 2005a. *Cervantes' "Don Quixote".* New York: Oxford University Press.

González Echevarría, Roberto. 2005b. "Introduction." *Cervantes' "Don Quixote".* Ed. Roberto González Echevarría. New York: Oxford University Press. 3-22.

González Martín, Vicente. 1997. "El refrán en la literatura española de los siglos XVI y XVII." *Paremia*, 6: 281-286.

Gorfkle, Laura J. 1993. *Discovering the Comic in "Don Quixote".* Chapel Hill, North Carolina: University of North Carolina Department of Romance Languages.

Grossman, Edith, tr. 2003. *Miguel de Cervantes. Don Quixote*. New York: HarperCollins.

Haller, Joseph. 1883. *Altspanische Sprichwörter und sprichwörtliche Redensarten aus den Zeiten vor Cervantes, in's Deutsche übersetzt, in spanischer und deutscher Sprache erörtert, und verglichen mit den entsprechenden der alten Griechen und Römer, der Lateiner der späteren Zeiten, der sämmtlichen germanischen und romanischen Völker mit einer Anzahl der Basken, endlich mit sachlichen, sprachlichen, geschichtlichen, literarhistorischen, biographischen, geographischen und topographischen Erläuterungen versehen*. Regensburg: G.J. Manz.

Hansen, Terrence L. 1959. "Folk Narrative Motifs, Beliefs, and Proverbs in Cervantes' *Exemplary Novels*." *Journal of American Folklore*, 72: 24-29.

Hart, Thomas R. 2002. "Sancho's Discretion." *Bulletin of Spanish Studies*, 79: 45-53.

Hasan-Rokem, Galit. 2007. "Literary Forms of Orality: Proverbs in Hebrew Translations of *Don Quijote*." *Proverbium*, 24: 189-206.

Hatzfeld, Helmut. 1947. "The Style of *Don Quixote*." *Cervantes Across the Centuries*. Eds. Angel Flores and M.J. Benardete. New York: Dryden Press. 94-100.

Hatzfeld, Helmut. 1949. *El "Quijote" como obra de arte del lenguaje*. Madrid: Patronato del IV Centenario del Nacimiento de Cervantes.

Hayes, Francis Clement. 1936. *The Use of Proverbs in the "Siglo de Oro" Drama. An Introductory Study*. Diss. University of North Carolina at Chapel Hill.

Hernandez, José Luis Alonso. 1984. "Interprétation psychoanalytique de l'utilisation des parémies dans la littérature espagnole." *Richesse du proverbe*. Eds. François Suard and Claude Buridant. Lille: Université de Lille. II, 213-225.

Hess-Lüttich, Ernest W.B. 1983. "Sprichwörter und Redensarten als Übersetzungsproblem. Am Beispiel deutscher Übersetzungen spanischer und türkischer Literatur." *Mehrsprachigkeit und Gesellschaft. Akten des 17. Linguistischen Kolloquiums Brüssel 1982*. Eds. René Jongen, Sabine De Knop, Peter H. Nelde, and Marie-Paule Quix. Tübingen: Max Niemeyer. II, 222-236.

Hutman, Norma L. 1984. "Don Quixote: Archetypal Baroque Man." *Approaches to Teaching Cervantes' "Don Quixote"*. Ed. Richard Bjornson. New York: Modern Language Association of America. 120-126.

Iventosch, Herman. 1980. "The Decline of the Humanist Ideal in the Baroque: Quevedo's Attack on the 'Refrán'." *Mester*, 9: 17-24.

Jehenson, Myriam Yvonne, and Peter N. Dunn. 2006 (2010). "Discursive Hybridity: Don Quixote's and Sancho Panza's Utopias." *Mi-

guel de Cervantes's "Don Quixote". New Edition. Ed. Harold Bloom. New York: Bloom's Literary Criticism. 127-144.

Johnson, Carroll B. 1983. *Madness and Lust. A Psychoanalytical Approach to Don Quixote*. Berkeley, California: University of California Press.

Joly, Monique. 1971. "Aspectos del refrán en Mateo Alemán y Cervantes." *Nueva Revista de Filologia Hispanica*, 20: 95-106. Also in Joly 1996: 239-255.

Joly, Monique. 1975. "Ainsi parlait Sancho Pança." *Les langues néolatines*, 69: 3-37. Also in Joly 1996: 257-297.

Joly, Monique. 1984. "Le discours métaparémique dans *Don Quichotte*." *Richesse du proverbe*. Eds. François Suard and Claude Buridant. Lille: Université de Lille. II, 245-260. Also in Joly 1996: 207-228.

Joly, Monique. 1991. "De paremiología cervantina: una reconsideración del problema." *Ínsula*, no volume given, no. 538: 23-24. Also in Joly 1996: 229-237.

Joly, Monique. 1996. "Parémiologie." In M. Joly. *Études sur "Don Quichotte"*. Paris: Publications de la Sorbonne. 205-297.

Krauss, Werner. 1946 (1975). *Die Welt im spanischen Sprichwort*. Wiesbaden: Limes. Leipzig: Reclam (much enlarged edition).

Krauss, Werner. 1959. "Die Welt im spanischen Sprichwort." In W. Krauss. *Studien und Aufsätze*. Berlin: Rütten & Loening. 73-91.

Krikmann, Arvo. 1974 (2009). *Proverb Semantics. Studies in Structure, Logic, and Metaphor*. Ed. Wolfgang Mieder. Burlington, Vermont: The University of Vermont.

Kuusi, Matti. 1957. *Regen bei Sonnenschein. Zur Weltgeschichte einer Redensart*. Helsinki: Suomalainen Tiedeakatemia.

Lacosta, Francisco. 1965. "El infinito mundo de los proverbios: *Don Quijote*." *Universidad* (Santa Fé), 65: 135-151.

Landa, Luis. 2013. "The Plebeian and the Cultivated Proverb in Miguel de Cervantes' *Don Quixote*." *Textures. Culture, Literature, Folklore*. For Galit Hasan-Rokem. Eds. Hagar Salamon and Avigdor Shinan. Jerusalem: Hebrew University of Jerusalem, Mandel Institute of Jewish Studies. I, 225-235 (in Hebrew), I, xviii-xix (English abstract).

Lathrop, Tom. 2006. "Edith Grossman's Translation of *Don Quixote*." *Cervantes*, 26: 237-255.

Leite de Vasconcellos, José. 1925. *A Figa. Estudo de etnografia comparativa*. Porto: Araujo & Sobrinho.

Leyva, J. 2004. *Refranes, dichos y sentencias del "Quijote"*. Madrid: Libdo0Hobby-Club.

Llosa, Mario Vargas. 2005 (2010). "A Novel for the Twenty-first Century." *Miguel de Cervantes's "Don Quixote". New Edition*. Ed. Harold Bloom. New York: Bloom's Literary Criticism. 57-68.

López del Arco, A. 1905. *Refranes de Sancho Panza. Aventuras y desventuras, malicias y agudezas del escudero de don Quijote*. Madrid: no publisher given.

MacKey, Mary. 1974. "Rhetoric and Characterization in *Don Quixote*." *Hispanic Review*, 42: 51-66.

Madariaga, Salvador de. 1934 (1961). *Don Quixote. An Introductory Essay in Psychology*. London: Oxford University Press.

Mal Lara, Juan de. 1568 (1958-1959). *La philosophía vulgar*. 4 vols. Sevilla: Diaz; rpt. Barcelona: Talleres de Gráficas Aymami.

Mancing, Howard. 1982a (2005). "Knighthood Compromised." *Miguel de Cervantes*. Ed. Harold Bloom. Philadelphia: Chelsea House. 7-35.

Mancing, Howard. 1982b. *The Chivalric World of "Don Quijote". Style, Structure, and Narrative Technique*. Columbia, Missouri: University of Missouri Press.

Mann, Thomas. 1934 (2001). "Voyage with *Don Quixote*." *Cervantes's "Don Quixote"*. Ed. Harold Bloom. Philadelphia: Chelsea House. 13-45.

Martín, Adrienne L. 2002. "Humor and Violence in Cervantes." *The Cambridge Companion to Cervantes*. Ed. Anthony J. Cascardi. Cambridge: Cambridge University Press. 160-185.

McGrath, Michael J. 2006. "Tilting at Windmills: *Don Quijote* in English." *Cervantes*, 26: 7-40.

Menéndez-Pidal, Ramón. 1947 (2005a). "The Genesis of *Don Quixote*." *Cervantes Across the Centuries*. Eds. Angel Flores and M.J. Benardete. New York: Dryden Press. 32-55. Also in *Cervantes' "Don Quixote"*. Ed. Roberto González Echevarría. New York: Oxford University Press. 63-94.

Mieder, Wolfgang. 1974. "The Essence of Literary Proverb Studies." *Proverbium*, no. 23: 888-894.

Mieder, Wolfgang. 1993 (2012). *Proverbs Are Never Out of Season. Popular Wisdom in the Modern Age*. New York: Oxford University Press; rpt. New York: Peter Lang, 2012.

Mieder, Wolfgang, ed. 1994 (2015). *Wise Words: Essays on the Proverb*. New York: Garland Publishing; rpt. London: Routledge.

Mieder, Wolfgang. 2004a (2012). *Proverbs. A Handbook*. Westport, Connecticut: Greenwood Press; rpt. New York: Peter Lang, 2012.

Mieder, Wolfgang, ed. 2004b. *"The Netherlandish Proverbs". An International Symposium on the Pieter Brueg(h)els*. Burlington, Vermont: The University of Vermont.

Mieder, Wolfgang. 2006a. "From 'Windmills in One's Head' to 'Tilting at Windmills': History and Meaning of a Proverbial Allusion to Cervantes' *Don Quixote*." *Proverbium*, 23: 343-418. With 38 illustrations.

Mieder, Wolfgang. 2006b. *"Tilting at Windmills": History and Meaning of a Proverbial Allusion to Cervantes' "Don Quixote"*. Burlington, Vermont: The University of Vermont. With 55 illustrations.

Mieder, Wolfgang. 2009. *International Bibliography of Paremiology and Phraseology*. 2 vols. Berlin: Walter de Gruyter.

Mieder, Wolfgang. 2011. *International Bibliography of Paremiography. Collections of Proverbs, Proverbial Expressions and Comparisons, Quotations, Graffiti, Slang, and Wellerisms*. Burlington, Vermont: The University of Vermont.

Mieder, Wolfgang. 2014. *Behold the Proverbs of a People". Proverbial Wisdom in Culture, Literature, and Politics*. Jackson, Mississippi: University Press of Mississippi.

Mieder, Wolfgang. 2015. "'All Men Are Created Equal': From Democratic Claim to Proverbial Game." *Scientific Newsletter*. Series: Modern Linguistic and Methodical-and-Didactic Researches (Voronezh State University of Architecture and Civil Engineering, Voronezh, Russia), no volume given, no. 1: 10-37.

Mieder, Wolfgang, and George B. Bryan. 1996. *Proverbs in World Literature. A Bibliography*. New York: Peter Lang.

Mieder, Wolfgang, and Stewart A. Kingsbury. 1994. *A Dictionary of Wellerisms*. New York: Oxford University Press.

Mieder, Wolfgang, Stewart A. Kingsbury, and Kelsie B. Harder. 1992. *A Dictionary of American Proverbs*. New York: Oxford University Press.

Montgomery, James H. 2009. "Selected Proverbs, Maxims, and Passages from *Don Quixote*." *Miguel de Cervantes Saavedra. Don Quixote*. Translated by J.H. Montgomery. Indianapolis, Indiana: Hackett Publishing. 835-844.

Morel-Fatio, Alfred. 1882. "'Al buen callar llaman Sancho'." *Romania*, 11: 114-119.

Mulinacci, Anna Paola. 1990. "'Cercar Maria per Ravenna': Da un proverbio, a un cantare, alla 'Fantesca' di G.B. Della Porta." *Italianistica: Revista di letteratura italiane*, 19: 69-77.

Murillo, L.A. 1990. *A Critical Introduction to "Don Quixote"*. New York: Peter Lang.

Nabokov, Vladimir. 1951-1952 (1983). *Lectures on "Don Quixote"*. Ed. Fredson Bowers. New York: Harcourt Brace Jovanovich.

Neumeister, Sebastian. 1994. "Geschichten vor und nach dem Sprichwort." *Kleinstformen der Literatur*. Eds. Walter Haug and Burghart Wachinger. Tübingen: Max Niemeyer. 205-215.

Norrick Neal R. 1985. *How Proverbs Mean. Semantic Studies in English Proverbs*. Amsterdam: Mouton.

Nuessel, Frank H. 1999 (2000). "Linguistic Theory and Discourse in *Don Quijote*." *Advances in Hispanic Linguistics: Papers from the 2nd Hispanic Linguistics Symposium*. Eds. Javier Gutiérrez-Rexach and Fernando Martínez-Gil. Somerville, Massachusetts: Cascadilla Press, 1999. I, 248-264 (esp. 258-261). Also in F. Nuessel. *Linguistic Approaches to Hispanic Literature*. New York: Legas. 97-114 (proverbs esp. 109-111).

Nuñez, Hernán. 1555 (2001). *Refranes o proverbios en romance*. Salamanca: Juan de Canova; rpt. eds. Louis Combet, Julia Sevilla Muñoz, Germán Conde Tarrio, and Josep Guia. Madrid: Guillermo Blázquez.

O'Kane, Eleanor S. 1950. "The Proverb: Rabelais and Cervantes." *Comparative Literature*, 2: 360-369.

Olmos Canalda, Elías. 1940 (1998). *Los refranes del "Quijote"*. Valencia: J. Nacher; rpt. Madrid: CIE Inversiones Editoriales.

Ormsby, John. 1885. "The Proverbs of *Don Quixote*." *The Ingenious Gentleman Don Quixote of La Mancha by Miguel de Cervantes Saavedra*. Translated by J. Ormsby. 4 vols. New York: Macmillan. IV, 367-395.

Paczolay, Gyula. 1997. *European Proverbs in 55 Languages with Equivalents in Arabic, Persian, Sanskrit, Chinese and Japanese*. Veszprém, Hungary: Veszprémi Nyomda.

Parr, James A., and Lisa Vollendorf, eds. 2015a. *Approaches to Teaching Cervantes's "Don Quixote"*. New York: Modern Language Association of America.

Parr, James A., and Lisa Vollendorf. 2015b. "Introduction." *Approaches to Teaching Cervantes's "Don Quixote"*. Eds. James A. Parr and Lisa Vollendorf. New York: Modern Language Association of America. 1-13.

Parr, James A., and Lisa Vollendorf. 2015c. "The Instructor's Library." *Approaches to Teaching Cervantes's "Don Quixote"*. Eds. James A. Parr and Lisa Vollendorf. New York: Modern Language Association of America. 17-31.

Percas de Ponseti, Helena. 1988. *Cervantes the Writer and Painter of "Don Quijote"*. Columbia, Missouri: University of Missouri Press.

Privat, Maryse. 1997. "Traduction et proverbes dans le *Don Quijote*." *Homenaje al professor Jesús Cantera Ortiz de Urbina*. No editors given. Madrid: Servicio de Publicaciones, Universidad Complutense (= *Revista de filología francesa*, 11-12 [1997]), 257-263).

Privat, Maryse. 1999. "Quelques proverbes du *Don Quijote* vus dans trois traductions français." *Paremia*, 8: 423-428.

Quint, David. 2003 (2005). "Cervantes's Method and Meaning." *Miguel de Cervantes*. Ed. Harold Bloom. Philadelphia: Chelsea House. 277-299.

Raymond, Joseph. 1851. *Attitudes and Cultural Patterns in Spanish Proverbs*. Diss. Columbia University (proverbs esp. 118-135).

Requena, Miguel. 2004. "Los refranes del *Quijote*." *Miguel de Cervantes. Don Quijote de la Mancha*. Ed. Francisco Rico. Barcelona: Galaxia Gutenberg. 882-895.

Rettenbeck, Lenz. 1953. *"Feige". Wort, Gebärde, Amulett. Ein volkskundlicher Beitrag zur Amulettforschung*. Diss. University of Munich.

Riley, Edward C. 1962. *Cervantes's Theory of the Novel*. Oxford: Clarendon Press.

Riley, Edward C. 1986a. *Don Quixote*. London: Allen & Unwin.

Riley, Edward C. 1986b (2005). "Ideals and Illusions." *Miguel de Cervantes*. Ed. Harold Bloom. Philadelphia: Chelsea House. 63-78.

Rivers, Elias L. 1984. "Voices and Texts in *Don Quixote*." *Approaches to Teaching Cervantes' "Don Quixote"*. Ed. Richard Bjornson. New York: Modern Language Association of America. 113-119.

Rodríguez Marín, Francisco. 1916 (1947). "Las frases del *Quijote*." In Francisco Rodríguez Marín. *Estudios Cervantinos*. Madrdrid: Ediciones Atlas. 597-599.

Rodríguez Marín, Francisco. 1947. *Estudios Cervantinos*. Madrid: Ediciones Atlas.

Rodríguez Valle, Nieves. 2005. "Paremias en *El Quijote* de 1605 como estrategias literarias." *Paremia*, 14: 105-115.

Rodríguez Valle, Nieves. 2008. "La 'creación' de refranes en el *Quijote*." *Paremia*, 17: 143-151.

Rodríguez Valle, Nieves. 2010. "Cervantes, creador de refranes en el *Quijote*?" *Actas del XVI congreso de la asociación internacional de Hispanistas. Paris, del 9 al 13 de julio de 2007*. Eds. Pierre Civil and Françoise Crémoux. Vervuert: Iberoamericana. 555-560.

Romera Pintor, Ángela Magdalena. 1999. "El refrán como componente cervantino en une nivela de Wieland." *Paremia*, 8: 457-462.

Romero Flores, Hipólito R. 1951. *Biografía de Sancho Panza. Filósofo de la sensatez*. Barcelona: Editorial Aedos.

Rosenblat, Ángel. 1971a. "Dignidad del habla popular: La naturalidad." Ángel Rosenblat. *La lengua del "Quijote"*. Madrid: Editorial Gredos. 43-56.

Rosenblat, Ángel. 1971b. "El refranero y el habla de Sancho." Ángel Rosenblat. *La lengua del "Quijote"*. Madrid: Editorial Gredos. 35-43.

Rosenblat, Ángel. 1971c. *La lengua del "Quijote"*. Madrid: Editorial Gredos.

Russell, P.E. 1985. *Cervantes*. Oxford: Oxford University Press.

Schipper, Mineke. 2003. *Never Marry a Woman with Big Feet. Women in Proverbs from Around the World*. New Haven, Connecticut: Yale University Press.

Serrano-Plaja, Arturo. 1970. *"Magic Realism" in Cervantes. "Don Quixote" as Seen Through "Tom Sawyer" and "The Idiot"*. Berkeley, California: University of California Press.

Sevilla Muñoz, Julia. 1993. "Fuentes paremiológicas francesas y españolas en la primera mitad del siglo XVII." *Revista de Filología Románica*, 10: 357-369.

Sevilla Muñoz, Julia. 2005. "Presupuestos paremiológicos de una propuesta metodológica para la enseñanza de los refranes a través de *El Quijote*." *Paremia*, 14: 117-128.

Sierra García, Jaime. 1994. *El refrán antioqueño*. Medellin: Editorial Lealon (on Cervantes esp. 328-351).

Sierra García, Jaime. 1997. "El refrán antioqueño en la obra de Cervantes." *Lingüistíca y Literatura*, 18, no. 31: 65-76.

Sobieski, Janet, and Wolfgang Mieder, ed. 2005. *"So Many Heads, So Many Wits". An Anthology of English Proverb Poetry*. Burlington, Vermont: The University of Vermont.

Spitzer, Leo. 1948 (2005a). "Linguistic Perspectivism in the *Don Quijote*". *Cervantes' "Don Quixote"*. Ed. Roberto González Echevarría. New York: Oxford University Press. 163-216.

Stavans, Ilan. 2015. *"Quixote": The Novel and the World*. New York: W.W. Norton.

Sullivan, Henry W. 1996 (2005). "The Two Projects of the *Quixote* and the Grotesque as Mode." *Miguel de Cervantes*. Ed. Harold Bloom. Philadelphia: Chelsea House. 225-241.

Suñé Benages, Juan. 1929. *Fraseología de Cervantes. Colección de frases, refranes, proverbios, aforismos, adagios, expresiones y modos adverbiales que se leen en las obras cervantinas*. Barcelona: Lux.

Tarán, Leonardo. 1984. "'Amicus Plato sed magis amica veritas'. From Plato and Aristotle to Cervantes." *Antike und Abendland*, 30: 93-124.

Taylor, Archer. 1948. "Folklore and the Student of Literature." *The Pacific Spectator*, 2: 216-223.

Thacker, Jonathan. 2015. "*Don Quixote* in English Translation." *Approaches to Teaching Cervantes's "Don Quixote"*. Eds. James A. Parr and Lisa Vollendorf. New York: Modern Language Association of America. 32-47.

Thompson, Emma. 1867. *Wit and Wisdom of "Don Quixote"*. New York: D. Appleton.

Vallés, Pedro. 1549. *Libro de refranes*. Çaragoça: Hernandez.

Vega Rodríguez, Pilar María. 1990. "Consideraciones paremiológicas cervantinas." *Actas del Primer Coloquio Internacional de la Asociación de Cervantistas, Alcalá de Henares 1988*. No editor given. Barcelona: Anthropos. 315-332.

Vega Rodríguez, Pilar María. 1999. "De nuevo sobre *El Quijote*: novela de burlas." *Espéculo: Revista de Estudios Literarios*, 11: 1-5.

Versini, Laurent. 2003. "Les proverbes de Sancho: De Cervantès à Challe." *Robert Challe: Sources et héritages*. Eds. Jacques Cormier, Jan Herman, and Paul Pelckmans. Louvain: Peeters. 25-39.

Vrtunski, Dushko. 1985. "O prevodenju poslovitsa u Servantesovom *Don Kikhotu*." *Mostovi*, 16, no. 63: 225-228.

Watt, Ian. 1996 (2005). "Don Quixote of La Mancha." *Miguel de Cervantes*. Ed. Harold Bloom. Philadelphia: Chelsea House. 191-223

Weiger, John G. 1979. *The Individuated Self. Cervantes and the Emergence of the Individual*. Athens, Ohio: Ohio University Press.

Weiger, John G. 1985. *The Substance of Cervantes*. Cambridge: Cambridge University Press.

Weiger, John G. 1988. *In the Margins of Cervantes*. Hanover, New Hampshire: University Press of New England.

Williamson, Edwin. 1984. *The Half-Way House of Fiction. "Don Quixote" and Arthurian Romance*. Oxford: Clarendon Press.

Wilson, F.P. 1970. *Oxford Dictionary of English Proverbs*. Oxford: Oxford University Press.

Woodward, Katharine Burchell. 1930. *Proverbs in "Don Quijote"*. M.A. Thesis Stanford University.

Zucker, George K, 1973. "La prevaricacion idiomática: Un recurso comico en el *Quijote*." *Thesaurus: Bulletin del Instituto Caro y Cuervo*, 28: 515-525.

Zuluaga, Alberto. 1997. "Verwendungsverfahren und Funktionen phraseologischer Äußerungen in *El Quijote*." *Phraseme im Text: Beiträge aus romanistischer Sicht*. Ed. Annette Sabban. Bochum: Norbert Brockmeyer. 237-258.

Zuluaga, Alberto. 2005. "Interpretación textolingüística de fraseoloxismos quixotescos." *Cadernos de fraseoloxía galega*, 7: 277-289.

Zurdo Ruiz-Ayúcar, María I. Teresa. 2014. "Recursos aplicados para la transmission del componente cultural en traducciones de *La Celestina* y del *Quijote*." *Paremia*, 23: 35-44.